# TRADE AND DEVELOPMENT REPORT 2021

## FROM RECOVERY TO RESILIENCE: THE DEVELOPMENT DIMENSION

Report by the secretariat of the
United Nations Conference on Trade and Development

**UNITED NATIONS**
Geneva, 2021

The designations employed and the presentation
of material on any map in this work do not imply
the expression of any opinion whatsoever on the
part of the United Nations concerning the legal
status of any country, territory, city or area or of
its authorities, or concerning the delimitation of
its frontiers or boundaries.

This publication has been edited externally.

United Nations publication issued by the
United Nations Conference on Trade and Development.

| UNCTAD/TDR/2021 |
| --- |
| *Sales No.* E.22.II.D.1 |
| ISBN: 978-92-1-113027-0<br>eISBN: 978-92-1-001027-6<br>ISSN: 0255-4607<br>eISSN: 2225-3262 |

# Contents

*Chapter 3*

IT'S THE END OF THE WORLD AS WE KNOW IT:
SURVEYING THE ADAPTATION LANDSCAPE

*Chapter 4*

FROM DE-RISKING TO DIVERSIFICATION:
MAKING STRUCTURAL CHANGE WORK FOR CLIMATE ADAPTATION

# List of figures

## *List of tables and boxes*

# Explanatory notes

## Classification by country or commodity group

The classification of countries in this *Report* has been adopted solely for the purposes of statistical or analytical convenience and does not necessarily imply any judgement concerning the stage of development of a particular country or area.

There is no established convention for the designation of "developing", "transition" and "developed" countries or areas in the United Nations system. This *Report* follows the classification as defined in the *UNCTAD Handbook of Statistics 2020* (United Nations publication, Sales No. E.21.II.D.1) for these three major country groupings (see https://unctad.org/en/PublicationsLibrary/tdstat45_en.pdf).

For statistical purposes, regional groupings and classifications by commodity group used in this *Report* follow generally those employed in the *UNCTAD Handbook of Statistics 2020* unless otherwise stated. The data for China do not include those for Hong Kong Special Administrative Region (Hong Kong SAR), Macao Special Administrative Region (Macao SAR) and Taiwan Province of China.

The terms "country" / "economy" refer, as appropriate, also to territories or areas.

References to "Latin America" in the text or tables include the Caribbean countries unless otherwise indicated.

References to "sub-Saharan Africa" in the text or tables include South Africa unless otherwise indicated.

## Other notes

References in the text to *TDR* are to the *Trade and Development Report* (of a particular year). For example, *TDR 2020* refers to *Trade and Development Report 2020* (United Nations publication, Sales No. E.20.II.D.30).

References in the text to the United States are to the United States of America and those to the United Kingdom are to the United Kingdom of Great Britain and Northern Ireland.

The term "dollar" ($) refers to United States dollars, unless otherwise stated.

The term "billion" signifies 1,000 million.

The term "trillion" signifies 1,000,000 million.

The term "tons" refers to metric tons.

Annual rates of growth and change refer to compound rates.

Exports are valued FOB and imports CIF, unless otherwise specified.

Use of a dash (–) between dates representing years, e.g. 2019–2021, signifies the full period involved, including the initial and final years.

An oblique stroke (/) between two years, e.g. 2019/20, signifies a fiscal or crop year.

A dot (.) in a table indicates that the item is not applicable.

Two dots (..) in a table indicate that the data are not available, or are not separately reported.

A dash (–) or a zero (0) in a table indicates that the amount is nil or negligible.

Decimals and percentages do not necessarily add up to totals because of rounding.

# Abbreviations

| | |
|---|---|
| BEPS | Base Erosion and Profit Shifting |
| BIS | Bank for International Settlements |
| BRICS | Brazil, Russian Federation, India, China and South Africa |
| CCRT | Catastrophe Containment and Relief Trust |
| CDOs | Collateralized Debt Obligations |
| CIS | Commonwealth of Independent States |
| CLOs | Collateralized Loan Obligations |
| CPB | Netherlands Bureau for Economic Policy Analysis |
| CRAs | credit rating agencies |
| DSSI | Debt Service Suspension Initiative |
| ECB | European Central Bank |
| ECLAC | Economic Commission for Latin America and the Caribbean |
| EITI | Extractive Industries Transparency Initiative |
| EIU | Economist Intelligence Unit |
| EU | European Union |
| FDI | foreign direct investment |
| FIRE | finance, insurance and real estate |
| FYP | Five-Year Plan |
| G20 | Group of Twenty |
| GDP | Gross Domestic Product |
| GFC | global financial crisis |
| GPM | Global Policy Model |
| GST | goods and services taxes |
| GVC | global value chains |
| HIPC | Heavily Indebted Poor Countries |
| IATA | Air Transport Association |
| ICTs | information and communications technologies |
| IFF | illicit financial flows |
| IIF | The Institute of International Finance |
| ILO | International Labour Organization |
| IMF | International Monetary Fund |
| IPCC | Intergovernmental Panel on Climate Change |
| ISDS | investor-state dispute settlement |
| ISM | United States Institute for Supply Management |
| KFW | Kreditanstalt für Wiederaufbau |
| MDRI | Multilateral Debt Relief Initiative |
| MERS | Middle East Respiratory Syndrome |
| MICs | middle-income developing countries |
| MNEs | multinational enterprises |
| MSCI | Morgan Stanley MSCI indices for equities |
| NAFTA | North American Free Trade Agreement |
| NBS | China National Bureau of Statistics |
| NEXGEM | JP Morgan Next Generation Markets Index |
| NPC | National People's Congress |
| ODA | official development assistance |
| OECD | Organization for Economic Co-operation and Development |
| OPEC+ | Organization of the Petroleum Exporting Countries Plus |
| PMI | Purchasing Managers' Index |
| PPPs | public-private partnerships |

| | |
|---|---|
| PRGT | Poverty Reduction and Growth Trust |
| QE | quantitative easing |
| SARS | Severe Acute Respiratory Syndrome |
| SCDIs | state-contingent debt instruments |
| SDGs | Sustainable Development Goals |
| SDRMs | sovereign debt restructuring mechanisms |
| SDRs | Special Drawing Rights |
| SMEs | small and medium enterprises |
| TRIMS | Trade Related Investment Measures |
| TRIPS | Trade Related Intellectual Property Measures |
| UNDESA | United Nations Department of Economic and Social Affairs |
| UNIDO | United Nations Industrial Development Organization |
| UNSD | United Nations Statistics Division |
| UNWTO | United Nations World Tourism Organization |
| VAT | value-added taxes |
| WB | World Bank |
| WESP | World Economic Situation and Prospects |
| WGP | world gross product |
| WHO | World Health Organization |
| WIOD | World Input-Output Database |
| WTI | West Texas Intermediate |
| WTO | World Trade Organization |

# OVERVIEW

## Introduction

Every crisis brings with it an opportunity. As the world economy recovers from the economic paralysis of the pandemic, there appears to be the chance to rethink the model of global governance that has guided the world economy for the past forty years but has largely failed to deliver on the promise of prosperity and stability.

There are some signs that 2021 could mark the beginning of a fairer, more resilient global economy, able to withstand interacting shocks and crises, and founded on a new consensus about the balance between the state, market, society and the environment. In the United States, the President's Council of Economic Advisors has acknowledged the need for a policy reset, both to fix the damage caused by past policies and to address new challenges, with a solid foundation built on investments, public as well as private, in workers, families, and communities.

The move away from simple market dogmas has also been apparent at the level of multilateral financial institutions. Both at the IMF and the World Bank, there has been a recognition that the economic thinking of the past would not deliver a more resilient system for the future. There has been an endorsement of big spending programmes, initiatives to tax the rich and curtail the power of monopolies, recognition of the role of targeted capital controls, an endorsement of a strongly interventionist policy agenda to backstop a green investment push.

It appears, in other words, that a new, global political economic consensus is emerging out of the crisis induced by the Covid-19 pandemic. But it would be premature to call time on belief in an unregulated free market.

The year 2021 marks the 40th anniversary of President Regan's inaugural speech that set the tone for the economic doctrine which prioritized private interests and markets over society and the state. Having gone global, the doctrine was institutionalized in the policies of national governments and international organizations where it retains its supporters. Even during the pandemic, austerity continued to guide the multilateral lending programmes to many developing countries; the G7 trade ministers called for deeper liberalization which would further narrow policy space for the state, while a good deal of the discussion of transitioning to a low-carbon economy has been focused on getting prices right.

What, then, is the likely path of post-Covid recovery? Will the world return, through a premature reversal to austerity, to a pre-pandemic state of affairs, marked by deepening and multi-faceted inequality, fractured economies, financial asset bubbles, corporate non-liability and environmental degradation? Will a more activist policy agenda persist but with only cosmetic efforts to address these underlying conditions? Or can a new way towards a fairer, balanced, resilient and climate-conscious development be found in the policy space opened by the pandemic?

Most advanced economies are rebounding in 2021 from the recession conditions, induced to stem the pandemic. Their key challenge is the medium and longer-term direction and nature of economic growth, both in terms of avoiding the policy reversals that marred the decade following the global financial crisis and making a definitive shift to a zero-carbon energy system, in line with the aims of the Paris Agreement.

The challenge facing developing countries is more immediate, with a combination of diminished fiscal space, increased indebtedness and limited vaccine roll out, holding back recovery and triggering divergence with advanced economies. Behind this divergence, however, lie decades of deepening economic and social divisions, an unstable insertion into global financial markets subject to mercurial flows of capital and diminished policy space. In many countries, these structural obstacles to a balanced recovery are compounded by shocks linked to warming global temperatures.

In the advanced economies, the initial response to the Covid-19 shock, following the policy playbook used in previous crises, was to cushion the blow to financial markets with a new round of quantitative easing. But governments in advanced economies soon found themselves in unfamiliar territory, as lockdowns triggered an economic blowback that required concerted and targeted measures to protect lives and livelihoods. Central Banks kept the liquidity injections going, but, unlike in 2007-09, governments also increased their spending to levels not seen since wartime, abandoning, in the process, previously sacrosanct policy positions. Even so, the drop in output during the second and third quarters of 2020 was unprecedented; even as economies began to unlock and confidence returned, the bounce back was marked by considerable unevenness across sectors, income groups and regions. Moreover, the income and wealth inequalities that emerged over the last four decades have, if anything, intensified, with the owners of financial and digital assets reaping the biggest gains from recovery.

Developing countries were hit particularly hard by the global lockdown of economic activity. It triggered a series of interconnected shocks which generated vicious economic cycles that came on top of existing debt vulnerabilities, tipping most regions in to a deep recession and some countries into default. Despite the fiscal squeeze and increased debt burdens, developing countries were left to manage the crisis largely on their own, forcing deep cuts in public employment and services. A faster than expected reflux of capital flows and recovery in commodity prices, as lockdown in the advanced economies were lifted, prevented a worst-case scenario emerging. Still, growth in most parts of the developing world remains weak, large debt overhangs have grown even larger, while variants of the virus threatening to revive new waves of the pandemic would derail fledgling recoveries in the more vulnerable economies. Even if the virus is contained, the fear of higher interest rates already undermines development prospects with the threat of another lost decade now a possibility.

As was the case with the first Report in 1981, this year`s Report coincides with the G7 countries again talking of the need to revitalize western democracy and build a new partnership with developing countries around infrastructure investment, including through an initiative for clean and green growth. Their call for a "building back better world" has struck a hopeful note. A promise to treat health and education as global public goods, a commitment to a sufficiently financed green revolution, an infusion of liquidity through a new allocation of SDRs, and the announcement of a minimum global corporation tax are all welcome departures from recent practice.

However, with a debt crisis looming, the climate crisis a reality for many countries and the Agenda 2030 in trouble even before Covid-19 hit, the willingness to acknowledge the scale of the challenge facing developing countries is still missing. There has been scant detail on the proposed reform agenda and even less on the resources available to lift all boats out of the immediate crisis and launch a just transition to a decarbonized world by 2050. The call from developing countries to waive the TRIPs agreement in the WTO – a necessary first step to enabling the local manufacture of vaccines – has, despite belated backing from the United States, been resisted by other advanced economies, whose deference to corporate interests is causing a new division in the global economy based on access to vaccines and freedom of movement. Furthermore, a general reluctance to pressure private creditors to the negotiating table gives little hope that the debt burden weighing on developing countries will be sufficiently eased to allow them to invest their way out of the multiple crises they currently face.

Forty years on, the conclusion of the first *Trade and Development Report* published in 1981 still rings true:

> The present situation thus appears to require a new development paradigm, and this paradigm will need to take explicit account of the fact that issues concerning the governance of the world economy, on the one hand, and long-term development objectives, are intermingled.

The big difference between then and now in linking long-term development objectives to the management of the global economy is the looming climate crisis. Whether or not a new policy paradigm emerges to help guide a just and inclusive transition to a decarbonized world is an open question; that a building back better world for people and the planet hinges on it is no longer in doubt.

## Growth divergence, inflation fears and new variants

Assuming no further shocks, global growth is projected to reach 5.3 per cent in 2021, decelerating somewhat to 3.6 per cent in 2022. These figures are the result of demand stimulus in advanced economies and economies issuing global currencies, but still reflect incomplete reactivation of the productive capacity idled in the recession of 2020. Growth performance by region is very uneven. Only developed countries show the expected growth spurt, while many developing economies will remain below pre-pandemic averages.

The unevenness reflects the different degrees of policy independence enjoyed by developed and developing economies. Most developed countries used the strong financial firepower afforded by the privileged status of issuers of international-reserve currencies. This was a necessary response, but it did not lead to the recognition that other countries, especially developing economies, needed support to implement similar policies.

The expansion of SDRs allocations, necessary to ease some policy constraints in developing economies, was agreed late and to an insufficient degree. A few developing countries, including Brazil, Indonesia and Turkey, did adopt strong fiscal and monetary responses, similar to those by developed countries, but recent developments suggest they are vulnerable to financial repercussions, including through currency markets. Also in the advanced economies, public money allowed the development of vaccines at record speed and the cornering of supplies. Manufacturers, who have struggled to produce enough doses for the developing world, have so far resisted calls to share technology, delaying the start of low-cost production in developing countries, and share technological know-how. By slowing down immunization, this stance aggravates the loss of life, facilitates the spread of new variants and makes booster doses necessary, compounding vaccine scarcity. This failure is even more dramatic than the inadequacies of the financial system because health infrastructure in developing countries is far weaker in comparison to most developed countries, and 'lockdowns' to contain the virus spread are futile, given widespread informality of jobs and inadequate social protection.

It is still unclear whether (or when) the current performance of the world economy will by sufficiently strong to recover pre-Covid trends (which in turn, were considerably lower than pre-2008 trends). In 2020-22, the global economy faces a cumulative income loss of about USD 13 trillion. If the global economy were to grow as in the early 2000s (approximately 3.5 per cent per year) it would return to its pre-pandemic trend only by 2030. Considering that global growth in 2017–2019 was already insufficient to reach the Sustainable Development Goals, reaching them in the current conditions requires unprecedented action, both in terms of degree and of multilateral coordination.

Prospects for maintaining the demand stimulus and advancing transformative public investment programmes over the longer term are clouded by the returning spectre of inflation, in both developed and developing economies. The facts, however, do not support the fears of inflation so often mentioned in some policy circles. Recent inflation spikes in the Euro Area will likely remain below target. In the United States, where inflation has recently surpassed the 2 per cent target, accelerating prices have been a common occurrence, especially in recovery years.

Evidence points to supply shortages as the main cause of the recent inflation spikes in commodity and energy exporting countries, as well as those that provide manufacturing inputs into global supply chains. Where inflationary shortages affect the labour market, establishing better working conditions, including wages and social protection, can help ease the shortage by attracting more workers and contain costs by stimulating productivity growth (which is positively correlated to high wage growth and good working conditions). This stands in stark contrast with the standard response, which attempts to contain inflation through wage repression but effectively drives down productivity, leading to higher real unit labour costs. Instead, in cases where inflationary shortages affect other inputs or commodities, as is often the case in developing economies, sensible responses should focus on engineering a strong recovery of investment, incomes and of production worldwide. This distinction of causes and the respective responses, however, are absent from policy discussions, which have focused on demand stimulus packages. Yet in many countries, slowing demand growth by terminating the stimulus packages would not stop inflation, since its source is imported inputs, including commodities.

## Debt vulnerabilities: Kicking the can down the road

Indebtedness has been growing across most regions since the start of the pandemic. With the exception of China and some oil exporting economies, debt burdens are too high and export revenues too low across the developing world. For almost all developing countries commodities are not a reliable source of income because their export revenues fluctuate due to frequent price swings. However, the frequently adopted approach of enhancing export potential by requiring developing countries to enter bilateral or plurilateral trade and investment agreements is no solution. One reason is that these agreements are not negotiated in the WTO, the functioning of which at least allows developing countries to form a united front.

Another reason is that the way these agreements regulate intellectual property rights and dispute settlement limits real technology transfer, preventing developing economies from competing with countries that are already industrially developed. Furthermore, the type of liberalization promoted by these agreements makes the global economy more vulnerable as it is mostly geared towards extreme financialization running counter the strategic need to manage finance, especially for developing countries.

Building protection against the vagaries of global finance is critical for developing countries. It should start with a proper evaluation of sovereign and private debt burdens and repayment profiles, which affect development strategies but also crisis response.

External debt sustainability is set to remain high over the coming years, as many developing countries face a wall of sovereign debt repayments in international bond markets. Excluding China, servicing existing sovereign debt in developing countries will generate payments of almost $1 trillion by 2030, the year earmarked for achievement of the Sustainable Development Goals (SDGs), including $571 billion in repayments of principals and $365 billion in interest. The total amount far exceeds the estimated investment target of 2 per cent of GDP required for the green transition. Debt reprofiling and relief, including debt cancellation, are necessary. But so far agreed measures have been mostly symbolic. The only lasting multilateral relief was provided by the IMF through the cancellation of debt service obligations in 29 countries, amounting to $727 million between April 2020 and October 2021.

The contrasting pre-pandemic experiences with debt management in the advanced and developing countries have carried over to the current crisis. Even with similar debt ratios, developed economies, especially those that issue reserve currencies, have continued to function smoothly and have seen growth pick up. Developing countries, in contrast, face the risk of a lost decade. The pandemic offered an important test-case, in which governments of developed countries were able to enact larger spending measures than developing countries with similar or even lower debt burdens. In the latter, domestic liquidity creation does not necessarily improve access to foreign currency, while fiscal deficits act as a deterrent to private foreign investors driven by short-term and speculative interests.

In terms of fiscal policy too, not only were developed countries able to provide much larger stimulus than developing countries, even though the actual stimulus in the former was often much smaller than initially announced. Yet developed countries were not chastised by the bond markets for their spending announcements as developing countries were. How stringent the constraints to fiscal policy really are in all countries becomes clear when we consider the prevalence in the stimulus packages of transfers compared to direct government spending. In many cases, government spending on goods and services contracted during the pandemic. While cash transfers have provided a critical lifeline, especially in the absence of robust social protection systems (as in most of the developing world), austerity in direct spending continued to affect policy decisions even during the pandemic.

## The perils of normalcy

The biggest threat to global recovery is a possible repeat of the post-2008 playbook, and a return to 'normalcy' in economic policymaking. In the wake of any crisis, reverting to pre-crisis ways of doing things is the easiest approach for policymakers, in advanced and developing countries alike. Even though the macroeconomic policy wisdom that has prevailed in recent decades has not played out well for the vast majority of countries, the pressures to contain government direct spending (and thus intervention in economic activities) remain strong.

Calls to enact new cuts have already returned, generally with the stated intention of reducing debt burdens. Commentary about the threat of inflationary pressures also contributes to the bias against fiscal spending. Meanwhile, calls to contain prices by increasing labour market flexibility have resumed. Fiscal austerity and downward pressure of labour income shares are supposed to help countries tap global demand with more competitive exports, hence the reignited attention to trade and investment agreements. Yet as previous Trade and Development Reports have argued, three decades of experiments in this direction have amply demonstrated just how faulty this strategy has been. No significant attempt has been made to support development, to reorient the global financial and payments system towards productive investment, to establish a debt workout mechanism, and to make trade more conducive to sustainable development.

Projections reflecting the continuation of these conditions into 2030 point to insufficient growth across the board. All economies would slow down, with the growth loss ranging between 0.6 and 1.2 percentage points, while the deflationary measures in each country would establish a global deflationary bias with negative feedbacks on all. Moreover, economies that typically recover thanks to exports and fiscal prudence will be the main losers since global trade will decelerate due to sluggish global demand, greater financialization and weaker wage growth, further constraining productivity growth.

The faster pace of financialization and the growth of speculative investment would raise the cost of government borrowing, especially in finance-constrained economies, thus deepening the pro-austerity measures. Disappointing growth aside, in this context developing economies will experience the greater vulnerabilities: both deficit economies subject to external bottlenecks and forced to rely on commodities, and surplus economies subject to double boom-bust cycles of commodity prices, exchange rate and domestic price shocks. Finally, these trends in trade and finance run counter to the climate stabilization goals, undermining the prospects of actual decarbonization of the global economy, which requires international cooperation for sustainable and efficient management of natural resources and therefore, alternative source of income for resource- abundant developing countries.

These projections invite a long overdue reflection on effective ways of sustaining growth and promoting structural transformation and economic development by internationally coordinated injections of effective demand, promotion of productive capacities and investment, enhancement of physical and social infrastructure and curbs to speculative finance. Global challenges clearly require multilateral responses.
The growing urgency of climate adaptation

July 2021 was the hottest month ever recorded on the planet, following on from the hottest year in 2020 which, itself, came after the hottest decade on record. Intense heatwaves, increasingly powerful tropical cyclones, prolonged droughts, rising sea levels, spreading diseases are just some of the threats accompanying the unrelenting rise in global temperatures, bringing with them ever greater economic damage and human suffering. And worse is to come. Even if we get our mitigation efforts together within this decade and manage to keep the global average temperature rise to 1.5°C above pre-industrial levels by the year 2100, the extreme climate events in 2021 serve as a foretaste of what an additional 0.4°C to the average global temperature has in store for communities and countries across the planet.

The consequences of rising global temperatures reflect, and are amplified by, existing structural inequalities within and across countries. The historical responsibility for global greenhouse gas emissions (the principal cause of global warming) lies squarely with the developed nations, which account for around two-thirds of the cumulative total of emissions in the atmosphere compared with just 3 per cent for Africa. Between 1990 and 2015, the wealthiest one per cent of the world`s population added more than double the carbon emissions of the bottom 50 per cent. And while some developing economies like Brazil, China, India, and South Africa have rising emissions, on a per capita basis they are still behind advanced countries and even the consumption-related emissions of their richest citizens are below counterparts in advanced economies.

For many developing countries rising global temperatures are compounding a vicious development cycle that has been constraining resource mobilization, widening income gaps and weakening state capacities for decades. Economies with underfunded health care systems, mal-developed infrastructure, undiversified production base and missing state institutions are more exposed not only to potentially large-scale environmental shocks but also a more permanent state of economic stress as a result of climate impacts.

Rising temperatures will hit growth prospects in developing regions the hardest; and all the more, the higher the increase above the 1.5°C target. But the nature of the adaptation challenge will vary across regions and sectors of the economy, making a one-size-fits-all response inappropriate. Extremely hot days are expected to primarily increase in the tropics, where temperature variability across years is lowest. Dangerous heatwaves are forecast to occur earliest in these regions, and they are expected to become widespread at 1.5°C global warming rise. As the most food insecure region with the largest rural population, Sub-Saharan Africa is likely to face deepening challenges. For scenarios ranging from a 1 °C to a 4 °C increase in global temperatures relative to pre-industrial levels, the continent's overall GDP is expected to decrease by 2.25 per cent to 12.12 per cent. In South Asia, more intense and frequent tropical cyclones, accelerated heatwaves and a rising sea level will continue to generate adverse impacts on the region. Middle East and North African countries face acute water shortages, where as many as 60 per cent of the region's inhabitants already experience a serious lack of water. East Asia and the Pacific, which have a quarter of the world's population already suffering from the most severe storms, cyclones and inundation globally, and will likely face the highest levels of climate-induced displacements.

Large portions of populations in low-lying coastal zones – 84 per cent in Africa, 80 per cent in Asia, 71 per cent in Latin America and the Caribbean and 93 per cent in the least developed countries can be especially affected. Critical infrastructure assets and networks like ports, airports, railways and coastal roads will also face devastation by rising sea levels which will cause permanent or even repeated damage and will impede access to food, materials, and other income-generating supplies to people and businesses.

## The risks of a risk-based approach

To date, the global policy response to the climate crisis has been divided between mitigation and adaptation measures. *Climate mitigation* focuses on slowing down and reducing emissions of greenhouse gases (GHG), through a mixture of more efficient energy use and the replacement of fossil fuels with renewable sources of energy. *Climate adaptation* centers on harnessing resilience and protection mechanisms to minimize the negative impact of climate change on lives and livelihoods. In practice, the two sets of measures are often difficult to separate, and in much of the agenda-setting discussion on climate, adaptation has remained a poor cousin of mitigation efforts. This is proving short-sighted and increasingly costly, particularly for developing countries, where adaptation challenge is both widespread and connected to a wider set of deep-seated social and economic vulnerabilities that have emerged in recent decades.

Conventional measures towards more resilient systems – across the economy, society and ecology- have borrowed from the available methodologies of risk management used in the financial system. Consequently, at all levels of development, governments have been told to strengthen their resilience to shocks by improving their data gathering and risk assessment techniques to better protect existing assets and by providing temporary financial support when shocks materialize. This approach has been appealing because no new methodologies and frameworks were necessary. Adopting and adapting already operational approaches was seen to deliver speedy response to the threat to lives and livelihoods.

In this traditional risk-management perspective, the problem of climate adaptation is not distinguished from most other types of risk and is being dealt with through disaster risk assessment and early warning systems, improved ecosystem management, and stronger social safety nets. The extension of this approach to the adaptation challenge can be more explicitly traced to the Sendai Framework for Disaster Risk Reduction that the United Nations General Assembly adopted in 2015 as a blueprint for disaster-related resilience and reacting to human-made hazards. The 2015 adoption of the Paris Agreement also stressed this approach with its focus on the reduction of risks related to climate change.

There is a problem, however, with this practice of climate risk management: it is retrospective, not forward-looking. The measures may provide partial resilience *now*, but by using scarce resources for adaptation to current climate hazards, these interventions preclude other future-oriented interventions and lock in path-dependent dynamics which reproduces current vulnerabilities. There is no guarantee that adapting to current climate variability would automatically reduce the vulnerability to future climate change.

The weakness of extending a risk-resilient approach to the adaptation challenge is its reliance on pricing and other market-assessment techniques which bias the approach towards what is predictable and incremental in nature, rather than what is uncertain and systemic. Given its roots in financial risk management, the approach privileges a return to (pre-crisis) normality and stability over a dynamic vision of change and new trajectories. In the case of many communities, this 'normality' means a return to persistent inequality. Preservation and coping therefore, take priority over transformation.

In the case of climate crisis, it is not simply insufficient, but counterproductive, leading to maladaptation. Application of conventional risk-resilience approaches are especially problematic in the current political context, where new social contracts are needed to regain citizens' trust in public policies and multilateral efforts. Tackling current global challenges like climate adaptation requires a new vision of common goals rather than emphasizing the avoidance of risks and worst-case scenarios that emerge from current circumstances.

A transformative approach to risks of climate change is required. The only lasting solution is to reduce the dependence of developing countries on a small number of climate sensitive activities through a process of structural transformation that can establish more resilient economies. It should move away from the core priority of de-risking and centre instead on an integrated, system-based vision that can deliver socio-economic resilience and diversified economies. This, in turn, requires the institutional capacity of a developmental State, equipped with greener industrial policies that are critical to advancing such an agenda.

## From de-risking to diversification

The success of today's advanced economies, as well as the catch-up economies of East Asia, rests on sustained economic growth closely tied to structural transformation. At its core, this involves two sets of combined and cumulative processes: a vertical shift in the production structure from the primary sector to manufacturing (and on to high-end services) on the one hand, and a more horizontal shift of resources from lower- to higher-productivity and more capital-intensive activities within and across both sectors. Together, these processes have, in almost all successful development experiences, facilitated a more diversified structure of economic activity, raised productivity and led to an improvement across a broad set of social indicators, including poverty reduction.

More diversified economies are also less vulnerable to external shocks which are likely to disrupt the growth and transformation process. This has, in recent years, been apparent with the heightened vulnerability of primary export-dependent economies to economic shocks that originate elsewhere in the global economy but it is also the case with climate shocks. Indeed, in many developing countries, particularly those located in tropical and sub-tropical regions, vulnerability to economic and climate shocks is compounding one another, locking countries into an eco-development trap of permanent disruption, economic precarity and slow productivity growth. Breaking out of that trap implies that the climate adaptation challenge in the developing world needs to be approached from a developmental perspective.

Not all past experiences, no matter how attractive, can, however, be easily adapted to contemporary realities. Today, developing countries confront the dilemma of having to pursue economic development while keeping emissions and resource consumption within the ecological limits of the planet. This challenge necessitates new strategies that pursue structural transformation in a climate constrained world. As that world wakes up to rebuilding economies after the Covid-19 shock, an opportunity to formulate, agree and implement a set of new policy choices that combine developmental and ecological concerns should not be missed.

Developing country policymakers face this challenge from a position of structural weakness in today's hyperglobalized economy and in terms of institutional weaknesses in their ability to mobilize domestic resources. One potentially offsetting advantage of economic latecomers is being able to draw on technologies already developed in more advanced economies to help speed up their transformation. This, however, is easier said than done, because developing countries face a number of obstacles to technology transfer, which are becoming more pronounced in the face of binding environmental constraints.

Macroeconomic priorities necessary in order to overcome those constraints will need to be based on pro-investment policies, as well as strategic collaboration and coordination between the private sector and the government. The former means abandoning austerity as the default policy framework to manage aggregate demand, the latter is needed to monitor the interdependence between investment and production decisions. These decisions concern identifying the areas where the most significant constraints to investment are; how effectively to channel public and private investment to the high-productivity activities; and monitor whether these investments are managed in such a way as to sustain a high-wage future for citizens and to increase long-term productivity. Such disciplining of investment is ensured through monitorable performance standards and a withdrawal of governmental support that fails to achieve its objective within a given period of time, as well as thorough checks on rent-seeking on the part of authorities and entrepreneurs.

One major benefit of green fiscal expansion is higher employment benefits. This is because expanding low-carbon sectors tend to be more labour intensive than shrinking high-carbon sectors. A recent study estimated that renewable energy, energy efficiency and grid enhancement will create around 19 million new jobs worldwide by 2050. As the job losses in the fossil fuel sector will be around 7.4 million, the net addition will be 11.6 million jobs. The greater job-generation capacity of a green path towards structural transformation may be of particular importance for economies where labour migration resulted in an expanding urban informal sector, including because existing technologies were too capital intensive for these economies' structural conditions, as for instance, in parts of Africa.

While climate-related investments on a global scale are needed to transform the global energy system to mitigate the rise in global temperatures, targeted national policies (and resources) are needed to address the adaptation challenge countries are facing from the rising temperature already baked into current patterns of growth. Aligning these global and national challenges is neither straightforward nor automatic. It requires strategic planning and policy intervention.

## Retrofitting the developmental State

Structural transformation, characterized by a shift in the production structure from the primary sector to manufacturing, has traditionally been the most successful way of achieving sustained economic growth and rising living standards. This avenue was followed by the now advanced economies, as well as a few successful late industrializers in East Asia. Their traditional fossil fuel-intensive model, however, cannot satisfy the aspirations of the many other developing countries that are trying to upgrade their national incomes through industrialization because it would take emissions and resource consumption beyond the limits of the planet's ecological capacity.

The answer to this problem is not to forsake industrial development in developing countries. Rather, it is to build a diversified low-carbon economic system, powered by renewable energy sources and green technologies, and where economic activities within and across sectors are interconnected through resource-efficient linkages. Such a solution maintains manufacturing as a central objective because important elements of structural transformation towards a more resilient low-carbon economy will, in most developing countries, continue to depend on the diversification into high-productivity high-wage activities. The energy transition, along with an emergent circular economy, can provide opportunities for a reduction of the carbon footprint of traditional manufacturing, as well as for the manufacturing of devices for a low-carbon economy.

The transition to renewable energy and progress with the circular economy can increase the scope for industrialization for a broad range of developing economies because they decouple economic activities endowed with natural resources. Sources of renewable energy – such as sun, wind and water – are more equally distributed than economically exploitable deposits of fossil fuels, and the circular economy allows extracting resources from used products and waste, thereby reducing the required quantity of new resources.

Many activities related to renewable energy production and the circular economy can economically operate at low scale, opening business opportunities for small firms and rural areas. This will not only help to diversify economic production structures and reduce many countries' dependence on the production of a narrow range of primary commodities, but it can enlarge developing countries' tax bases and foster domestic resource mobilization as a source of development finance. These activities can also help to relax countries' balance-of-payments constraints. Relying on domestic production of energy and food requirements, thereby reducing the import of raw materials, may allow for a sizable reduction of imports, what will liberate scarce foreign exchange for imports of capital goods for industrialization and economic catch-up.

None of these transformations are likely to occur without a developmental State. Successful structural transformations have generally relied on proactive government policies and effective regulations. In addition to undertaking large-scale public investment and financing the investment push required for green structural transformation through green financial instruments, it will involve green industrial policy and state-society relations that not only break existing fossil-fuel interests but also establish clear rules, the enforcement of which can govern the new green investment trajectories and ensure a legitimacy base that can rely on a wide range of societal groups.

Retrofitting the developmental State to deal with adaptation (and mitigation) challenges can still draw lessons from previous success stories. First, there is the need for strong administrative and institutional capacities for the state to formulate industrial policy and lead structural transformation. Experience with the Covid-19 pandemic and the uncertainties associated with climate adaptation suggest that governments should also possess dynamic capabilities to handle partial and at times contradictory evidence; build synergies from multiple tiers of governance; quickly repurpose existing infrastructure; and learn from other governments.

A second lesson concerns the importance of *mechanisms of accountability* of policymakers and implementation agencies, such as through reporting requirements and other obligations to disclose information, combined with more general checks through auditing, independent courts and the press.

A third lesson involves embeddedness – the close relationships between private actors and government officials that can ensure a mutual exchange of information and common understandings. Embeddedness will be particularly important for green industrial policies because societal transition will involve a broad set of stakeholders and reflect broad societal consensus. Combined, the second and third lessons constitute reciprocal control mechanisms.

A final, and related, lesson concerns the state not being too close to private interests and willing to employ disciplining devices to sanction abuse of its support and to discontinue failing projects and activities. Disciplining abusive practices requires clearly defined objectives, measurable performance indicators, appropriate monitoring and evaluation routines, and government autonomy in deciding where and when to apply disciplining devices, as well as where and what experimental approaches to apply, and where and when to change course if something goes wrong.

Given the scale of adaptation needs and the fact that those who suffer the most are the least responsible for the cause of the problem and least able to pay for them, it is clear that advanced economies will be the main source of finance. However, domestic resource mobilization will need to be strengthened, including through more active Central Banks and dedicated public banks.

A climate conscious developmental State must catalyse a public investment-led strategy of diversification. Locally-led climate finance efforts need to be driven by principles that ensure the most effective way of responding to governance and climate challenges and risks, including: i) community-led planning that is anchored within and is supportive of existing devolved institutions, and that promotes ii) social inclusion of climate marginalized people; iii) a process that is flexible and adaptive management towards the creation of resilience investments, with iv) an emphasis on public goods provisioning.

The complexity of systemic risks requires the state to become a regulator and coordinator of private green finance and not simply "de-risk" the opportunity for others to make profit and take more than their share of the benefit. These should be seen as a means to avoid the destructive tendencies of today's ultra-liquid financial sector, where the embedded search for yield is inconsistent with the global needs of climate mitigation, let alone the more localized needs of adaptation.

As central banks around the world were able to help support governments directly during the Covid pandemic, the post-Covid recovery period provides an opportunity to consider how they could also follow this path to support climate-related investments. At the very least, central banks could do more to discontinue support for carbon-intensive and maladaptive activities which means a change in the current programmes that continue to give financial support to fossil fuel industries. In addition to properly regulating the financial sector, Central Banks should also use a fuller range of tools to create and guide finance to green activities. Collateral policy is one of the main tools towards greener central banking: central banks should adjust their collateral regulations and accept financial institutions' green bonds as collateral.

## Reforming adaptation governance I: International finance

At the most basic level, addressing climate change makes structural transformation a global task, in which the advanced economies should take the lead in undertaking profound changes in their patterns of production and consumption but where significant structural and technological changes are also necessary even in the least developed countries. A climate-conscious developmental State must be able to combine the challenges of climate adaptation and mitigation with the longstanding goals of higher productivity jobs, rising living standards and closing the economic and technological gaps with more advanced economies.

The imperative of scaling up climate investment and directing it to where it is needed, requires that the international trade and financial systems are geared to supporting structural transformation, particularly in developing countries. This is currently not the case, particularly when it comes to the adaptation challenge. Aligning ambition and action will require a concerted reform effort at the multilateral level.

In the run up to the Copenhagen COP in 2009, the UNFCCC estimated that annual worldwide costs of adapting to 2 degrees of warming would be between $49 to 171 billion by 2030, with developing countries facing a $34 to 57 billion bill. A decade later, the delay in responding has been costly. Annual adaptation costs in developing countries is now estimated at USD 70 billion, reaching USD 140–300 billion in 2030 and USD 280–500 billion in 2050. Current funding reaches less than a half of current needs and will not reach the 2030 target without a fundamental change of track.

At present, assistance from the international community for climate adaptation continues to rely on an ad hoc combination of official development assistance, multilateral lending and self-insurance schemes against catastrophic risk. This, however, is woefully insufficient to address the systemic impact of recurrent and increasingly frequent climate change-related shocks. For many countries, the result has been an endless cycle of punctuated development and rising indebtedness.

From a development perspective, the challenge of climate adaptation puts the onus on grant-based finance or highly concessional lending mechanisms as key to meeting the adaptation challenge. Two levels of reform for financing the adaption challenge can be identified at the international level: first, steps in support of the climate conscious developmental State to mobilize financial resources for mitigation and adaptation investments, and second, reforming the approach to climate governance internationally.

The first set of reforms should focus on the following:

- **ODA commitments** and pledges need to be met and go further, to increase the proportion of additive finance designated for climate change adaptation and resilience building. *Grants and extremely concessional loans* are essential for adaptation. These could be financed by a green bond and a tax à la Tobin tax, or through the repurposing of fossil fuel subsidies. This must take account of specific country requirements in least developed countries and lower-middle income countries and fossil-fuel exporting economies that need a gradual restructuring of these carbon-intensive industries and an appropriate safety net system to meet climate debt.
- **Debt relief and debt restructuring** for developing countries should be put firmly on the climate agenda. An obvious starting point would be the debt of the V20 countries but linking the climate and debt crises highlights the need for more systemic reforms to the international debt architecture.
- **The multilateral development banks** need additional capital to support more green investments and less fossil fuel or polluting activities and their activities aligned with the Paris Agreement and their "build forward better" commitments, withdrawing from oil, coal and gas and building in transition processes that support people and those industries to make the leap. Policy conditionalities will need to be pruned back and their AAA straitjacket should be relaxed to support experimental or new green technologies and enterprises. G7 countries should use their shareholder power to guide MDBs in this direction. *Regional Development banks* and multilateral development banks could also buy developing countries' green bonds, guaranteeing a more stable demand for such bonds and easier access to long-term capital for developing countries. This could also have a favourable impact on their yields and, consequently, help to mitigate the external service burden, to an extent.
- **Green bond markets** are one way to help raise long-term financing. Yet regulatory standards lag behind the growth of these markets and greenwashing is rife. Given the scale of the challenge, the regulatory framework for the green bond market needs to be supported by *corresponding levels of financing and staffing*, at national and international levels.

The second step would be declaring the adaptation challenge a global emergency and establishing appropriate mechanisms to govern what is effectively, a global public good. This would reflect the reality already experienced by the developing economies struggling to fund climate adaptation needs, help establish a framework to enable them to access finance on appropriate terms and adapt green technologies to their national growth trajectories.

Some seventy-five years ago, the Marshall Plan helped deliver shared prosperity among the war-torn economies. Today, climate change is a challenge to humanity that requires a similarly integrated, anticipatory and strategic approach. Several pathways are discussed in this Report. However, a global, green-oriented structural fund would support realignment of developing countries and deliver funding for both adaptation and mitigation initiatives as an urgent priority. This would generate dividends not only for the developing countries, but for advanced economies too.

## Reforming adaptation governance II: International trade

Many of the initiatives that are gaining momentum in the context of reforming the multilateral system continue to adhere to a view of free markets and capital flows that bears little resemblance to the deep divisions and asymmetries that structure the contemporary global economy. This agenda has done little to advance inclusive development, nor is it likely to provide meaningful support to meeting global emission targets. Pursuing it further is, instead, likely to jeopardize any notion of a just transition for developing countries, by adversely impacting existing export capacities and reducing their policy and fiscal space at a time when it needs to expand to build resilience against future shocks.

Liberalization of trade in environmental goods and services is being pushed at the WTO. While there is no consensus on what goods should be included in the list of environmental goods, most developing countries are net importers of environmentally related goods as identified in the combined list of environmental goods (CLEG). Tariffs on these environmentally related goods are on average 5 to 6 per cent in developing countries with maximum tariffs exceeding 100 per cent on some products, while these tariffs are below 1 per cent in most developed countries. In 2019, tariff revenue collected on these goods by developing countries amounted to USD 15 billion. Trade liberalization in these products will therefore entail a substantial loss of tariff revenue for developing countries.

Environmental services were already classified under a limited range for the negotiations on the General Agreement on Trade in Services (GATS). However, there are attempts to widen the scope of environmental services to include services like engineering, architecture, design, general management, construction. Any resulting commitments in these services will take away the flexibility that the positive list approach in the GATS offered to the developing countries in terms of liberalizing their services trade. Furthermore, there is a risk that forcing the liberalization of vital public utilities would lead to negative development outcomes. This will create an environment of conflicted interests, because public goods will then be delivered for profits. This will further restrict developing countries' ability to use public procurement as a policy tool to achieve social objectives.

Trade liberalization agenda is also being pushed in the context of the circular economy, on the grounds that trade restrictions in the form of export bans may hinder related activities to reuse, repair, refurbish, remanufacture and recycle. However, the calls for the liberalization of trade in remanufactured or recycled goods and waste, dating back to 2004 in the WTO have been rejected by many developing countries, worried that second-hand, refurbished, or remanufactured goods may lock their economies into outdated and less efficient technological solutions and therefore would delay the achievement of environmental goals. Concerns were also raised over liberalizing trade in waste and scrap as that would put additional pressure on the waste management systems of developing countries, especially those which lack a sound regulatory framework for waste management and the associated infrastructure capacities. Furthermore, imports of second-hand clothes and footwear were found to have significant negative impacts on the revamping of the textiles and leather industries, especially in Africa, and on consumer health, human dignity, and culture.

Greenhouse gas emissions in traded goods and services account for around a quarter of of global carbon emissions. This suggests that trade policy, and in particular international trade rules, will play a secondary role in reshaping the climate agenda. Rather than building a trade and environment agenda which pushes trade liberalization, such an agenda should focus on facilitating green technology transfers and providing climate finance to developing countries. Given that structural transformation in a climate constrained world requires a shift from high- to low (and no) -carbon technologies, it can only be achieved when it is approached in an integrated manner by an effective developmental State, with technological change occurring alongside productivity growth, expanding employment opportunities, and rising living standards.

In today's interconnected global economy, the organization of global production through global value chains (GVCs) has caused many carbon emitting production activities to be shifted to developing countries, while associated low-carbon pre-production and post-production activities have been retained by the lead firms and mainly based in the developed countries. The comparative energy efficiency in the North therefore cannot be de-linked from the energy inefficiency in the South. This implies that measures such as Cross Border Adjustment Mechanisms (CBAM), which impose carbon tariffs on imports from developing countries into developed countries, cannot be evaluated independently of these structural conditions. Such mechanisms impose on developing countries the environmental standards that developed countries are choosing. This goes against the principle of common but differentiated responsibility enshrined in the Paris Agreement. Achieving coherence between special different treatment (SDT) and the UNFCCC principle of 'common but differentiated responsibilities' (CBDR) can offer a better point of departure for a development-oriented approach to the trade-climate nexus.

A first step in aligning SDT and CBDR would be to widen non-reciprocal SDT measures to expand policy space for climate and development initiatives. Legal tools such as waivers and peace clauses can help to diminish the number of restrictive rules and extent of regulatory chill, as well as to expand the policy space for developing countries. Advanced economies can provide supportive incentives, such as optional preference schemes that provide ringfenced climate financing additional to ODA or preferential market access in exchange for progress towards nationally determined contributions (NDCs), which could accelerate climate action without resorting to measures with anti-developmental effects.

As a step towards such an arrangement, the international community could support initiatives to transform rules governing intellectual property rights, such as through a WTO Ministerial Declaration on TRIPS and Climate Change, with a view to expanding TRIPS flexibilities for developing countries in relation to climate-related goods and services. This could provide a basis for innovative mechanisms for promoting access to patent-protected critical green technologies. Other initiatives that could support this agenda include the open-sourcing of key green technologies as global public goods and South-South cooperation on low-emission research and design.

## Conclusion

After decades of growing inequalities, polarizing pressures and a pandemic that has destroyed jobs on an unprecedented scale, the economic recovery provides an opportunity to rebalance the distribution of income within and between countries. But, in spite of calls by G7 leaders for "building back a better world", separate economic worlds may in fact be rising from the ashes of 2020, with little chance of them being unified without concerted reform measures at the national and international levels.

A better world will only emerge from the pandemic if strong economic recoveries are promoted and supported in all regions of the global economy, if the economic gains from recovery are skewed towards middle and lower-income households, if health provision, including ready access to vaccines, is treated as a truly global public good and if there is a coordinated big investment push across all countries into carbon-free sources of energy.

# GLOBAL TRENDS AND PROSPECTS: POSITIVE VIBRATIONS OR WAITING IN VAIN?

## A. Introduction

At this writing, eighteen months have passed since the Covid-19 outbreak was declared a pandemic by the WHO. It has tested the responsiveness of governments and the resilience of economic systems everywhere; it has changed social behaviour and personal habits in ways previously unthinkable. The dedication of essential workers has shone through dark times, while the scientific community has harnessed the power of collaborative research and public money to develop a vaccine at breakneck speed.

At the same time, the pandemic has exposed just how unprepared countries, including the wealthiest, are for unexpected shocks, a point underscored by a series of extreme weather events this year, and just how deeply divided the global economy has become. Four decades of eroding government services, heightened inequalities, unchecked financialization and impunity for financial and corporate elites have taken their toll.

On the economic front, the dramatic collapse of output, as countries locked down to contain the spread of the virus, was so dramatic as to trigger unprecedented responses. Massive Central Bank action in rich countries stabilized financial markets and unparalleled (at least in recent times) government spending cushioned firms and households against the worst of the downturn. A global recovery began in the second half of 2020, as countries adopted less draconian ways to manage the health risks, and is still unfolding, even as regional and country prospects vary widely amid disparities in fiscal space, new virus variants and uneven vaccination rates.

Global growth is expected to hit 5.3 per cent this year, the fastest in almost half a century, with some countries restoring (or even surpassing) their output level of 2019 by the end of 2021. The global picture beyond 2021, however, remains shrouded in uncertainty.

Next year will see a deceleration in global growth but for how long and by how much will depend on policy decisions, particularly in the leading economies. Even assuming no further shocks, a return to the pre-pandemic income trend could, under reasonable assumptions, still take until 2030 – a trend that, it should be remembered, itself reflected the weakest growth rate since the end of the Second World War. This is a worrying prospect for many countries. The damage from the Covid-19 crisis has exceeded that from the global financial crisis (GFC) in most parts of the global economy but has been particularly draining in the developing world. The recent decision by the IMF Executive Board to allow a $650 billion issue of special drawing rights (SDRs), the largest in its history, offers a glimmer of hope but the international community has still to acknowledge the scale of the challenge facing many developing countries.

Any crisis does, however, bring with it an opportunity. The scope and scale of governmental support in 2020–21, particularly in advanced economies but also in some emerging markets, broke new ground, or, for those with a sense of history, rediscovered old territory. This response brushed aside entrenched policy dogmas and opened the political space to change the balance of power between the state and the market in managing the economy even as it has served to highlight the constraints on fiscal and policy space that many countries continue to face in a world of footloose capital. In less than a year President Biden's wide ranging policy initiatives have begun to effect concrete change. Domestically, legislation to expand social protection, financed through more progressive taxation, breaks with a long-term trend that has transferred income to the top and risk to the bottom of the income distribution. Internationally, the support from the United States for the new SDR allocation, global minimum corporate taxation, and a waiver of vaccine-related intellectual property rights in the World Trade Organization (WTO) anticipate a renewal of multilateralism that could begin to rein in hyperglobalization and resolve the deepening environmental crisis.

Whether or not the world builds back better from the pandemic will not, however, depend on the actions of a single country but on concerted efforts to rebalance the global economy. Hurdling the barriers to greater prosperity will depend on improved coordination of the policy choices made in leading economies over the coming years as they push to maintain the momentum of recovery and build resilience against future shocks (see Chapter II). The reluctance of other advanced economies to follow the lead of the United States on the vaccine waiver is a worrying sign and a costly one; on one recent estimate, the cumulative cost (in terms of lost income) of delayed vaccination will, by 2025, amount to $2.3 trillion with the developing world shouldering the bulk of that cost (EIU, 2021).

But coordination among the leading economies will not be sufficient either. Renewed international support is needed for developing countries, many of which face, given their limited access to vaccines and the spread of new virus variants, a spiralling health crisis, even as they struggle with a growing burden of debt and face the prospects of a lost decade. That effort should also prompt us to rethink – or, perhaps, revive – the role that fiscal policy can play, beyond the countercyclical interventions of late. Delivering the necessary support will also require the kind of systemic reforms to the international economic architecture that were promised after the global GFC but were quickly abandoned in the face of resistance from the winners of hyperglobalization (*TDR 2017*). And amid all these efforts, policymakers will need to stay wary of inflation scaremongering that would derail progress before it has really taken off.

This chapter is organized into four sections. Section B outlines key developments in the global economy in 2020–21, focusing, in particular, on misguided fears of inflation and the role of fiscal policy and public debt beyond the pandemic. Section C analyses the situation of developing countries in the system of global finance, focusing on the issue of debt sustainability and counter-cyclical measures. Section D reviews the trends in global trade and commodities markets. Section E surveys regional macroeconomic trends in greater depth.

# B. The Global Economy: Building Back Separately?

## 1. Global growth prospects

The global economy is set for a strong recovery in 2021, albeit with a good deal of uncertainty clouding the details at the regional and country levels over the second half of the year. As in the past, policy makers continue to pay undue attention to financial markets, whose horizon rarely stretches beyond quarterly macroeconomic and earnings data and whose sentiment appears jittery even in the face of small changes in leading indicators.

After a 3.5 per cent fall in 2020, UNCTAD expects world output to grow 5.3 per cent this year, partially recovering the ground lost in 2020. However, considering the average annual global growth rate of 3 per cent in 2017–2019, world income will still be 3.7 per cent below where its pre-pandemic trend would have put it by 2022 (Figure 1.1). Based on the nominal

gross domestic product (GDP) estimates for this year, the expected shortfall represents a cumulative income loss of about USD 10 trillion[1] in 2020–21. Looking ahead UNCTAD expects world output to grow 3.6 per cent in 2022 (Table 1.1).

Despite this two-year boost to the global economy, it will take several years for world income to recover the loss from the Covid-19 shock. Assuming, for example, an annual growth rate of 3.5 per cent from 2023 onwards (an optimistic assumption), global output will only revert to its 2017–2019 trend by 2030. Since the pre-Covid 19 trend was, as discussed in previous *Reports*, unsatisfactory – average annual global growth in the decade after the 2009–10 financial crisis was the slowest since the end of the Second World War – this is a prospect that should raise alarm in policy circles.

**TABLE 1.1  World output growth, 1991–2022**
*(Annual percentage change)*

| Country groups | 1991–2000[a] | 2001–2008[a] | 2009–2018[a] | 2009 | 2010 | 2011 | 2012 | 2013 | 2014 | 2015 | 2016 | 2017 | 2018 | 2019 | 2020 | 2021[b] | 2022[b] |
|---|---|---|---|---|---|---|---|---|---|---|---|---|---|---|---|---|---|
| **World** | **3.0** | **3.6** | **2.9** | **-1.3** | **4.5** | **3.3** | **2.8** | **2.7** | **3.1** | **3.1** | **2.7** | **3.4** | **3.2** | **2.5** | **-3.5** | **5.3** | **3.6** |
| **Africa** | **2.5** | **5.7** | **3.0** | **3.9** | **5.6** | **-1.0** | **8.0** | **0.7** | **3.3** | **2.6** | **1.7** | **3.4** | **3.3** | **2.9** | **-3.4** | **3.2** | **2.9** |
| North Africa (incl. South Sudan) | 3.1 | 5.4 | 1.0 | 3.7 | 4.7 | -11.1 | 13.3 | -6.8 | -0.3 | 1.7 | 2.7 | 5.1 | 4.1 | 3.2 | -5.2 | 4.2 | 3.1 |
| South Africa | 2.1 | 4.4 | 1.8 | -1.5 | 3.0 | 3.3 | 2.2 | 2.5 | 1.8 | 1.2 | 0.4 | 1.4 | 0.8 | 0.2 | -7.0 | 4.0 | 2.3 |
| Sub-Saharan Africa (excl. South Africa and South Sudan) | 2.1 | 6.5 | 4.8 | 5.7 | 7.1 | 5.7 | 6.1 | 5.5 | 5.9 | 3.4 | 1.5 | 3.0 | 3.5 | 3.4 | -1.5 | 2.5 | 2.9 |
| **America** | **3.5** | **2.8** | **2.0** | **-2.5** | **3.3** | **2.3** | **2.3** | **2.1** | **2.2** | **2.3** | **1.1** | **2.2** | **2.6** | **1.7** | **-4.4** | **5.6** | **2.9** |
| Latin America and the Caribbean | 3.2 | 3.9 | 1.9 | -2.1 | 6.2 | 4.6 | 2.7 | 2.9 | 1.1 | 0.3 | -0.9 | 1.3 | 1.1 | 0.1 | -7.1 | 5.5 | 2.6 |
| Central America (excl. Mexico) and Caribbean | 3.1 | 4.8 | 3.3 | -0.7 | 3.5 | 3.9 | 3.6 | 3.3 | 3.3 | 4.2 | 2.9 | 3.0 | 3.1 | 2.1 | -8.1 | 3.9 | 2.9 |
| Mexico | 3.2 | 2.2 | 2.6 | -5.3 | 5.1 | 3.7 | 3.6 | 1.4 | 2.8 | 3.3 | 2.6 | 2.1 | 2.2 | 0.0 | -8.3 | 6.2 | 2.8 |
| South America *of which:* | 3.2 | 4.3 | 1.5 | -1.3 | 6.9 | 4.9 | 2.3 | 3.3 | 0.3 | -1.1 | -2.5 | 0.8 | 0.4 | -0.2 | -6.5 | 5.5 | 2.5 |
| Argentina | 4.0 | 5.0 | 1.2 | -5.9 | 10.1 | 6.0 | -1.0 | 2.4 | -2.5 | 2.7 | -2.1 | 2.7 | -2.5 | -2.1 | -9.9 | 6.7 | 2.9 |
| Brazil | 2.8 | 3.7 | 1.1 | -0.1 | 7.5 | 4.0 | 1.9 | 3.0 | 0.5 | -3.5 | -3.3 | 1.3 | 1.8 | 1.4 | -4.1 | 4.9 | 1.8 |
| North America *of which:* | 3.6 | 2.5 | 2.0 | -2.6 | 2.6 | 1.7 | 2.2 | 1.9 | 2.6 | 2.9 | 1.7 | 2.4 | 3.0 | 2.1 | -3.7 | 5.7 | 3.0 |
| Canada | 3.0 | 2.5 | 1.9 | -2.9 | 3.1 | 3.2 | 1.8 | 2.3 | 2.9 | 0.7 | 1.0 | 3.0 | 2.4 | 1.9 | -5.4 | 5.1 | 2.9 |
| United States | 3.6 | 2.6 | 2.0 | -2.5 | 2.6 | 1.6 | 2.3 | 1.8 | 2.5 | 3.1 | 1.7 | 2.3 | 3.0 | 2.2 | -3.5 | 5.7 | 3.0 |
| **Asia (excl. Cyprus)** | **4.3** | **5.9** | **5.2** | **2.4** | **7.8** | **6.0** | **5.0** | **5.4** | **4.9** | **4.9** | **4.9** | **5.1** | **4.6** | **3.8** | **-1.1** | **5.9** | **4.7** |
| Central Asia | -3.3 | 8.5 | 5.5 | 3.3 | 7.6 | 8.1 | 6.0 | 6.9 | 5.6 | 3.5 | 3.2 | 4.5 | 4.7 | 4.7 | -0.3 | 4.3 | 3.1 |
| East Asia *of which:* | 4.4 | 5.8 | 5.3 | 2.8 | 8.0 | 5.9 | 5.2 | 5.5 | 5.0 | 4.8 | 4.7 | 5.2 | 4.8 | 4.3 | 0.3 | 6.7 | 4.7 |
| China | 10.6 | 10.9 | 7.9 | 9.4 | 10.4 | 9.6 | 7.9 | 7.8 | 7.4 | 6.9 | 6.7 | 6.9 | 6.7 | 6.1 | 2.3 | 8.3 | 5.7 |
| Japan | 1.2 | 1.2 | 1.0 | -5.7 | 4.1 | 0.0 | 1.4 | 2.0 | 0.3 | 1.6 | 0.8 | 1.7 | 0.6 | 0.3 | -4.7 | 2.4 | 2.1 |
| Republic of Korea | 6.8 | 4.9 | 3.2 | 0.8 | 6.8 | 3.7 | 2.4 | 3.2 | 3.2 | 2.8 | 3.0 | 3.2 | 2.9 | 2.0 | -0.9 | 3.9 | 2.8 |
| South Asia *of which:* | 4.8 | 6.7 | 5.9 | 4.0 | 8.7 | 5.6 | 3.4 | 5.0 | 6.1 | 6.4 | 8.0 | 6.6 | 4.9 | 3.1 | -5.6 | 5.8 | 5.7 |
| India | 5.9 | 7.6 | 7.0 | 5.0 | 11.0 | 6.2 | 4.8 | 6.1 | 7.0 | 7.9 | 8.2 | 7.2 | 6.6 | 4.6 | -7.0 | 7.2 | 6.7 |
| South-East Asia *of which:* | 4.9 | 5.7 | 5.1 | 2.0 | 7.8 | 4.9 | 6.0 | 5.0 | 4.5 | 4.7 | 4.8 | 5.3 | 5.1 | 4.4 | -3.9 | 3.5 | 4.7 |
| Indonesia | 4.2 | 5.2 | 5.4 | 4.6 | 6.2 | 6.2 | 6.0 | 5.6 | 5.0 | 4.9 | 5.0 | 5.1 | 5.2 | 5.0 | -2.1 | 3.6 | 4.9 |
| *Western Asia (excl. Cyprus) of which:* | 4.1 | 5.5 | 4.1 | -1.3 | 5.7 | 8.0 | 4.6 | 4.9 | 3.3 | 3.8 | 3.2 | 2.3 | 2.1 | 1.3 | -2.9 | 3.5 | 3.2 |
| Saudi Arabia | 1.7 | 4.5 | 3.7 | -2.1 | 5.0 | 10.0 | 5.4 | 2.7 | 3.7 | 4.1 | 1.7 | -0.7 | 2.4 | 0.3 | -4.1 | 2.7 | 3.3 |
| Turkey | 3.9 | 6.0 | 6.0 | -4.8 | 8.4 | 11.2 | 4.8 | 8.5 | 4.9 | 6.1 | 3.3 | 7.5 | 3.0 | 0.9 | 1.8 | 3.9 | 3.6 |
| **Europe (incl. Cyprus)** *of which:* | **1.6** | **2.5** | **1.2** | **-4.5** | **2.4** | **2.0** | **0.1** | **0.5** | **1.7** | **1.9** | **1.8** | **2.5** | **2.0** | **1.5** | **-6.2** | **4.3** | **3.0** |
| European Union (EU 27) *of which:* | 2.1 | 2.1 | 1.1 | -4.4 | 2.3 | 1.9 | -0.7 | 0.0 | 1.6 | 2.3 | 2.0 | 2.8 | 2.1 | 1.6 | -6.2 | 4.0 | 3.3 |
| Euro area *of which:* | 2.1 | 1.9 | 1.0 | -4.5 | 2.2 | 1.7 | -0.9 | -0.2 | 1.4 | 2.1 | 1.9 | 2.6 | 1.9 | 1.3 | -6.6 | 4.1 | 3.4 |
| France | 2.0 | 1.8 | 1.0 | -2.9 | 2.0 | 2.2 | 0.3 | 0.6 | 1.0 | 1.1 | 1.1 | 2.3 | 1.8 | 1.5 | -8.0 | 5.2 | 3.4 |
| Germany | 1.6 | 1.3 | 1.6 | -5.7 | 4.2 | 3.9 | 0.4 | 0.4 | 2.2 | 1.5 | 2.2 | 2.6 | 1.3 | 0.6 | -4.9 | 2.2 | 3.2 |
| Italy | 1.6 | 0.9 | -0.3 | -5.3 | 1.7 | 0.7 | -3.0 | -1.8 | 0.0 | 0.8 | 1.3 | 1.7 | 0.9 | 0.3 | -8.9 | 5.5 | 3.0 |
| Russian Federation | -4.7 | 6.8 | 1.3 | -7.8 | 4.5 | 4.3 | 4.0 | 1.8 | 0.7 | -2.0 | 0.2 | 1.8 | 2.5 | 1.3 | -3.0 | 3.8 | 2.3 |
| United Kingdom | 2.9 | 2.5 | 1.7 | -4.1 | 2.1 | 1.3 | 1.4 | 2.2 | 2.9 | 2.4 | 1.7 | 1.7 | 1.3 | 1.4 | -9.9 | 6.7 | 2.1 |
| **Oceania** *of which:* | **3.7** | **3.4** | **2.7** | **1.9** | **2.4** | **2.7** | **3.7** | **2.1** | **2.8** | **2.6** | **2.9** | **2.7** | **2.8** | **1.9** | **-2.4** | **3.1** | **2.8** |
| Australia | 3.8 | 3.4 | 2.6 | 1.9 | 2.4 | 2.7 | 3.9 | 2.1 | 2.6 | 2.3 | 2.8 | 2.5 | 2.8 | 1.8 | -2.5 | 3.2 | 2.8 |
| **Memo items:** | | | | | | | | | | | | | | | | | |
| **Developed (M49, incl. Republic of Korea)** | **2.5** | **2.5** | **1.7** | **-3.5** | **2.8** | **1.7** | **1.3** | **1.4** | **2.0** | **2.3** | **1.7** | **2.4** | **2.4** | **1.7** | **-4.7** | **4.7** | **2.9** |
| **Developing (M49)** | **4.9** | **6.7** | **5.2** | **3.3** | **8.1** | **6.3** | **5.6** | **5.1** | **4.9** | **4.5** | **4.3** | **4.9** | **4.6** | **3.7** | **-1.8** | **6.2** | **4.7** |

*Source:* UNCTAD secretariat calculations, based on United Nations Global Policy Model; United Nations, Department of Economic and Social Affairs (UNDESA), National Accounts *Main Aggregates* database, and *World Economic Situation and Prospects* (WESP): *Update as of mid-2021*; ECLAC, 2021; Organisation for Economic Co-operation and Development (OECD), 2021; International Monetary Fund (IMF), *World Economic Outlook, April 2021;* Economist Intelligence Unit, *EIU CountryData database*; JP Morgan, *Global Data Watch*; and national sources.

*Note:* Calculations for country aggregates are based on GDP at constant 2015 dollars.
   a  Average.
   b  Forecasts.

Such an environment would not get the 2030 Agenda for Sustainable Development back on track and would hinder efforts to mobilize the additional resources needed to address the climate challenge. Moreover, if unanticipated shocks – whether of an epidemiological, financial or climatic nature – hit again, or policy efforts to sustain the current recovery begin to falter, the negative economic impact of Covid-19 would last longer. This is an outcome that cannot be dismissed lightly, given what happened in the aftermath of the GFC and the current, broken state of international policy coordination (see also Chapter II).

The recovery has to date been unbalanced, reflecting fault lines that were present before the pandemic. There have been substantial differences in GDP growth between regions and countries, with many developing countries falling behind; a sectoral divide between the recovery in services and goods production but also within the service sector between booming financial and digital services and the depressed hospitality and entertainment sectors; and a sharp divergence in income (and wealth) gains amongst social groups. So far, the world economy appears to be building back separately.

In most regions, but particularly in the developing world, the damage from the Covid-19 crisis has been much greater than after the GFC, notably in Africa and South Asia (Figure 1.2). Geographically, as of mid-2021, post-lockdown growth accelerations were concentrated mostly in North America, with close

**FIGURE 1.1**  **World output level, 2016–2022**
*(Index numbers, 2016 = 100)*

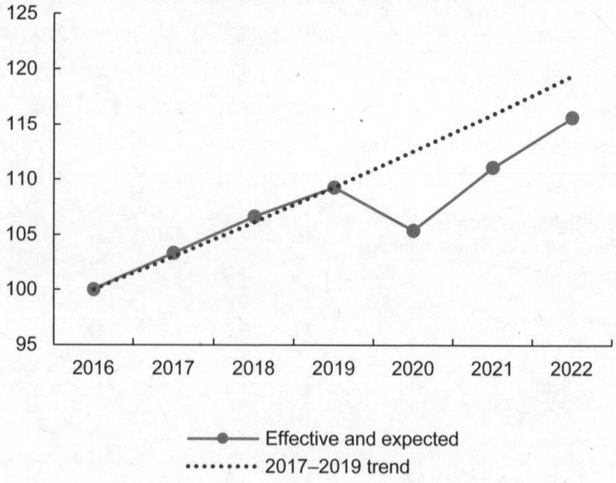

Legend:
—●— Effective and expected
·········· 2017–2019 trend

*Source:*  See Table 1.1.

regional trade linkages reinforcing a strong fiscal stimulus and monetary accommodation in the United States, and in East Asia, where an infrastructure investment drive (through state-owned enterprises) in China has helped growth ripple across the region.

Regional trends in the world economy are surveyed in the final section of this chapter. Here, an initial evaluation of differences in the speed of recovery can be made by examining expected cumulative GDP growth between 2019 and 2021 in countries in the Group of Twenty (G20)[2] (Figure 1.3).

**FIGURE 1.2**  **The economic impact of GFC, 2009–2010, vs. Covid-19, 2020–2021**

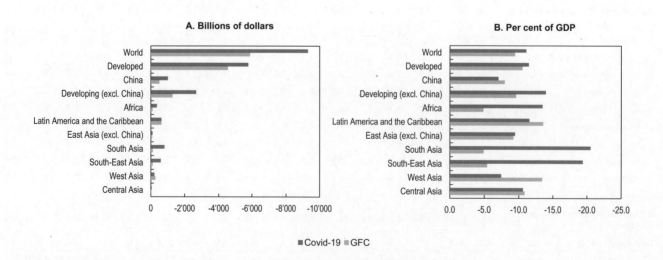

*Source:*  UNCTAD secretariat calculations, based on official data and estimates generated by United Nations Global Policy Model.
*Note:*  Estimated loss from GFC corresponds to the accumulated income loss of 2009 and 2010, relative to 2006 to 2008 trend; and the estimated loss from Covid-19 corresponds to the accumulated income loss of 2020 and 2021, relative to 2017 to 2019 trend.

The standout performances, on this measure, have taken place in the two G20 countries that avoided a recession in 2020: China and Turkey. In the case of China, an early lockdown policy, combined with massive testing and related public health measures, followed by a rapid vaccine roll out from the middle of 2021, helped to contain the spread of the virus and allow for a relatively swift rebound of activity. On the demand side, the maintenance of domestic investment projects and the post-lockdown surge in the foreign demand for industrial goods have helped maintain the pace of recovery, although concerns remain about the financial position of some highly indebted state-owned enterprises and the danger of new virus variants.

Turkey did see a sharp contraction in the second quarter of 2020, but this was followed by strong growth in the third quarter, largely thanks to accommodative monetary policy and the ensuing credit boom. Despite a resurgence in infections during the second quarter of 2021, growth has been driven by the country's industrial sector and budgetary support to businesses from the government. Rising prices and pressures on the lira are, however, clouding growth prospects for the second half of 2021, raising concerns about its sustainability.

China's growth and the resulting demand for manufactures is expected to help the Republic of Korea make a full recovery from the pandemic in 2021. The same holds for Australia, albeit less rapidly due to extended lockdowns in 2021, and propelled by commodity exports rather than manufactures. In contrast, despite the expansion in net export demand of goods, sluggish domestic demand is expected to keep GDP in Japan below its pre-Covid level.

India suffered a contraction of 7 per cent in 2020 and is expected to grow 7.2 per cent in 2021, while Indonesia had a milder contraction of 2.1 per cent in 2020 and is expected to grow 3.6 per cent in 2021, which is fairly weak given its growth rates in recent years. As the discussion of regional trends shows in section E, the recovery in India is constrained by the ongoing human and economic cost of Covid-19, and the negative impact of food price inflation on private consumption.

Rising commodity prices will help recovery in oil-exporting countries, albeit unevenly. The Russian Federation will almost triple its 2019 GDP growth of 1.3 per cent this year, but a similar bounce back will not hold for Saudi Arabia, due to the greater reliance of its economy on oil production and OPEC's output

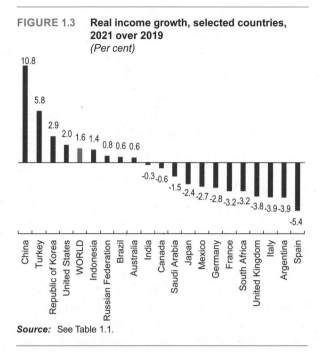

**FIGURE 1.3** **Real income growth, selected countries, 2021 over 2019**
*(Per cent)*

*Source:* See Table 1.1.

quotas (even if it raises them). The spike in commodity demand and relative prices will also be insufficient to raise South Africa's 2021 GDP above its 2019 level, due to a weak investment climate (which pre-dates the pandemic) and stringent fiscal constraints.

In the Americas, the fast recovery in the United States recovery is expected to raise GDP to 2 per cent above its pre-Covid-19 level. This should help Canada to approach its 2019 level. In contrast, despite the pull of demand of the United States, Mexico will fall short of its pre-Covid-19 income in 2021 because of its relatively deeper recession and small domestic fiscal relief in 2020. Argentina is in a similar situation due to tight financial constraints, resulting in large part from its heavy pre-pandemic external borrowing. Brazil should grow slightly above its 2019 GDP this year, thanks to the positive effect of higher commodity exports and a relatively larger and well-targeted fiscal stimulus than in Mexico and Argentina.

Europe is experiencing a disappointing growth recovery, despite a very accommodative monetary policy stance adopted by the ECB. The policies agreed by eurozone governments have been too little and too late. In numbers, despite the recovery in its net exports, the German GDP in 2021 is expected to be almost 3 per cent below its 2019 level. The recovery tends to be even weaker in France, Italy and the United Kingdom, where Brexit disruptions have counteracted the effects of fiscal expansion and rapid vaccine roll out. Europe's historical coordination problem will be felt hardest in Spain and Italy, where the 2021 GDP is expected to be 5.6 and 3.8 per cent below their pre-pandemic level, respectively.

In terms of the sectoral composition of the recovery, the disruptive effects of the pandemic on some global value chains and the rebound in the demand for goods have created bottlenecks (Goodman and Chokshi 2021). The problem has been most acute in semiconductors, which has had a knock-on impact on electronics and auto production in many countries (King et al., 2021), and construction materials, which raised the cost of residential investment (AGC 2021).

In the service sector, as of mid-2021, output was still depressed in relation to its pre-pandemic level in many economies, especially in personal urban services (Furman and Powell III 2021). The increased adoption of remote work is expected to have a long-lasting negative effect on business travel and lodging (McKinsey 2021), but the reopening of many economies after their vaccination drives should see a partial recovery in personal recreational services by the end of 2021 and beginning of 2022 (European Commission, 2020).

Even in the United States, where the economy is recovering quickly from the Covid-19 shock, there was still a large gap between the rebound in the demand for goods and the demand for services in the beginning of 2021 (Figure 1.4). Since services account for most jobs in advanced economies, the rebound to pre-pandemic levels in the United States labour market is likely to be incomplete during 2021, especially if we measure labour slack by the employment-population ratio of prime-age workers *and* factor in the previous negative impact of the GFC (Figure 1.5).

## 2. Inflationary Pressures: Nothing to Fear but Fear Itself

The initial economic impacts of Covid-19 were the deep recession and lower inflation. However, since the second half of 2020, due to a combination of the quick recovery of global aggregate demand and some adverse supply shocks, prices have been accelerating in the world's advanced economies.

Globally, the rise in commodity prices has pushed the cost of basic inputs higher. Since mid-2020, metal and oil prices have been on the rise and, in May of 2021, annual food inflation reached almost 40 per cent, its highest value in ten years according

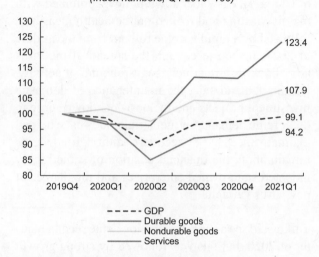

**FIGURE 1.4**  **Real GDP and personal consumption expenditures in the United States, 2019–2021**
*(Index numbers, Q4 2019=100)*

----- GDP
—— Durable goods
—— Nondurable goods
—— Services

***Source:*** United States Bureau of Economic Analysis.

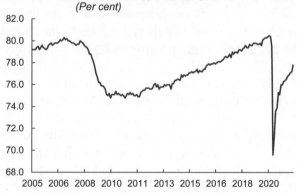

**FIGURE 1.5**  **Employment-population ratio in the United States, January 2005–July 2021**
*(Per cent)*

***Source:*** St. Louis Federal Reserve bank.

to the FAO food price index. The increase in food prices has contributed to the rise in the world hunger index since the pandemic, with the greatest harm in developing countries (see Box 1.4 and FAO, 2021a). The pandemic has caused bottlenecks in global value chains, especially in sectors that depend heavily on semiconductors, which, in turn, has raised the price of capital goods and durable consumer goods around the world, with a stronger impact in advanced economies. Figure 1.6 shows the inflation history of the main economies of the world since 2005.

Unsurprisingly, prices have been accelerating faster in countries which had been experiencing higher inflation before the pandemic due to exchange-rate pressures, such as Argentina and Turkey (see Figure 1.7). In Brazil, domestic political factors drove a depreciation of the domestic currency relatively faster than in other developing countries, while a severe drought pushed the economy to use more expensive sources of electrical power. In mid-2021, the two adverse shocks increased inflation to almost 9 per cent, prompting the Brazilian Central Bank to hike its short-run interest rate.

Currency depreciations and commodity price rises also pushed inflation up in Mexico, South Africa, and the Russian Federation, but so far at a

more moderate pace than in Brazil. As of mid-2021, these three economies have registered consumer price inflation between 4 and 6 per cent, which, in turn, has prompted the Central Banks in Mexico and the Russian Federation to tighten monetary policy.

In India, consumer inflation was already at 6 per cent before the pandemic. The Covid-19 shock caused a temporary dip in prices, but as the economy recovered and food prices accelerated, the country returned to a 6 per cent inflation rate in mid-2021.

**FIGURE 1.6**   **Consumer inflation, selected economies, December 2005–December 2020**
*(Per cent)*

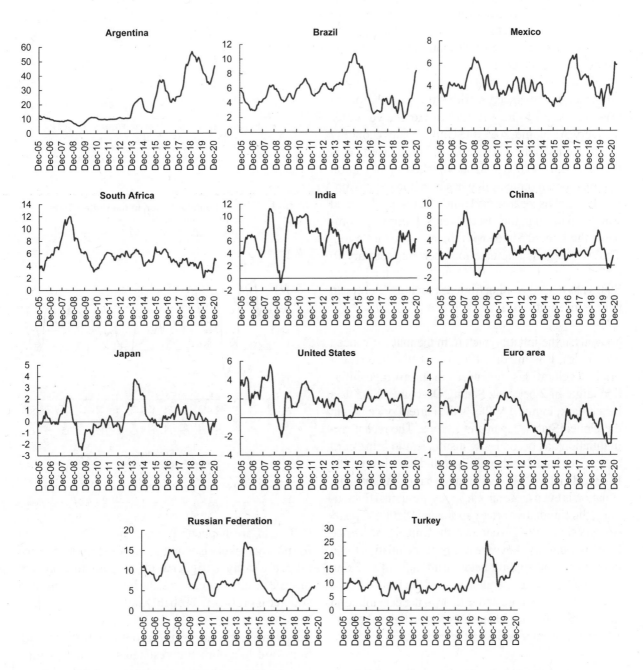

***Source:*** UNCTAD secretariat calculations based on Refinitiv data.

In contrast, in China, the government had been adopting restrictive measures to fight inflation before the Covid-19 shock. In mid-2020, the sudden stop of the economy increased the impact of the restrictive measures and pushed the economy briefly into deflation. As the economy recovered, inflation became positive again, yet still low (around 2 per cent) by international standards.

In the advanced world, Japan is still struggling with a deflationary trend, meaning the recent acceleration in prices has been insufficient to offset the deflationary pressures caused by the pandemic. A more moderate version of the Japanese story is unfolding in Europe, where inflation has been on the rise, but still not sufficiently to compensate for almost eight years of effective price stagnation with annual increases below the target of 2 per cent.

So far, in the advanced world, stronger inflationary pressures seem to be a feature of the United States recovery. As of mid-2021, the United States economy registered its highest consumer inflation in ten years (5.4 per cent), which some have taken as indication that macroeconomic policy has been too expansionary. To emphasize how the United States has deviated from its pattern in the last ten years, Figure 1.8 compares the United States with the euro area inflation. The two regions fluctuate together, but contrary to what happened after the GFC, inflation in the United States has been deviating from its previous "European path" since mid-2021.

To analyse the inflation picture in the main advanced economies, it is important to see whether the recent price accelerations deviate from an average inflation target of 2 per cent. Setting December 2005 as a benchmark, Figure 1.9 shows the current price gap in the United States, Japan and Europe. The recent rise in inflation has been clearly insufficient to bring euro area prices back to where they would have been if the ECB had met its 2 per cent inflation target. In Japan, the situation is even more striking. Despite annual fluctuations, the cumulative price gap shows inflation of just 5 per cent since 2005. In contrast, the United States price index ran slightly above the two per cent inflation trend until 2014, and slightly below it from 2014 to 2020. The recent price acceleration pushed the United States price index once more above the two per cent inflation trend, which in turn will probably lead to tighter Federal Reserve monetary policy in the near future.

Temporary inflation spikes are normal after deep recessions; they occurred in the recovery from the

**FIGURE 1.7** **Variation in exchange rate of selected currencies vis-à-vis the dollar of the United States, selected time periods, 1 Jan. 2020–30 Jul. 2021**
*(Per cent)*

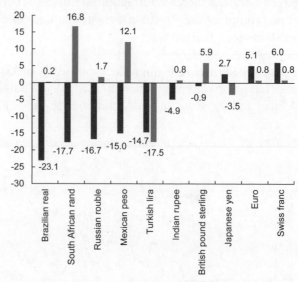

■ 1 Jan. 2020–31 Jul. 2020   ■ 31 Jul. 2020–30 Jul. 2021

*Source:* UNCTAD secretariat calculations, based on Refinitiv data.
*Note:* A positive value corresponds to an appreciation.

**FIGURE 1.8** **Consumer inflation in the United States and the euro area**
*(Per cent)*

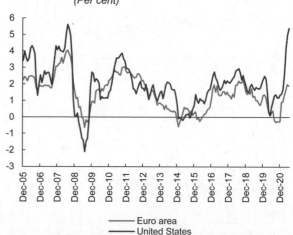

—— Euro area
—— United States

*Source:* UNCTAD secretariat calculations based on Refinitiv data.

GFC and are happening again now. The question for policy makers is whether or not temporary price hikes are likely to trigger a self-perpetuating process of accelerating price rises. Is inflation becoming a structural problem? Probably not.

To see why, it is necessary to put inflation expectations and long-term interest rates into the picture. If the inflation shock is temporary, expected inflation remains anchored on the government's target and long-run interest rates show a reversion to the mean. Focusing on the United States, which sets the standard for bond markets elsewhere, Figure 1.10 shows the 10-year breakeven inflation implicit in United States Treasury Securities. The number is the expected inflation that makes the return on inflation-indexed bonds equal to the return on non-indexed bonds. Because of risk aversion, the breakeven inflation tends to overestimate expected inflation by a constant value.

As of mid-2021, the 10-year breakeven inflation implicit in the United States government bonds was 2.4 per cent, a substantial increase from the depth of the Covid-19 shock in 2020, when this variable fell to 0.5 per cent. However, when the change in expected inflation is put in historical perspective, the recent increase seems to be a return to normal. The same thing happened after the GFC and the current breakeven inflation is approximately equal to its value in 2005–07 and 2011–13. So far, there is no evidence of rising inflation expectations in the United States economy. In fact, the recent increase in expected inflation seems to be a correction of the low-inflation forecasts that predominated in 2014–19.

Inflation tends to become a problem when it ignites a price-wage spiral that feeds on itself, as happened in many economies during the 1970s, when two oil shocks and a productivity slowdown in overheating economies led to a cost-induced inflation, wage increases, and another round of cost-induced inflation. Today, because of the relatively lower bargaining power of workers in the United States economy, it is unlikely that the recent price acceleration will turn explosive. On one side, (see Figure 1.11) the United States labour market does show a recovery in real wages, which started before Covid-19 and for statistical reasons was amplified during the critical months of the pandemic (lower-wage workers lost their jobs and this pushed the mean real wage up). However, on the other side, the recent increase in real wage is happening after 35 years of stagnation, meaning it is simply too early to state that the current recovery will start a wage-price spiral.

The inflationary impact of the real wage depends on labour productivity. If the real wage grows but labour productivity grows faster, the labour share of output falls. As a result, the profit share goes up and prices may even fall, if firms decide or are forced to pass the gain to customers (Barbosa-Filho and Taylor 2006; *TDR 2020*). The data from the United States economy shows an increase in the workers' share of

**FIGURE 1.9**  **Price gap from a 2 per cent inflation trend, selected economies, December 2005–April 2021**
*(Index numbers, December 2005=100)*

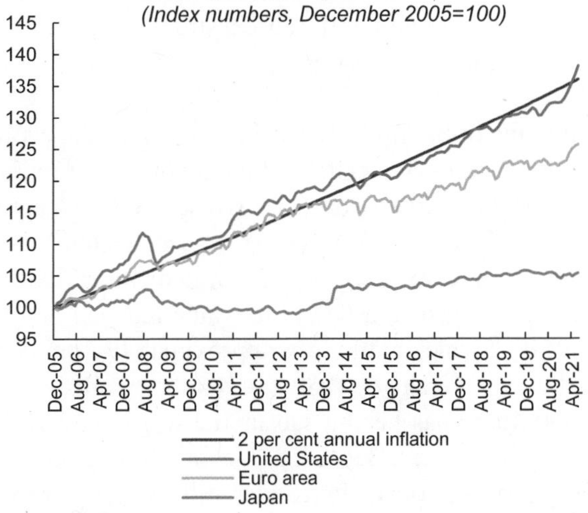

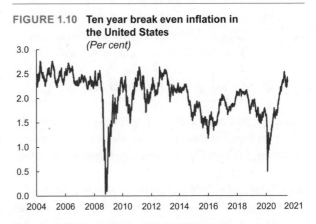

*Source:* UNCTAD secretariat calculations, based on national sources.

**FIGURE 1.10**  **Ten year break even inflation in the United States**
*(Per cent)*

*Source:* FRED, Federal Reserve Bank of St. Louis.

**FIGURE 1.11**  **Real wage in the United States, January 1979–March 2021**
*(Index numbers, 2010=100)*

*Source:* FRED, Federal Reserve Bank of St. Louis.

income immediately after the Covid-19 shock and subsequently a fall, but like with the real wage rise, it is too early to know whether these fluctuations in income distribution will cause a structural change in inflation, for two reasons.

First, the initial impact of a sudden stop of the economy is to reduce profits, and the labour share jumps up for temporary reasons; and as discussed in Chapter II, this may already have been reversed. Second, even with the recent increase, the United States labour share only just returned to its value reached before the GFC, which in turn was approximately 5 per cent below its average in 1980–90. In other words, since 2000, there has been a substantial wage squeeze in the United States. Because of the low starting point in 2019, firms in the United States still have large profit margins to absorb a higher real wage without raising inflation. In an extreme case, the economy's recovery and initial increase in the labour cost may push firms to innovate, which, in turn, raises productivity and accommodates the higher real wage without excessive inflationary pressures (Storm and Nastepaad 2012).

## 3. Fiscal Policy and Public Debt

In developed countries the aggressive spread of the virus prompted a set of equally aggressive measures to counter its paralyzing consequences. In contrast, most of the developing world faced the same financial, structural and political constraints that had hampered their ability to intervene in the economy over previous decades, resulting – in most cases – in an exacerbation of domestic and international inequities.

However, even in countries with fiscal space, there is a risk of premature withdrawal of fiscal (as well as monetary) stimulus. While a consensus has emerged about the need for significant public sector intervention, there is no clear agreement yet about its composition or duration. If, as in previous recessions, state intervention is confined to absorbing the immediate shock, it is likely that the deep sources of instability will not be addressed.[3] If that becomes the case, the much-heralded post-pandemic paradigm shift in policymaking would prove to be more a matter of rhetoric than reality.

The lesson from previous crises and recovery experiences strongly suggests that the political space created by the pandemic should be used to re-assess the role of fiscal policy in the global economy, as well as the practices which have widened inequalities.

## (a) Speculation and austerity: tame one to stop the other

At the onset of the pandemic, most governments were quick to announce large spending packages, as recommended by international organizations (IMF, 2020a; TDR 2020). Yet, in the absence of an internationally coordinated effort, the global stimulus was not as effective as it could have been. In many cases, actual measures were insufficient and considerably smaller than initial announcements (see Box 1.1).

According to IMF data, 41 developing countries actually reduced their total expenditures in 2020, 33 of which nonetheless saw their public debt-to-GDP ratios increase. A similar divergence is evident also within the group of developed economies (Box 1.1, Table B1.1),[4] but Figure 1.12 shows how the constraints between the two groups remain significantly different: developed countries were able to increase their total primary outlays, relative to the past, significantly more than developing countries with similar or lower public debt ratios in 2019.

To understand why this has happened, two relevant factors are worth recalling. First, while modern economies are structured to create money for the purpose of public and private spending, liquidity creation does not necessarily improve access to foreign currency for developing countries, an essential requirement to sustain spending in an open and financialized system (TDR 2020), nor for developed countries in common currency arrangements (Izurieta, 2001). Second, under these conditions, a government's budgetary strategy is subject to private, mostly foreign, investors' willingness to lend, which is, under current structures and practices, influenced by a short-term and speculative logic and a pro-austerity bias (Chandrasekhar, 2016). As such, global financial markets as currently structured exert considerable influence on policy, to the detriment of its public functions (Nesvetailova and Palan, 2020).

Agreement on practical solutions to reduce fiscal constraints has proven elusive. Actions taken over the past months to lessen foreign exchange constraints on developing economies have been narrow in scope and temporary in nature: the G20 granted a suspension of the debt servicing of bilateral loans to a small number of countries, and the IMF and the World Bank offered emergency credit. No significant action was taken regarding private financial claims, or to address the urgent need of direct assistance (in cash, services or

**BOX 1.1**   Fiscal stimuli in 2020: An ex-post assessment

In response to the economic damage caused by the pandemic and accompanying lockdowns, governments across the globe adopted a series of fiscal stimulus measures and support packages during 2020. Key components of these packages included the channelling of significant resources to specific economic sectors, the provision of temporary wage support or replacement schemes, increases in unemployment benefits in terms of both amount and duration, direct cash transfer to households, as well as the ramping up of health expenditures (*TDR 2020*).

While these fiscal packages differed considerably across countries, particularly between developed and developing countries, they were in many cases of an unprecedented scale and scope. At the time of their introduction, estimates were tentative relying on the announcements made by the governments. Now that data is available for 2020, it is possible to derive more detailed estimates and compare them to recent historical benchmarks.

*Table B1.1* summarizes the main findings for selected economies.[18] The table compares *a priori* announcements of the fiscal responses with the estimates of the effectively applied fiscal stimuli. These are separated into two categories:

(a)  additional amount of Government spending (*G*) on goods, services and investment. These are direct injections to the stream of aggregate demand; and

(b)  transfers (including subsidies and unemployment benefits) from the Government to the private sector (*T*), net of taxes and contributions to social security (after rebates and deferrals are taken into account). These are additions to the flow of income for the private sector.

Estimates of *G* and *T* are based on levels of spending and transfers that would have likely materialized absent the pandemic. The relevant benchmark for government spending on goods, services and investment (*G*) is their trend level in real terms. For net transfers (*T*) the benchmark is the average proportion of GDP of past years, applied to the level of GDP of 2020 (to take account of the fact that the bulk of such flows depends, in large part, on the level of economic activity and incomes generated).

### Main observations

*i.   Large gaps between announcements and actual stimuli*

As can be seen from *Table B1.1*, there are substantial differences between the announced and effective size of the Covid-19 fiscal stimuli measures introduced in 2020. This is particularly the case for several developed countries, namely Australia, Canada, Germany, Japan and the United Kingdom. In these countries, the actual size of the Covid-19 fiscal stimuli packages was between 6 and 9 percentage points of GDP lower than the announced size of these packages.

**TABLE B1.1**   **Estimated size of Covid-19 fiscal stimuli, 2020**
*(Per cent of GDP)*

|  | Government Spending (G) | Government Transfers (T) | G + T | Announced measures |
|---|---|---|---|---|
| Argentina | -0.5 | 4.1 | 3.3 | 3.8 |
| Australia | 0.1 | 10.0 | 10.2 | 16.1 |
| Canada | -0.4 | 8.8 | 8.3 | 14.7 |
| France | -0.5 | 4.6 | 3.3 | 7.6 |
| Germany | 0.5 | 3.0 | 3.3 | 11.0 |
| India | -0.9 | 3.4 | 2.4 | 3.3 |
| Italy | 0.5 | 4.9 | 5.4 | 6.8 |
| Japan | 0.3 | 7.5 | 8.0 | 15.5 |
| Mexico | 0.2 | 1.8 | 2.0 | 0.7 |
| Republic of Korea | -0.5 | 2.0 | 1.8 | 3.4 |
| South Africa | -0.4 | 4.2 | 4.2 | 5.3 |
| Spain | 0.2 | 4.7 | 4.9 | 4.1 |
| Turkey | -0.5 | 1.7 | 1.4 | 1.0 |
| United Kingdom | 2.1 | 5.6 | 7.1 | 16.3 |
| United States | -0.4 | 9.2 | 9.1 | 10.6 |

**Note:**

**G**   refers to general Government gross fixed capital spending and consumption spending in goods and services (excluding payments or transfers) and is estimated as that above the trend over the recent past (2017–2019).

**T**   refers to net transfers from the Government to the private sector. It encompasses transfers, including subsidies and all payments to other sectors (including unemployment benefits and direct income transfers), minus government revenues (including personal current taxes and contributions to government social security); and it is estimated as the difference with its past average (2017–2019) as a proportion of GDP applied to 2020 GDP.

There are various possible explanations for the discrepancies. Although the initial announcements intended to show the strength of the policy responses to the Covid-19 shock, the packages may have included outlays that were already budgeted, and which would have occurred absent the pandemic. Moreover, spending in other areas was in many cases cut to compensate for the increases in Covid-19-related outlays. Likewise, included in the packages were tax deferrals and accelerated spending measures that would have taken place later in the same cycle, i.e. spending brought forward from the fourth quarter to the second quarter. Lastly, the announced packages often included spending presumably to be deployed in 2021 or beyond.

### ii. Significant divergences between developed and developing economies

The results underscore that the size of the stimuli enacted by governments of most developed countries are significantly larger than those of developing countries.[19] Policymakers in developing countries are particularly vulnerable to the policies imposed on them by international investors, credit-rating agencies and lending institutions to cut debt ratios (even if these are smaller than those of developed economies). Furthermore, their vulnerability to external economic shocks requires greater caution when increasing public debt because of recurring private sector bankruptcies prompting government bailouts. Finally, larger fiscal programmes in developing countries tend to involve larger current account deficits, which cannot be filled by domestic liquidity injections alone without triggering currency vulnerabilities.

### iii. Biases in the composition of the fiscal packages

Another key result from Table B1.1 is that actual additional government spending ($G$) was systematically lower than net transfers to the private sector ($T$), in addition to the fact that direct spending was either only marginally larger than historic norms or even smaller. This is relevant from a macroeconomic perspective for two reasons. First, the impact of direct spending on aggregate demand is larger than that of reductions of taxes or increases of transfers (*TDR 2013*; *TDR 2019*). With larger multipliers, funds injected into the economy represent a more effective cushion to economic shocks. Second, while not all goods and services can receive a demand boost during a lockdown, many can and should. For example, medical services, training, production of equipment; educational programmes online to maintain or improve labour skills; planning activities to lay down infrastructure projects, and more.

Thus, the bulk of fiscal stimulus came in the form of net transfers ($T$), i.e. tax cuts, income transfers, additional or extended unemployment benefits, and subsidies. There is no denying that programmes to protect the incomes of households, especially of those who were out of work, have been necessary during the pandemic. This is especially the case for wage-earners in the lower income deciles, who live from pay-check to pay-check, both in developed and developing countries. In the latter case, moreover, where a large proportion of workers are involved in informal sectors and activities relying on personal contact, such transfers represent the only effective livelihood support tool. Other forms of financial support via existing welfare or unemployment benefits programmes are out of reach for the majority of households in developing economies. By contrast, the prevalence of transfers over direct spending in developed economies is harder to justify, all the more while public spending, educational and health-related, as well as infrastructure provisions were partially left unattended or even reduced in some cases.

The unprecedented build up in household savings in some countries in 2020, resulting in part from the additional net transfers enacted, cannot be ignored. To mention the clearest example, households in the United States[20] increased their savings in 2020 from \$1.2 to \$2.9 trillion[21] — representing nearly 8 per cent of GDP, while the economy contracted by 3.5 per cent. In this case, as in most other cases, the build-up of savings was concentrated in the upper income deciles (Rennison, 2021), while low-earning households continue to remain financially constrained, as well as subject to more precarious employment prospects (Dua et al., 2021). Not unrelated to such disparities is the observation that an outsized share of the build-up in household savings during 2020 was funnelled towards stock markets, thus fuelling financial speculation and inflating equity prices as opposed to propping up real spending and demand within the economy. In this way, the over-reliance on transfer payments can not only prove ineffective, it can also be destabilizing as well as increase wealth inequality (Stiglitz and Rashid, 2020).

Finally, while fiscal support and stimulus measures have the primary aim of counteracting a downturn in economic activity in order to keep businesses afloat and maintain employment, as well as providing assistance to households in need, they also represent an opportunity to plan and undertake investments in physical and social infrastructure, including education, that will boost productivity and push towards more sustainable and resilient productive models (Jotzo et al., 2020). This is especially pertinent when economies face the imminent challenge of revamping the productive structure and consumption patterns to drastically reduce greenhouse gas emissions.

While the immediate priority of fiscal measures in 2020 was to support households and businesses, the chance to capitalize on fiscal injections to boost aggregate demand with proactive investments that have a long-lasting and positive impact in terms of productivity, growth and climate goals was largely missed, as evidenced by the broadly subdued nature of government spending in 2020. Fiscal packages, moreover, have tended to exacerbate the disparities between developed and developing economies, with lasting consequences.

FIGURE 1.12  **Additional primary outlays in 2020 relative to inherited debt ratios in developing and developed economies[5]**

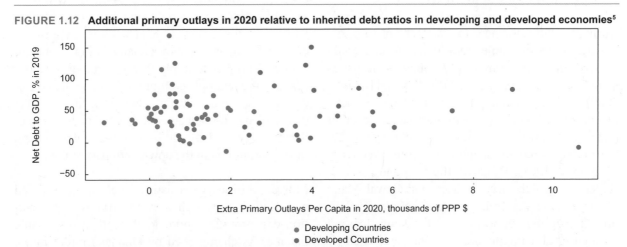

*Source:* UNCTAD secretariat calculations from IMF WEO database, April 2021.
*Note:* Extra primary outlays refer to the difference between the primary outlays of the general government in 2020 and its average over the period 2016–2019. *Developing economies are:* Albania, Algeria, Barbados, Bolivia, Bosnia and Herzegovina, Botswana, Brazil, Cabo Verde, Cameroon, Chile, Colombia, Djibouti, Dominican Republic, Egypt, Equatorial Guinea, Eswatini, Ethiopia, Fiji, Ghana, Guyana, Indonesia, Islamic Republic of Iran, Jordan, Kazakhstan, Kenya, Lebanon, Lesotho, Liberia, Mali, Mauritania, Mexico, Morocco, Namibia, Niger, Nigeria, North Macedonia, Oman, Pakistan, Panama, Paraguay, Peru, Saudi Arabia, Serbia, South Africa, St. Vincent and the Grenadines, Taiwan Province of China, Trinidad and Tobago, Turkey, Uruguay, Yemen, Zambia. The grouping excludes former transition economies that are part of the European Union, the Solomon Islands and the Seychelles and all the countries for which data is not available. *Developed economies are:* Australia, Austria, Belgium, Canada, Denmark, Finland, France, Germany, Ireland, Israel, Italy, Japan, Korea, Luxembourg, Netherlands, New Zealand, Portugal, Spain, Sweden, Switzerland, United Kingdom United States. It excludes former transition economies and all the countries for which data is not available.

equipment, let alone waivers on patents) to combat the health crisis.

Thus, while massive amounts of public money were used by the major Central Banks to keep private credit institutions afloat, governments in developing countries continued to experience severe constraints both on servicing their external debt and supporting production, exports, income and employment throughout the pandemic. The overriding concern continues to be avoiding domestic actions that could trigger financial turmoil or anticipating when the major Central Banks will decide to withdraw their massive liquidity injections or raise their interest rates (see Box 1.2). Moreover, fear of upsetting private creditors has prevented many eligible countries from taking advantage of the G20 Debt Service Suspension Initiative: only 46 of 73 eligible countries have participated (World Bank, 2021a).

Hence, whilst the pandemic has brought back the shock-absorbing dimension of fiscal policy into the mainstream of counter-cyclical demand management,

it is clear that additional steps are necessary to guarantee that all countries can employ even those minimal fiscal measures in line with their own domestic circumstances and to the benefit of global recovery and financial stability.

This view, long held by many developing countries, has recently received support from some G7 members. United States Treasury secretary Janet Yellen has finally endorsed a proposal to create $650bn of new SDRs, an important, if still insufficient, step in the right direction (see Section C). Similarly, supportive signals have emerged in the European Union, where member countries have no lender of last resort and, according to Mario Draghi, former ECB president and current Italian Prime Minister, "we must reason on how to allow all [EMU] member states to issue safe debt to stabilize economies in case of recession" (Draghi, 2021, *our translation*). Since Italy holds the G20 presidency in 2021, there is hope that this argument can also be extended beyond the borders of the European Union.

With these small steps in the right direction, the debate will continue. But the world has not yet absorbed the central lesson. For the state to re-emerge as a central institution of *public* policy, the autonomy and impunity enjoyed by global finance over the past decades need to be seriously circumscribed.

### 4. Timing counter-cyclical measures or targeting development?

During the GFC, the need to rescue the private sector after years of ample credit creation once again showed the limits of monetary policy as an instrument to smooth out recessions (Godley and Izurieta, 2009). This experience helped revive the legitimacy of active fiscal policy as a temporary shock absorber that should, however, be promptly withdrawn, leaving market forces to shape the eventual recovery (Bernanke, 2008). By 2010, the G20 and the IMF started to signal the need for fiscal withdrawal. Many of these same voices have since recognized their mistake. Public support ended too soon, leaving economies in a fragile situation and threatened by debt deflation (IMF, 2012; Fatàs and Summers, 2015).

Mindful of this experience, since the beginning of the pandemic a consensus seems to have materialized in favour of maintaining fiscal and monetary support beyond the immediate recovery (*TDR 2020*; IMF, 2020b). However, the question remains whether fiscal policy will remain a countercyclical tool for macroeconomic emergencies, or if it merits a more structural role to promote development and sustained job creation (Costantini, 2020), especially in developing economies where leaving structural change to market forces has, invariably, ended in disappointment (see Figure 1.13).

A fiscal policy that withdraws stimulus at the earliest possible point in the cycle, even if extended to prevent possible damage to long-term growth from skill obsolescence or debt deflation, cannot play its necessary structural role. The current approach, despite giving fiscal policy a relatively longer span of action, continues to imply that governments cannot actively prevent or pre-emptively reduce the size of downturns, which simply occur from time to time despite demand-management policy. The function of fiscal policy then should be solely countercyclical, mostly prompted in the downward part of the cycle.

More ambitiously, measures such as guaranteed minimum income schemes and progressive taxation can provide a floor to the fall in disposable income. As championed by Gunnar Myrdal in the 1930s, and more recently suggested by Haughwout (2019) and Orszag et al. (2021), public investments, pre-approved and scheduled to start at the earliest manifestation of a downturn, can also play a similar role.[5] But this type of proactive steps rarely materialize, and did not in 2020, when the fiscal response was disproportionately geared toward transfers (see Box 1.1).

**FIGURE 1.13  Public and private investment in selected country groups, 1995–2016**
(Per cent of GDP)

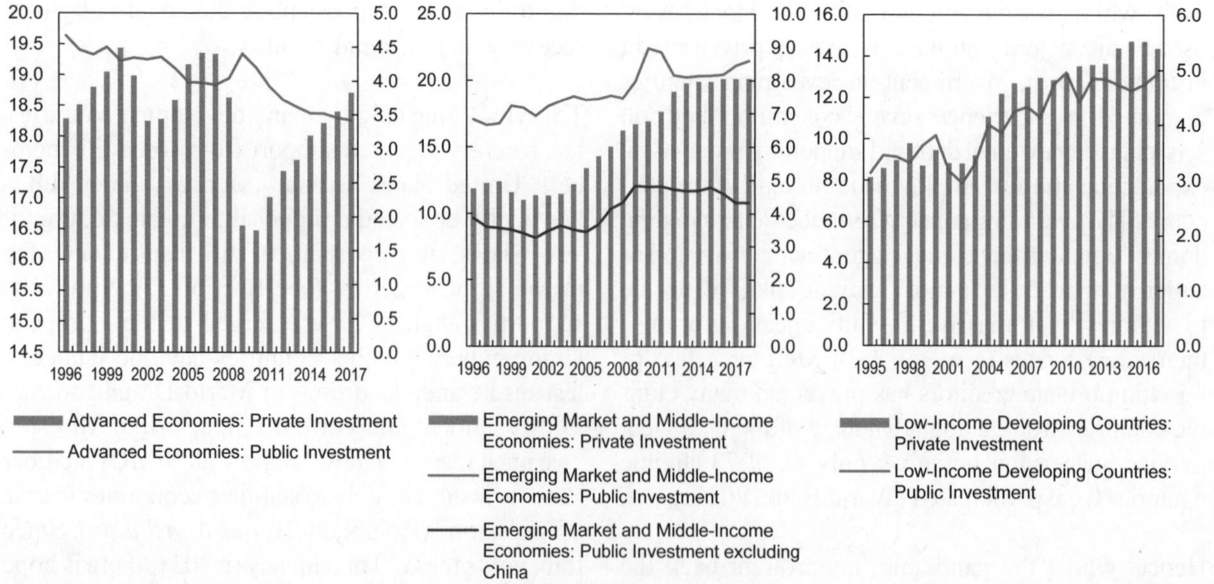

Advanced Economies: Private Investment
Advanced Economies: Public Investment

Emerging Market and Middle-Income Economies: Private Investment
Emerging Market and Middle-Income Economies: Public Investment
Emerging Market and Middle-Income Economies: Public Investment excluding China

Low-Income Developing Countries: Private Investment
Low-Income Developing Countries: Public Investment

*Source:*  IMF, Fiscal Monitor. April 2020.

**BOX 1.2**    The rocky road to public debt sustainability: A developmental perspective

In an accounting framework for the closed economy, where international and macroeconomic constraints, as well as policy and institutional feedbacks are put aside, it is possible to identify the specific relation between primary budget balance, interest rate, and rate of GDP growth that, given an initial debt to GDP ratio, guarantees, on average, its stability over time (Domar, 1944; Blanchard et al., 1990; Pasinetti, 1998). In particular, if the interest rate that applies to the stock of debt is higher than the rate of growth of income (that determines the size of GDP), the primary budget must be in surplus to avoid an unrelenting increase in the debt ratio.

Real world situations, as reviewed in the *TDR 2020* (Chapter IV) are far more complex, given a variety of exogenous factors (domestic and external to each economy) that alter the 'r minus g' measure, such as changes in expectations or sudden external shocks affecting exchange and interest rates (Barbosa-Filho and Izurieta, 2020). But there are also different ways in which structural constraints and policy choices influence the fiscal budget, the rate of economic growth, prices and interest rates. Indeed, frameworks of policy analysis that target public debt sustainability by means of primary budget surpluses and assume that economies are organically geared to grow, with small oscillations around technologically driven output potential and well-tuned expectations about prices and interest rates, are misleading.

Alternative paths ahead need to rely on a different set of internationally agreed financial conditions, with respect to liquidity provision as well as debt management and restructuring, and most importantly on a more realistic set of assumptions about the functioning of developing economies, as discussed below.

By abandoning the mainstream approach to macroeconomic analysis, a first question is about the correct interpretation of fiscal deficits in the circumstances at hand (Godley and Izurieta, 2004). For instance, a deficit today can be an indication that the government is spending too little rather than too much: it may conceal an austerity policy that is reducing growth to a point that budget cuts do not produce the desired reduction in net spending while eroding fiscal revenues. This would not only worsen current conditions but threaten debt sustainability. Conversely, deficits can be a sign that the government is supporting a growth strategy, investing in social and physical infrastructure, growth capacity and the expansion of the productive potential. If those policies are successful and sustained for a sufficiently long period, debt-to-GDP ratios may not only be stable but possibly declining over time. As the growth rate of income exceeds the real interest rate, a moderate primary deficit (rather than a surplus) could become a structural feature of a successfully developing economy. Within this long-term perspective, it makes sense to allow the debt-to-GDP ratio to increase and, depending on the stage of a country's development, until the targets of sustainable growth and wellbeing are achieved.

Conversely, especially in economies operating with unemployed or underemployed resources, when governments cut their budgets to reduce public debt, they affect aggregate private income to the extent that unemployment tends to increase, especially those of the income groups which are more reliant on public services. They also constrain the ability of private wealth holders to acquire non-risky public debt as assets, thus increasing overall portfolio risks (Lysandrou and Nesvetailova, 2020). All this affects the resilience of the economy and of the society to economic shocks. Similarly, if the size of the public sector shrinks, for example due to privatizations, a larger part of the economy depends on private expectations. As a result, income fluctuations tend to be larger and increasingly driven by unchecked and fickle private credit movements.

In sum, public debt solvency indicators and targets of any kind gain some meaning only in the presence of a framework that determines the macroeconomic relationship among variables as well as the appropriate horizon for the analysis (Costantini, forthcoming). The problem is that access to finance is a pre-requisite for determining the timing and direction of the development process as well as of any reconfiguration of the debt sustainability profile when external shocks occur or international macroeconomic conditions change significantly.

Indeed, even if macroeconomic dynamics are put aside, several factors can stand in the way of public debt sustainability, which are especially relevant in developing economies, where a significant proportion of assets and liabilities of the public sector are denominated in foreign currency (Barbosa-Filho, 2021). A speculative attack on the domestic currency, leading to exchange rate depreciations, inflationary spirals and interest rate adjustments can derive from political instability in response to contractionary fiscal policies, triggering a vicious circle of growth collapse, rising fiscal deficits and a debt crisis. Several other outcomes are possible, exposing as a common feature that aiming at primary surpluses becomes an elusive means to contain debt ratios, be it because changes in expectations could adversely affect the discount rates when fiscal prudence is interpreted as a worrying sign of trouble ahead (Guzman and Lombardi, 2017), or because shocks beyond policy control alter exchange rates or foreign interest rates. The accounting framework can be expanded to allow for the real-world case where governments also hold fixed-income financial assets, which can soften the required fiscal adjustment when either governments accumulate fixed assets at a faster rate of GDP growth, or when the interest rate on assets is greater than on liabilities. For most developing economies, where the accumulation of financial assets is limited and where most often the interest payments on fixed assets or loans are low, debt dynamics can be worsened (Akyüz, 2021). Exchange rate complications would tend to exacerbate these patterns, because earnings on foreign reserves are typically lower than debt payments, and even more so when foreign interest rate premiums rise faster than the pace of domestic currency depreciations after external shocks or changes in foreign investors' expectations (Barbosa-Filho, 2021).

More generally, the liquidity risk associated with an expansionary fiscal policy is higher, the tighter the balance of payment constraint. This means that different stages of development are associated with typical liquidity risk configurations (Akyüz, 2007). On the one hand, least developed countries and low-income developing countries have trouble accessing credit and exports are often the only source of foreign currency. On the other hand, middle and high-income developing countries can sometimes be the destination of speculative capital inflows which can overwhelm the domestic financial and credit market, induce misallocation of assets and push inflation and imports.

From this point of view, it is market discipline, or being exposed to liquidity risk, that prevents countries spending their way to a structurally sustainable path. If, partly, mitigating liquidity risks can be an immediate national policy target, addressed for example by price and capital controls, it is mainly something that only international coordination can tackle and solve, creating the policy space needed for a reduction of the external dependency of countries on global finance. Achieving the required degrees of policy coordination around a pro-development revamp of the global financial architecture is not trivial and, in many respects, may look unachievable. But intermediate steps carried out at regional or South-South level of cooperation can help approach the goal (Kregel, 2016; *TDR 2019*).

The widespread, underlying assumption is that the economy's growth and development path is fully determined by its factors of production and technology with cyclical and mostly self-correcting features. In this view, "well-crafted automatic stabilizers are the best way to deliver fiscal stimulus in a timely, targeted, and temporary way" (Boushey and Shambaugh 2019: 5). Since in normal times no such support should be present, these programs should "contain triggers, which assure markets that neither excess spending nor premature austerity will harm the economy going forward" (Altman et al., 2019: 3).

However, it has been amply documented that such counter-cyclical expansions do not allow economies to develop sufficiently or for a sufficiently long time to *sustain* the increase in potential output that results from a stable growth of income, aggregate demand and technical progress (McCombie, 2002; Ocampo et al., 2009; Storm and Naastepad, 2012). For instance, for the United States, Storm (2017), Taylor (2020), and earlier Minsky (1969) show that the failure to contribute to income generation and effective aggregate demand has produced subdued productivity growth and a systematic displacement of jobs from high- to low-wage sectors. Celi et al.

(2018) show how austerity and an abandonment of industrial policy in Southern Europe have produced slow productivity growth, increased dependency on imports and, in many cases, high private indebtedness.

Sustained fiscal support is even more necessary for developing countries. Wade (1992) shows this in the NIEs of East Asia centred on the simultaneous promotion of exports and domestic absorption as the infrastructure and technology transfers triggered the expansion of the industrial sector.[6] Meanwhile, Palma (2011) shows that the abandonment of active import substitution policies in Latin America brought premature de-industrialization and productivity slowdown (see also Khan and Blankenburg, 2009; Tregenna, 2016).

The countercyclical approach to fiscal policy not only appears inappropriate to face the great challenges of reducing inequality and mitigating the impact of climate change, but it is even detrimental to its own declared objective of fiscal sustainability (see Box 1.2). Decades spent in (often failed) pursuit of balanced budgets have intensified the cyclical fluctuations of income and employment, at the same time reducing fiscal space in the downturn.

# C. Global Finance and Developing Country Vulnerabilities

As highlighted in previous *Reports* (see Chapter II), developing countries have integrated into global financial markets: since the 1990s high-income emerging market economies, and more recently, low- and middle-income so-called frontier economies.[7] This change has left them vulnerable to the volatility and procyclical nature of private capital flows. Subject primarily to external factors (such as monetary and fiscal policy decisions in the United States or commodity price movements) rather than local factors, these flows pose substantive challenges for the management of macroeconomic imbalances, debt sustainability and monetary and fiscal spaces in developing countries (see also Section B.3).

The ongoing Covid-19 pandemic has thrown these vulnerabilities into sharp relief. As Figure 1.14 shows, the deterioration of net capital flows to developing countries in the initial phase of the pandemic was led by record portfolio outflows in the first quarter of 2020, amounting to $127 billion. Since then, the picture has been one of much reduced, but still volatile, portfolio flows, with outflows of $21 billion in the second quarter of 2020 followed by inflows

of $51.6 billion in the second half of the year, and another round of outflows ($34.5 billion) in the first quarter of 2021. From the second quarter of 2020, massive outflows of 'other investments', totalling just under $370 billion between the 2020Q2 and 2021Q1, have accounted for overall net negative capital flows to developing countries in this period.[8] By contrast, FDI flows to developing countries have remained stable overall, despite their initial reduction in the first quarter of 2020.

This broad picture shrouds more complex dynamics of net capital flows to developing countries in the wake of the pandemic, including uneven regional impacts (see also Figure 1.14 right hand side - By region).

Net portfolio flows to developing countries are largely driven by non-resident investment in debt and equity (*TDR 2020*: 6; UNCTAD 2021: 3; IMF, 2021). Following the record negative shock to these flows in the first quarter of 2020 that hit all developing regions, the earlier-than-expected return of portfolio funds is likely to have been bolstered by prospects

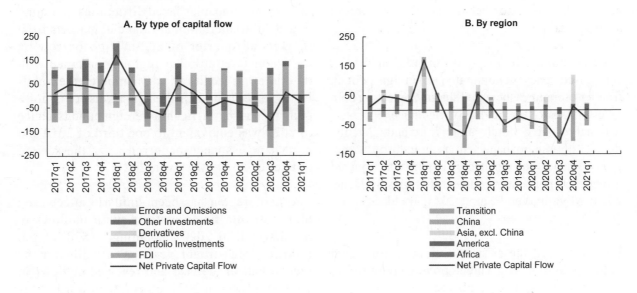

**FIGURE 1.14   Net private capital flows to developing countries, 2017–2021**
*(Billions of dollars)*

***Source:*** UNCTAD secretariat calculations based on national data.
**Note:** Negatives values indicate outflows. The samples of economies by country group are as follows:
*Transition Economies:* Kazakhstan, Kyrgyzstan, the Russian Federation and Ukraine. *Africa:* Botswana, Republic of Cabo Verde, Egypt, Ghana, Mauritius, Morocco, Mozambique, Namibia, Nigeria, South Africa, the Sudan and Uganda. *Latin America:* Argentina, the Plurinational State of Bolivia, Brazil, Chile, Colombia, Ecuador, El Salvador, Mexico, Nicaragua, Paraguay, Uruguay and the Bolivarian Republic of Venezuela. *Asia excluding China:* Hong Kong (China), India, Indonesia, Jordan, Lebanon, Malaysia, Mongolia, Pakistan, Philippines, Saudi Arabia, Singapore, Sri Lanka, Thailand and Viet Nam.

of a substantive new allocation of SDRs and by a growing consensus around the need to recycle unused SDRs from advanced to developing countries (see Box 1.3), whereas investor expectations of rising long-term interest rates in the United States have driven outflows in early 2021 (Wheatley, 2021). While the high volatility and reduced volume of portfolio flows since the second half of 2020 reflect financial markets' uncertainty regarding the future trajectory of the virus and to uneven economic recovery patterns in developed and developing countries, their impact on developing countries has been amplified by deepening financial vulnerabilities after the GFC of 2007–09.

As pointed out previously (*TDR 2020*, Box 1.1), this new round of financial integration was marked by a number of trends. First, the expansion of the external balance sheets of emerging market economies gained momentum,[9] with asset managers from advanced economies, in addition to targeting foreign-currency denominated corporate bond markets, increasing their participation in domestic sovereign bond markets. While greater reliance on domestic-currency denominated public debt mitigates the currency mismatch in the balance sheets of developing country governments, it also creates maturity mismatches, arising from the prohibitive costs of issuing long-term government securities in most developing countries. It also shifts the currency risk to global lenders, thus heightening exposure to speculative, non-resident investor behaviour (Berensmann et al., 2015).

Second, non-resident portfolio investments in foreign-currency denominated sovereign debt in frontier economies increased sharply, reflecting both investors' search for yield and dwindling public international resource mobilization. Third and relatedly, the rise of asset management as an industry within global finance has resulted in highly synchronized pro-cyclical portfolio investment strategies (Haldane, 2014; Miyajima and Shim, 2014; Raddatz et al., 2017).[10]

Fourth, during the crisis, sovereign ratings and outlooks by the "Big Three" private credit rating agencies (CRAs) have played an increasingly problematic role in further limiting access to international financial markets, just as beleaguered developing countries needed it most, to help bolster financial (and fiscal) breathing space. In addition to driving up refinancing costs in these markets, CRAs hampered the effective implementation of international emergency initiatives, such as the G20 Debt Service Suspension Initiative (DSSI). While participation in the DSSI was not considered a default event, seeking equal treatment under the terms of this initiative from private creditors has been deterring participating countries from taking such action (Li, 2021; Griffith-Jones et al., forthcoming).

As a result of these vulnerabilities, strongly net negative, if fluctuating, portfolio flows to developing countries translated into a vicious cycle of currency depreciations, weakening debt sustainability and reduced fiscal spaces. During 2020, emerging market currencies depreciated against the United States dollar by more than 20 per cent and some frontier economies' currencies by between 20 to 50 per cent,[11] triggering hikes in sovereign credit spreads and driving up the value of their foreign-currency denominated debt, thus also affecting private borrowers' balance sheets and refinancing risks (Hofmann et al., 2020).

A stop-go pattern of portfolio flows has been particularly prevalent in Africa and in Latin America and the Caribbean (LAC). In 2020 in Africa, portfolio outflows were the primary factor reducing the regions' total private capital inflows. Although, in 2019, the region recorded portfolio inflows of just over $39 billion, this trend was all but wiped out in 2020. Most African governments and companies faced difficulties in issuing new debt in international financial markets from the second quarter of 2020. High borrowing costs compared to other regions combined with deteriorating credit ratings, hampered their ability to raise capital in these markets. It is not a coincidence that African sovereign bond issuance in 2020 was equivalent to one third of 2019 and almost no issuance occurred after the second quarter of 2020 (Munevar, 2021).

The LAC region has been similarly affected by high portfolio flow volatility, with outflows in the first half of 2020 amounting to $30 billion, followed by a partial reversal at $19 billion in the second half of the year and renewed outflows in the first quarter of 2021, albeit at a lower level (-$2.6 billions). At the same time, while FDI flows into African regions have remained fairly stable, the LAC region has seen a brief but sharp decline in FDI in the second half of 2020, returning only partially to more normal levels, compared to pre-crisis trends, in the first quarter of 2021.

**BOX 1.3**     Money for something: Moving on to an expanded role for Special Drawing Rights

The record new allocation of Special Drawing Rights (SDRs) of $650 billion (or around 457 billion SDRs at the current SDR/$ exchange rate[22]) – approved by the IMF's Board of Governors in August 2021 – more than doubles the total stock of SDRs (currently SDR 204 billion) amounting to more than 2.5 times the general allocation of SDRs made in 2009 following the global financial crisis.

First created by IMF in 1969, SDRs are an international reserve asset to supplement the foreign exchange reserves of member countries. They represent a potential claim on freely usable currencies of IMF members[23] for use in transactions between member states' central banks and between them and IMF, but not directly for operations in private markets (see also *TDR 2020*, Box 4.5).

TABLE B1.2     **Proposed 2021 SDR allocation to developing country groups**
*(as per cent of total allocation, in billions of current United States dollars, and as per cent of 2019 GDP, international reserves and short-term debt)*

| Country group | No. of countries | Quota (% of total SDRs) | 2021 Allocation (billion USD) | SDR/ GDP | SDR/ Reserves | SDR/ ST debt |
|---|---|---|---|---|---|---|
| Transition economies | 18 | 4,2 | 27,52 | 1,1% | 3,8% | 23,8% |
| Low-income developing countries (LICs) | 29 | 1,4 | 9,21 | 1,9% | 18,4% | 70,3% |
| Middle-income developing countries (MICs) | 58 | 9,6 | 62,12 | 0,8% | 4,8% | 19,4% |
| High-income developing countries (HICs) | 45 | 22,2 | 144,01 | 0,6% | 2,5% | 6,3% |
| **Total all developing countries and transition economies** | **150** | **37,4** | **242,86** | **0,7%** | **3,1%** | **8,9%** |

*Source:*   UNCTAD secretariat calculations, based on World bank, IMF and national sources.
 *Note:*   As per World bank International Debt Statistics, Short Term (ST) debt includes all debt with an original maturity of one year or less and interest in arrears on long-term debt.

SDRs are unique: they are allocated to IMF member states without eligibility criteria, do not create new debt[24], while boosting a country's international reserves and providing unconditional liquidity support with regard to a country's macroeconomic policies. For developing countries, simply holding SDRs as a reserve asset may benefit the way they are perceived by global investors and credit rating agencies (see also *TDR 2020* and Hawkins and Prates, 2021).

The 2021 SDR allocation is, however, based of IMF's historical quota system which, as has long been noted, favours developed countries.[25] Of the 190 IMF member countries, 40 developed countries will receive roughly 63 per cent of this allocation (around $407 billion) and 150 developing countries, taken together, will receive just over 37 per cent ($243 billion) of this allocation, which on average accounts for 0.7 per cent of their combined 2019 GDP (see Table B1.2). While the quantum of the proposed SDR allocation for low-income countries (LICs) is significantly smaller than for other country groups, at $9.2 billion, its relative shares to GDP at 1.9 per cent, of reserve assets at 18.4 per cent and of short-term debt at 70.3 per cent show how potentially important this SDR allocation is to LICs. By contrast, the economic impact of the new SDR allocation is considerably less in MICs, many of which, including Small Island Development States (SIDS), face particularly high levels of debt as well as environmental vulnerabilities.

It is not only the historically skewed quota system for SDR allocations that rankles but the low utilization rate of SDR allocations by developed countries. As shown in Table B1.3, 71 per cent (108) of IMF members have employed their SDRs. But whereas 82 per cent of SIDS have made use of 44 per cent their SDR allocations and 69 per cent of LICs have used 86 per cent of their allocations, the 65 per cent of developed countries that employed their allocations made use of only 13 per cent of their allocations. This raises the question of whether (and how), in addition to new allocations, voluntary reallocations of unused SDRs (sometimes referred to as SDR recycling) from developed to developing member states could be undertaken.

### *SDR recycling: Old wine in new bottles?*

Broad estimates for SDR recycling from the Group of Seven (G7) to developing countries (excluding the planned new 2021 SDR allocation) suggest a figure in the region of $100 billion (Reuters, 2021). Compared to $266.5 of the new SDR allocation going to these countries, and if broadened beyond the G7, such SDR recycling could be significant. The most prominent proposals for such SDR recycling currently mooted include channelling SDR reallocations through of IMF's poverty reduction growth trust (PRGT) and the establishment of a separate

IMF Resilience and Sustainability Fund for vulnerable economies including MICs, aimed at supporting their Covid-19 recovery and promoting climate change (Shahal and Jones, 2021). The idea is that recycled SDRs (to IMF) will be used to boost the funding of concessional IMF lending facilities. This, however, not only compromises the non-debt creating characteristic of SDRs, but recycling SDRs through IMF lending facilities runs the danger of stripping them of their role as policy-unconditional liquidity support that (indirectly) helps to free up much needed fiscal space in developing countries.

**TABLE B1.3**    **Utilization of existing SDR allocations by country group, as of 31 May 2021**

| Country group (total number of counties in brackets) | Share of countries that utilized past SDR allocations | SDR utilization (Share of allocation) |
|---|---|---|
| Transition economies (18) | 67% | 38% |
| Low-income developing countries - LICs (29) | 69% | 86% |
| Middle-income developing countries - MICs (44) | 73% | 63% |
| High-income developing countries - HICs (31) | 68% | 35% |
| Small Island Developing States - SIDS (28) | 82% | 44% |
| Total all developing economies (150) | 72% | 47% |
| Developed countries (40) | 65% | 13% |
| Total  (190) | 71% | 28% |

*Source:*   UNCTAD secretariat calculations, based on World Bank, IMF and national sources.
  *Note:*   LICs and MICs exclude SIDS.

Other proposals include the creation of earmarked funds outside the IMF, such as a Covid-19 response investment fund, a Global Vaccine Fund or a Global Social Protection Fund, but without clear answers as to how country eligibility criteria, potentially competitive priority setting for ear-marked purposes and the more detailed functioning of such funds in regard to their lending activities should be designed (e.g. Ghosh, 2021). The alternative is to allow decision-making in developed countries with a low utilization rate of their allocated SDRs to lend or donate unused allocations to developing country partners on a unilateral basis (e.g. Plant, 2020).

### A bolder option: Leveraging SDRs for multilateral cooperation to achieve global goals

Under the pressure of global emergencies quick responses will inevitably entail working within given structures to achieve the best short-term outcome. But this should not obscure the urgent need to move beyond the use of SDRs solely as a "fire-fighting" crisis-response tool.[26] The most obvious option would be a further and deeper review of IMF's quota system to address current biases in favour of developed countries. Given the many years it took to arrive at the marginal 14th General Quota Review, implemented in 2016, this is also the least realistic option due to lack of political consensus. Another still challenging, but perhaps more achievable, option is the creation of new ear-marked types of SDRs – such as Special Environmental Drawing Rights or Special 2030 Agenda Drawing Rights – to establish SDR-based global funds for purposes that command a high degree of collective and multilateral support. Under this proposal, participating countries would develop national investment plans to meet specific (environmental and/or SDG-related) targets and specify budgetary requirements. For countries that cannot self-finance these plans, a zero-interest loan facility at the IMF could be put into place, whose maximum funding capacity would be measured using Special Purpose Drawing Rights that link claims on these directly to planned earmarked investments (*TDR 2019*: 92-93). This would have several advantages:

i.   It would de-link an *expansion* (and more regular use) of *new types* of SDRs from the IMF quota system.

ii.   It would provide a flexible and, in principle, unlimited mechanism for the predictable, stable and affordable financing of environmental and development targets and objectives without mechanical reliance on counter-productive policy conditionalities or ad-hoc eligibility criteria.

ii.   It could also channel recycled 'standard' SDRs in coordinated fashion towards complementary global environmental and developmental goals.

While this idea, as with other proposals,[27] will likely require changes to IMF's Articles of Agreements, action is urgent, if the achievement of interrelated environmental and developmental goals is to be taken seriously.

Looking at both parts of Figure 1.12 in conjunction, it becomes clear that net private capital flows to developing regions in 2020 and the first quarter of 2021 have been dominated by a few emerging market economies, in particular China, as well as other emerging Asian economies and to a lesser extent, large emerging market economies in Latin America. For these countries, changes in the net external assets of their residents are significant, since the expansion of their external balance sheets over the last decade has involved the build-up not only of international reserves but also of other foreign assets (Akyüz, 2021). Although China was the main recipient of net portfolio and foreign direct investments between mid-2020 and the first quarter of 2021 (with non-resident portfolio inflows and FDI much larger than Chinese portfolio and direct investments abroad), as mentioned, substantive outflows of Chinese other investments in corporate and commercial bank deposits overseas, bank lending abroad and, to a lesser extent, trade credits and advances, have been important in accounting for net negative capital flows to developing countries overall in this period (SAFE, 2021; Westbrook and Zhou, 2021). While other Asian economies have, throughout 2020 and into 2021, seen the largest portfolio outflows of all regions – including substantive non-resident investor flight from domestic sovereign bond markets in some cases – the region overall has benefited most from inflows of other investments as well as from strong FDI, in particular, into India (UNCTAD, 2021a; World Bank, 2021).

### 1.  Debt sustainability in developing countries: No sign of relief on the horizon

Even though spiralling sovereign debt crises were avoided in 2020, developing countries' external debt sustainability further deteriorated, revealing growing pressures on external solvency in addition to immediate international liquidity constraints. Growing optimism about financial resilience in developing countries is premature.

The external debt stocks of developing countries reached $11.3 trillion in 2020, 4.6 per cent above the figure for 2019 and 2.5 times that for 2009 ($4.5 trillion).[12] The slower growth of these stocks in 2020 compared to average annual growth rates between 2009 and 2020 (7.7 per cent) reflects a combination of more limited access to international financial markets, increased reliance on concessional financing sources and the temporary impact of partial debt

service payment suspensions through the G20 DSSI for low-income economies. Rising commodity prices from around the 2020Q2 helped to alleviate balance of payment constraints in developing country commodity-exporters, but also were a contributory factor to inflationary pressures and to rising food insecurity in commodity-importing developing countries, while the recovery of remittances has been very gradual (Malik, 2021) and tourism revenues have remained subdued (see Section D). But these rebounds, as well as the gradual return of global investors to some developing countries (see above), have been insufficient to compensate the impact of their drastic collapse in the first half of the year on the ability of developing countries to service their external debt obligations.

At the same time, substantive debt relief has not materialized. The only lasting multilateral relief is being provided by the IMF through the cancellation of debt service obligations in 29 countries due to it, amounting to $727 million between April 2020 and October 2021. The G20 DSSI delivered around $5.7 billion in debt service suspensions by participating bilateral creditors to 46 out of 73 eligible recipient countries in 2020, with a further $7.3 billion expected to apply in the first half of 2021.[13] This not only is at best a proverbial drop in the bucket, but also will increases debt repayment burdens from the end of the DSSI in December 2021 for participating countries who will have to add suspended payments to their repayment schedules from 2022. The provision of emergency concessional financing by the IMF, the World Bank and – to a lesser degree – other multilateral development banks,[14] while required, also represents new debt that needs to be serviced.

Numerous sovereign debt crises across the developing world have, therefore, been postponed rather than resolved. As Figure 1.15 shows, the external debt stocks of developing countries have been growing faster than their export earnings again since 2018, with this trend clearly accelerating in 2020, pointing to rising external solvency constraints. The consequent strong rise in the ratio of total external debt stocks to exports from 110 per cent in 2019 to 129 per cent in 2020 for developing countries overall has been driven by much sharper increases, from higher levels, in low-income developing countries (from 179 per cent in 2019 to 220 per cent in 2020), least developed countries (from 158 to 202 per cent, respectively) and in particular, in small island developing states (SIDS), from 158 to no less than 293 per cent in the space of a year. This trend has been most pronounced in African countries and the LAC region (Figure 1.16, right side).

Debt service on total external debt, as a percentage of exports, thus rose to 15.8 per cent in 2020 for all developing countries, from 14.7 per cent in 2019 and compared to an annual average of 11.3 per cent between 2009 and 2020. This figure reached 17.5 per cent in middle-income countries and an unprecedented 34.1 per cent in SIDS, both country groups with a substantive exposure to the refinancing of public external debt in international financial markets and to growing shares of private in total external debt. In this context, it is worth recalling that the 1953 London Agreement on German external debt considered that the amount of export revenues that West Germany could spend on debt servicing should be limited to 5 per cent of the total in any year in order not to impede its post-war recovery (*TDR 2015*: 134).

Pressures on external debt sustainability are set to remain high over the coming years since many developing countries face a wall of upcoming sovereign debt repayments in international bond markets (Figure 1.16). Taken together, developing countries (excluding China) face total repayments on sovereign bonds already issued to a value of $936 billion until 2030, the year earmarked for achievement of the Sustainable Development Goals (SDGs), consisting of $571 billion in repayments of principals and $365 billion in coupons or the annual interest rate paid on a bond's face (or nominal) value.

Of particular concern are countries in sub-Saharan Africa, many of whom are low-income countries. At the time of writing, the third wave of the pandemic is rampant across the African continent with very low levels of vaccination, and there is no assurance that countries in sub-Saharan Africa will be in a position to meet bond obligations scheduled for 2023, nor that they will have time to recover by 2025, a watershed year in which these countries need to repay $13 billion (in principal outstanding and coupon disbursement).

In mostly middle-income LAC countries, the wall of sovereign bond debt immediately following the pandemic is also palpable, with over $25 billion due in 2024 and 2025. Both regions also face high coupon disbursement burdens (or shares of coupon disbursements in total repayments on foreign-currency denominated sovereign bonds due in any one year under the period of observation), well above those in other developing countries (excluding China), in particular in the first half of this decade. This challenge reflects the fact that countries in these regions pay higher coupon or annual interest rates on their sovereign bonds in international financial markets than the average for developing countries as a whole (Munevar, 2021). Thus, the data highlights the consequence of historically high coupons in LAC countries, with the coupon disbursement burden well above 60 per cent until 2023, only gradually falling in subsequent years to reach 16 per cent in 2030. For countries in sub-Saharan Africa, the coupon disbursement burden is very high at the start of the period

**FIGURE 1.15** **Total external debt to export revenues, developing countries, 2009–2020**
(*Percentage*)

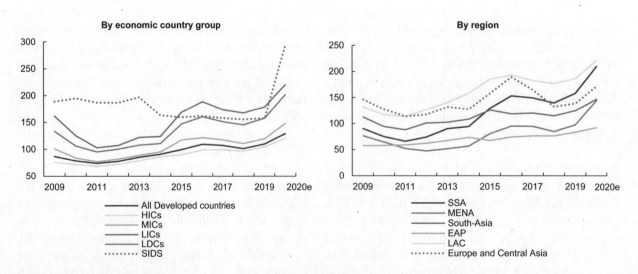

*Source:* UNCTAD secretariat calculations, based on World Bank International Debt Statistics.
*Note:* 2020 = estimates.

**FIGURE 1.16** **Sovereign bond repayment profiles, selected regions, 2021–2030**
*(Billions of current United States dollars (left scale) and percentage of total debt service (right scale))*

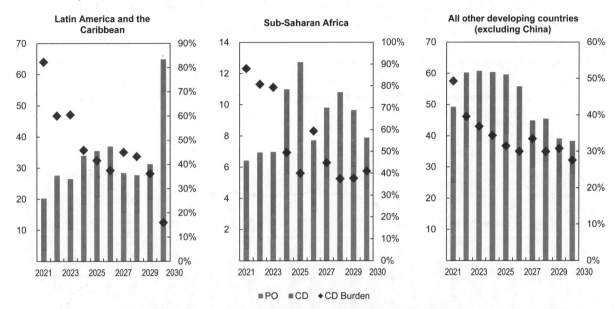

PO= Principal outstanding and maturing. CD=Coupon disbursement (left-hand side).
CD Burden= Coupon disbursement burden (per cent of total debt service, right-hand side).

*Source:* UNCTAD secretariat calculations based on Refinitiv.
*Note:* Sovereign bonds included are those issued in foreign currencies. Coupon disbursements reflect currently available information and may under-estimate the coupon disbursement burdens since a number of sovereign bond contracts have variable interest rates (coupons) over the period under consideration. Red dot represents the average coupon, as of current information available.

at over 80 per cent, and although it then declines somewhat, is still estimated to stand at 41 per cent of the total debt servicing bill in 2030.

Beyond sovereign bond debt, the overall composition of external debt has changed, with public and publicly guaranteed long-term external (PPG) debt overtaking private non-guaranteed long-term external (PNG) debt as the main component of developing countries' external debt profiles in most countries since 2018, a trend clearly reinforced by the onset of the Covid-19 pandemic. While PNG debt became a driving factor of developing countries' overall indebtedness in the aftermath of the GFC (see *TDR 2019*), the recent faster growth of PPG compared to PNG debt reflects the stronger reliance on public borrowing in times of crises. Thus, while PPG debt grew at 8.7 per cent in 2020 – well above its average annual growth rate since 2009 of 7.5 per cent – PNG debt grew at only 2.9 per cent. Current shares of PNG debt, in both long- and short-term external debt, nevertheless remain high by historical standards (amounting to 48 and 34.7 per cent, respectively, in 2020), entailing considerable contingent liabilities for public sectors.

Finally, and to fully grasp the severity of the situation, it is necessary to look beyond external debt

burdens to the evolution of public debt burdens overall, as an indicator of pressures on fiscal space and on repayment capacities in developing countries. As Figure 1.17 shows, the economic fallout from the Covid-19 pandemic has, unsurprisingly, spurred a build-up in public debt as government revenues have collapsed and health and social expenditure has increased. As a percentage of government revenues, total gross government debt reached unprecedented levels in sub-Saharan Africa (364 per cent) and LAC (300 per cent), surpassing high levels at the start of the century. In the case of sub-Saharan Africa, this also means that the success of the multilateral debt relief initiatives of the 1990s and early 2000s has been obliterated. Such high levels of public debt are more typically associated with advanced countries, whose management of this degree of indebtedness benefits from far lower debt service costs and the ability to issue internationally accepted domestic currencies to finance their government budget deficits. For developing countries, the outcome is likely to be higher balance of payments constraints. While the degree of policy space and the link between the fiscal and external constraints varies across developing countries (see *TDR 2020*, p. 98-100), there is little reason to doubt current IMF projections that these high public debt ratios will continue into 2026.

Given this outlook, more concerted and bolder international action is urgently needed to reduce the debt overhang in developing countries through substantive debt relief and outright cancellation. The alternative to addressing structural solvency constraints and putting developing countries' external debt burdens on a more sustainable, long-term footing is another lost decade for development marked by developing countries struggling under unsustainable debt burdens rather than investing in more promising approaches after the pandemic and achieving the 2030 Agenda.

**FIGURE 1.17  Gross government debt to government revenues, selected developing country regions and advanced economies, 2000–2026**
*(Per cent)*

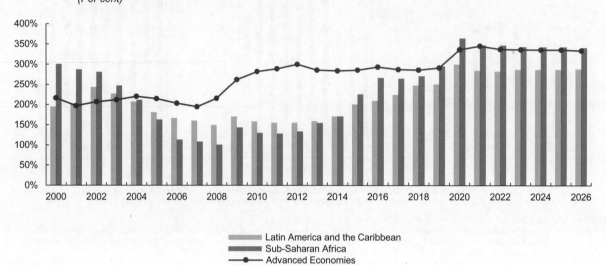

Latin America and the Caribbean
Sub-Saharan Africa
Advanced Economies

*Source:*  UNCTAD Secretariat calculations, based on IMF WEO April 2021. Country grouped by IMF WEO country classification.
*Note:*  2021 to 2026 = estimates.

# D. Trends in International Trade

## 1.  Goods and services

Extraordinary measures such as lockdowns, quarantines and travel restrictions had dramatic effects on trade; the international flow of goods and services dropped by 5.6 per cent in 2020. Nevertheless, this downturn proved less severe than had been anticipated, as month-on-month merchandise trade flows in the latter part of 2020 rebounded almost as strongly as they had fallen earlier (Figure 1.18). The modelling projections underpinning the economic growth results in Section B yield an annual real growth of global trade in goods and services of 9.5 per cent in 2021. Still, the recovery has been extremely uneven, and scars will continue to weigh on the trade performance in the years ahead.

Risks remain tilted to the downside. First, the recent uptick in international trade may be short-lived, as it partly reflects an inventory restocking cycle in early 2021 after very low inventory-to-sales ratios were registered in many developed economies. Furthermore, the pandemic-induced shift in consumption habits, notably the relative increase in demand for goods, is expected to shift back as demand patterns normalize in high-contact sectors. This dynamic could boost trade in services if the rollout of vaccines improves worldwide. Yet, as of mid-2021, the spread of the Delta variant, including in the advanced economies with relatively high vaccination rates, is a reminder of just how fragile and uncertain the current situation is. The new variant could also prolong bottlenecks in international shipping caused by the pandemic, resulting in delays and price hikes in container shipping rates.

Apart from these near-term effects, trade tensions between the United States and China remain elevated. Similarly, global disputes over trade more broadly remain unresolved. These wrangles include the failure to end a deadlock on appointments to the Appellate Body of the World Trade Organization

**FIGURE 1.18  World merchandise trade, January 2015–May 2021**
*(Index numbers, average 2010 = 100)*

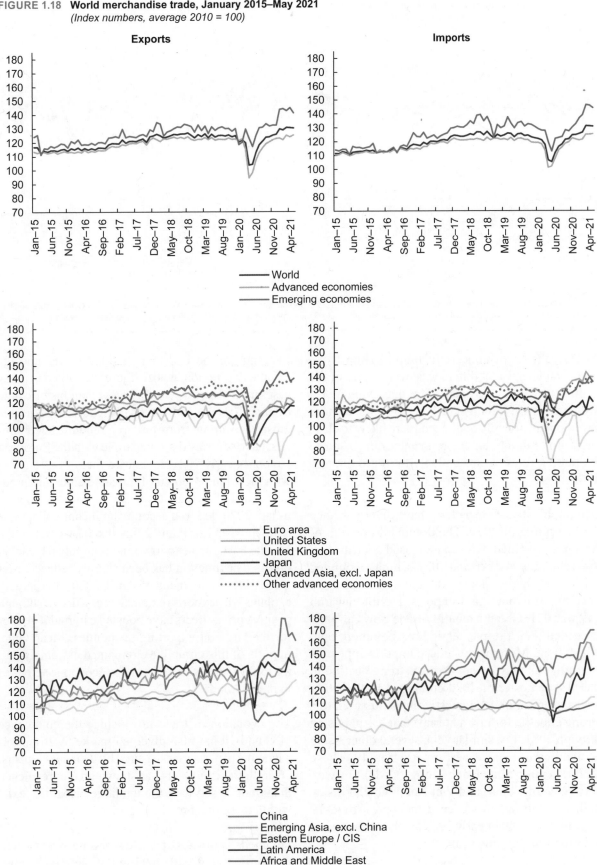

**Source:**  CPB Netherlands Bureau for Economic Policy Analysis, World Trade Monitor database.
**Note:**  Country group classification in this figure relies on Ebregt (2020).

**FIGURE 1.19**   **Metric tons of world exports by vessel type, 1 January 2020–31 May 2021**
*(Index numbers: average 2019 = 100 ; 31-day centred moving averages)*

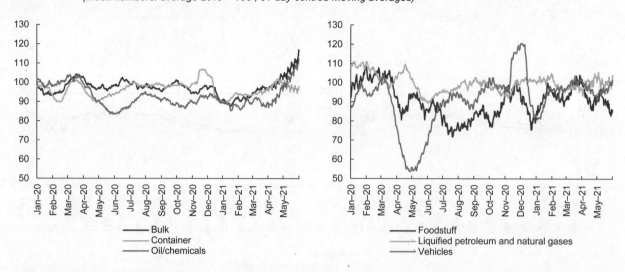

Bulk
Container
Oil/chemicals

Foodstuff
Liquified petroleum and natural gases
Vehicles

**Source:**   UNCTAD secretariat calculations, based on Cerdeiro et al. (2020) and AIS data collected by MarineTraffic (available at UN COMTRADE Monitor).
**Note:**   Data after 15 June 2021 were not used because by the cut-off date the coverage was still insufficient to get a meaningful world aggregate.

(WTO), the highly uncertain future of the Doha Round and persistent differences over reform of the multilateral trading system. The upcoming WTO Ministerial in December, where calls for a more development-friendly trade agenda are likely to clash with efforts to add an environmental dimension to the trading rules, seems unlikely to iron out major differences.

Geographically, trade patterns have diverged since the beginning of 2020. The dominant position of Asia has prevailed, with an increased contribution to world trade in 2020 and 2021. China rebounded earlier and sharper than most other countries, both in terms of exports and imports. During the first half of 2021, China's monthly trade flows already exceeded their pre-pandemic levels by more than 10 per cent. Moreover, Chinese imports appear as an outlier as they do not show a strong decline in the first semester of 2020 compared to their historical trend. Robust domestic investment led to a strong appetite for raw materials that has persisted through 2021. In a similar vein, several other Asian economies have also performed strongly. These include, inter alia, Hong Kong (SAR), Taiwan (Province of China) and Viet Nam, which all saw their monthly exports exceed their pre-Covid-19 peak by late 2020 or early 2021 and have continued to surge through this year.

A number of other large economies saw their monthly merchandise trade flows, both exports and imports, close to the pre-Covid-19-crisis peaks by mid-2021.

Lagging are the United Kingdom, Africa and the Middle East region, whose figures remained in many cases more than 20 per cent below their historic high by mid-2021. In the United Kingdom, weaknesses mostly resulting from post-referendum uncertainties, have severely disrupted trade with the European Union. In early 2021, lockdown measures, together with the winding-down of a rush to stockpile products ahead of the end of the Brexit transition period in late 2020, led to a second significant collapse of trade flows in less than 12 months. In Africa and the Middle East, total export volumes largely depend on oil. As its extraction has been sharply reduced after the OPEC+ agreement of April 2020, this largely explains why exports remain depressed, even though positive price effects have boosted external revenues for the large oil-exporting economies. Meanwhile, imports of this group have remained extremely flat, mirroring the subdued rebound in economic activities in these countries.

The evolution of trade flows since the emergence of Covid-19 has also diverged markedly from pre-pandemic patterns, as measured by their components. Overall, trade in goods has shown greater resilience than trade in services, though large disparities exist within these two broad categories.

For goods, estimates of world seaborne exports from Cerdeiro et al. (2020) track maritime merchandise trade by their respective vessels in real time (Figure 1.19). These can be used as proxies to unravel specific patterns in real time, which is especially relevant in the current environment. As seaborne trade represents more than half of the value of all trade in goods – compared to 'air' and 'other transport modes' (i.e. mostly land) which account respectively for only 12 per cent and 31 per cent of the global freight services in 2019 (WTO, 2020) – these data provide a good sense of what is currently happening to these specific segments.

Seaborne transportation also experienced mixed patterns. As for the other dimensions of trade, data point to a multi-paced recovery. Containers, which represent roughly two thirds of the world maritime transport in terms of metric tons of cargo, registered a kind of W-shaped trajectory between March 2020 and June 2021.[15] Overall, this type of vessels did not register more than 5 per cent decline in activity in the first half of 2021 compared to 2019 and 2020, though a misallocation of containers led to a significant surge in shipping costs, especially from East Asia to Europe (see below). By contrast, compared to 2017 and 2018, container shipments were about 18 per cent lower, reflecting trade disputes and general subdued economic activities preceding the Covid-19 shock.

For the other two main categories of maritime transport – i.e., bulk and oil/chemicals, both accounting for slightly less than one fifth of the total – the patterns also differ markedly. Bulk has been much more constant than any other type of cargo. Indeed, the Covid-19 shock is hardly visible in the data when compared to previous oscillations. In the second quarter of 2021, however, it gradually increased, to reach an all-time high towards the end of May amid strong demand for raw materials.

Tanker shipping, by contrast, oscillated between the 2020Q1 and 2021Q1 at a level roughly one-tenth below its pre-pandemic plateau. Gas shipments have been relatively resilient while vehicles point to a deep drop in March-April 2020 due to the closure of many automotive assembly plants and the decline in the purchasing of vehicles in Europe and North America. After this episode, vehicle shipments rebounded quickly owing to the release of pent-up demand, especially in Asia, followed by a continued increase in the second half of 2020.

In trade in services, the shock from the pandemic has been sharper, with key sectors within this catch-all category still suffering severely from the pandemic-related disruptions. Tourism, at one-fourth of the total and thus the largest component of trade in services prior to the pandemic, dropped to only one

tenth in 2020 due to the collapse in travel and remains heavily depressed. Recent estimates point to global financial losses of $2.4 trillion in 2020 followed by another $1.7–2.4 trillion in 2021 depending on the scenarios for the rest of the year (UNCTAD, 2021b). Aside from these projections, recent data shows that in January–May 2021, international tourist arrivals worldwide remained 85 per cent lower than their corresponding levels of 2019. Asia and the Pacific continued to register the largest declines with a 95 per cent drop in international arrivals during the first five months of 2021, compared to the same period two years ago. The situation was slightly better in North America and the Caribbean, though the evolution in these figures still point to declines of 70 per cent and 60 per cent, respectively (UNWTO, 2021a).

Confidence in this industry has been slowly rising as the vaccination rollout in some key source markets together with policies to restart tourism safely have boosted hopes for a rebound in some locations. However, uncertainty remains high due to the uneven rollout of vaccines and the surge of new variants, which altogether tend to have a greater impact on long-haul destinations given the likelihood to have greater asymmetries in terms of health conditions and lesser harmonization of travel measures against Covid-19. In this context, almost half of all experts saw a return to 2019 levels only in 2024 or later (UNWTO, 2021b).

Transport, accounting for about one sixth of trade in services, registered its lowest level of activity since 2010, with a 19-per cent drop in 2020. Apart from the sea transport described above, which weathered the crisis relatively well, except for most of the world's 1.7 million commercial seafarers who have been left stranded by the pandemic, air transport services remain severely depressed as passenger flights struggle to recover. In this context, airlines passenger revenues were down 74 per cent in the first quarter of 2021, compared to the same quarter in 2019. By contrast, air cargo has registered intense activity owing to the pandemic-induced logjams in maritime transport that prevent on-time delivery for high-value goods. The sudden rush for medical appliances and PPE at the onset of the pandemic and the subsequent rise of e-commerce, have further supported this subsector. In this context, cash-strapped airlines have converted passenger planes to cargo carriers as they looked for alternatives to limit their financial losses. This switch led to a year-on-year increase in cargo revenues by 50 per cent during the first quarter of 2021, though it was insufficient to compensate for the sharp loss in passenger flows, which resulted in a 65 per cent drop in overall revenues.[16]

As of mid-2021, several other types of trade in services remain depressed. These include commercial, maintenance and repair, construction and to a lesser extent personal, cultural, and recreational services. By contrast, trade in ICT, insurance, pension, and financial services, have benefitted to an extent from pandemic-induced effects, such as the rise of activities being conducted over the Internet due to social distancing and remote work.

Aside from these specific developments, disruptions of all kinds have interrupted international trade in 2020 and 2021. Some of these disruptions still weigh on the outlook. Crippling supply chain bottlenecks that may have bolstered shipping profitability have also increased pressure on supply chains and thus trade. By early 2021, maritime freight rates surged, surcharges proliferated, service reliability declined, congestion in ports increased while delays and dwell times went up (UNCTAD, 2021c).

Supply chains have come under considerable pressure over the last year for a variety of unrelated reasons: the surge in consumer demand for manufactured goods, especially in the United States; transport capacity constraints; shortages affecting equipment and container; renewed virus infections in some parts of the world, including in Yantian terminal, a critical international container port in China; and a week-long blockage of the Suez Canal caused by the grounded container ship *Ever Given*. These disruptions are holding up the recovery for some major industries, especially in Europe. In parallel, the self-isolation of workers in large factories or warehouses, like in the United Kingdom also disrupted the production of manufactured goods. Automotive industry plants, for instance, had to close temporarily due to missing critical components and parts or at least to cut production because of labour shortages. Together, these experiences heightened the push back against long-haul trade, extended supply chains and the over-reliance on single-source suppliers.

## 2. Commodity markets

Commodity prices have, through mid-2021, continued their upward trajectory observed since mid-2020, with all commodity groups recovering to pre-pandemic levels, and some groups far exceeding those. The aggregate commodity index registered a drop of over 35 per cent from December 2019 to April 2020

– the date at which the price index reached its lowest point – with fuel commodities experiencing a fall of just shy of 60 per cent during this period (Figure 1.20).

The imbalance between global oil supply and demand explains the unprecedented decline of international crude oil prices. A subsequent agreement reached by OPEC+ members in April 2020 to reduce daily oil production by 10 million barrels a day – the largest ever coordinated cut in production – proved effective in stabilizing crude prices.

A slightly positive trajectory for minerals, ores and metals during the first months of 2020 reflects the significant price gains registered for precious metals, a main refuge for financial investors during times of market uncertainty. These gains compensated the decline in the prices of industrial metals as international demand for these materials plunged.

Lastly, the commodity groups of food, beverages and vegetable oilseeds saw fairly moderate price declines at the beginning of 2020. Despite the weakening aggregate demand outlook and the sharp drop in fuel prices (which particularly affects the prices of biofuel crops such as corn and soybeans), as well as record high production for some food groups (particularly grains), the downward pressure on food prices during the first few months of 2020 was not as acute as that of other commodity groups. This was in part due to their lower income elasticity of demand. Similarly, increasing concerns regarding food security amidst the spread of the pandemic – particularly for poorer developing nations – due to disruptions in supply chains and transport networks also served to attenuate the downward pressure on food prices. The implementation of trade restrictions (including export bans) and increased imports with the intention of stockpiling certain food commodities further eased any downward pressure on prices. These factors account for the modest price declines in these commodity groups during the initial phase of the pandemic.

By the end of 2020, the aggregate commodity price index laid only marginally below the level observed in December 2019. The only group which remained significantly below the level observed prior to the pandemic was fuels, which ended 2020 with their price level 18 per cent below that registered a year earlier. By contrast, the prices of minerals, ores and metals and of vegetable oilseeds and oils, ended the year over 30 per cent above their pre-pandemic levels. In the case of metals, a ramping up of investment

**FIGURE 1.20 Monthly commodity price indices by commodity group, January 2002–May 2021**
*(Index numbers, 2002 = 100)*

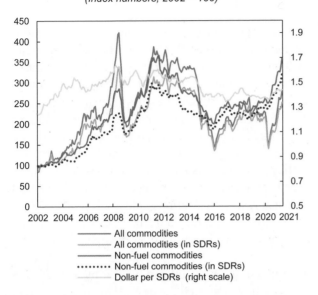

Legend:
- All commodities
- All commodities (in SDRs)
- Non-fuel commodities
- Non-fuel commodities (in SDRs)
- Dollar per SDRs (right scale)

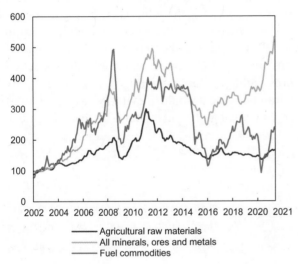

Legend:
- Agricultural raw materials
- All minerals, ores and metals
- Fuel commodities

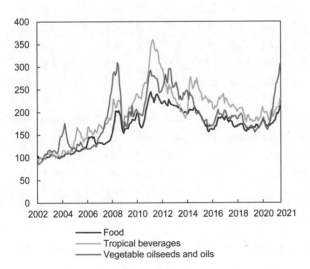

Legend:
- Food
- Tropical beverages
- Vegetable oilseeds and oils

*Source:* UNCTAD secretariat calculations, based on *UNCTADstat*. For more detailes on the data sources see https://unctadstat.unctad. org/wds/TableViewer/tableView.aspx?ReportId=140864.

spending in infrastructure projects in China as well as the Chinese authorities' decision to replenish strategic stockpiles led to a vertiginous increase in import demand for industrial metals such as copper and iron ore during the second half of the year. At the same time, the closure of key mines in Brazil due to virus outbreaks constrained supply and applied further upward pressure on the prices of these metals. Likewise, in the cases of food and vegetable oilseeds, increased demand for soybeans and wheat from China, coupled with lower-than-usual rainfalls in key producers in South America – due to the periodic cooling of ocean surface temperatures in the Pacific known as La Niña – which resulted in depressed grain volumes, lifted the prices of these agricultural goods towards the end of the year.

In 2021, the positive trajectory of commodity prices from the trough observed in the second quarter of 2020 has continued. The aggregate commodity index registered an increase of 25 per cent from December 2020 to May 2021, mainly due to the price of fuels, which surged by 35 per cent, while that of minerals, ores and metals registered an increase of 13 per cent.

The principal factors on the demand side exerting upward pressure on industrial commodity prices in 2021 include the ongoing rebound in industrial output in China and the strong recovery observed in the United States. These developments helped lift growth prospects and provide greater buoyancy to industrial commodities in 2021. Similarly, the Biden Administration's initial proposals to ramp up investment spending on major infrastructure projects further raised the growth outlook, and particularly boosted the demand for commodities such as aluminium, copper, iron ore and crude oil in the near term. Yet, subsequent revisions and clarifications of the investment plans point to a significantly smaller increase in spending than that originally indicated, dampening the expected boost to demand.

Similarly, the surge seen in the prices of industrial metals in 2021 has been supported by supply constraints. Copper prices, which rose by 24 per cent over the course of the first half of 2021, have been lifted by mining disruptions in Peru and Chile. Likewise, iron ore prices, which surged by 38 per cent during the same period, were bolstered by disruptions to supply in Australia. Adding to the upward pressure on metal prices have been problems with regards to transportation of these goods largely due to increased congestion at strategically important ports, as well as difficulties with shipping personnel linked to quarantine requirements in certain locations. Finally, the strong recovery in fuel prices has also increased transportation costs.

Moderating somewhat the uptick in the price of minerals, ores and metals has been the negative, albeit mild, trajectory in the price of gold. The downturn corresponds to a decline in demand for the commodity – which is seen as a safe asset – as the real yield on United States Treasury securities has nudged upward in 2021.

The commodity groups of food, beverages, and vegetable oilseeds and oils saw increases of 17 per cent, 13 per cent and 26 per cent, respectively, through the first half of 2021. Food insecurity concerns continue to be a factor in driving up prices. Meanwhile, sustained robust demand from China – particularly for feed commodities such as soybeans and maize as the country's livestock sector recovers from an outbreak of African Swine Fever – has been a factor driving global demand for these goods. The surge in fuel prices has also boosted the prices of grains and oilseeds that are used as biofuels.

On the supply side, the previously mentioned adverse weather conditions linked to La Niña towards the end of 2020 and into 2021 have severely affected grain production in South America and the United States, adding upward pressure to grain prices in 2021.

Despite the continued buoyancy in commodities prices since mid-2020, sources of fragility remain. In June 2021, the suggestion that the Fed may move to tighten policy earlier than had been previously envisaged was sufficient to drive down the prices of raw materials such as copper and lumber – both of which are key inputs in the construction sector – in the week following the Fed's announcement. Strategic policy turns can also sway the trajectory of prices. For instance, in June Chinese authorities released national reserves of various industrial metals, including copper, aluminium and zinc, in order to moderate their steep price increases over the first half of 2021.

Continued curbs on oil production by the OPEC+ alliance has supported the upward movement in fuel prices. Maintaining these limits on supply is contingent on adherence to the agreed output cuts within the OPEC+ framework. Recent fractious negotiations among OPEC+ members to extend production curbs highlights the possibility of loosening supply restraints, which would inevitably lead to a swift ramping up of global oil output. The sharp decline in

---

TABLE 1.2    **World primary commodity prices, 2008–2021**
*(Percentage change over previous year, unless otherwise indicated)*

| Commodity groups | 2008 | 2009 | 2010 | 2011 | 2012 | 2013 | 2014 | 2015 | 2016 | 2017 | 2018 | 2019 | 2020 | 2021[a] |
|---|---|---|---|---|---|---|---|---|---|---|---|---|---|---|
| All commodities[b] | 33.4 | -31.6 | 24.3 | 28.6 | -3.0 | -3.7 | -7.9 | -36.2 | -9.4 | 17.4 | 16.0 | -7.4 | -15.9 | 43.5 |
| Non fuel commodities[c] | 22.2 | -17.8 | 26.1 | 18.9 | -12.7 | -6.5 | -8.0 | -18.9 | 2.3 | 9.1 | -2.2 | 0.1 | 4.2 | 41.0 |
| Non fuel commodities (in SDRs)[c] | 18.3 | -15.7 | 27.3 | 14.9 | -10.0 | -5.7 | -8.0 | -11.9 | 3.0 | 9.4 | -4.2 | 2.5 | 3.4 | 34.5 |
| All food | 32.6 | -10.4 | 12.0 | 24.0 | -6.5 | -9.6 | -0.8 | -15.6 | 3.6 | -1.3 | -6.5 | -2.0 | 6.5 | 28.1 |
| Food and tropical beverages | 31.1 | -2.2 | 11.6 | 23.6 | -9.9 | -9.1 | 3.8 | -14.2 | 2.2 | -1.6 | -6.7 | 0.3 | 3.6 | 13.7 |
| *Tropical beverages* | 19.2 | 1.1 | 19.8 | 31.2 | -22.4 | -19.8 | 24.1 | -10.3 | -3.3 | -3.1 | -8.5 | -5.1 | 4.8 | 8.2 |
| *Food* | 34.9 | -3.2 | 9.1 | 21.1 | -5.6 | -6.0 | -1.2 | -15.4 | 4.0 | -1.2 | -6.1 | 1.9 | 3.3 | 15.2 |
| Vegetable oilseeds and oils | 35.2 | -24.1 | 13.0 | 24.8 | 0.7 | -10.5 | -9.6 | -18.8 | 7.0 | -0.5 | -6.2 | -6.9 | 13.4 | 61.8 |
| Agricultural raw materials | 8.4 | -16.4 | 37.0 | 24.5 | -19.2 | -8.8 | -11.8 | -13.3 | -0.4 | 5.3 | -1.8 | -3.9 | -2.0 | 16.6 |
| Minerals, ores and metals | 19.7 | -12.9 | 33.6 | 20.5 | -6.9 | -9.5 | -12.8 | -17.2 | 4.6 | 11.3 | 1.3 | 6.2 | 15.5 | 34.6 |
| Minerals, ores and non-precious metals | 17.5 | -25.4 | 39.0 | 12.2 | -16.8 | -2.0 | -14.6 | -24.8 | 1.4 | 25.7 | 2.6 | 3.4 | 3.7 | 62.7 |
| Precious metals | 23.4 | 7.5 | 27.5 | 30.8 | 3.4 | -15.8 | -11.0 | -9.9 | 7.1 | 0.4 | 0.0 | 8.9 | 26.3 | 14.3 |
| Fuel commodities | 37.9 | -38.6 | 23.1 | 32.0 | -0.5 | -1.2 | -7.5 | -44.4 | -17.5 | 25.9 | 27.5 | -12.6 | -32.1 | 54.8 |
| **Memo item:** Manufactures[d] | 4.9 | -5.6 | 1.9 | 10.3 | -2.2 | 4.0 | -1.8 | -9.5 | -1.1 | 4.7 | 4.7 | -2.1 | 1.4 | |

***Source:*** UNCTAD secretariat calculations, based on UNCTAD, *Commodity Price Statistics Online*; and United Nations Statistics Division (UNSD), *Monthly Bulletin of Statistics*, various issues.
***Note:***   In current dollars unless otherwise specified.
   *a*   Percentage change between the average for the period January to May 2021 and  January to May 2020.
   *b*   Including fuel commodities and precious metals. Average 2014-2016 weights are used for aggregation.
   *c*   Excluding fuel commodities and precious metals. SDRs = special drawing rights.
   *d*   Unit value of exports of manufactured goods of developed countries.

oil demand and prices in the first half of 2020 caused a string of bankruptcies among shale producers in the United States, as well as a severe drop in investments in new shale production facilities. However, going forward persistently high oil prices would likely translate into greater investment and production in the United States.

Looking beyond 2021, the shift towards renewable energy sources has important implications for the commodities sector, and not necessarily in the direction one might assume, particularly in the short-term. In the case of certain materials such as copper, lithium and cobalt, the move away from internal combustion engines will lead to a strong uptick in their demand as these products are key inputs in

electric vehicles. The recent proposal put forward by the European Union to ban the sale of new petrol and diesel cars by 2035 will only bolster this trend. Moreover, copper is not only used in electric vehicles but is also a key input for green infrastructures such as solar and wind energy. The green transition will therefore actually exert sustained upward pressure on the demand and prices for certain commodities. In fact, somewhat paradoxically, the investment drive to build the renewable energy infrastructure required for the green transition – with the accompanying rise in employment and economic growth associated with this investment push – will likely provoke, in the nearer term, an increase in the prices of the very same traditional energy commodities that this green infrastructure will later replace.

# E. Regional Trends

## 1. North America and Europe

In 2020, the GDP of the United States contracted 3.5 per cent, the worst recession since the end of the Second World War. While all components of private demand contributed to the drop, a sharp fall in private consumption was responsible for three-quarters of the contraction, despite massive transfers from the Federal government. In response, the government expanded its net contribution to aggregate demand by the largest amount on record, including through the $1.9 trillion (9 per cent of GDP) American Rescue Plan, but this only offset the downturn by a small fraction.

After slowing down amid the second wave of Covid-19 contagion in 2020 Q4, the recovery picked up again in 2021 Q1–Q2, as sanitary restrictions eased, and the impact of stimulus packages cascaded through the system. The expansion was driven by private consumption (especially of durable goods), professional services and residential investment; individual cash transfers ended by mid-year. Overall, growth is projected to be 5.7 per cent in 2021 and 3 per cent in 2022.

In Canada GDP contracted by 5.4 per cent in 2020, dragged down by consumption and investment spending, like in the United States, despite a substantial increase of government's contribution to aggregate demand. However, recovery has been moderately strong in 2021, partly thanks to an expansion of spending for social protection and partly on the

back of fast growth in the United States. Growth is projected to reach 5.1 per cent in 2021 and 2.9 per cent in 2022.

In Europe, between March 2020 and 2021 Q2, the three largest economies of the eurozone repeatedly went into lockdowns with adverse effects on growth. Indeed, France, Germany and Italy registered, respectively, -8.0, -4.9 and -8.9 per cent in 2020, while growth rates in the first quarter of 2021 relative to the first quarter of 2020 were negative for Germany and Italy (-3 and -1 per cent, respectively). In response, governments introduced extraordinary measures, which prevented layoffs and many bankruptcies and preserved the accumulation of aggregate private savings. In France, the total primary outlays of the general government grew by 12.8 per cent; in Germany by 13.5 per cent. Italy saw an 18.8 per cent increase, which reflects the extremely austere budgetary policies of the previous years.

At the same time, the intra-eurozone differences reflect a long-standing lack of coordination in the area, with the strongest economy, Germany, running a relatively small primary fiscal deficit-to-GDP ratio, 3.5 per cent, while the same ratio was 7.9 per cent in France and 6 per cent in Italy, the hardest hit eurozone economy. European Union-level measures were unprecedented but insufficient to overcome this structural limitation. In particular, ECB's support, including a € 1.85 trillion emergency bond purchasing program, reduced, but did not eliminate, the yield spread between national government bonds and guaranteed liquidity access to banks and firms.

In France and Germany, the fiscal effort more than compensated the steep fall in primary incomes of households but could not prevent the dramatic reduction in personal consumption, most of which was concentrated in the sectors directly affected by the public health restrictions. In Italy, total after-tax household income fell slightly despite a 10.6 per cent increase in social transfers in cash and an almost 50 per cent increase in its non-pension share from 2019. The fall in personal consumption was almost twice as large as that in the other two economies (11.8 per cent). Investment shrank at a similar rate everywhere and across the spectrum of activities, but most dramatically in the transport sector. Overall, there was no significant disruption in exports and net external demand bounced back quickly with the recovery of the global economy and an easing of travel restrictions, especially in Italy and Germany.

As the three countries progress with vaccinations and ease public health restrictions for the summer, tourism and consumption are projected to resume, together with some private investment. Both fiscal and monetary supports will remain in place for the time being, while early signs of pressure on prices have generally been taken as temporary. With growth expected in the remaining quarters of the year, and barring any new negative health developments, the real growth rate in 2021 is expected to reach 5.5 per cent for Italy and 5.2 per cent for France. The projected rate for Germany is 2.2 per cent, reflecting the smaller contraction of the past year together with the significant contraction of the first quarter. These rates will leave the respective economies below 2019 GDP levels. Given the already stagnant pre-Covid-19 conditions, prolonging a recovery beyond the bounce-back will depend on the capacity of new planned fiscal stimulus to expand public and private investment in a durable way, reinforcing domestic demand.

The European Union has suspended its fiscal rules throughout 2022, allowing room for further expansionary fiscal policies. Moreover, in June 2021, the European Union Commission began disbursement of the Next Generation EU funds, which will finance stimulus measures complementing the national budgets. The national recovery plans (only partly funded by European Union grants) include public investments which amount to an estimated 6.4 per cent of 2019 GDP spread over 6 years in Italy, 4.1 per cent in France and 0.7 per cent in Germany. Considering the small size of these investment programs, the outcome of the ongoing debate about reforming the fiscal rules, as well as the criteria for the ECB bond purchasing programs, is crucial. Uncertainty on the matter is especially binding for Italy, which is the only country of the triad that we do not project to return to the 2019 GDP level in 2022, when it is projected to achieve a 3.0 per cent GDP growth rate. France and Germany with respectively 3.4 per cent and 3.2 per cent growth rates next year are both expected to reach previous levels in 2022.

The United Kingdom's GDP fell by nearly 10 per cent in 2020, the second largest contraction in the region, largely owing to plummeting domestic demand. The government's net contribution to aggregate demand increased more than 10 per cent of GDP compared with 2019, a record amount, partially absorbing the shock. A second wave of Covid-19 infections, met with restrictions to economic activity and school closures, led to a large contraction of retail sales in 2021 Q1, which brought GDP down by 1.5 per cent and its level 8.7 per cent below where it was in the last quarter of 2019. However, during this period employment began to recover. For 2021, growth is projected at 6.7 per cent and for 2022 at 2.1 per cent, assuming no more restrictions will be imposed and employment will continue to recover toward its 2019 level. However, post-Brexit adjustment processes still weigh over medium-term growth prospects of the United Kingdom.

## 2. Latin America and the Caribbean

The Latin American and the Caribbean region was severely hit by Covid-19, with high contagion and mortality rates, together with a sharp economic downturn. The GDP of the whole region fell 7.1 per cent in 2020 and is expected to grow just 5.5 per cent in 2021. Latin America is also struggling with rising inflation, due to the international spike in food prices, and volatile exchange rates, caused by the region's overspecialization on commodity exports and high exposure to speculative international capital flows (Campello and Zucco, 2020).

The Mexican economy contracted 8.3 per cent in 2020 and is expected to rebound 6.2 per cent this year. Part of the recovery reflects the booming United States economy, through higher Mexican non-oil exports. The other part is domestic, due to the easing of social distancing and the vaccination of the general population, which should pull up the demand for urban services. Fiscal policy has been a drag, since

Mexico continues to have the smallest fiscal impulse to fight the Covid-19 recession. In contrast, despite the increase in the short-term interest rates, monetary policy has tended to remain neutral, as the Bank of Mexico raised its base interest rate in line with the increase in expected inflation. The acceleration of the economy in the second half of 2021 will create a positive base effect for 2022, helping the economy grow 2.8 per cent next year, slightly above the country's pre-Covid-19 growth trend.

In Brazil, despite the heavy human cost of the pandemic, the economy contracted by just 4.1 per cent in 2020, the smallest impact among the largest Latin American economies. Expansionary fiscal and monetary policy helped Brazil wither the economic impact of Covid-19 and, in 2021, the recovery in commodity prices and a gradual phase out of the fiscal stimulus is expected to help GDP grow by 4.9 per cent. On the upside, vaccination and services' demand tend to accelerate in the second half of 2021. On the downside, supply shortages from hydropower plants have been pushing inflation up, which in turn is forcing the Brazilian Central Bank to hike the short-term interest rate to a contractionary level. The negative forces and political uncertainty associated with Brazil's next presidential election is likely to weigh on prospects in 2022, with growth slowing to just 1.8 per cent .

Similar to Mexico, Argentina's GDP was also heavily affected by the Covid-19 shock, falling by almost 10 per cent in 2020. The country's pre-pandemic recession and balance-of-payments problems also account for the sharp contraction, since the Argentine government had limited flexibility to attenuate the pandemic shock. In 2021, the increase in commodity prices, especially of food items, reduced the country's financial constraint and is expected to help the economy grow by 6.7 per cent. Going forward, the structural public and foreign-exchange imbalances remain a challenge, together with rising inflation. Assuming the government manages its foreign liabilities and the central bank avoids a wage-price spiral, economic growth is estimated at 2.9 per cent in 2022, a positive result in view of the Argentine performance before Covid-19.

The Andean economies have also been hard hit by Covid-19 in 2020, with double-digit GDP contraction in Peru, and a fall between 6 per cent and 8 per cent in Colombia, Chile, and Ecuador. The recovery in commodity prices, especially copper in the case of Chile, is helping most of the region recover to nearly 6 per cent this year. The exception is Ecuador, where the currency peg limits the stabilizing role of fiscal and monetary policy. For 2022, the Andean economies can expect to return to their pre-Covid-19 trend, growing around 3.4 per cent.

Finally, the reduction in tourism and remittances from the United States pushed Central America (ex-Mexico) and the Caribbean into a deep recession in 2020, with double-digit GDP contractions in many island economies. In contrast, assuming vaccination accelerates and most of the restrictions on international traveling come down, the region tends to recover fast by the end of 2021 and return to its pre-pandemic 3.0 per cent growth trend in 2022.

## 3. The Russian Federation and Central Asia

In 2020, the Russian Federation GDP dropped by 3 per cent, slightly better than some of the official expectations, which had forecast a 3.9 per cent contraction. Like in other oil-exporters, the decline is accounted for by Covid-19 restrictions internally, as well as sharp fall in the external demand for energy exports. More specifically, the downward dynamics of GDP in 2020 was affected by the 5 per cent fall in final consumption, and the net trade balance, where deceleration in imports (-13.7 per cent) dominated over exports (-5.1 per cent).

In 2021, recovery was observed across most economic sectors, with manufacturing, investment, retail trade, as well as people's disposable incomes, growing, after having dropped by 2 to 5 per cent, on average, in 2020. By mid-2021, consumer activity had reached its pre-pandemic levels. The major factor that has slowed growth internally was a 6.4 per cent inflation of food prices. It pushed the overall inflation rates above the Central Bank's target, prompting the central bank to raise interest rates repeatedly in 2021. In 2021, inflation is projected at 4.6 per cent. The financial buffers built during the two decades of relative prosperity have allowed the government to add stimulus which sustained aggregate demand during the pandemic. The key to the 2021 growth has been growth in consumption, continued decline in Covid-19 cases (at least until the summer of 2021), and investments, which were partly funded out of the National Wealth Fund (NWF). The July 2021 decision by OPEC to expand the volume of oil extraction has further brightened the prospects for short-term recovery. UNCTAD estimates that the Russian GDP will growth by 3.8 per cent in 2021 and by 2.3 per cent in 2022.

The Central Asian region, which includes the countries in the Eurasian Economic Union, registered a mild contraction of 0.3 per cent in 2020. The sharp downturn in economic activity in many of the region's key trading partners and the drop in the international price of commodities (amongst which hydrocarbons and industrial metals represent key export products for several countries in the region) during the first half of 2020 were partially offset by the introduction of targeted fiscal and monetary support measures and a recovery in external demand, particularly from the European Union, during the second half of the year. For 2021, UNCTAD expects relatively moderate growth of 4.3 per cent, as the continued recovery in external demand and international commodity prices provide the main impetus for growth, while a winding down of fiscal support measures and more restrictive monetary policy stances in several countries in the region inhibit the rebound in economic activity. A growth rate of 3.1 per cent is expected for 2022 as domestic demand recovers more fully from the economic shock of the pandemic.

The region's largest economy, Kazakhstan, was particularly affected by the drastic reduction in the international price of crude oil, its main export, during the first half of 2020. The subsequent stabilization and recovery in international crude prices, together with the application of substantial fiscal and monetary stimulus measures helped to moderate the economic contraction in 2020, at 2.6 per cent. For 2021, the Kazakh economy is expected to register growth of 3.6 per cent as the rebound in global demand, a gradual uptick in international oil prices and production helps to boost economic activity. UNCTAD expects a moderate acceleration of growth in 2022, to 4.0 per cent, as an increase in production in the country's energy sector and recovering domestic demand will help to drive productive activity.

## 4. East Asia

East Asia was the region which demonstrated most resilience in 2020, registering a growth rate of 0.3 per cent. Likewise, the region is expected to register the most dynamic recovery in 2021 with 6.7 per cent growth estimated for 2021, moderating to 4.7 per cent in 2022.

East Asia's growth pattern is driven mostly by China, where the imposition of restrictions following the initial outbreak and subsequent mass test and trace programmes proved largely successful in containing the virus within the country. The Chinese economy is expected to comfortably outperform the minimum target of 6 per cent growth set for this year by the authorities, accelerating to 8.3 per cent in 2021 as a continuing recovery of global demand and the country's role as a key player in the global supply chains of electronics and communications goods as well as healthcare equipment and vaccines will provide a strong boost to the export sector. Similarly, a gradual bounce back in domestic demand is expected, albeit partly contingent on the success of the domestic roll-out of vaccines. For its part, continued support from the government for new infrastructure projects will ensure a healthy expansion of public expenditures.

UNCTAD expects the growth rate to moderate to 5.7 per cent in 2022, as fiscal and liquidity support measures wind down. More stringent macroprudential policies and a tightening of regulations in the financial and real estate sectors, amid elevated debt burdens and rising housing prices, should also restrain growth.

In the Republic of Korea during 2020, containment policies which proved to be very effective without causing excessive disruptions to productive activities helped minimize the negative impact of the pandemic. However, an unexpected rise in infections at the end of 2020 necessitated the introduction of tighter restrictions and social distancing rules, which in turn had a detrimental impact on employment and private consumption. Tempering this downturn in consumption was the positive performance of the export sector which, much like in China, enjoyed buoyant demand, in particular, for electronic and communications equipment. The combination of these factors resulted in only a modest contraction of 0.9 per cent in 2020.

An expansion of 3.9 per cent is expected in 2021, as the country's external sector benefits from strong international demand for its exports of consumer electronics, semiconductors and automobiles. For its part, investment spending remains resilient helped by public outlays on digital and infrastructure in the context of the Korean Green New Deal. Likewise, the fiscal and monetary support measures introduced by the government during 2020 have largely remained in place, along with increased public expenditures targeted towards lower income households and small businesses in 2021. UNCTAD expects a moderation of the growth rate in 2022 to a fairly robust 2.8 per cent, as policy support, an uptick in investment and private consumption, and continued strength of the export sector drive the expansion in economic activity. However, rising debt levels among households, elevated real estate prices and growing inequality remain policy concerns for the government.

During 2020, Japan experienced a double hit from the two consecutive quarters of contraction in 2019Q4 and 2020Q1, and the ensuing Covid-19 shock, producing an annual contraction of 4.7 per cent, which could have been more severe without the remarkable growth of government spending in goods and services. This stimulus played its role in creating a good momentum in the second half of the year, but was halted due to a severe second wave of the pandemic, leading to a fall in GDP of 1.0 per cent in the first quarter of 2021. The government continued to support the shocked economy but at a more moderate pace. Private sector activity shifted to positive territory from the second quarter onwards, but as restrictions and lockdowns continue to different degrees, growth will only stabilize from the fourth quarter and into the year 2022.

The Olympics, held under lockdown, will have a very marginal effect on effective demand. Net external demand, which has been disappointing since 2019 is expected to play a more favourable role, pulled by the global rebound and assuming that bottlenecks in global value chains are overcome. Given all uncertainties, growth for 2021 is projected at 2.4 per cent. In 2022, external demand will likely gain firmer traction, leading to more private sector activity and consumer demand. By contrast, the fiscal stance will likely shift towards adjustment, responding to pressure to contain the rise of debt. On these assumptions, the economy will yield 2.1 per cent growth, a stronger performance than the pre-Covid-19 average, but barely overpassing at the end of the year the level of 2019.

## 5. South Asia

South Asia suffered a sharp contraction of 5.6 per cent in 2020, with the region's economic activity brought to a halt due to widespread restrictions. Deficient public healthcare systems and high levels of informality magnified the impact of the pandemic in terms of both health and economic outcomes, which was reflected in a stark rise in poverty rates. UNCTAD expects the region to expand by 5.8 per cent in 2021, with the more vigorous recovery signalled at the beginning of the year muted by a rapid surge in infections during the second quarter of 2021. Moreover, the limited progress made in terms of vaccine rollouts continues to leave the countries

of the region susceptible to future outbreaks. For 2022, UNCTAD expects the region's growth rate to moderate to 5.7 per cent.

India, which experienced a contraction of 7.0 per cent in 2020, showed a strong quarterly growth of 1.9 per cent growth in the first quarter 2021, on the back of the momentum of the second half of 2020 and supported by government spending in goods and services. Meanwhile, a severe and broadly unanticipated second wave of the pandemic, compounded by bottlenecks in the vaccine roll out, hit the country in the second quarter, on top of rising food and general price inflation, forcing widespread lockdowns and drastic consumption and investment adjustments.

Income and wealth inequalities have widened, and social unrest has increased. The Central Bank estimates another sharp contraction (quarter-on-quarter) in the second quarter followed by a rebound afterwards. Given the inherent fragilities in coping with the pandemic and restoring employment and incomes, growth in 2021 as a whole is estimated at 7.2 per cent, insufficient to regain the pre-Covid-19 income level. Going forward, assuming away a resurgence of the pandemic to the degree experienced in the second wave, a revitalization of private sector activity, subject still to a slow recovery of jobs, is likely to be matched with a more adverse policy environment, especially on the fiscal front, and with continuing pressures on the trade balance. On these conditions, the economy is expected to decelerate to 6.7 per cent growth in 2022.

## 6. South-East Asia

South-East Asia registered a contraction of 3.9 per cent in 2020, as several of the larger economies in the region, notably Malaysia and the Philippines, struggled with elevated and persistent infection rates that were met with restrictions on population movements. The economic fallout of these restrictions was predictably severe. In Indonesia, the contraction of output was not as severe as other countries in the region, at 2.1 per cent, as the country benefitted from its relatively limited reliance on external demand and tourism flows, and less-stringent lockdowns. Those countries reliant on tourism (particularly Thailand) were especially hard hit by the widespread travel restrictions that were introduced to limit the spread of the pandemic. One positive note in the region was Viet Nam, which registered an economic expansion in 2020. The country's success in containing the virus helped to ensure a quick bounce back in activity, while the export sector also performed well as global demand recovered during the second half of the year.

The prospect of a more rapid recovery in 2021 has been interrupted by a resurgence in infection rates throughout the region and the reintroduction of lockdowns (including in Indonesia, Malaysia and Thailand), with a knock-on effect on travel and tourism. Even in the case of Viet Nam, a significant increase in the number of cases was registered towards the end of the first quarter of 2021. Moreover, the slow pace of vaccinations and the prospect of a withdrawal of policy support measures have acted as further drags on growth in the region. In Indonesia, the region's largest economy, although significant public investments in infrastructure will help boost economic activity, the rise in infections will dampen the recovery in household consumption, resulting in growth of 3.6 per cent in 2021, a weak expansion compared to the growth rates observed prior to the pandemic.

UNCTAD expects the region to expand by 3.5 per cent in 2021, increasing to 4.7 per cent in 2022. A significant factor behind the expectation of a somewhat subdued recovery is the prospect of a relatively slow reversal of the numerous job losses suffered in 2020, many of which were low-skilled jobs in the services sector. As such, the bounce back in private consumption is expected to be gradual.

## 7. Western Asia

Western Asia registered a contraction of 2.9 per cent in 2020, as the oil-exporting countries in the region suffered the simultaneous shocks from the pandemic and the precipitous drop in the demand and price of oil during the first months of 2020. As in the case of other oil exporters, a gradual uptick in crude prices during the second half of 2020 as global demand recovered did drive a partial recovery in oil revenues. UNCTAD expects the region to expand by 3.5 per cent in 2021 as international crude prices continue to return to the levels observed prior to the onset of the pandemic. Virus-related disruptions to economic activity will continue to hamper the recovery, although the economic impact of these outbreaks have proven to be less severe than those observed during 2020. For 2022, the region is expected to grow by 3.2 per cent as domestic demand increasingly gains traction and global demand remains firm.

The economy of Saudi Arabia contracted by 4.1 per cent in 2020 as the government's efforts to provide budgetary support to households and firms was compromised by the growing pressures coming from the sharp reduction in fiscal revenues due to the drop in oil prices. For 2021, the Saudi economy is expected to register a modest bounce back in growth of 2.7 per cent. The somewhat subdued recovery is explained in part by the relevant authorities' decision to make additional cuts in oil production beyond those agreed in the OPEC+ quota agreement. A reversal of these self-imposed cuts along with a winding down of the production caps from the OPEC+ agreement and the rebound in global oil demand will help growth pick up during the second half of 2021. For 2022, UNCTAD expects the economy to expand by 3.3 per cent as domestic demand recovers more fully and a planned ramping up of public investments coming from the country's sovereign wealth fund takes hold.

Turkey was one of the few countries to register an expansion in 2020, with growth of 1.8 per cent. Despite suffering a deep contraction in the second quarter, a period of record growth ensued during the third quarter as a substantial cut in the Central Bank's policy rate prompted real interest rates to turn significantly negative. At the same time, a change in banking regulations compelled the country's banks to extend credit lines. These moves triggered an unprecedented credit boom and a subsequent sharp uptick in economic activity. For 2021, UNCTAD expects the Turkish economy to grow by 3.9 per cent. Although a resurgence in infections and consequent introduction of restrictions hampered the recovery during the second quarter of the year, the government's response in providing budgetary support to businesses, along with a pickup in the export sector thanks to the rebound in external demand and the sustained resilience of the country's industrial sector will help to boost economic activity during the latter part of the year. UNCTAD expects an expansion of 3.6 per cent in 2022 as domestic demand gains more traction and provides a greater impetus to growth. However, the country continues to face severe vulnerabilities due its outsized reliance on short-term capital flows and the elevated level of foreign-currency denominated debt obligations among its domestic firms.

## 8. Oceania

Oceania registered a contraction of 2.4 per cent in 2020. The negative result was the first in almost 30 years for the region. However, UNCTAD expects a robust rebound in economic activity in 2021, with an estimated growth rate of 3.1 per cent for this year, followed by 2.8 per cent growth in 2022. The region's performance is determined to a large degree by that of its largest economy, Australia, which accounts for over 80 per cent of the region's total GDP.

After contracting by 2.5 per cent in 2020, the Australian economy is experiencing a rapid rebound, following the growth momentum that started in the second half of the year thanks to strong fiscal and monetary stimuli. Commodity prices and favourable supply in the exporting sectors also helped. This led to a rapid recovery of household consumption and business investment in the first quarter of 2021, especially as the full border isolation and partial internal lockdowns helped contain the pandemic despite the scarcity of vaccines.

However, new headwinds have emerged. On the domestic front, new partial lockdowns in relatively populated areas were needed, affecting private activity and confidence. On the external front, while the rapid rise of commodity prices continues to boost export earnings, tensions with China, the main export market, present a potential constraint on the rebound. All in all, UNCTAD projects the Australian economy to grow at 3.2 per cent in 2021. Growth will moderately decelerate to 2.8 per cent in 2022, partly as the main private and external growth drivers resume a more 'normal' pace, and partly because of curbs on government spending in goods and services, which have already started in early 2021 and will gather pace going forward.

## 9. Africa

Most African economies have entered a phase of cyclical recovery in 2021 after the pandemic brought an unprecedented recession of 3.4 per cent, which wiped out years of development gains. In this context, the entire continent is expected to grow 3.2 per cent in 2021, before slowing to 2.9 per cent in 2020. The underlying level of activity, however, remains depressed, and scars will endure. This is particularly unfortunate because several large sub-Saharan African economies – such as Angola, Nigeria, and South Africa – had already been stuck in low growth trajectories since the middle of the last decade. As a result, current estimates predict that the regional GDP per capita will not return, even in the best-case scenario, to its pre-pandemic level before 2024. In particular, South Africa, which experienced a contraction of 7 per cent in 2020, is expected to grow by a moderate 4 per cent in 2021 and by 2.3 per cent in 2022. As tens of millions of African citizens have already fallen back into extreme poverty (World

Bank, 2021a and 2021b), such development will make the SDGs even more elusive.

The economic upturn has in many cases rested on improved external conditions, especially in developed economies and China, which have supported African exports. In parallel, exchange rates have continued to rebound, for example in Botswana, Morocco, and South Africa, after being severely hit in March–April 2020. By mid-2021, exchange rates of these three economies reached levels that were close to their pre-pandemic ones, if not higher. By contrast, foreign exchange rates have trended downward in several other countries, notably in Nigeria where acute hard-currency scarcity has forced multiple devaluations since the beginning of the Covid-19 crisis. Fortunately, the terms of trade of major commodity-exporters have reversed after reaching a trough during the second quarter of 2020. PMI indicators for manufacturing activities (and services when available) have been, almost always, above the 50-point mark in Kenya and South Africa during the last quarter of 2020 and the first half of 2021. By contrast, they have mostly remained in contraction territories in Egypt and in Nigeria during this period.

In situations of subdued economic activity and generally low inflation pressures, monetary policies have often been accommodative, despite soaring food prices that have created tensions, especially in Central and West Africa. Nevertheless, several countries have registered double-digit inflation (or even triple-digit in the case of Sudan). These include, inter alia, Zimbabwe, South Sudan, Angola, Libya, Zambia, Nigeria, and Ethiopia, which all face stagflationary threats.

On the fiscal front, pressure has mounted to reduce, or even withdraw completely, the (limited) support that a handful of countries had initially been able to introduce in response to the Covid-19 shock. The fact that many governments have lost control of the public debt trajectory due to the widening budget deficits (sometimes reaching double-digit figures) and growing government debt (often by at least 15 percentage points of GDP) has significantly constrained public demand. Meanwhile, external financial assistance has fallen dismally short of what was deemed necessary to cope with the social, sanitary, and economic needs. Official Development Assistance to sub-Saharan Africa averaged US$ 27.1 billion in 2018 and 2019 but fell to US$22.6 billion in (OECD, 2021) In the outlook period, a resumption of tourism and the rollback of pandemic-induced restrictions should provide some relief to the region. The gradual increase in oil production for OPEC+ African countries will also support export revenues. Yet, these positive elements will fall short of taking many African economies out of their low-growth environment. Moreover, the weak recovery has recently been jeopardized by the third wave of virus infection, starting in June 2021, given the lagging vaccine rollout.[1] Such outbreaks will hamper the situation, especially if fast-spreading variants develop. Though at this stage it remains unclear how strong this negative effect will be, there is no doubt that no serious improvement will be made until vaccination campaigns reach the herd immunity threshold. Prior to that, sectors linked to the hospitality industry, though not only these ones, will remain heavily depressed. The situation will therefore remain dramatic in most of the tourist-reliant economies, which have already experienced the largest shocks.

In this outlook, two main factors could further damage economic prospects. One is elevated food prices (see Box 1.4.), which have already exacerbated hunger across the continent. The other is renewed social protests and conflicts – which have already escalated in several parts of sub-Saharan Africa, including in Central African Republic, Eswatini, Ethiopia, Mozambique, the Sahel region, and South Africa – as these now threaten to hinder the recovery, with potentially long-lasting economic consequences. Should these factors persist, they will add to Covid-19 related shocks – such as the disruption of education, the worsening of health, and the setback of investment – whose negative effects have already altered the growth prospects for the years ahead.[17]

---

**BOX 1.4**    Increased food insecurity amid rising food prices

The global goal of achieving 'zero hunger' by 2030 (SDG 2) seems increasingly out of reach as the number of people facing acute food insecurity and requiring urgent food, nutrition and livelihoods assistance has been on the rise. In 2020, at least 155 million people, across 55 jurisdictions, faced a situation of food crisis or worse (IPC/CH Phase 3 or above).[28] This represents an increase of about 20 million people from 2019 and roughly a 50 per cent increase from 2016. In absolute terms, the situation was particularly acute in Afghanistan, the Democratic Republic of the Congo, Sudan and Yemen, since in each country, at least 2 million people were categorized in an emergency phase or worse (IPC/CH Phase 4 or above), requiring urgent action to save lives and livelihoods (FSIN and GNAFC, 2021). The FAO (2021b) estimates that globally 45 countries, including 34 in Africa, 9 in Asia and 2 in Latin America and the Caribbean, will need external assistance due to severe food insecurity.

While conflict is often the main reason behind hunger, climate disruption and economic shocks, aggravated by the Covid-19 pandemic, have further compounded the situation. In this context, international food prices have rising from the second quarter of 2020 after 5 years of relative stability; the FAO Monthly Food Price Index increased steadily by 37 per cent between May 2020 (a 4-year low) and May 2021 (a 10-year high).

On domestic markets, increasing food prices – particularly in import-dependent countries that experienced currency depreciation – weighed heavily on household access to food. In parallel, damaged public finances often constrained governments' capacity to support vulnerable households as needs increased. In this context, six countries – Argentina, Brazil, Nigeria, South Sudan, Sudan, and Zimbabwe – saw prices of one or more basic food commodity at abnormally high levels in mid-2021 that could negatively impact on access to food (FAO, 2021a).

Overall, food crises are becoming increasingly protracted and the ability to recover from new adverse events is becoming more difficult. Conflicts, the Covid-19 pandemic, and prolonged economic stress are expected to extend food crises beyond 2021.

---

# Notes

1    Based on 2015 constant dollars and exchange rates.

2    Since the European Union is one of the G20 economies, together with Germany, France, and Italy, we

included Spain as the 20th economy in figure 1 to avoid double counting.

3    The full impact of expansionary fiscal measures on income distribution across households is still

not clear. There is also a growing debate about the impact of monetary policies, although with only a very small percentage of the population directly benefiting from the massive monetary injections by Central Banks that eased liquidity constraints and prevented financial meltdown, its magnifying effect on wealth inequality seems more certain (Petrou, 2021).

4    Not incidentally, a large proportion of countries are expected to engage in aggressive austerity packages down the road (Ortiz and Cummins, 2021).

5    For a historical account of the concepts see Costantini (2018).

6    See *TDR 1994* and *TDR 1996*, also Storm and Naastepad, 2005; Wade, 2014.

7    Defined, by the IMF, as those economies "that resemble emerging markets with regards to international market access" (IMF 2020, p.46).

8    Other investments conventionally include other equity, currency and deposits, loans, insurance and pensions, trade credits and advances, guarantee schemes as well as Special Drawing Rights (SDRs).

9    This expansion and the changes in the composition of emerging economies' foreign liabilities and assets have amplified the susceptibility of gross external assets and liabilities and of net foreign asset positions to variations in asset prices and exchange rates, entailing large transfers of wealth and income from emerging economies to advanced economies (see *TDR 2019* and Akyüz, 2021).

10   Haldane A (2014). The age of asset management? Speech by Mr. Andrew G Haldane, Executive Director, Financial Stability. Bank of England, at the London Business School. London. 4 April.

11   UNCTAD secretariat calculations, based on Refinitiv. See also UNCTAD (2021) and IMF (2021).

12   Unless otherwise indicated, figures quoted in the text are UNCTAD secretariat calculations based on World Bank, IMF and national sources.

13   See https://www.imf.org/en/About/FAQ/sovereign-debt.

14   Between March 2020 and June 2021, Covid-19-related lending by the IMF to 85 countries amounted to $113 billion (see: https://www.imf.org/en/Topics/imf-and-covid19/COVID-Lending-Tracker#REGION), while the World Bank committed $104 billion for the period between April 2020 and June 2021. According to the World Bank, this has been as high as the commitments of all other multilateral development banks taken together. See: https://www.worldbank.org/en/news/factsheet/2020/10/14/world-bank-covid-19-response.

15   The first dip relates to the great lockdown of the spring 2020. The second happened during the first quarter of 2021, reflecting a mixture of new lockdowns in some large economies, together with the traditional seasonal slowdown in international trade which occurs during the first two months of the year.

16   IATA (2021). Airlines Financial Monitor, May. Available at https://www.iata.org/en/iata-repository/publications/economic-reports/airlines-financial-monitor---may-2021/.

17   World Bank (2021a). Sub-Saharan Africa: Macro Poverty Outlook. Spring Meeting 2021. World Bank. Washington DC. World Bank (2021b). Middle East and North Africa: Macro Poverty Outlook. Spring Meeting 2021. World Bank. Washington DC.

18   In reading the estimated size of the Covid-19 stimuli packages, it is important to take note of the extent of the economic shock in the case of each country. This is particularly so for those countries that are part of the European Union, where, as discussed in section E, the differences in the scale of fiscal stimuli also respond to the disparities in the magnitude of the shock to economic activity in each country.

19   Problems of data availability and comparability did not allow straightforward inclusion of smaller developing economies or LDCs, which would most likely show even greater disparities.

20   The United States stands out among developed economies for its outsized reliance on direct income transfers in its Covid-19 fiscal support measures. As discussed in section B, the dependence on these transfers for providing support to households in the midst of the pandemic points to the inadequacies and poorly calibrated nature of the country's existing welfare protection systems.

21   United States Bureau of Economic Analysis, GDP (Advanced) Estimate of 2021 second Quarter, Table 8.

22   At the SDR/US$ exchange rate of 0.7026 on 7 July 2021.

23   Currently, SDRs can be exchanged for US dollars, euros, renminbi, Japanese yen, and pound sterling.

24   The use of SDRs is not entirely cost-free, since when countries use (or reduce) their allocated holdings of SDRs in transactions with the IMF or other member countries, they incur an interest charge at a non-concessional rate. Net interest payments due to the IMF are based on the difference between a country's cumulative allocation of SDRs and its effective holdings. The same interest rate applies for allocations and holdings, as set by the IMF based on a weighted average of representative interest rates on 3-month debt in the money markets of the five SDR basket currencies. At present, this rate stands at a mere 0.05 per cent per year, reflecting strongly accommodative

25  monetary policies in issuer countries of SDR basket currencies.

25  The current IMF quota formula is a weighted average of GDP (50 per cent), openness (30 per cent), economic variability (15 per cent) and international reserves (5 per cent). This systematically favours the status quo of the distribution of economic power between developed and developing countries rather than facilitating the use of SDRs for agreed global goals, including inclusive and sustainable development.

26  UNCTAD has been a longstanding advocate of linking SDRs to development finance (see Park, 1973).

27  Thus, Plant and Andrews (2021) suggest that proposals limited to the use or recycled 'standard' SDRs' for current Covid-19 responses would require changes

28  to the IMF's legal and policy framework (including its Articles of Agreement).

28  The scale of the Integrated Food Security Phase Classification (IPC) and the Cadre Harmonisé (CH) ranges between 1 (none/minimal) and 5 (catastrophe/famine).

29  The reader should note that generally T is used to described net or gross taxes, that is transfers from the private sector to the government. Here the definition carries the opposite sign so that the difference dT (as presented above) is interpreted as a fiscal stimulus.

30  Net Transfers from the Government to the Private Sector encompass the sum of government transfers to the private sector (including unemployment benefits and direct income transfers) minus taxes and contributions to government social security.

# References

Akyüz Y (2007). Debt sustainability in emerging markets: A critical appraisal. Working Paper No. 61. Department of Economic and Social Affairs (DESA).

Akyüz Y (2021). External balance sheets of emerging economies: Low-yielding assets, high-yielding liabilities. *Review of Keynesian Economics.* 9(2): 232–252.

Barbosa-Filho N (2021). Public debt dynamics with two currencies. Background Report to UNCTAD Trade and Development Report 2021. March.

Barbosa-Filho NH and Izurieta A (2020). The risk of a second wave of post-crisis frailty in the world economy. *International Journal of Political Economy.* 49(4): 278–303.

Barbosa-Filho N and Taylor L (2006). Distributive and demand cycles in the US economy: A structuralist Goodwin model. *Metroeconomica.* 57(3): 389-411.

Berensmann K, Dafe F and Volz U (2015). Developing local currency bond markets for long-term development financing in Sub-Saharan Africa. *Oxford Review of Economic Policy.* 31(3-4): 350–378.

Bernanke BS (2008). Testimony: Before the Committee on the Budget, U.S. House of Representatives. *The Economic Outlook.* 17 January.

Blanchard OJ, Chouraqui JC, Hagemann R and Sartor N (1990). The sustainability of fiscal policy: New answers to an old question. Working Paper No. 1547. National Bureau of Economic Research.

Boushey H and Shambaugh J (2019). Introduction. In: Boushey H, Nunn R and Shambaugh J eds. *Recession Ready: Fiscal Policies to Stabilize the American Economy.* Brookings. Washington, D.C:5–9.

Campello D and Zucco C (2020. The Volatility Curse: Exogenous Shocks and Representation in Resource-Rich Democracies. Cambridge University Press. Cambridge.

Celi G, Ginzburg G, Guarascio D and Simonazzi A (2018). *Crisis in the European Monetary Union: A Core-Periphery Perspective.* Routledge. New York.

Cerdeiro DA, Komaromi A, Liu Y and Saeed M (2020). World Seaborne Trade in Real Time: A Proof of Concept for Building AIS-based Nowcasts from Scratch. Working Paper No. 20/57. International Monetary Fund.

Chandrasekhar CP (2016). Development planning. In: Reinert ES, Ghosh J and Kattel R eds. *Handbook of Alternative Theories of Economic Development.* Edward Elgar Publishing. Cheltenham (United Kingdom) and Northampton, MA (United States):519–532.

Costantini O (2018). Invented in America: Birth and evolution of the cyclically adjusted budget rule, 1933–61. *History of Political Economy.* 50(1): 83–117.

Costantini O (2020). The Eurozone as a trap and a hostage: Obstacles and prospects of the debate on European fiscal rules. *Intereconomics.* 55(5): 284–291.

Costantini O (Forthcoming). Debt sustainability and the Sustainable Development Goals. Working paper. UNCTAD.

Domar E D (1944). The 'burden of the debt' and the national income. *The American Economic Review.* 34(4): 798–827.

Draghi M (2021). *Intervento all'Adunanza solenne di chiusura dell'anno accademico dell'Accademia Nazionale dei Lincei.* Available at https://www.

governo.it/it/articolo/lintervento-del-presidente-dra-ghi-all-accademia-dei-lincei/17314.

Dua A, Ellingrud K, Lazar M, Luby R, Petric M, Ulyett A and Van Aken T (2021). Unequal America: Ten insights on the state of economic opportunity. *McKinsey and Company*. 26 May.

Ebregt J (2020). The CPB World Trade Monitor: Technical description (update 2020). CPB Background Document. CPB Netherlands Bureau for Economic Policy Analysis. The Netherlands.

EIU (2021). How much will vaccine inequity cost? Report. The Economist Intelligence Unit.

FAO (2021a). Food Price Monitoring and Analysis. Bulletin No.6. Food and Agriculture Organization. 13 July.

FAO (2021b). Crop Prospects and Food Situation - Quarterly Global Report No. 2. July. Food and Agriculture Organization.

Fatás A and Summers LA (2015). The permanent effects of fiscal consolidations. Discussion Papers No.10902. Centre for Economic Policy Research.

FSIN and GNAFC (2021). *Global Report on Food Crises*. Food Security Information Network (FSIN) and Global Network Against Food Crises (GNAFC). Rome.

Furman J and Powell III W (2021). Worker pay has fallen in 2021 when adjusted for inflation. *Peterson Institute for International Economics*. July 30. Available at: https://www.piie.com/research/piie-charts/worker-pay-has-fallen-2021-when-adjusted-inflation.

Godley W and Izurieta A (2004). Balances, imbalances and fiscal targets: A new Cambridge view. Cambridge Endowment for Research in Finance. University of Cambridge.

Godley W and Izurieta A (2009). The US economy: weaknesses of the 'strong' recovery. *PSL Quarterly Review*. 62:248–251.

Goodman P and Chokshi N (2021). How the World Ran Out of Everything. *New York Times*. 1 June.

Griffith-Jones S and Kraemer M (2021, forthcoming). Credit ratings and developing economies. UNDESA Working Paper.

Guzman M and Lombardi D (2017). Assessing the appropriate size of relief in sovereign debt restructuring. Research Paper No. 18-9. Columbia Business School.

Haldane A (2014). Managing global finance as a system. Speech by Andrew Haldane, Executive Director and Chief Economist of the Bank of England, at Birmingham University. Birmingham, 29 October.

Haughwout A (2019). Infrastructure investment as an automatic stabilizer. In: Boushey H, Nunn R and Shambaugh J eds. *Recession Ready: Fiscal Policies to Stabilize the American economy*. Brookings. Washington, D.C: 129–152.

Hofmann B, Shim I and Shin HS (2020). Emerging market economy exchange rates and local currency bond markets amid the Covid-19 pandemic. Bulletin No. 5. Bank for International Settlements. Available at https://www.bis.org/publ/bisbull05.htm.

IMF (2012) *World Economic Outlook: Coping with High Debt and Sluggish Growth*. October. International Monetary Funds. Washington, D.C. Available at https://www.imf.org/en/Publications/WEO/Issues/2016/12/31/World-Economic-Outlook-October-2012-Coping-with-High-Debt-and-Sluggish-Growth-25845.

IMF (2020a). *World Economic Outlook: The Great Lockdown*. April. International Monetary Fund. Washington, D.C. Available at https://www. imf. org/en/Publications/WEO/Issues/2020/04/14/weo-april-2020.

IMF (2020b). *Fiscal Monitor*. April. Available at https://www.imf.org/en/Publications/FM/Issues/2020/04/06/fiscal-monitor-april-2020.

IMF (2020c). The evolution of public debt vulnerabilities in lower-income economies. Policy Paper No. 20/003. International Monetary Fund.

IMF (2021). Global Financial Stability Report: Preempting a Legacy of Vulnerabilities. April. International Monetary Fund. Washington, D.C.

Izurieta A (2001). Can countries under a common currency conduct their own fiscal policies? Working Paper No. 337. Levy Economics Institute of Bard College.

Jotzo F, Longden T and Anjum Z (2020). Fiscal stimulus for low-carbon compatible COVID-19 recovery: Criteria for infrastructure investment. Working Paper No. 2005. Centre for Climate Economics and Policy. Australian National University.

Khan M and Blankenburg S (2009). The political economy of industrial policy in Asia and Latin America. In: Cimoli M, Dosi G and Stiglitz JE eds. *Industrial Policy and Development: The Political Economy of Capabilities Accumulation*. Oxford University Press. Oxford.

Kregel J (2016). The Clearing Union Principle as the Basis for Regional Financial Arrangements in Developing Countries. Report prepared for UNCTAD Seminar on Debt Sustainability, held in Geneva in November 2016.

King I, Wu D and Pogkas D (2021). How a chip shortage snarled everything From phones to cars. Bloomberg. 29 March. Available at https://www.bloomberg.com/graphics/2021-semiconductors-chipsshortage/.

Li Y (2021). Debt relief, debt crisis prevention and human rights: The role of credit rating agencies. Report of the Independent Expert on the effects of foreign debt and other related international financial obligations of States on the full enjoyment of all human rights, particularly economic, social and cultural rights. 21 February, A/HRC/46/29. Available at https://www.ohchr.org/EN/HRBodies/HRC/RegularSessions/Session46/Documents/A_HRC_46_29_AdvanceEditedVersion.docx.

Lysandrou P and Nesvetailova A (2020). This time was different: The global safe asset shortage and shadow banking in socio-historical perspective. Working Paper Series No. 2020-01. City Political Economy Research Centre.

Malik H (2021). Remittances are still helping many emerging markets, but Nigeria is an outlier. *Tellimer*. 9 May.

McCombie J (2002). Increasing returns and the Verdoorn Law from a Kaldorian perspective. In: McCombie J, Pugno M and Soro B eds. *Productivity Growth and Economic Performance: Essays on Verdoorn's Law*. Palgrave Macmillan. London: 64–114.

Minsky HP (1969: reprinted 2013). Policy and poverty. In: Minsky HP. *Ending Poverty: Jobs not Welfare*. Ford Foundation and Levy Economics Institute. New York: Chapter 3.

Miyajima K and I. Shim I (2014). Asset managers in emerging market economies. Quarterly Review. September. Bank for International Settlements.

Munevar D (2021). Sleep now in the fire: Sovereign bonds and the Covid-19 debt crisis. *Eurodad*. 26 May. Available at https://d3n8a8pro7vhmx.cloudfront.net/eurodad/pages/2307/attachments/original/1621949568/sovereign-bond-report-FINAL.pdf?1621949568

Nesvetailova A and Palan R (2020). *Sabotage: The Business of Finance*. Penguin. London.

Ocampo J A, Rada C and Taylor L (2009). *Growth and Policy in Developing Countries: A Structuralist Approach*. Columbia University Press. New York.

Orszag PR, Rubin RE and Stiglitz JE (2021). Fiscal resiliency in a deeply uncertain world: The role of semiautonomous discretion. Policy Brief No. 21-2. Peterson institute for International Economics.

Ortiz I and Cummins M (2021). Global austerity alert: Looming budget cuts in 2021-25 and alternative pathways. Working Paper. Initiative for Policy Dialogue.

Palma JG (2011). Why has productivity growth stagnated in most Latin American countries since the Neo-Liberal reforms? In: Ocampo J A and Ros J eds. *The Oxford Handbook of Latin American Economics*. Oxford University Press. Oxford: 568–607.

Park YS (1973). The link between special drawing rights and development finance. Essays in International Finance No. 100. Princeton University.

Pasinetti LL (1998). The myth (or folly) of the 3% deficit/GDP Maastricht 'parameter'. *Cambridge Journal of Economics*. 22(1): 103–116.

Raddatz C, Schmukler SL and Williams TS (2017). International asset allocations and capital flows: The benchmark effect. *Journal of International Economics*. 108 (C): 413–430.

Rennison J (2021). How the Fed's fine intentions feed US wealth inequality. *Financial Times*. 26 July.

SAFE (2021). *2020nian Zhongguo guoji shouzhi baogao [2020 China' balance of payments report]*. State Administration of Foreign Exchange. Available at https://www.safe.gov.cn/safe/2021/0326/18626.html.

Stiglitz J and Rashid H (2020). Which economic stimulus works? *Project Syndicate*. 8 June. Available at https://www.project-syndicate.org/commentary/stimulus-policies-must-benefit-real-economy-not-financial-speculation-by-joseph-e-stiglitz-and-hamid-rashid-2020-06.

Storm S (2017). The new normal: Demand, secular stagnation, and the vanishing middle class. *International Journal of Political Economy*. 46(4): 169–210.

Storm S and Naastepad CWM (2005). Strategic factors in economic development: East Asian industrialization 1950–2003. *Development and Change*. 36(6): 1059–1094.

Storm S and Naastepad CWM (2012). *Macroeconomics beyond the NAIRU*. Harvard University Press. Cambridge (USA).

Taylor L (2020). *Macroeconomic Inequality from Reagan to Trump: Market Power, Wage Repression, Asset Price Inflation, and Industrial Decline*. (with Ömer Ö) Cambridge University Press. Cambridge.

Tregenna F (2016). Deindustrialization and premature deindustrialization. In: Reinert ES, Ghosh J and Kattel R eds. Handbook of Alternative Theories of Economic Development. Edward Elgar Publishing. Cheltenham (United Kingdom) and Northampton MA (United States): 710–728.

UNCTAD (2021a). Out of the frying pan…Into the fire? Update to TDR 2020. March 2021. (United Nations Publication. Geneva).

UNCTAD (2021b). Covid-19 and Tourism: An Update. UNCTAD. Geneva.

UNCTAD (2021c, forthcoming). *Review of Maritime Transport 2021*. (United Nations publication. New York and Geneva).

UNCTAD (*TDR 1994*). *Trade and Development Report 1994*. (United Nations publication. Sales No. E.94.II.D.26. New York and Geneva).

UNCTAD (*TDR 1996*). *Trade and Development Report 1996*. (United Nations publication. Sales No. E.96.II.D.6. New York and Geneva).

UNCTAD (*TDR 2013*). *Trade and Development Report, 2013: Adjusting to the Changing Dynamics of the World Economy*. (United Nations publication. Sales No. E.13.II.D.3. New York and Geneva).

UNCTAD (*TDR 2015*). *Trade and Development Report 2015: Structural Transformation for Inclusive and Sustained Growth*. (United Nations publication. Sales No. E.16.II.D.5. New York and Geneva).

UNCTAD (*TDR 2017*). *Trade and Development Report, 2017: Beyond Austerity – Towards a Global New Deal*. (United Nations publication. Sales No. E.17.II.D.5. New York and Geneva).

UNCTAD (*TDR 2019*). *Trade and Development Report, 2019: Financing a Global Green New Deal*. (United Nations publication. Sales No. E.19.II.D.15. New York and Geneva).

UNCTAD (*TDR 2020*). *Trade and Development Report, 2020: From Global Pandemic to Prosperity for All: Avoiding another Lost Decade*. (United Nations publication. Sales No. E.20.II.D.30. New York and Geneva).

UNWTO (2021a). *World Tourism Barometer Statistical Annex*. Volume 19. Issues 4. July. United Nations World Tourism Organization. Madrid.

UNWTO (2021b). *World Tourism Barometer*. Volume 19. Issues 3. May. United Nations World Tourism Organization. Madrid.

Wade R (1992). East Asia's economic success: Conflicting perspectives, partial insights, shaky evidence. *World Politics*. 44(2): 270–320.

Wade R (2014). 'Market versus state' or 'Market with state': How to impart directional thrust. *Development and Change*. 45(4): 777–798.

Westbrook T and Zhou W (2021). China's banks are bursting with dollars, and that's a worry. *Reuters*. 2 June. Available at https://www.reuters.com/world/china/chinas-banks-are-bursting-with-dollars-thats-worry-2021-06-01/.

Wheatley J (2021). Rate expectations: Developing countries threatened by US inflation. *Financial Times*. 5 June.

World Bank (2021a). *Debt Report*. Edition II. April. Available at https://pubdocs.worldbank.org/en/247471617652072581/Debt-Report-2021-Edition-II.pdf.

World Bank (2021b) *Global Economic Prospects*. June. World Bank Group. Washington D.C.

WTO (2020). *World Trade Statistical Review 2020*. World Trade Organization. Geneva.

# Annex: Methodological Note for Box 1.1

The estimates for $G$ and $T$ in Table B1.1 are calculated on the basis of the decomposition of the following two identities. The identities are valid in both nominal and constant values; in this note, unless otherwise specified, constant values (chained) are used:

(1)  $Y_x = C_x + I_x + G_x + NX_x$   with $Y_x$: GDP, $C_x$: Private Consumption spending, $I_x$: Private Investment spending, $G_x$: Total Government Consumption and Investment spending, $NX_x$: Net Exports.

(2)  $-NL_{Gx} = T_x + G_x \Leftrightarrow T_x = -NL_{Gx} - G_x$   with $NL_{Gx}$: Net Lending by the General Government sector, $T_x$: Net Transfers *from* the Government to the private sector[29], $G_x$: Total Government Consumption and Investment spending.

For the selection of countries in Table B1.1, annual data for $G_x$ is extracted from National Accounts datasets, as expressed in equation (1). Likewise, annual data on $NL_{Gx}$ is extracted from Government accounts or fiscal data for these countries.

In order to estimate $dG$, that is the additional amount of Government consumption and investment spending relative to the expected level in 2020, first the expected level of Government consumption and investment spending in 2020 ($\hat{G}_{2020}$) is estimated as the average growth rate of $G_x$ ($\widehat{growth}[G]$) over the last 3 years, 2017 to 2019, applied to $G_{2019}$:

$$\hat{G}_{2020} = G_{2019} * (1 + \widehat{growth}[G])$$

and $dG_{2020}$ as the difference between the expected and observed value of $G_{2020}$:

$$dG_{2020} = G_{2020} - \hat{G}_{2020}$$

In order to estimate $dT$, that is the additional amount of Net Transfers from the Government to the Private Sector[30] relative to the expected level in 2020, first the expected level of Net Transfers in 2020 ($\hat{T}_{2020}$) is estimated as the average ratio of $T_x / GDP_x$ ($\widehat{ratio}[T]$) over the last 3 years, 2017–2019, applied to the value of GDP in 2020 ($GDP_{2020}$):

$$\hat{T}_{2020} = \widehat{ratio}[T] * GDP_{2020}$$

and $dT_{2020}$ as the difference between the expected and observed value of $T_{2020}$:

$$dT_{2020} = T_{2020} - \hat{T}_{2020}$$

For simplicity, the variable $dG_{2020}$ is presented as $G$ and the variable $dT_{2020}$ is presented as $T$ in Table B1.1.

# THE TROUBLED HISTORY OF BUILDING BACK BETTER: FROM THE 1980s DEBT CRISIS TO COVID-19

## A. Introduction

President Ronald Reagan was fond of citing Thomas Paine's declaration, penned at the height of the American Revolution, that "we have it in our power to begin the world over again". Although Reagan did not begin the neo-liberal revolution, which was stirred by disruptive economic and political events during the 1970s, his assuming the reins of the world's most powerful state, in January 1981, was a catalytic moment in the rise of a new policy consensus. The promise was a better future for all, by releasing mobile capital, nimble entrepreneurs and efficient market forces from the dead hand of government oversight and regulation.

UNCTAD's *Trade and Development Report* was launched that same year and has over the subsequent four decades borne witness to the consequences of the new consensus as it spread beyond the Anglo-Saxon world, through many international institutions, to the developing world.

Even in the face of overwhelming evidence that this era has been marked by recurring crises, an unprecedented concentration of wealth and power and growing economic insecurity, too many policymakers remain committed to the idea that markets are naturally competitive and automatically self-righting. To a large degree, this dogma has reflected a reckless disregard, notably among the more fundamentalist proponents of hyperglobalization, of the anarchic impulses of hot money, the predatory practices of big finance and the destructive power of unrestrained movements of capital across borders.

That neglect culminated in the global financial crisis whose origins, in the activities of large Western banks, were impossible to ignore and whose destructive consequences forced policy makers, as much in panic as from conviction, to abandon some of the totems of the policy consensus. Governments promised to build back better. The 2009 meeting of the G20 in London signalled a desire to change course:

> We start from the belief that prosperity is indivisible; that growth, to be sustained, has to be shared; and that our global plan for recovery must have at its heart the needs and jobs of hard-working families, not just in developed countries but in emerging markets and the poorest countries of the world too; and must reflect the interests, not just of today's population, but of future generations too.

In the end, the grip of conventional policy wisdom and the gravitational pull of financial markets proved too strong. Any hope of building back better had, by the end of the last decade, faded away.

With lives, as much as livelihoods, under threat, the Covid-19 crisis has exposed just how fragile the world has become; it has also served as a reminder that if we are to build back better this time around, the invisible hand of financial markets will not deliver the money on the right scale, to the right places at the right time. Beginning the world all over again will require a much more collective effort, within and across countries.

The next section positions the analysis provided by the *Trade and Development Report* in response to the shocks, setbacks and crises that have hampered development during the era of hyperglobalization and underscores its abiding call for an inclusive global economic governance. Section C looks at what might happen if the policy proposals that were widely adopted during that era were to return once the pandemic subsides and sounds an "amber warning" about the supercharged asymmetries that would follow. Section D considers some of the measures that advanced economies, in particular,

have undertaken during the crisis to address inequality, unchecked corporate power and the looming climate crisis; while in the right direction, these have been too tentative and could, given the lack of policy coordination, blowback on developing countries. If a new policy consensus is to emerge it will need to be made of sterner stuff. The final section highlights some broad policy themes that have emerged during the Covid-19 crisis which could provide just that.

# B. The Trade and Development Report at 40

## 1.  Swimming Against the Tide

In 1981, the advanced economies were still grappling with the stagflationary pressures unleashed in the previous decade. Inflation and unemployment remained at elevated levels. Investment was sluggish or falling. Political tensions added to an atmosphere of anxiety and confusion. Confusion was also apparent at the international level; the consensus agreed at Bretton Woods had already been upended by the release of the dollar from its link to gold, the opening of capital accounts and volatile movements in private capital flows. Some large international banks faced solvency issues due to shaky loans to developing countries.

Against this backdrop, the G7 countries met in Ottawa in July 1981 "to revitalize the economies of the industrial democracies". Doing so, they insisted, hinged on defeating inflation by cutting government borrowing and controlling the money supply, a signal that the era of Keynesian demand management was over. They also insisted that revitalization would require more fundamental changes in expectations about growth and earnings, in labour relations, in support for industry, in the direction and scale of investment, and in energy use and supply (G7, 1981).

Acknowledging the realities of an interdependent world and "the serious economic problems in many developing countries", the G7 also confirmed their commitment to strengthen international cooperation and expressed a desire to discuss common challenges at the International Meeting on Cooperation and Development in Cancun later in the year.

During the previous decade, many developing countries had made economic strides thanks to higher commodity prices, above all oil, increased investment and faster growth. With growing economic

confidence fuelling heightened political ambition, negotiations had been launched at the United Nations to fashion a more development-friendly international economic order. However, the structural foundations of many economies were still weak and growth spurts proved ephemeral. The low real cost of debt (in terms of the volume of exports needed to cover interest payments) and high commodity prices had encouraged massive borrowing through syndicated bank loans. With much higher interest rates and much slower growth in advanced countries, financial stresses began to emerge in some heavily indebted economies.

UNCTAD's first *Trade and Development Report* landed in 1981 amidst these shifting economic currents. The *Report* warned that the global conditions for promoting a long-term development agenda were disappearing and that the deteriorating situation in many countries·signalled a pending "development crisis". Its message, which has become a recurring theme across the subsequent four decades, was that faster growth in developing countries is of mutual benefit to developed countries but achieving "it will require intensified international cooperation and concerted efforts by governments since market forces alone cannot be relied upon to achieve the required transformation and structural reforms". In 1981, this was a message at odds with the direction of policy in the North.[1]

Signs of a changing policy direction, since tagged with a neo-liberal label, were already discernible in the mid-1970s but had moved up a political gear with the election in 1979 of Margaret Thatcher in the United Kingdom and of Ronald Reagan the following year in the United States.[2] A last hurrah of Keynesian demand management came with the Government of Francois Mitterand in France, elected a few months before the first *Report* was launched, but a turn to austerity soon came from the pressure of capital flight and a widening current account deficit. Despite the desires expressed in Ottawa, the Cancun Summit proved to be the end of negotiated changes to the international economic order when President Reagan made it clear that the focus of his Administration would be on supporting domestic policies in countries willing to "encourage economic freedom" and not reform of the existing multilateral architecture.

The resulting policy shift extolled the virtues of smaller government and the benefits of freeing markets from regulatory discipline and oversight. As competitiveness trumped employment as the measure of economic success, liberalization moved to the centre of the policy stage with tight monetary policy cast in the sole supportive macroeconomic role. The promise was simple: freed from government intervention, particularly regulation on international capital movements, and wage-price spirals, increased competition would spur entrepreneurship, stimulate investment and bolster wealth creation with the gains trickling down to even the poorest strata of society and spreading globally through free trade and heightened capital flows.

## 2. A Lost Decade

Economic reality was proving very different; as Paul Volker (1978), Chair of the United States Federal Reserve, pushed interest rates into double figures, a strengthening dollar and falling demand for commodities, turned the liquidity strains and financial stresses in developing countries into solvency crises. Mexico's default in 1982 cast suspicion on other sovereign borrowers and the flight of private capital triggered debt crises across much of the South. The 1982 *Report* warned that with a further narrowing of the range of "feasible policies open to developing countries to promote their own development" and with "the spirit of international cooperation ... on the wane", the development crisis was set to intensify.

In the absence of timely concessional multilateral support, stringent retrenchment measures were inevitable. Structural adjustment programmes, backed by a very different development policy paradigm from the one envisaged in the *Report*, and subsequently christened the "Washington Consensus" (Williamson, 1990), became commonplace in developing countries as a condition for renewed access to multilateral financing. The damage these programmes caused along with

their failure to produce a macroeconomic environment that supported long-term investment was extensively documented across subsequent *Reports*.

As the advanced countries began to recover, a very different global economy emerged from what Volcker himself, somewhat euphemistically, described as "the controlled disintegration of the world economy" that followed the floating of the dollar. This world economy would require different governance arrangements – "mutual contingency planning" among the monetary authorities of the systemically important economies – from those established at the Bretton Woods Conference (Volcker, 1978). These arrangements were underpinned by a new growth regime in the United States led by an expanding financial sector and related service industries, a strong dollar, persistent trade deficits and a drive to boost overseas profits through increased foreign investment flows, tighter intellectual property rights and an incessant search for cheaper sources of labour.

The payments and exchange rate regime became more and more intertwined with the free movement of capital and the international trade regime operating through a mixture of tariff reductions negotiated largely by advanced economies under the GATT and unilateral discretionary trade restrictions adopted by those same countries. The 1984 *Report* anticipated the fault lines and asymmetries that would come to characterize the emerging global landscape: creditors would be favoured over debtors, large producers over small, profits over wages, with the interests of developed countries prioritized over those of developing countries in international fora.

Overcoming the crisis posed by an unsustainable burden of debt would, ideally, have involved a combination of accelerating growth, lower interest rates and increased capital flows on appropriate terms. In their absence, the lack of a well-designed and impartial framework for the timely resolution of external debt problems became increasingly apparent. Ad hoc and creditor-friendly restructuring exercises, beginning with the Baker Plan in 1985, offered some limited rescheduling but with the onus on spending cuts and deflationary adjustment in indebted countries. In response, the 1986 Report proposed an alternative approach built around new principles of debt restructuring, drawing in part on the United States Bankruptcy Code, a temporary standstill on debt servicing and the establishment of an independent debt workout mechanism tasked with undertaking debt restructuring on a fair and timely basis.

As the decade came to an end, the 1989 Report concluded that moving beyond the lost decade would require a significant relaxing of the external constraint on growth in developing countries, along with a new social contract (and accompanying fiscal reforms) that could more equitably share the costs of further adjustment and the fruits of any subsequent recovery. A relaxation of sorts had started with commercial banks selectively writing down some of their loans, and the Brady Plan, launched in 1989, offering more extensive debt relief by converting outstanding loans into tradeable bond instruments, paving the way for the return of middle-income Latin American countries to international capital markets. A more equitable social contract, however, was not on the table.

### 3. Birth of the Hot

With the easing of acute economic distress – and the fall of the Berlin Wall in November 1989 – the contours of a hyperglobalized economy became clearer. The deregulation of financial markets and the opening of the capital account gave way to the buying and selling of financial assets, shareholder governance and rising levels of debt. The removal of tariff barriers continued but negotiations turned to agreeing rules in support of deeper integration and the spread of international production networks with heightened protections for the corporations managing them. The drive to privatize state-owned assets gave way to the promotion of public-private partnerships and a business environment that would attract foreign direct investment. Policy makers were told that they had no more grounds to debate these changes than they did the changing of the seasons (Blair, 2005), countries could either "integrate themselves into the international economy or become marginalized from it and thus fall farther and farther behind in terms of growth and development" (Camdessus, 1997).

The break-up of the Soviet Union as the new decade got under way opened up a wider front for market-based reforms and at a faster pace described as "shock therapy". The 1993 Report warned that transition economies had seen more shock than therapy. Still, a new world order was promised which would, according to United States President George H. W. Bush, offer "new ways of working with other nations . . . peaceful settlement of disputes, solidarity against aggression, reduced and controlled arsenals and just treatment of all peoples" (Nye, 1992); on the musings of one enthusiastic observer this signalled "an end to history" (Fukuyama, 1992).

History, it turned out, was not so obliging. The changing face of global interdependence in a world of footloose capital and the new threats this posed, particularly for developing countries, became an abiding theme of subsequent *Reports*. Particular attention was given to how trade and capital account liberalization, combined with pro-cyclical fiscal and monetary policies, could disrupt growth and development. The misalignment of macroeconomic prices, the shortening of investment horizons and the fuelling of asset bubbles which could go bust when sudden shifts in market sentiment triggered rapid capital outflows and heightened payment pressures, led to retrenchment, job losses and rising poverty. And despite the assurances that financial innovation was conquering market risk, the 1995 Report expressed a growing concern about the rapid growth of derivative instruments generating systemic risks which, in the absence of international cooperation, could cause a wider breakdown in financial markets.

Foreign capital did begin flowing back to Latin America from the early 1990s, but many developing countries, particularly in sub-Saharan Africa, continued to struggle with the legacies of the debt crisis. Only with the Highly Indebted Poor Countries initiative (HIPC), launched by the IMF and the World Bank in 1996, did their situation begin to change. At the same time, the dangers of rapid financial liberalization were becoming apparent in some of the most successful developing countries in East Asia. The 1994 Report warned that capital account liberalization there had triggered a surge of short-term inflows ("hot money"), taking advantage of higher local nominal interest rates, that could just as quickly flow out. As investors became nervous about growing current account deficits and turned their speculative antennae to booming markets in the United States, a reversal of flows put pressure on local exchange rates. The collapse of the Thai baht in July 1997 proved highly contagious, dragging Thailand and several neighbouring economies into a vicious financial spiral and triggering a sharp recession. Contagion from the crisis continued to ripple across other emerging markets through the end of the decade.

The 2000 Report concluded that the initial policy response to the East Asian crisis, marshalled in large part by the international financial institutions, had been unnecessarily severe, with the burden carried by wage earners, small and medium sized enterprises and the poor. Recovery only began once austerity measures were reversed and governments allowed to play a more positive role, including, in the case

FIGURE 2.1  **The slowdown in global economic growth, 1971–2020**
*(annual and decadal geometric average, percent)*

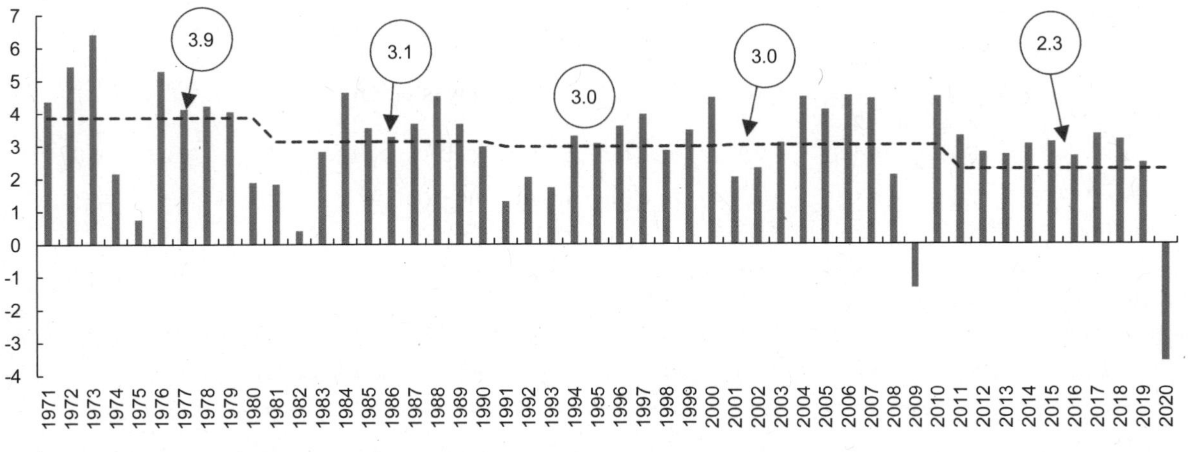

*Source:* UNCTAD secretariat, based on UNCTADStat; and World Output series for *TDR* production.

of Malaysia, through the effective use of selective capital controls. A fundamental lesson drawn from the experience was that even in developing countries with a strong growth record, in a financialized global economy excessive reliance on foreign resources and markets leaves growth prospect vulnerable to external shocks.

Among advanced countries, the 1990s was America's decade. A short-lived recession at the beginning of the decade gave way to stronger growth linked to accommodative monetary policy and the euphoria surrounding the information and communication technology revolution; investment, productivity and employment all picked up while inflationary pressures remained subdued. The stock market rose precipitously leading the Chair of the Federal Reserve to warn of "irrational exuberance" but he showed no enthusiasm to dampen it. The European Union, by contrast, suffered a more prolonged downturn, as it struggled with the newly adopted Maastricht Treaty. A weak recovery from the mid-1990s did, however, inject sufficient confidence in a sub-section of the bloc to launch a currency union under the Euro at the end of the decade. Japan, by contrast, was unable to find a sustainable adjustment path away from the massive financial bust at the end of the previous decade, with short-lived stop-and-go cycles holding back growth over the course of the decade.

Along with these uneven growth performances, the persistence of high unemployment and accelerating deindustrialization were taxing policy makers across advanced countries. Adjusting to market forces was not it turned out quite as smooth as textbooks implied,

leaving residual pockets of poverty and deprivation even as growth picked up. The 1995 Report rejected the suggestion, gaining political traction at the time, that growing trade with developing countries was the main culprit and instead highlighted a combination of weak demand, uneven investment growth and labour market deregulation resulting from policy choices aligned with their increasingly financialized economies. The Report warned that cutting wages in an attempt to boost competitiveness would, by reducing domestic demand, only further weaken employment conditions.

Overall, average annual global growth in the 1990s failed to register a significant improvement over the previous decade despite the surge in capital flows (Figure 2.1). Per capita growth in many developing countries continued to lag advanced economies, signalling their further falling behind (Table 2.1). However, a pick-up of growth in South Asia and continued strong growth in East Asia, now including the rapidly transforming China, was a sign that the international economic landscape was changing.

## 4.  Winners and Losers

While faith in efficient markets continued to dominate economic policy making. governments in advanced economies were beginning to worry about persistent imbalances in the global economy. Trade imbalances and accompanying financial instability caused by inconsistent macroeconomic policy stances both within and across the main advanced countries had been a running concern of the Report during the 1980s. The growing current account surplus of Japan

**TABLE 2.1 Average annual per capita growth, by region 1951–2020**
(PPP)

| | World | Developed (M49 incl. Republic of Korea) | Developing (M49) | Central Asia | East Asia (incl. Japan and Republic of Korea) | South Asia | South-East Asia | West Asia (incl. Israel) | Latin America | North Africa | Sub-Saharan Africa |
|---|---|---|---|---|---|---|---|---|---|---|---|
| 1951–1959 | 3.0 | 3.6 | 2.8 | | 5.1 | 1.4 | 2.5 | 4.1 | 2.3 | 2.6 | 1.9 |
| 1960–1969 | 3.5 | 4.4 | 3.1 | | 5.4 | 2.8 | 1.9 | 4.7 | 2.6 | 6.8 | 1.9 |
| 1970–1979 | 2.6 | 2.4 | 3.6 | | 3.9 | 1.2 | 4.2 | 4.6 | 3.5 | 2.1 | 0.9 |
| 1980–1989 | 1.0 | 2.0 | 0.8 | -0.5 | 4.0 | 2.0 | 3.1 | -2.8 | -0.3 | -1.4 | -0.9 |
| 1990–1999 | 1.0 | 1.1 | 2.2 | -4.7 | 2.9 | 3.3 | 3.4 | 1.1 | 1.2 | 0.8 | -0.6 |
| 2000–2009 | 2.4 | 1.8 | 4.0 | 6.9 | 4.6 | 4.5 | 3.7 | 2.4 | 1.6 | 2.5 | 2.4 |
| 2010–2019 | 2.1 | 1.7 | 3.0 | 4.3 | 3.5 | 4.7 | 4.2 | 2.1 | 0.8 | 0.2 | 1.4 |
| 2020 | -4.5 | -4.6 | -3.9 | -2.0 | -0.3 | -6.7 | -4.4 | -4.4 | -7.9 | -5.8 | -4.7 |
| 2000–2008 | 2.9 | 2.5 | 4.3 | 7.5 | 4.9 | 4.6 | 4.0 | 3.1 | 2.2 | 2.8 | 2.6 |

**Source:** The Conference Board (April 2021). Total Economy Database. See https://www.conference-board.org/data/economydatabase/total-economy-database-productivity.

had provoked particular anxiety in the United States and, in the absence of effective international coordination, triggered a series of ad hoc responses which disrupted international trade. Imbalances widened further in the 1990s, on the back of persistent policy divergences, compounded by the export success of the newly industrialized East Asian economies. The resulting global imbalances exposed the lack of policy coordination in an increasingly interdependent world that, the 2000 Report warned, would most likely be resolved in a disorderly manner and to the disadvantage of developing countries. Subsequent *Reports*, up to the global financial crisis, continued to warn of the danger of a hard landing.

The logic of free trade promised widespread gains for developing countries. However, more than a decade of rapid opening up had seen only a small number of developing countries, mainly from East Asia, posting a strong record of catch-up growth, while elsewhere the lost decade of the 1980s was lengthening into the early years of the new decade. The anomalous success of the "miracle" economies began to raise questions about the policy advice coming from Washington. A major World Bank study, commissioned by the Japanese Government, attributed its success to a tighter embrace of market-friendly policies (implicitly endorsing its own advice to other developing countries). But this account was quickly contested by a growing body of scholarly research which highlighted the key role of strategic trade and industrial policies employed by strong developmental states in promoting structural transformation and compensating for the competitive disadvantages their firms faced in international markets. UNCTAD's own

research, presented in various *Reports*, confirmed that active policy measures had helped to animate a robust profit-investment-export nexus in the most successful East Asian economies and highlighted the role of effective public institutions willing and able to dialogue with the private sector and with sufficient policy space to support, guide and, where necessary, discipline businesses in order to achieve a fast pace of investment and technological upgrading.

Recognizing that there were losers, within and across countries, as well as winners in a globalizing world went against the trickle-down logic promoted by market fundamentalism. As parts of the international community became concerned that a narrow focus on growth conditions was neglecting the wider challenge of "an enabling environment for people to enjoy long, healthy and creative lives" (UNDP, 1990), "human development" emerged as an important theme during the 1990s. While this approach helped to broaden the policy discussion in international development circles, it concentrated exclusively on the policy challenges posed by extreme poverty and social deprivation. The 1997 Report broke with this line of thinking by shifting the debate from those at the bottom of the economic pyramid (the poverty challenge) to those at the top, recognizing that widening income gaps had become endemic to hyperglobalization and that the behaviour and influence of an increasingly disconnected elite, of both households and firms, was having a disproportionate impact on the direction and prospects of the wider economy.

The Report detailed the trend of rising inequality in countries at all levels of development with a hollowing out of the middle-class in the North while middle-income countries in the South were falling further behind. This, the Report argued, was best explained by a combination of policy decisions, particularly tight macroeconomic policies and rapid liberalization, and the new rules of the international economy that favoured footloose capital and put downward pressures on wages.

The flip side of these trends was a rising share of profits in national income, but rather than delivering the promised boost to productive investment this was instead leading to a shortfall in aggregate demand, rising levels of debt and slower growth, with investors shifting attention from the productive economy to the buying and selling of existing assets. The rentier economy had emerged. The Report warned that if left unchecked the resulting economic fragilities and political tensions would eventually produce a backlash against globalization. Violent demonstrations at the WTO meeting in Seattle in November 1999 were an early sign of growing discontent.

## 5. Growth Picks up; Imbalances Widen

As had been predicted in previous *Reports*, not only were liberalized financial markets becoming a greater source of volatility, but the increasing integration of the global economy also meant that shocks (both real and financial) were being transmitted much more rapidly across sectors, countries and regions. Meanwhile, developing countries were still being strongarmed into dismantling capital controls on the promise of increasing market efficiency. The possibility that financial instability could spread from "emerging markets"[3] was signalled by the so-called Tequila crisis which hit the Mexican bond market in 1994, while the collapse of Long-Term Capital Management in 1998 – overexposed to the Russian bond market – brought the role of hedge funds, as conduits of contagion, to the attention of policy makers. In both cases, swift bailout operations by monetary authorities in the United States proved successful. However, the dotcom bust in 2000, persisting through 2001, provoked a more active response from the Federal Reserve (amplified by the terrorist attack on New York and Washington), along with other Central Banks, who rapidly reduced interest rates and injected liquidity on a large scale and for a prolonged period, in an effort to stabilize and revive financial markets.

These large-scale injections also spilled over to developing countries through increased capital inflows

as investors became less risk averse in their search for higher yields. A sense of returning economic optimism was given a further boost with the confirmation of China's membership to the WTO, along with a recovery in global trade. For the first time since the 1970s, growth across the South exhibited a simultaneous pick up and poverty numbers finally began to fall, albeit dominated by their rapid drop in China. High and rising commodity prices – that became known as a "super-cycle" – fed growth across developing countries; and with growth in advanced economies on a slower trajectory, the long-promised convergence – narrowing income gaps between developed and developing countries – finally looked like it would happen.

As interest rates dropped and financial markets picked up, policy makers in advanced countries convinced themselves that they had discovered the holy grail of macroeconomic stability. Economists (retrospectively) announced the arrival of "a great moderation" (Bernanke, 2004), with some announcing the end of economic depressions (Lucas, 2003). The Chair of the Federal Reserve, Alan Greenspan (2005), suggested that a combination of financial innovation and Central Bank foresight had finally given Adam Smith's invisible hand the room to deliver stability and vibrancy across the entire global economy.

The big question was whether these trends were sustainable. With policy making becoming ever more closely tied to the calculations of unregulated financial markets and the ever-shortening investment horizons of footloose capital, there were reasons to be doubtful. As outlined in the 2001 Report, various initiatives pursued in different forums in the hope of finding a system of international governance compatible with flexible exchange rates and large-scale capital flows had failed to make meaningful progress. In the absence of a multilateral system to match the reach of global financial markets, a dualistic system had emerged where heightened surveillance and disciplines on developing countries coexisted with a laisser-faire approach towards the policies of systemically important advanced countries, whose domestic financial systems, including private international creditors, were left to be governed through voluntary arrangements. Such a system, the Report concluded, was both crisis prone and skewed against the needs of developing countries.

Picking up on previous reform proposals aimed at making international finance work for development, the Report called for improved multilateral surveillance and coordination of economic policies in the major economies; stronger regulation and supervision of international capital flows; increased official financing, including on concessional terms; new ways to manage and restructure debts in a fairer and timely fashion; greater coherence in the formulation of policies relating to finance and development, including a significant pruning of policy conditionalities attached to adjustment programmes.

Concerns were also growing over the governance of international trade. The ambiguous outcome of the Uruguay Round had been discussed in the 1996 Report and the 1999 Report concluded that the predicted gains for developing countries had been exaggerated due to a combination of non-tariff barriers restricting access to Northern markets and various trade-related measures that reduced their policy space. The gap between what the 2002 report called "the rhetoric and reality of a liberal international economic order" was even more apparent with the spread of international production networks. While opening up new export opportunities for developing countries, participation in these networks depended on a significant increase in imported intermediate inputs and the sacrifice of policy space to the large corporations managing these networks – a privatization of governance, making it increasingly difficult for participating countries to diversify into higher value-added activities.

The 2002 Report concluded that while developing countries were now trading more than before, many were earning less from doing so. Manufacturing enclaves with few links to the wider domestic economy did little to boost employment, investment, value added and productivity growth, and in some cases, as examined in the 2003 Report, the rapid pace of liberalization had led to "premature deindustrialization" as countries experienced declining shares of manufacturing employment and output at relatively low levels of income and a downgrading to less technology intensive activities.

On a more positive note, the East Asian growth story had demonstrated potential benefits from closer regional trade and investment flows, raising the possibility that replicating such arrangements, along with closer south-south cooperation and integration, could help sustain the growth momentum in the South. The opportunities and challenges were examined in various *Reports*, while insisting that they should not be taken as a substitute for effective multilateral arrangements and a warning that their impact would be compromised

if these arrangements continued to squeeze policy space through badly designed trade and investment agreements, excessive lending conditionalities and the further encouragement of pro-cyclical capital flows.

## 6.  A Feature not a Flaw

In 2007 the Report again raised concerns that persistent global imbalances combined with the outsized presence of highly leveraged institutional investors in a position to benefit from and, up to a point, influence, macroeconomic price movements across countries, were posing a systemic risk to the global economy. Combined with complex financial instruments that promised to spread the impact of risky investments and the search for yields well in excess of growth in the real economy, the danger of "irrational exuberance" had become a permanent feature of financialized economies, along with the limits of self-regulating markets to discipline such behaviour.

The warning proved prescient, the optimism of the new millennium was shattered by the financial crisis that had been building since August 2007 and broke across the global economy with the collapse of Lehman Brothers in September 2008. While the crisis was incubated in the increasingly reckless practices of the United States mortgage market, it was the culmination of a highly leveraged financial system which had become untethered from the productive economy. The impact was as swift as it was devastating, with investors resorting to panic selling in the hope of minimizing losses. As financial contagion crisscrossed markets and continents, the global economy went into recession for the first time since the Second World War.

Judgement was swiftly forthcoming. A distressed Alan Greenspan told a congressional hearing that he had discovered "a flaw" in his thinking about the virtues of free markets while a group of eminent economists in the United Kingdom informed the Queen that there was "a failure of the collective imagination of many bright people". The head of the IMF, Dominic Strauss Kahn, concluded, more correctly, that the crisis had "devastated the intellectual foundations of the last twenty-five years".

Recognizing that a global crisis on this scale required collective actions beyond the efforts of a small club of Western economic powers, the response was broadened to include key emerging economies with the new G20. At its London meeting in April 2009, the G20 called for large-scale coordinated fiscal expansion to stem the crisis. The new United States Administration had already announced a three-year $720bn stimulus package – 1.6 per cent of GDP annually – prior to the meeting but the real gamechanger was China's two-year $586bn spending package, some 4.3 per cent of its GDP annually. The sense of a shifting geo-political landscape was given further expression with the first summit of the BRICS countries in June 2009.

The London meeting promised a series of ambitious reforms to prevent a repetition of the crisis, restore growth and build back better (G20, 2009). Its ability to deliver, however, proved underwhelming. Once the balance sheets of the big international banks at the centre of the crisis had been cleaned up and financial markets had regained their nerve, the advanced economies made the turn, in varying degrees, to austerity. The revealed preference of policy makers in Europe and the United States in particular was for global financial stability; global prosperity mattered less.

The Report in 2011 warned that with a concerted shift to fiscal consolidation while the private sector was still deleveraging, neither a further loosening of monetary policy nor a rehabilitated financial sector, would, separately or together, produce a strong recovery. Moreover, given the likelihood of subsequent financial shocks, not only would the poverty challenge be set back in many developing countries but the growing calls for a transition to a more climate friendly economy would go unheeded.

A year before President Obama pronounced inequality "the defining challenge of our times", the 2012 Report returned to the issue of rising inequality and its links to economic stagnation. Confirming that the policy factors and structural forces that had been identified in the late 1990s continued to make for a highly unequal world, the Report also noted that there had been some regional improvements, particularly in Latin America, since the opening years of the new millennium, as a boost to job creation (in both the public and private sectors) from rising commodity prices and accelerating growth was amplified by a new policy turn which supported public spending on social services and income support schemes. Still, in the absence of reforms to international governance, continuing vulnerability to shocks and high levels of economic informality would, the Report concluded, continue to pose significant barriers to tackling inequality in many developing countries.

What eventually emerged from the crisis was a new variant of hyperglobalization in which new forms of non-bank finance were allowed to flourish beyond the (limited) regulatory oversight of banks introduced after the crisis,[4] Central Banks would continue to prime financial markets through their balance sheet transactions, and new sources of rent extraction were created through monopolistic practices in concentrated markets and on digital platforms.

In the United States, the stock market soared as large corporations used their profits to buy back their own shares and acquire rival companies, while budget cuts, weak domestic investment and wage stagnation held back a strong recovery and generated growing precarity. Similar polarizing pressures were visible elsewhere albeit with remaining welfare provisions in some countries softening more extreme outcomes.

The exception to post-crisis austerity and malaise was China. Its unprecedented fiscal stimulus in response to the global financial crisis shifted the impetus of growth towards domestic demand, particularly investment, which rose to $6.2 trillion by 2019 from $2.8 trillion in 2010 (compared to $4.5 and $2.8 trillion respectively in the United States), and continued to underpin a strong export performance, despite an appreciating currency and the targeted tariff increases adopted by the Trump Administration. While China's trade surplus did begin to fall after 2014 it remained in positive territory while overseas lending, including to other developing countries, began to rise, linked, in part, to its Belt and Road Initiative launched in 2013. However, the deceleration of growth over the course of the decade and the continued build-up of domestic debt, particularly at the provincial and corporate levels, along with growing inequality brought a threat of unspeculative bubbles. Turbulence on the Shanghai stock market in 2015 and 2016 was a warning to policy makers that financial balance sheets needed a clean-up.

## 7. A New Normal versus a New Deal

The failure to deliver the promised reforms after the global financial crisis raised uncomfortable questions about the effectiveness of the multilateral system in a hyperglobalized world of footloose capital, growing market concentration, sluggish global demand, weak investment and mounting indebtedness. Still, 2015 saw the launch of the Agenda 2030 and agreement in Paris on reducing carbon emission levels to mitigate the climate crisis, which together offered an ambitious and transformative agenda for the global economy. However, in the absence of a programme of systemic reforms to address the entrenched asymmetries of hyperglobalization and to provide the financial support needed for a big investment push to meet the agreed goals and targets, the odds of their timely delivery were soon lengthening.

Taking lessons from the efforts of the Roosevelt Administration in the United States to build back better from the Great Depression of the 1930s, the 2017 Report, argued that a Global New Deal was needed to end austerity and create decent jobs, rein in the rentier economy and harness finance to serve wider social interests. "Effective internationalism" the report concluded "continues to rest on responsible nationalism and finding the right balance remains at the heart of any meaningful multilateral agenda".

As the decade ended, advanced countries had failed to find significant new resources for the IMF or to deliver the (even limited) funding promised a decade earlier for the Green Climate Fund, had abandoned the multilateral trade negotiations launched in Doha, focusing instead on bilateral and plurilateral deals, and had made little progress on global tax reform. The limited attempts at financial regulation (including through the efforts of the Financial Stability Board and the, delayed, third stage of the Basel Accords) had done little to rein in the predatory activities of a new generation of private creditors, leaving many highly indebted developing countries struggling against an unforgiving legal system, with some already in default.

The IMF in its final *World Economic Outlook* of the decade expressed concerns about the danger of policy missteps against a backdrop of downside global risks. UNCTAD also worried about policy missteps, but the bigger problem was the rules of the international economic game which constrained productive investment, generated intolerable levels of inequality, and indulged, if not actively encouraged, predatory corporate behaviour. A deepening sense of insecurity continued to permeate the lives of too many people across the global economy. The potential dangers coming from an emerging rentier class, that the Report had warned about at the end of the 1990s, had now become a fully-fledged rentier economy that had acquired global reach. In the face of weak and unstable growth, persistent financial fragility, growing economic polarization and rising geo-political tensions, the 2019 Report warned that a global recession was a clear and present danger.

## 8. Back to the Future

Covid-19 was the straw that broke this sclerotic camel's back. The immediate response to the shock, following the policy playbook of previous crises, was to cushion the blow to financial markets with a new round of quantitative easing. But governments in advanced economies soon found themselves in unfamiliar territory, as lockdowns to contain the pandemic triggered an economic blowback that required concerted and targeted measures to protect lives and livelihoods. Central Banks kept the money tap open, but governments also increased their spending to levels not seen since wartime, abandoning, in the process, previously uncontested policy positions. Even so the drop in output during the second and third quarters of 2020 was unprecedented and even as economies began to unlock and confidence return, the bounce back was marked by considerable unevenness across sectors, income groups and regions. Moreover, the income and wealth inequalities that emerged over the last four decades have, if anything, intensified, with the owners of financial and digital assets reaping the biggest gains from recovery.

Lockdowns hit developing countries hard triggering a series of interconnected shocks which generated vicious economic cycles that on top of existing debt vulnerabilities, tipped most regions in to a deep recession and some countries into default. Despite the fiscal squeeze and increased debt burden, developing countries were left to manage the crisis largely on their own, forcing deep cuts in public employment and services.

A faster than expected reflux of capital flows and recovery in commodity prices, as lockdown in the advanced economies were lifted, prevented a worst-case scenario emerging. Still, as discussed in the previous chapter, growth in most parts of the developing world remain weak, large debt overhangs have grown even larger, while variants of the virus are threatening to revive new waves of the pandemic that will derail fledgling recoveries in more vulnerable economies.

But even if the virus is contained, the fear of higher interest rates is again stalking development prospects with the threat of another lost decade a possibility. In response, last year's Report, much like the first, called for a coordinated global recovery plan based on a change of policy direction in the advanced economies which would sustain recovery and build resilience and reforms to the international architecture that could better coordinate those efforts and support developing countries in adopting similar measures. So far, the international community has failed to deliver.

In an odd sense of déjà vu, this year's Report coincides with the G7 countries again talking of the need to revitalize western democracy and build a new partnership with developing countries around infrastructure investment, including through an initiative for clean and green growth. Their call for a "building back better world" has struck a hopeful note. A promise to treat health and education as global public goods, a commitment to a sufficiently financed green revolution, an infusion of liquidity through a new allocation of SDRs, and the announcement of a minimum global corporation tax are all welcome departures from recent practice.

However, with a development crisis looming, the climate crisis a reality for many countries and the Agenda 2030 in trouble even before Covid-19 hit, the willingness to acknowledge the scale of the challenge facing developing countries is still missing. The G7 countries provided little detail on their proposed reform agenda and even less on the resources they would commit to lift all boats out of the immediate crisis and launch a just transition to a decarbonized world by 2050. The call from developing countries to waive the TRIPs agreement in the WTO as a necessary first step to enabling the local manufacture of vaccines has, despite belated backing from the United States, been resisted by other advanced economies, whose defence of large corporate interests is causing new fissures in the global economy, based on access to vaccines and freedom of movement. Furthermore, a general reluctance to bring private creditors to the negotiating table gives little hope that the debt burden weighing on developing countries will be sufficiently eased to allow them to invest

their way out of the multiple crises they currently face.

What is missing is a bold, human-centred narrative that breaks out of the technocratic, finance-influenced tropes about economic growth and connects shared global policy challenges to improvements in the everyday lives of people in Bogota, Berlin, Bamako, Busan or Boston. Policy should address worries about not only their job security but whether the job they have will guarantee a secure future for themselves and their families, whether the taxes they pay will deliver the public services that they want and the social protection they need if things go awry, whether the debts they acquire to put a roof over their head, food on the table or their children through school will be a lifelong burden and whether the planet itself will continue to sustain a meaningful life for their children and grandchildren.

Forty years on, the conclusion of the first *Trade and Development Report* still rings true:

> The present situation thus appears to require a new development paradigm, and this paradigm will need to take explicit account of the fact that issues concerning the management of the world economy, on the one hand, and long-term development objectives, are intermingled.

The big differences between then and now in linking long-term development objectives to the management of the global economy are the widening income and wealth gaps in countries at all levels of development and the looming climate crisis. Whether or not a new policy paradigm emerges to help guide a just and inclusive transition to a decarbonized world is an open question. That a building back better world for people and the planet hinges on that new paradigm is, quite simply, no longer in doubt.

## C. Living in the Past

In the wake of any crisis, reverting to pre-crisis practices is a temptation for policymakers, in advanced and developing countries alike. But, as discussed in the previous section, the economic policy wisdom that has prevailed in recent decades has not played out well for the vast majority of countries, and particularly since the global financial crisis. Even when successful performers appear,

their achievements often come under very specific circumstances, making generalized policy choices unclear. Moreover, as has again been demonstrated this year with the emergence of new strains of the virus and extreme weather events, there are many imponderables that can upset projected economic trends. Even the immediate future is uncertain and beyond that, more so.

In this section, and with these caveats in mind, we examine the risks of a return to pre-crisis "normalcy" as a target of post-pandemic recovery for policy makers. The UN Global Policy Model (GPM)[5] is employed to map out the plausible impact of a pre-defined set of policies on economic performance, assuming away exogenous shocks. The policy assumptions made in the scenario period draw on data from previous post-crisis periods over recent decades, as well as current and ongoing policy debates and announcements by governments, central banks and other relevant players. The scenario assumes that policy responses in the post-pandemic period will be oriented to: (a) tightening fiscal spending aiming at cutting deficits below 3 per cent of GDP; (b) labour market deregulation leading to continuing pressures on wage shares, so that wages rise at a slower pace than productivity until the unemployment rates approaches pre-covid levels; (c) continuing injections of liquidity by central banks aimed at inducing private investment; (d) continuing measures to liberalize capital markets (including through advancing trade and international investment agreements).

Whether such a configuration of policies will materialize is a matter of political conjecture. The intent here is to provoke a rigorous ex-ante reflection on the risks inherent in a return to policy normalcy.

## 1. The growth picture

Table 2.2 presents the estimated growth rates to 2030 in the main regions of the world if the return to policy normalcy is adopted. It shows that the world economy is likely to slow down after the rebound of 2021 continues in 2022 (see Chapter I). The deceleration is such that the average rate of growth for the period 2023–2030 will be lower than that of the post-GFC of 2007–09, and lower still than the post 'dot.com' crisis of 2000–01.[6] We call this deceleration in recovery growth rates *growth loss*. We calculate the loss of growth comparing the growth rates in this simulated scenario of post-Covid recovery with these earlier periods of recovery from 1980 onwards. We show that post-Covid growth loss compared with the earlier periods is substantial for all regions, albeit with variation among them.

Our scenario suggests that Developed America will exhibit a narrower growth loss than other developed regions by virtue of what appears to be a relatively more proactive approach to macroeconomic management. The striking outcome of the policy scenario is the more severe projected growth decelerations for developing economies. The scenario yields a narrower growth loss in Latin America than in other developing regions, due, in part to its historically lower growth performance, but also to economic ties with the relatively better performing Northern neighbours, and to the resurgence of more proactive governments in some countries. The nearly 5 percentage points shortfall in China is not, however, a sign of economic malaise but rather, a continuation of its policy-driven restructuring, incorporated in the scenario design. At this level of aggregation, the resulting growth average for China will still outperform the rest of the world.

---

TABLE 2.2 **Economic growth of world regions, 2001–2030**
*(annual per cent, based on constant dollars at market rates)*

| | 2019 | 2020 | 2021 | 2022 | 2025 | 2030 | "average 2001–07" | "average 2010–19" | "average 2023–30" | growth loss relative to past recoveries |
|---|---|---|---|---|---|---|---|---|---|---|
| **World** | 2.45 | -3.67 | 5.33 | 3.59 | 2.54 | 2.44 | 3.54 | 3.13 | 2.54 | -0.80 |
| Developed America | 2.14 | -3.69 | 5.67 | 3.03 | 2.29 | 2.04 | 2.53 | 2.28 | 2.22 | -0.18 |
| Europe | 1.46 | -6.93 | 4.46 | 2.88 | 1.21 | 1.19 | 2.53 | 1.67 | 1.28 | -0.82 |
| Developed Pacific | 0.94 | -3.46 | 2.84 | 2.35 | 1.45 | 1.33 | 2.24 | 1.97 | 1.45 | -0.65 |
| China | 6.11 | 2.30 | 8.34 | 5.75 | 4.73 | 4.34 | 10.96 | 7.80 | 4.59 | -4.79 |
| East Asia excluding China | 3.17 | -3.57 | 3.72 | 4.48 | 3.17 | 3.08 | 5.15 | 4.76 | 3.15 | -1.80 |
| South Asia | 3.49 | -5.57 | 5.68 | 5.62 | 3.43 | 3.65 | 6.72 | 5.89 | 3.64 | -2.67 |
| Western and Central Asia | 1.81 | -2.72 | 3.69 | 3.07 | 2.34 | 2.18 | 5.15 | 4.02 | 2.34 | -2.25 |
| Latin America and Caribbean | -0.87 | -6.70 | 5.46 | 2.53 | 1.94 | 1.80 | 3.36 | 1.83 | 1.93 | -0.67 |
| Africa | 3.50 | -3.58 | 3.16 | 2.70 | 2.54 | 2.38 | 5.30 | 2.70 | 2.51 | -1.49 |

*Source:* United Nations Global Policy Model. Historic data compiled from United Nations Secretariat and IMF databases; projections 2021 to 2030 are estimated.

*Note:* Regions as defined in Table 1.1 (for modelling purposes, the Republic of Korea is included in 'Developed Pacific').

---

## 2. The triggers of the slowdown

The domestic policy conditions that contribute critically to the growth outcomes presented above are aggregated at global level in Figure 2.2(a). As it is known, the ratio of government spending in goods and services on GDP has been subject to a marked fall since the 1980s (*TDR 2013, 2017*; Izurieta et al., 2018), ascribed to the doctrine of small government. Expansionary policies have occasionally swung into action to counter recessions, as with the GFC (and even more so with the Covid-19 shock) but were followed by tighter budgets, particularly through declining government spending, as policy makers confronted the inevitable rise in government debt caused by recession (Costantini, 2015; Lavoie and Seccareccia, 2017). Cutting the fiscal budget is not the only means to reduce debt ratios, is ineffective in most cases and undermines growth (Jayadev and Konczal, 2010; Storm and Nastepaad 2012; Blanchard et al., 2015). But it has, nonetheless, been the preferred policy option adopted after recent crises.

The scenario starts from the assumption of a general return to tighter fiscal stances, recognizing that in some instances (China, the European Union, North America, and a handful of developing countries in East Asia and Latin America) the resort to austerity points to a relatively softer line. Yet, in most of the mentioned cases the expected magnitudes of direct injections to the flow of expenditure in goods and services are marginal (see Chapter I). At the same time, the current ratios of government

debt are unprecedented and there is little to suggest the adoption of a sustained policy prescription to reduce debt burdens by fiscal expansion (see also *TDR 2019*). Thus, fiscal policy in the scenario is modelled to cut fiscal deficits to less than 3 per cent of GDP by the end of the decade, resulting in the pace of government spending shown in the Figure 2.2 (a).[7]

Figure 2.2 (a) also shows the historic pattern of global wage shares. As discussed in previous *Reports*, wage share compression has been the norm in most countries since the 1980s. From 2000 to 2019 the decline was nearly 4 percentage points of World Gross Product (WGP). As discussed in the next section, wage shares appear to have fallen further after the Covid-19 shock. Our scenario assumes that wage shares will keep falling moderately, at a pace similar to that experienced in the post-GFC, especially until the pre-crisis rate of employment is restored, which will take a few years.[8] This is because policy-makers, facing a weakening of aggregate demand due to induced fiscal tightening, and being wary of excessive demand push by the private sector (for fear of inflationary pressures or financial fragility), would tend to privilege the option of increasing export competitiveness to gain market share. In the current policy paradigm, a weakening of labour's bargaining power appears as the default option to induce lower unit costs.[9]

The combined set of domestic policy conditions is mirrored in a continuing acceleration of the pace of financialization, highlighted by the rising trend of the

**FIGURE 2.2  Main drivers of the scenario: global aggregates, 2001–2030**

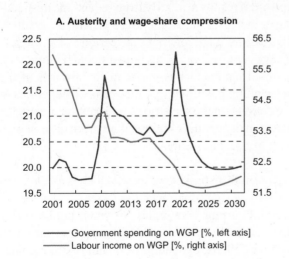

A. Austerity and wage-share compression

——— Government spending on WGP [%, left axis]
——— Labour income on WGP [%, right axis]

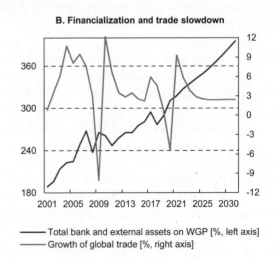

B. Financialization and trade slowdown

——— Total bank and external assets on WGP [%, left axis]
——— Growth of global trade [%, right axis]

**Source:**  United Nations Global Policy Model. Historic data compiled from United Nations Secretariat and IMF datasets; projections 2021 to 2030 are estimated.

ratio of external and bank financial assets on WGP (figure 2.2(b)).[10] This, in part, reflects policymakers' preference to gain net export demand through opening up to external markets by deepening trade and financial agreements (Kohler and Cripps, 2018). But it is also partly the result of continuing reliance on monetary easing and liquidity creation to support productive investment (Dow, 2017; Epstein, 2019; Gabor, 2021). As is well-known, would-be investors in productive activities facing sluggish aggregate demand would rather seek profitable investment opportunities in the financial sector (Bhaduri et al., 2015). The line showing the growth of import demand is not an assumption but an endogenous result of the policy stances. As indicated in the graph, pronounced cyclical fluctuations of trade growth follow the rhythm of the major economic crises. The model captures the sensitivity of import volumes to global conditions of demand, the weak impact of reducing tariffs barriers, and the negative effect of an accelerated pace of financialization that diverts funds away from credit for production and employment creation (see also *TDR 2016*).

### 3. Unfavourable conditions for most developing regions

The key assumptions of a return to normal policies play out under the current structure of global governance. This structure includes the heightened power of corporate players and the growing burden of (public and private) debt worldwide, which impose deeper vulnerabilities for most developing economies that do not issue currencies traded on international markets. As discussed in Chapter I, the structure of private finance generates waves of inflows and outflows beyond the control of policymakers, amplifying the worst aspects of current governance.[11]

Thus, developing economies are increasingly forced to aim at securing the needed foreign exchange to meet their external commitments by exporting. Depending on initial conditions, availability of resources, externally determined price fluctuations, etc., few of them can become successful (net-) exporters. And even then, they will need to rely on deflationary policies to contain the growth of imports and related financial leakages. Most other developing economies will likely remain in structural deficit and facing greater costs of external finance (McCombie and Thirlwall, 1994; Barbosa-Filho and Izurieta, 2020). Regarding developed economies, the self-inflicted limits to growth brought about through wage-share compression, inadequate public sector

demand and accelerated financialization are likely to amplify the trend towards rising macro-financial imbalances.

On this basis, macroeconomic patterns can be mapped as either finance-constrained (most developing economies) or financed-unconstrained (developed economies). Within each category surplus-biased and deficit-biased economies can be further distinguished. China is presented separately as it no longer matches the conditions of surplus economies (with growth depending increasingly on domestic demand), nor of financially constrained economies (given advances in the international use of its currency as well as the abundance of held reserves). Their current account configurations are shown in Figure 2.3.[12]

The current account performances of these groups in the scenario period are the endogenous result of the interplay of the assumed domestic policies, the financial constraints mentioned above, and the expected behavioural responses of the private sector in each of the economies under exam. These elements, discussed below, will help explain economic growth patterns.

Current account positions are, by accounting, exactly equal to the combined public and private sector net lending positions (shown in Figure 2.4 for each set of countries). As all lines represent ex-post flows of savings (disposable income of either public or private sectors minus current and investment expenditure), movements downwards indicate injections to effective demand and conversely movements upwards represent leakages. The graphs per se do not reveal whether the shrinking of a deficit (movement upwards) results primarily from reductions of spending or increases of income. But a general observation that can be made of 'normal' periods of growth is that government revenues hold a stable relation with national income. Thus, movements upwards of the net-lending position of public sectors (reductions in the deficits) in the scenario period capture mostly the extent of expenditure cuts resulting from the assumed shift to fiscal austerity.

A pattern from past experience, which is extended to 2030 by design of the scenario, is the bias in current account surplus economies for small public sector deficits. In the process of moving from larger to smaller deficits, expenditures do not rise at the pace of revenues. Thus, by withdrawing public sector demand from the flow of income generation, *unless* corresponding additional spending is done by their

**FIGURE 2.3  Current account, selected groups, 2001–2030**
*(Per cent of GDP)*

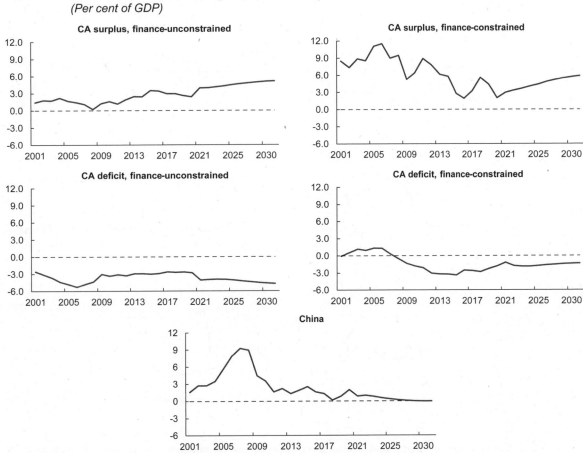

*Source:*  See Figure 2.2.
 *Note:*  Current account surplus, finance-unconstrained economies include the European Union and other economies of Western Europe, Israel, Japan and the Republic of Korea. Current account deficit, finance-unconstrained economies include Australia, Canada, New Zealand, United Kingdom, and the United States of America. Current account surplus, finance-constrained economies include major developing economies of East Asia (excluding China), of Western Asia (excluding Israel) and the Russian Federation. Current account deficit, finance-constrained economies include all other developing economies.

private sectors, these economies would be imposing deflationary pressure on the rest of the world. In other words, the resulting net withdrawal of spending relative to income by surplus economies implies a reduction of income potential in partner economies.

Thus, given the assumed shifts towards fiscal austerity, growth performance would mostly depend on private sector behaviour, which, in turn, is affected by financial conditions. To illustrate this, it is worth recalling the post-GFC responses in China. As in all other groups, the global shock of 2008–09 was met with a sudden increase of the fiscal deficit. But the sharpest injection to aggregate demand came from the private sector (movements downwards of the net-lending position). This was facilitated by financial conditions created to support investment. And such conditions were extended far into the post-GFC period with the double effect of generating fast growth

domestically and contributing to global demand. A similar configuration is extended into the post-Covid recovery, with the notable difference that it is expected that there will be greater emphasis on supporting household demand than on business investment. Needless to say, liquidity provisions to sustain private sector spending carry financial risks (*TDR 2020*), but to the extent that the Chinese economy does not issue a currency that can be easily traded in global financial markets, and flows of capital are carefully managed, those risks can be closely monitored.

In the other surplus economies, the large fiscal deficits in 2021 shrink relatively quickly in the scenario period. In the first four years, finance-unconstrained economies cut 71 per cent of the public deficit, while finance-constrained economies 62 per cent. Meanwhile, the export-bias of these economies, which also contributes to a continuing

**FIGURE 2.4  Private and public sectors net lending, 2001–2030**
*(Per cent of GDP)*

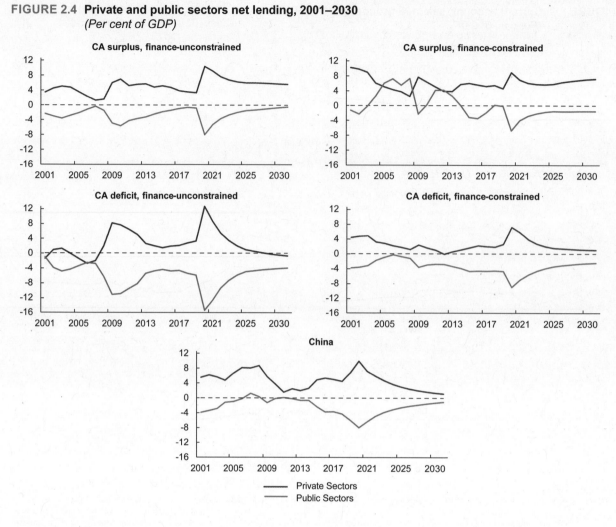

*Source:* See Figure 2.2.
  *Note:* For country groupings, see Figure 2.3.

compression of wage-shares, results in cuts of the large surpluses of their private sectors, but by only 30 per cent (finance-unconstrained economies) and 16 per cent (finance-constrained economies). In sum, considerably greater cuts in public spending than additions to private spending induce growth decelerations, domestically and abroad. This behaviour turns out to be very similar to that of the post-GFC.

Among these surplus economies, the central difference is referenced by financial conditions. Finance-unconstrained (developed) economies have induced considerably large private sector net lending positions (savings) during the Covid-19 shock,[13] and maintain moderately large private savings levels in the post-Covid period, by expanding liquidity (generated electronically by Central Banks) which make domestic and international portfolio investment attractive on the back of asset appreciations.

Meanwhile, private sector savings behaviour in surplus finance-constrained (developing) economies is more dependent on international financial conditions than domestic monetary stimuli. The allocation of private savings into financial assets is typically biased in favour of investments abroad, denominated in reserve currencies, while the flows of borrowing are mostly dependent on external 'push' factors. And especially in conditions of growth slowdown and potential global financial instability, private sector savings in these economies tend to increase and to divert more assets abroad.[14] This, in turn, forces governments to assume higher costs (interest rate premium) to finance their budgets. As costs add to the fiscal deficit, greater shares of expenditure cuts have to be enacted to achieve degrees of fiscal 'consolidation' similar to those of the finance-unconstrained economies. Thus, the domestic deflationary impact of similar paces of fiscal austerity are greater for developing economies. In the policy conditions postulated in this scenario, finance-constrained surplus economies will likely experience a combination of growth slow-down (where both domestic and external sources of demand weaken) and greater volumes of domestic private capital shifting abroad, especially as growth decelerates.

In economies tending to current account deficits, the main growth drivers rest on domestic demand. For finance-unconstrained (developed) economies, while fiscal austerity may predominate, the targets of fiscal adjustment seems to be more moderate than elsewhere, in part because of the privilege conferred on economies that can issue internationally accepted currencies without severe market pressures, and in part because their economic structure is geared to partially rely on public sector injections to demand ('soft-budget constraint', as per Galbraith, 2008). What is more, domestic creation of liquidity has proven to be an effective and powerful means to accelerate the pace of private sector demand (reducing or eliminating their net-lending positions), backed by asset appreciations (Godley and Lavoie 2007: 74–77; Costantini and Seccareccia, 2020). By virtue of the international status of their currencies (which may even trigger more inflows from abroad when international conditions falter), they are able to feed, via credit booms, increasing private sector spending.

By contrast, deficit finance-constrained (developing) economies cannot pursue a meaningful relaxation by domestic liquidity creation; public sector deficits shrink through the adoption of austerity measures and while private sector surpluses may shrink (contributing effectively to aggregate demand), private consumption or investment are likely to depend heavily on foreign inflows, which are (i) beyond the control of local policy makers, and (ii) costly, risky and volatile. Furthermore, in these economies which are structurally constrained and subject to boom-bust cycles, a significant portion of their private expenditure involves imports of manufacturing goods that cannot be generated domestically because industrialization requires affordable and stable financing. Thus, effective demand may not weaken as much as in surplus finance-constrained economies but keeping growth going induces an increasingly greater risk of financial instability.

### 4. Overcoming the dilemmas of interdependence

Given the current macro-financial structure of the world economy, a return to pre-Covid-19 policy

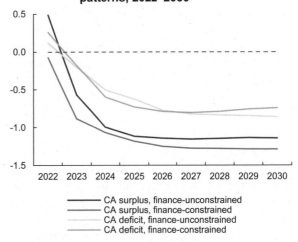

**FIGURE 2.5 Projected growth performance according to macro-financial patterns, 2022–2030**

CA surplus, finance-unconstrained
CA surplus, finance-constrained
CA deficit, finance-unconstrained
CA deficit, finance-constrained

**Source:** See Figure 2.2.
**Note:** For country groupings, see Figure 2.3.

normality marked by fiscal austerity, wage constraint and loose monetary and financial policy, will impose heavy burdens on developing countries.

Just as in the period leading to the GFC, this policy mix seems to deliver robust growth for as long as financial risks are kept in check. It may be tempting to think that reinstating similar policy stances in the post-Covid period may speed up growth for long enough so that the benefits outweigh the potential losses of, say, another global financial crisis. But this would be wishful thinking. By replicating similar policy triggers and analysing the world economy in a model that takes into account the configuration of external imbalances and financial constraints, we have shown that a marked slowdown of growth is the more likely outcome, and sooner, rather than later.

Policymakers in surplus economies have typically justified this set of policy options by offering reassurance that their emphasis on financial resilience and fiscal prudence warrants their economic growth performance. But it will not be so this time around. Figure 2.5 shows the timeline of growth losses of the four types of economies in the scenario period.[15] The series measure the losses in economic growth of these groups, in per cent terms each year, relative to the average of economic growth of the same economies along all the recovery periods since the 1980s. The two sets of surplus economies are likely to lose the most, of around 1.2 percentage points of growth each year. Between these two groups, the finance-constrained (developing) economies will experience relatively sharper hits. Current account deficit economies will also exhibit considerable slowdowns, to the tune of about 0.8 percentage points of growth each year, provided that systemic shocks from the build-up of financial vulnerabilities are averted. Needless to say, in the event of a significant financial collapse under current global conditions, neither deficit nor surplus economies will be spared considerable pain.

The rationale for this adverse outcome for surplus, financially well-off economies,[16] is fairly straightforward. First, this time around, in most parts of the world, wage-shares have reached rock-bottom levels. Employees, small farmers and informal workers are remunerated at levels far below their historical contributions to output generation. This creates unprecedented pressures for either underconsumption or overborrowing.

Second, a return to fiscal austerity aimed to cut deficits is likely to trigger an acceleration of effective demand shortfalls. This is because, on the one hand, the predominance of global finance will raise the costs of public debt implying greater cuts in real public sector spending, as noted earlier. On the other, fiscal multipliers are higher at lower levels of aggregate activity, which in turn implies that austerity cuts will have a greater negative impact on aggregate demand.

Third, public sector spending in goods and services relative to national income has been declining through the last decades. As clearly explained in Minsky (1982), and widely corroborated by decades of observation after the Great Depression, smaller public sectors make it harder to counter cyclical fluctuations of demand, which makes economies more vulnerable to private sector shocks.

Fourth, financial innovation and deeper globalization make it considerably easier and more attractive to shift resources potentially available for spending and investment into speculative activities with no direct effect on global demand (Nesvetailova, 2007).

Finally, as demonstrated in earlier *Reports*, the combination of wage share compression, austerity and smaller public sectors, and greater financialization impose further constraints on import growth, weakening global trade.

Therefore, the global deflationary impact of this combination is likely to be severe and will affect most dramatically economies which rely relatively more heavily on external demand than on domestic conditions, and most especially developing economies among them. The slow growth predicament facing surplus economies in the event of a widespread return to past policies should serve to motivate policymakers to seek more effective ways to sustain growth by combinations of injections to demand and tighter reins on speculative finance. And to the extent that growth is a globally intertwined outcome, policies to achieve it ought to be internationally coordinated.

## D. From Economic Recovery to Building Back Better

Avoiding the policy mistakes of the past is necessary but not sufficient to recover from Covid-19. A better world will only emerge from the pandemic if strong economic recoveries are supported and coordinated in all regions of the global economy, if the economic gains from recovery are skewed towards middle and lower-income households, if health provision, including ready access to vaccines, is treated as a truly global public good and if there is a massive investment push across all countries into carbon-free sources of energy.

These are all demanding challenges in their own right, made all the more so because they are also closely interconnected. with the need for simultaneous progress on all fronts, moreover, policy makers can no longer disregard the complexity of the challenge by offering a simplistic narrative about things falling in to place if prices are right. As the previous section showed, reverting to business-as-usual will by the end of the decade leave an even more fragile and fragmented world. That world now needs planning, not platitudes.

Thinking about how to make connections on all these fronts can help concentrate minds and actions on some of the basic elements of a successful strategy, and, in the process, make the challenge facing policy makers less daunting. In particular, with success on all fronts depending on boosting productive investment, creating decent jobs and narrowing wealth and income gaps, this section considers some of the policy responses adopted in the advanced economies since Covid-19 with respect to reducing inequality, countering corporate rent-seeking and advancing green investments.

## 1. Avoiding separate development

After decades of growing inequalities and polarization pressures (*TDR, 2017, 2020*) and a pandemic that has destroyed jobs on an unprecedented scale, the economic recovery provides an opportunity to rebalance the distribution of income within and between countries. But, in spite of calls by G7 leaders for "building back a better world", separate economic worlds may in fact be rising from the ashes of 2020, with little chance of them being unified without concerted reform measures at the national and international levels.

A full spectrum of the impact of the Covid-19 crisis on inequality, within and across countries, will not emerge for some time (Ferreira, 2021). But with vaccines still a distant hope for the majority of the world's population, the gap in living standards between the developed and developing economies, which narrowed for some years from the start of the new millennium, is likely to widen again. In most developing countries, fiscal and monetary expansion has been constrained largely by external factors: the limited appetite of financial markets for debt issued in local currencies, the risk of being forced into an austerity program, should the need for IMF assistance arise, and the ebb and flow of international capital movements. As discussed in the previous section, failure to address these constraints will see a repetition of the lopsided recoveries of the past. Moreover, developed countries have been reluctant to agree on a multilateral mechanism for orderly debt workouts, clinging, instead, to the belief that a mixture of enlightened market responsibility, ad hoc reprofiling exercises and fiscal discipline will eventually alleviate the stress from undue debt burdens (see Chapter I sections B and D).

Most importantly, many of the policies developed countries are relying on for immediate relief and longer-term growth – including fiscal and monetary expansion, support for their high-tech sectors and protection for traditional sectors and trade in intangibles – could, without effective international coordination and compensating measures, impede the ability of developing countries to recover from the Covid-driven recession. In fact, historically low interest rates in developed countries combined with the speculative appetite of investors for high returns have led to large capital inflows into some emerging and commodity markets, including food, with adverse consequences for food security in the rest of the world (see Chapter I section C). Moreover, without scaled-up multilateral financial support for investments in climate mitigation, the foreign exchange constraint is likely to tighten further on many developing countries as their exports become the target of carbon adjustment taxes. Meanwhile, the health emergency in developing countries is ongoing. As a result, developing countries are, more than ever, likely to come under pressure to cut labour costs and public services, in a futile attempt to export their way to recovery, further exacerbating inequality at home.

In contrast, a budding recovery in developed countries has been driven by a fiscal expansion, which has supported household incomes, and by monetary policies that made sure financial breakdown was avoided when the economy was at its most vulnerable and that firms had access to cheap credit to remain sufficiently liquid during lockdowns. Going forward, growth is set to continue as long as the current policies are maintained and could even gain more momentum, at least to the extent that concerns about climate change encourage investments in green technologies to accelerate (see next section).

However, underlying structural problems that predate the pandemic continue to cast a shadow over future stability. The danger of separate recovery paths among countries has its counterpart in a K-shaped recovery across households and which reflect existing patterns of domestic inequality. On the one hand, as noted in Chapter I, CEO compensation rose by over 18 per cent during 2020 and an astounding 1,322 per cent since 1978. On the other, a large section of the American labour force on the minimum wage of $7.25 per hour actually earned a higher weekly income being unemployed during the pandemic from the $300 federal benefits than they did working (Matthews, 2021). In this context, the monetary measures employed during the crisis have been double-edged: these undoubtedly prevented a financial crash but have helped also to fuel massive asset appreciations, contributing significantly, in the process, to income and wealth inequality.

As discussed in the previous section, as financialization has become a ubiquitous feature of the global economy, and a spur to rent-seeking behaviour, an unbalanced macroeconomic policy mix has been present in virtually all developed countries since the bursting of the dotcom bubble in 2000, but similar trends can also be found in some emerging

**FIGURE 2.6  Housing, shares and output in developed countries, first quarter 2000 to first quarter 2021**

*(Real price index, 2010q1 =100)*

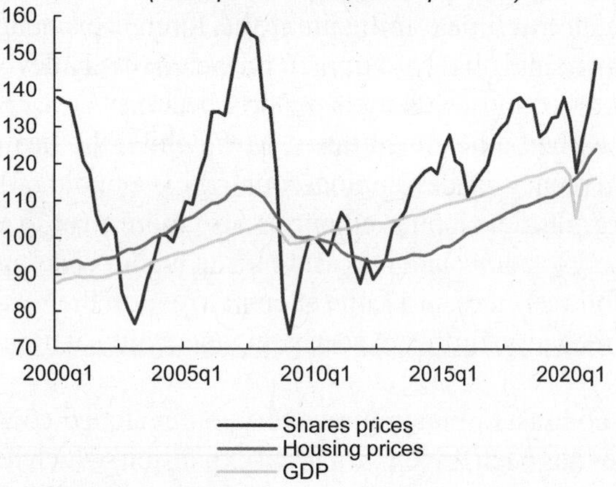

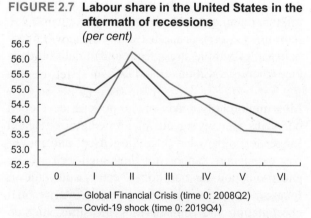

- Shares prices
- Housing prices
- GDP

*Source:* OECD and IMF data.

*Note:* Average indices weighted by nominal GDP. Data available for 42 countries: AUS, AUT, BEL, BRA, CAN, CHE, CHL, CHN, COL, CZE, DEU, DNK, ESP, EST, FIN, FRA, GBR, GRC, HUN, IDN, IND, IRL, ISL, ISR, ITA, JPN, KOR, LUX, LVA, MEX, NLD, NOR, NZL, POL, PRT, RUS, SVK, SVN, SWE, TUR, USA, ZAF.

economies. If ignored by policy makers, a separate recovery for the financial sector compared to other parts of the economy, extending the disconnect already visible from before Covid-19, will pose an obstacle, and probably an insurmountable one, to building back better. Figure 2.6 which shows how, since the global financial crisis, house and share prices have, worldwide, become closely correlated with each other on a sharply upward trend and increasingly disconnected from a more sluggish output trend, provides a measure of the policy challenge (see also Annex Figure 1).

If a pattern of separate development is to be avoided, much is likely to depend on policymakers in advanced economies confronting the inequality challenge head on. In the United States, Covid-19 caused, cumulatively, the largest number of deaths per thousands of inhabitants among developed countries with a disproportionate number of women and minorities, and low-income families. The shock hit an already fractured economy split between "lead" sectors, with high wages and high productivity, and "lagging" sectors with low wages and low productivity (*TDR 2020*; Taylor, 2020). By 2019, decades of wage repression, weak social protection and industrial offshoring had left half the labour force (80 million workers) in precarious conditions, often in debt and with limited access to health care.

Against this already polarized economy, changes in income distribution during the pandemic have

followed a familiar script: as the recession wiped out profits, the labour share initially increased, in part thanks to discretionary government interventions, such as stimulus checks and increased unemployment benefits, only to decrease again as a result of layoffs. With small oscillations, five quarters after the recessions first hit, the labour share appears set on a downward trend. The timing is very similar to the one registered during the global financial crisis in 2008 and 2009, with the impact somewhat harder (Figure 2.7).

Sector level data are still incomplete but aggregate data already provide clear indications of rising inequality: While unemployment soared in 2020 and remains 2 percentage points above its 2019 level, total wage payments have already recovered. In fact, they surpassed pre-recession levels in the fourth quarter of 2020, when unemployment was still at 7 per cent. This suggests that some of the workers who remained employed during the pandemic saw their incomes increase. As this is unlikely the case for essential workers, it probably reflects income gains for workers in the prime economy who worked remotely in high productivity, high wage sectors including high-tech and pharmaceuticals (BIS, 2021; Gould and Kandra, 2021). In other words, economic recovery in the United States has not yet happened for a large share of the labour force.

In 2020 and the first half of 2021, government payments and discretionary relief measures including stimulus checks, mortgage forbearance and a moratorium on evictions staved off a deeper social and economic crisis, helped alleviate the plight of

**FIGURE 2.7  Labour share in the United States in the aftermath of recessions**

*(per cent)*

- Global Financial Crisis (time 0: 2008Q2)
- Covid-19 shock (time 0: 2019Q4)

*Source:* US Bureau of Economic Analysis. National Income and Production Accounts (NIPA), Table 1.10; released 29 July 2021.

*Note:* i. The wage share is the proportion of 'Compensation of Employees' over Gross Domestic Income (GDI).
ii. The wage bill of Q2 2021 is the officially published (preliminary) figure. GDI for 2021Q2 was generated assuming the same trend of GDP.

those at the bottom of the income ladder – with a significant drop in the poverty rate in 2021 on some estimates, (Parolin et al., 2021) – and could possibly make the United States economy more efficient in the longer run. However, reversing decades of wage repression requires more than temporary measures and discussions from early 2021 about direct government intervention by raising the minimum wages seem to have faded.

The large cash transfers contributed less to GDP growth and employment creation than direct spending in goods and services would have because a portion of the transfer has been saved. This is a well-known effect of cash transfers and in the initial phase of the crisis, it was probably consistent with the objective of keeping people at home. But the increase in personal savings was massive in 2020, in excess of 12 per cent of GDP. To what extent this was fuelled by saved stimulus checks is still unclear, but it seems realistic that most of the increase was caused by capital gains on existing assets. Regardless, the combination of financial transfers to the private sector and expansionary monetary policy has fuelled growth of financial and real estate prices driving up wealth inequality further.

The path of the recovery, and whether it will be inclusive or not, hinges on the deployment of investment and labour market policies, which are articulated in legislative proposals currently under discussion. The recent social protection measures are mostly set to expire in 2021. As measures are phased out and pressures to reduce the public debt mount, fiscal policy may revert to austerity counteracting the impact of the recovery plans.

Avoiding this path will be key to ensuring an inclusive recovery. One challenge for the government going forward is how to persuade households to spend some of the savings accumulated during the pandemic. If most of the savings are held by the middle class, what is holding them back from spending them is probably insufficient confidence in future economic security or excessive confidence in financial returns. This can be addressed with policies that strengthen job security and wage growth, public investment and less expansionary monetary policy. If most of the savings are held by the wealthy, channelling them to real spending likely requires increasing marginal tax rates to transfer part of the wealth to the government, which can make productive use of it. A wealth tax, paid on total assets in the manner that homeowners pay property taxes, would break

new ground in ensuring equitable taxation, and help reverse existing inequalities.

A broad plan would include enhancements of physical infrastructure – with public investment programs and incentives for private investment aiming at decarbonizing the economy – and of "social infrastructure" such as the introduction of free childcare and higher education, which aim at generating wage and productivity growth. The plan also recognizes the importance of manufacturing as a driver of productivity growth and outlines a vision in which offshoring is partially reversed and corporate concentration reined in. With $4.5 trillion in spending[17] over a time span of eight years, the proposal would amount to 2.5 per cent of GDP annually starting in 2022, enough to have an initial impact on the long-standing problems of inequality and underinvestment.

As discussed in the previous chapter, the European Union suffered a more severe recession than the United States largely because of widespread and extended lockdowns. Although the private sector curbed its spending, employment did not contract as much as in the United States thanks to stricter dismissal regulations. Extensive social protection systems helped sustain disposable income but consumers' willingness to spend is still at historical lows, as signalled by a saving rate of 21 per cent of disposable income (mid-2021), compared to 12 per cent in the United States (long-term rates are similar).

This may, in part, be owed to insufficient financial support offered by governments in 2020. But it is also likely to reflect a skewed recovery of incomes in 2021, which privileges the highest earners, who save proportionally more. Data are not yet conclusive on this issue but a major challenge in achieving an inclusive recovery in the European Union is posed by increasing inequality as a result of widening economic dualism.

In the European Union's three largest economies – France, Germany and Italy – productivity growth has been low or negative for two decades, with wages in low-productivity sectors losing substantial ground to wages in high-productivity sectors (Capaldo and Ömer, 2021). Labour shares have decreased substantially but most of the loss has been borne by workers in already low-wage occupations. In Italy a severe deterioration of productivity growth has offset the decline of the labour share but a large share of workers has nonetheless suffered decades of wage repression. Research indicates that a major factor of these developments has been the combination of austerity and emphasis on export competitiveness (Capaldo, 2015; Capaldo and Izurieta, 2013), which has undermined two key components of aggregate demand – public spending in goods and services and household spending.

In this context, an inclusive recovery in the European Union depends on restoring dynamism to consumption and investment, which requires sustained wage growth, public investment and continued commitment to strong social protection systems. Current fiscal rules and the emphasis on export competitiveness present serious hurdles which recently adopted recovery plans have not yet addressed.

As discussed in the next section, the "Next Generation European Union" plan is a good starting point to revive public investment and make sure it occurs in strategic sectors such as renewable energies, transport and agriculture. But to accomplish the targeted transformation and an inclusive economic recovery, member states would have to add substantially more to it at the national level. However, European Union rules foresee a return to austerity in 2023, after a temporary suspension of the deficit reduction mandated by the Stability and Growth Pact, which could prevent member states from effectively ramping up spending to bolster the recovery. At the same time, continued emphasis on trade expansion and cost cutting reforms (affecting government spending as well as wages) threaten to widen the gap between workers in lead sectors and those in the lagging sectors, adding to widening income gaps and further undermining the prospects for an inclusive recovery.

## 2. Taming the rentiers

As discussed above, an abiding theme of past *Reports* is the link between hyperglobalization and the rise of a rentier economy dominated by large corporations. Their control over key strategic assets and long global reach affords them a dominant market position from which abusive, and oftentimes predatory, business practices proliferate. Considerable evidence has accumulated over the last two decades indicating the growing extent of abusive market power and its distortionary impact, at both the national and global levels. The pandemic has, if anything, extended these practices, particularly through intellectual property rights and the control of digital technologies.

In both developed and developing countries, the perception that the benefits from globalization have been unfairly skewed to large conglomerates is reinforced by their ability to pay little or no tax on the rents they extract.

A stark example is the increasing share of corporate profits – oftentimes classified as FDI – that passes through empty corporate shells rather than being invested in productive activities in the receiving economies (Damgaard et al., 2019). This type of transaction can be used for intra-company financing or to hold intellectual property and other assets. For tax-optimization purposes, it is concentrated in a few tax havens (Delatte et al., 2020), depriving many countries of a fair share in the benefits of globalization. Evidence on the exploitation of loopholes and tax havens or low-tax jurisdictions shows, for example, that companies from the United States generate more investment income from Luxembourg and Bermuda than from China and Germany (*TDR 2018*).

The origins of such practices can be traced back to the very foundations of the regime of international business taxation, whose broad principles were agreed during the early years of the 20th century and have remained intact until very recently. These principles assigned the taxation of active business income to source jurisdictions – where the business was located – while passive income such as investment income or rent fell to the jurisdiction where the investors resided.[18] The concept of source taxation, which has been the mainstay of international business taxation, had both technical and political flaws. Since a large portion of global trade takes place in the form of intra-firm trade between subsidiaries within the same company (*TDR 2015*), companies often transfer large portions of profitable activities to subsidiaries in low-tax jurisdictions, also known as tax havens, so that the income appears to originate there.

The fallout from the GFC of 2007–2009 prompted renewed attempts, at both national and international levels, to target tax abuse and the secrecy jurisdictions that facilitate these practices (*TDR 2014*: chap. VII). Policymakers in leading economies have been focusing their attention, in particular, on the abusive practices of large digital corporations. During the pandemic, several European Governments, along with the European Commission, have pushed for improved surveillance of these corporations and stronger antitrust enforcement. The new United States Administration has also set out to strengthen antitrust laws and enforcement with the clearly stated aim of rewriting the rules of corporate behaviour more generally (*Financial Times*, 2021).

The main multilateral response was the launch in 2013 of the Base Erosion and Profit Shifting (BEPS) project by the OECD (see *TDR 2019*: Chapter V). It was given a boost in 2020 with the launch of the Inclusive Framework to deliver a multilateral, consensus-based solution to the tax challenges arising from the digitalization of the economy (OECD, 2021a).

The latest step forward was the agreement in early July 2021 by 132 member jurisdictions out of the 139 entities for a two-pillar solution to address those tax challenges with respect to taxing rights between jurisdictions and the losses of public revenues due to profit shifting activities (see OECD, 2021a: Annex A for the details). Subsequently, G20 Finance Ministers endorsed the key components of the Inclusive Framework agreement. These include the reallocation of profits of multinational enterprises under Pillar One and an effective global minimum tax of at least 15 per cent under Pillar Two. G20 also called on the Inclusive Framework to swiftly address the remaining issues, finalize the design elements within the agreed framework and provide an implementation plan for the two pillars by October 2021. Meanwhile, it invited the Inclusive Framework member jurisdictions that have not yet joined the agreement to do so (G20, 2021).

This achievement has been presented as a gamechanger for several reasons. Technically, it reaffirms the need to consider MNEs as unitary businesses, displacing the ineffective arm's length principle. Moreover, by applying a minimum tax rate to all multinational groups with consolidated revenues over €750 million (not only the ones linked to the digital economy), it simplified the scope of negotiations and narrowed the room for further delays.

Politically, the deal should help reinvigorate multilateralism, including by deescalating trade tensions between some key G20 members after several advanced economies announced that they would pursue their own path to tax major tech giants, which led the previous United States Administration to threaten retaliatory trade measures. Economically, the two-pillar package also promises to bring much needed tax revenue (OECD, 2021a), with estimates up to $275 billion per year (Cobham, 2021), and to dent, if not eliminate, the global race to the bottom on corporate taxation.

As is often the case in the issue of taxation, the devil is in the details, and the details of implementing the latest agreement are yet to be finalized. However, since, according to some calculations, corporate tax avoidance through profit shifting in low-tax countries 'saves' these firms from $500-$600 billion dollars in tax payments world-wide (Shaxson, 2019), one would expect the new system to affect companies' bottom line. However, despite the publicity surrounding the proposals for the new global tax, share prices have failed to register significant change. This suggests that business analysts are not persuaded that the new tax regime will change much.

There are at least three areas of concern about the global efficacy of the reform. First, there is a risk that it would still be possible to game the system (de Wilde, 2021). The more complex the system, the greater the probability of creating loopholes. Moreover, Devereux and Simmler (2021) find that this reform would affect only 78 of the world's 500 largest MNEs, because, under Pillar One, the tax applies only to companies with revenues above $20 billion that earn a rate of return on revenue above 10 per cent. Their study reveals that reducing the revenue threshold for MNEs from $20 billion to €750 million (the threshold of Pillar Two) would increase the number of companies affected by a factor of 13, even though the authors acknowledge that the relative gain of reducing the threshold below $5 billion is small relative to the increase in the number of companies involved.

Second, there is a risk that developing countries will gain very little from this reform, because major grey areas and other contentious issues remain to be addressed. These include: the complexity of the new rules creating a significant burden for tax administrations around the world, especially in developing countries who face a shortage of highly-trained tax experts in their public administration; the low level of the tax rate; the limited reallocated tax-base under Pillar One with special carve-outs already promised for extractives and regulated financial services; the timing of the implementation with legal and political haggling shift the start date to well beyond 2023; the final allocation of taxing rights between firms' home and host countries currently based on MNE sales in each country (as favoured by the OECD and its members) and giving headquarter countries the first right to top up the tax on undertaxed profits, which would see G7 countries receiving more than 60 per cent of additional revenues (Cobham, 2021).

Third, a number of unresolved problems specifically concern the United States system of taxation. The United States has traditionally adhered to the principle of capital export neutrality (CEN), which is based on the idea that system of business taxation should be neutral about a resident's choice between domestic and foreign investments. For that purpose, the United States introduced the principle of tax deductions, so that United States firms could deduct losses generated abroad from their domestic taxation. A number of large companies have taken advantage of the system of tax deductions to reduce their tax to the minimum; Amazon, for instance, is paying nearly no tax at all world-wide by taking advantage of this system (Fair Tax Mark, 2019; Phillips et al., 2021).

It is not, as yet, clear how the existing United States system of deductions of taxation will work with the new multilateral proposals, and how it will affect the operation of global corporate structures. Furthermore, the United States also needs to address the inconsistency between the G7 proposal and its so-called Global Intangible Low-Taxed Income tax (GILTI), introduced by the previous Administration. In an attempt to prevent United States companies from moving their intangible assets, the 2017 Tax Cuts and Jobs Act had set the GILTI tax rate in a range of between 10.5% and 13.125%.

In the absence of an agreement that would have resolved all the above-mentioned risks and uncertainties, a group of leading tax experts have devised a more equitable, far less complex, and more practical proposal for a global anti-base erosion tax (Cobham et al., 2021; Picciotto et al., 2021). This relates to a minimum effective tax rate (METR), which could be introduced by a coalition of willing countries, whether they are home to MNEs, host of MNEs, or both. As the authors stress, this would still not be a complete solution. Changes would be needed to tax treaties to ensure a taxable nexus for significant economic presence and to allow a switch-over rule. However, in their view, progress on ensuring a minimum effective tax rate should not depend on securing signature and ratification by all States of a multilateral treaty – as is necessary for Pillar Two – because such a ratification process would in practice give all States a veto on implementation, which would be fatal. By contrast, the METR provides a practical and pragmatic basis for a feasible consensus of willing States to create a critical mass for progress toward effective reforms, since its adoption would contribute to, rather than impede, momentum for a more comprehensive multilateral agreement in a more distant time horizon.

## 3. Making green recovery packages work

Nothing highlights the importance of connecting policies adopted today to the prospects of a better future tomorrow than the dangers posed by rising global temperatures. Keeping the rise in global temperatures to below 1.5C is, arguably, the preeminent challenge facing the global policy community (IPCC, 2021), albeit one that is inseparable from the redistribution of economic resources within and across countries.

The *Trade and Development Report 2019* laid out a global strategy that could mitigate the threat of global warming whilst simultaneously addressing the inequities and fragilities of a financialized world. Climate protection requires a massive wave of new investments to rewire energy systems and other carbon-emitting sectors. Such a wave of green investment, the *Report* showed, could be a major source of jobs and income everywhere but the existing constraints on developing countries would mean that new sources of finance are required, including a significant scaling up of support from the international community in line with its commitment to common but differentiated responsibilities, along with the policy space needed to tailor industrial policies to the local demands of a just transition.

Given the uneven global economic landscape, rapid progress in this direction will, however, hinge on the immediate actions of the largest players, particularly China, the United States and the European Union. The United States and the European Union account for close to half of the stock of $CO_2$ emissions in the atmosphere. China, which is still a developing economy, accounts for much less than either (the more so on a per capita basis) but is now the world's largest emitter. Together, these three economies account for well over half of the 34 billion metric tons of emissions being pumped into the atmosphere each year (Table 2.3).

As Table 2.3 also shows, over the 20-year period 1999 – 2018, all three economies managed to lower their emissions relative to GDP, and by similar amounts—a 2.5 per cent average annual decline in China, a 2.2 per cent decline for the United States and 2.1 per cent decline in the European Union. Of course, the broad economic trajectories were distinct over this period. China's economy grew rapidly, at 9.0 per cent per year, so that the country's absolute level of emissions rose at a 6.5 per cent average annual rate, even while its emissions/GDP ratio declined. Economic growth was much slower in the United States and European Union over this period and, as a result, the absolute level of emissions did decline, by 0.1 per cent per year in the United States and a slightly larger 0.8 per cent per year in the European Union. However, and unlike China, in both cases, investment levels have been moving in the wrong direction, particularly in the public sector.

Despite the differences between the three big economic blocs, the fundamental requirement for advancing climate stabilization remains the same for all: to cut their absolute emissions levels, regardless of their respective economic growth rates. All three economies face formidable challenges to accomplish this. This is because the single most important action required for eliminating $CO_2$ emissions is to phase out the consumption of oil, coal, and natural gas to produce energy since burning fossil fuels is responsible for about 70–75 per cent of global $CO_2$ emissions. Correspondingly, it is imperative to build a new energy infrastructure in all three economic areas, as well as throughout the global economy. The cornerstones of this new global energy infrastructure will need to be high efficiency and clean renewable energy sources, primarily solar and wind power.

In terms of policy design, a critical first question to ask is: what will be the investment spending requirements for transforming the energy infrastructures in China, the United States and European Union and, more generally, throughout the global economy? Estimates, including the 2020 *Report*, converge around a finding that, on a global basis, total clean energy investment spending in the range of 2–3 per cent of GDP per year will be necessary for this project to succeed. This figure can be somewhat lower or higher in individual countries, depending on the extent to which a country's clean energy infrastructure has advanced to date. For China, the United States and European Union, it is likely that investment spending will need to be sustained at this roughly 2–3 per cent of GDP level.[19]

With economies other than China, the United States and the European Union currently generating about 48 per cent of global emissions, it follows that the clean energy transition will have to advance throughout the rest of the global economy as well. The climate programs for China, the United States and European Union will therefore also need to be evaluated in terms of how much they contribute toward achieving the IPCC targets on a global basis, not simply within their own national or regional economies. However, in this regard, the principle of common but differentiated responsibilities places

**TABLE 2.3**  **$CO_2$ Emissions and Economic Growth for China, United States and the European Union, 1999–2018**
*(per cent)*

| | $CO_2$ emissions in 2018 billions of metric tons | Share of 2018 global $CO_2$ emissions | $CO_2$ emissions and GDP annual growth, 1999–2018 | | |
| --- | --- | --- | --- | --- | --- |
| | | | Growth of emissions/ GDP | GDP growth | Emissions level growth |
| China | 10.3 | 30.2 | -2.5 | 9.0 | 6.5 |
| United States | 5.0 | 14.7 | -2.1 | 2.0 | -0.1 |
| European Union | 2.9 | 8.5 | -2.2 | 1.4 | -0.8 |

*Source:* https://data.worldbank.org/indicator for $CO_2$ emissions and emissions/GDP figures; https://fred.stlouisfed.org/ for real GDP growth figures. Emissions growth figures derived from GDP growth and emissions/GDP ratios.

the onus for concerted international action on the developed economies.

The two basic ways through which government policy can advance a clean energy transformation are through either direct public-sector investments or a range of regulations and incentives to encourage private-sector investment. These regulations/incentive policies for private investment include carbon taxes or carbon caps, long-term contracts for clean energy suppliers with guaranteed prices (i.e. "feed-in tariffs"), and various forms of subsidized financing.

Achieving the right mix between public and private investment will be critical to the success of the overall project. The *TDR 2019* argued that public investment should take the lead given that achieving the required spending levels by private investors faces very high sunk costs, political risks, illiquidity and uncertain returns. Private investments depend on the calculations of expected profitability by private business owners and financial markets. As a recent IMF Working Paper has noted, closing the resulting gap between private and social returns is, under these conditions, difficult using market-based instruments. On the other hand, the advantage of higher levels of private investment for the clean energy transition is that they will relieve pressures on public-sector budgets to deliver the overall spending amounts required.

There will be large-scale job creation resulting from both the public and private-sector investments to build clean energy infrastructures. Climate stabilization projects in China, the United States and European Union and throughout the world should therefore include measures to establish high job quality standards and to ensure that these newly-created jobs are fully available to women and other disadvantaged population cohorts. At the same time, it is unavoidable that workers and communities that are currently dependent on the fossil fuel industry will face significant economic losses as that industry is phased out. For China, the United States and the European Union, and throughout the global economy, fair and effective transition policies for these negatively impacted workers and communities should also be incorporated into their overall clean energy transition projects.

A transition led by public investment and jobs rich, to a decarbonized future underpins the calls, already heard before Covid-19 hit, for green new deals. The massive mobilization of fiscal and monetary resources in advanced countries to respond to the pandemic has suggested that there is an opportunity to globalize this idea. Under the banner of "a building back better world" there has been much talk by G7 economies of launching the kind of green recovery that was promised in response to the global financial crisis but was quickly abandoned in the face of austerity measures adopted in the advanced economies.

A premature resort to austerity appears less likely at the current moment than it did after the GFC. However, a survey of the initial recovery packages adopted in the world's 50 largest (mainly advanced) economies found that only 2.5 per cent of the spending went to greening the recovery (UNEP, 2021). The challenge ahead will, therefore, be maintaining a public investment drive over the coming decade and beyond whilst scaling-up the climate component. In this context it is important to understand the current policy positions, and the respective strengths and weaknesses, of the major economic players.

### (a) Policies of the United States

Between 2017–2020, under the Trump Administration the federal Government undertook no new climate initiatives and weakened most existing federal regulations and reduced sources of financial support to address climate change. The United States also withdrew from the Paris Climate Agreement in 2017. One of the first acts of the Biden Administration in January 2021 was to rejoin the Paris Agreement and has since then advanced a range of further initiatives aiming to put the United States economy onto a viable climate stabilization path. Most broadly, in alignment with the IPCC's global emissions reduction targets,

the new Administration has committed to reducing United States $CO_2$ emissions by 50 per cent as of 2030 and to become a net zero emissions economy by no later than 2050.

In terms of specific measures to achieve these broad goals, the most significant initiative to date is the proposed 8-year, $2.7 trillion American Jobs Plan, introduced in March 2021. Between 35–40 per cent of the total spending allocation, or about $130 billion per year, would be allocated to investments that can directly contribute to reducing $CO_2$ and other greenhouse gas emissions. The American Jobs Plan would also provide significant support for R&D on climate issues as well as just transition initiatives for workers and communities that are currently heavily dependent on the fossil fuel industry. In separate proposals, the Biden Administration also advocates financial support, in unspecified amounts, for climate stabilization measures in developing economies.[20]

This level of federal Government funding for climate stabilization would be unprecedented for the United States. But even if something close to this measure does become law, it is still not clear that the proposed funding levels would be adequate for achieving the Administration's stated climate goals, i.e. of a 50 per cent emissions reduction by 2030 and net zero emissions by 2050.

In line with the estimates noted above that 2–3 per cent of GDP will be needed to finance the clean energy transformation, overall clean energy investments in the United States—including both public and private investments—should range between $450–$500 billion per year to reach the 50 per cent emissions reduction target as of 2030. The American Jobs Plan would provide about 25–30 per cent of the total investment required. Public funding from state and local governments can also contribute, but, for the most part, the amounts are likely to be much smaller than what the federal Government provides. This raises the question of the prospects for mobilizing most of the remaining 75 per cent of the needed funding from private investors.

Private clean energy investment spending in the United States has been on an upward trajectory for over a decade. But to date, the level of private clean energy investment spending remains far below the required level. For 2019, the year before the onset of the COVID-induced recession as well as the most recent year for which full data are available, total private sector clean energy investments amounted to about $60 billion in renewable energy and $40 billion in energy efficiency.[21] This total of $100 billion therefore could contribute about 20 per cent of the amount that is required.

To mobilize private funds at the level required will depend on a strong set of incentives to support clean energy and energy efficiency and disincentives to discourage fossil fuel consumption. The most impactful such measures would be some combination of carbon taxes and carbon caps. Carbon taxes or caps do presently operate in 12 United States states that account for a quarter of the population and one-third of United States GDP.[22] These states have achieved lower emissions levels relative to the United States average. But they have not succeeded in inducing private clean energy investment spending to a level close to the amount required. Part of the problem is that neither carbon tax or carbon cap policies have been designed in the United States states to avoid the significant problems that can accompany these measures. One major problem is that increasing the price of fossil fuels affects lower-income households more than affluent households, since energy costs account for a higher share of lower-income households' consumption. An effective solution to this problem is to rebate to lower-income households a significant share of the revenues generated by the tax to offset the regressive distributional impacts of such taxes. But such rebate policies have not yet been enacted in any state.

Overall, for the United States to transition onto a viable climate stabilization path will require some combination of significantly greater levels of public investment as well as stronger and more effectively designed regulations of private investment than those operating at present or are under current discussion within either the Biden Administration or at the United States state level.

## (b) European Union policies

The European Union is advancing the world's most ambitious climate stabilization program, what it has termed the European Green Deal. Under this plan, the region has pledged to reduce emissions by at least 55 per cent as of 2030 relative to 1990 levels, a more ambitious target than the 45 per cent reduction set by the IPCC. The European Green Deal then aligns with the IPCC's longer-term target of achieving a net zero economy as of 2050.

Beginning in December 2019, the European Commission has been enacting measures and introducing further proposals to achieve the region's emission reduction targets. The most recent measure to have been adopted, in June 2021, is the Next Generation EU Recovery Plan, through which €600 billion—one-third of the overall €1.8 trillion euro investment seven-year budget—will be allocated toward financing the European Green Deal.[23] In July 2021, the European Commission followed up on this spending commitment by outlining 13 tax and regulatory measures with these major features:

- Expansion of carbon taxes within the European Union Emissions Trading System;

- A Carbon Border Adjustment Mechanism through which importers will pay fees for importing carbon-intensive products such as steel, cement or aluminium;

- Tighter alignment of overall taxation policies with the European Green Deal objectives;

- Raising energy efficiency levels and expanding renewable energy supplies;

- A faster rollout of low-emissions transport modes and the infrastructure and fuels to support them;

- Tools to preserve and grow forests and other natural carbon sinks;

- A socially fair transition aiming to spread the costs of tackling and adapting to climate change.[24]

In terms of the mix of public investments, regulations and other incentive to promote private investments, the European Green Deal apparently aims to rely primarily on regulations and other private-sector inducements. The €600 billion allocated over seven years through the NextGenerationEU Recovery Plan would amount to an average of about €85 billion per year. This is equal to less than 0.6 per cent of European Union GDP over this period (assuming that the European Union grows at a modest 1.5 per cent per year over this period). Private spending levels to transform the region's energy infrastructure, as well as forestry and agricultural practices, would therefore need to provide the remaining roughly €250 billion per year—or 75 per cent of total spending—to be on a viable stabilization path both for 2030 and 2050.[25]

As noted above, considerable uncertainty is, unavoidably, associated with relying on private investments induced by regulations and incentives as opposed to direct public investment spending for building a clean energy infrastructure. Thus, one recent study concluded that achieving the European Union's 55 per cent emission reduction target as of 2030 would require a tripling of the carbon price as of 2030 relative to what would be needed to reach a 40 per cent emissions cut by 2030.[26] Implementing this steep of a carbon price increase would undoubtedly face stiff political opposition, especially in the absence of rebates to counteract this new tax burden on lower- and middle-income people.[27] The 2018 Yellow Vest Movement in France emerged precisely in opposition to President Macron's proposal to enact a carbon tax without including substantial rebates for non-affluent citizens

As such, as with the United States case, the prospects for the European Green Deal to succeed as a climate stabilization program will almost certainly entail much higher levels of public investment support than has been proposed to date through the NextGenerationEU Recovery Plan.

### (c) China policies

Unlike the United States and the European Union, China has not yet committed to achieving the IPCC's emission reduction targets for 2030 or 2050. However, in his September 2020 address to the United Nations General Assembly, President Xi was the first world leader to set out a set of targets for his country: emissions would continue to rise until they peak in 2030 and then begin declining to reach net zero emissions by 2060. commitment was the trigger for others to increase their ambition (Tooze, 2020). In addition, China has stated its endeavour to reduce its reliance on coal; emissions from burning coal are currently about 30 per cent greater than those from oil and 70 per cent greater than from natural gas.

China's position is that its situation, as both an historically low emitter and a developing country, is distinct because it is proceeding along a much more rapid economic growth trajectory than either the United States, European Union or other advanced economies.

China, as a fast-growing developing economy, does, undoubtedly, face more formidable challenges than either the U.S or European Union in achieving major emissions reductions. But it is still the case that if China does not achieve the IPCC's targets within

its own economy, these targets will be unattainable on a global scale. It follows that the risks the IPCC describes as resulting from failing to meet these targets — intensifying heat extremes, heavy precipitation, droughts, sea level rise, and biodiversity losses — will become increasingly severe, including in China itself.

China does, moreover, have a record of overachieving in advancing climate stabilization projects. As a major case in point, following the 12th Five-Year-Plan (2011–2015) in which solar and wind manufacturing were listed as strategic industries, the Government implemented a series of industrial policies, including public financing, feed-in-tariffs, local content requirement, and R&D support, which enabled China to become a leading global manufacturer of solar and wind power. When low domestic demand for solar energy became a bottleneck for this project, the Government responded by facilitating the growth of a domestic solar market. As a result, China managed to install over 130 GW of solar capacity by 2017. This exceeded by 24 per cent, and three years ahead of schedule, the Government's solar installation target of 105 GW by 2020 (Finamore, 2018). Primarily as a result of this and related initiatives by Chinese policymakers, the average global price of solar panels has also fallen by about 80 per cent since 2009.

China has been active in financing clean energy investments in developing economies through its Belt and Road Initiative, including in collaboration with international partners.[28] By contrast, the G7 economies did not commit to significantly raising their own global green financing commitments at their 2021 Cornwall meeting in the United Kingdom.[29]

China has also implemented extensive programs for transitioning workers out of the fossil fuel industry and into other occupations. In 2016, it was estimated that roughly 1.8 million coal and steel industry workers needed to be relocated into other occupations when various coal and steel operations were closed. China's central Government announced in February 2016 a series of policy measures to support the reemployment for laid-off workers including an earmarked fiscal package of 100 billion RMB (about 15.4 billion USD).[30]

In short, China has successfully mounted a highly ambitious set of industrial and financial policies to move its economy onto a viable climate stabilization path. At the same time, China is likely to remain as the primary source of global $CO_2$ emissions over the next 20 to 30 years unless it substantially accelerates its emissions reduction program.

For different reasons, China, the United States and the European Union all need to mount significantly more ambitious climate stabilization programs in order for their respective initiatives to provide the necessary leadership for achieving the IPCC's emission reduction targets. In particular, these economic blocks need to commit higher levels of public investment to the global clean energy investment project. Of course, policies to induce private clean energy investments are also critical. But, as with private investment activity more generally, there will inevitably be high levels of uncertainty associated with achieving the increases in private investment at the scale necessary to reach a viable global climate stabilization path.

A basic constraint with increasing public investment is how to find significantly greater sources of public funding. The need to raise additional public revenues through more progressive tax systems, should be considered in all countries, conscious of local demands and pressures. But in fact, most of the funds needed to bring global clean energy investments to scale can be made available without a significant increase in taxes, by channelling resources from other sources, including:

- Transferring funds out of military budgets;

- Eliminating fossil fuel subsidies and transferring a significant proportion of these funds into clean energy investments;

- Mounting large-scale green bond purchasing programs by the United States Federal Reserve, the European Central Bank, and the People's Bank of China.

- Leveraging the lending power of public development banks, at the national, regional and international levels

A great deal of analysis and program design will, no doubt, need to be accomplished in order to make these proposals workable, and with countries opting for different mixtures of these potential sources of finance.[31] But one critical starting point for this work will be to raise levels of cooperation between China, the United States and the European Union, both on specifics of public financing for clean energy investments as well as more generally across all aspects of the global climate stabilization project.

## E. Towards a new economic settlement

Speculating on the future direction of economic policy after Covid-19 is complicated by the extemporaneous nature of the response to the pandemic in many countries, as well as the high degree of uncertainty at the current juncture. Moreover, the global financial crisis stands as a warning that directions taken under the pressures of a particularly stressful moment may not persist once those pressures ease.

Under the circumstances, it is perhaps not surprising that a good deal of attention has been given to the actions and pronouncements of the new Administration in the United States with some already anticipating "the dawn of a new economic era" (Tooze, 2021) and others a "new variant" of capitalism (Elliot, 2021).

The President's Council of Economic Advisors (2021) has been forthright in acknowledging the need for a policy reset both to fix the damage caused by past policies and to address new challenges:

For the past four decades, the view that lower taxes, less spending, and fewer regulations would generate stronger economic growth has exerted substantial influence on United States public policy. Over this period, the United States has underinvested in public goods such as infrastructure and innovation, and gains from growth have accrued disproportionately to the top of the income and wealth distribution.

The economic theory underlying President Biden's American Jobs Plan and American Families Plan is different. These proposed policies reflect the empirical evidence that a strong economy depends on a solid foundation of public investment, and that investments in workers, families, and communities can pay off for decades to come.

A nascent break with past policy prescriptions – and the emergence of a new consensus (Sandbu, 2021) – is detectable in the multilateral financial institutions, with their endorsement of big spending programmes, taxing the rich and curtailing the market power of big business (Georgieva et al., 2021), their acknowledgement that capital flows need to be more effectively managed including, under some circumstances, through capital controls (Adrian and Gopinath, 2020) and their endorsement of a strongly interventionist policy agenda to backstop a green investment push (IMF, 2020). Another bastion of neo-liberal policy thinking, the OECD, has also encouraged its members to spend big and protect jobs (Giles, 2021) and has recognized that socially inclusive and cohesive outcomes will require "a fundamental reappraisal of the relationship between state, society, the economy and the environment" (OECD, 2021b).

Others, however, have warned that the death of neo-liberalism is exaggerated (Galbraith, 2021), stressing its adaptability to changing circumstances (Slobodian, 2021) and pointing to new strains that will extend the power and influence of under regulated financial markets (Gabor, 2021). Some have also pointed to the policy continuities attached to the lending programmes of multilateral financial institutions during the pandemic (Ortiz and Cummings, 2021) and by the call from G7 trade ministers for deeper liberalization and a further narrowing of policy space (Davies et al., 2021). A greener variant of neo-liberalism has also been observed determined to ensure that the transition to a low-carbon high-digital future remains market-centred and capital-friendly by getting the price of carbon right, promoting a new generation of financing instruments that abide by ESG standards, greening corporate social responsibility and harnessing the wealth of billionaires and the power of big data to save the planet.

To date, most of the talk of a new consensus has been delivered by voices from the North and often with an eye on the 10-point policy checklist synthesized into the previously mentioned "Washington Consensus". While Williamson never endorsed all the policy recommendations enshrined in that Consensus, he did support its claim that there was no alternative to "outward-oriented market economies subject to macroeconomic discipline" (Williamson, 1993) and its underlying mission to abandon the "intellectual apartheid" that had restricted the application of some policies to particular categories of countries (Williamson, 2004).

Whatever the record of this one size fits all policy agenda, it is not the approach needed by policy makers facing the multiple and intertwining challenges that will shape development outcomes over the coming decade. If there is to be a genuine break with the past 40 years, governments must not only confront the vested interests that have built up considerable economic and political capital from the skewed distribution patterns under hyperglobalization but also acknowledge the deep structural constraints and vulnerabilities that have continued to obstruct sustainable growth and development prospects. Doing so will have to allow for greater flexibilities in the setting of policy priorities by developing countries and ensure sufficient policy space for the measures needed to manage ambitious goals and resulting trade-offs, along with differential treatment in support of their efforts to mobilize the resources needed to pursue the 2030 Agenda.

That said, the Covid-19 crisis has already opened the door to taboo breaking approaches to policy making that could help countries, at all levels of development, navigate towards a better future. These would include a recognition that:

1. *Governments are not households*. The Covid 19 crisis has not only seen advanced country governments spend on an unprecedented scale it has forced them to abandon the idea that budgets should always be balanced and instead to embrace, whether implicitly or explicitly, a functional approach to government finance which allows governments to spend first and tax later, and under certain conditions to spend solely with state-issued money (*TDR 2020*). Recognizing this opens up a discussion on the determinants of fiscal space, particularly in developing countries, where external factors have a much greater influence on the spending capacity of governments and where reforms to the multilateral financial institutions, as well to the domestic tax system, can help provide greater room for both counter-cyclical and social expenditures.

2. Revisiting *Central Bank independence*. Central banks have, since the last crisis, moved away from a singular focus on inflation targeting into economic fire-fighting through their balance sheet operations. This approach has continued in the current crisis including, in some cases, direct lending to the private sector. Accepting that Central Banks are the lynchpin of a credit making machine, necessarily extends their regulatory authority, including over the shadow

banking system, taming boom-bust credit cycles and more broadly extends their risk horizon to include wider threats to financial stability, such as from climate change and rising inequality. Given such wider responsibilities, greater democratic oversight is appropriate.

3. *Resilience is a public good.* The idea that "no one is safe until everyone is safe" clearly extends to challenges beyond the immediate health crisis and while some elites appear desperate to find ways to isolate themselves from economic, health and environmental shocks, Covid-19 has reinforced the idea that resilience is a public good, in the sense that it is both non-excludable and non-rivalrous, and one with global dimensions. Resilience is, no doubt, the responsibility of the state, delivered through a robust public sector with the resources to make the necessary investments, provide the complementary services and coordinate the multiple activities that building resilience involves. Countries need universal systems of basic services and social protection, but this imperative also raises specific challenges for developing countries over how to adapt the goals of a developmental state to the challenges, including financial challenges, posed by protecting citizens against shocks. In this respect, funding world-wide resilience will require new and ambitious thinking on the mobilization and dispersion of financial resources.

4. *Finance is too important to be left to markets.* Wall Street, and its counterparts elsewhere, has not been good at providing long-term, affordable finance even as its indulgence of speculative excess has undermined resilience at country and community levels; rates of capital formation have been too low in many countries and at all levels of development. Equally, the willingness to allow parts of the financial system to operate in the shadows, beyond regulatory oversight, has proved damaging, along with the discredited idea that they are disposed to regulate themselves. A financial system that accords a more significant role to public banks, breaks up and guards against the emergence of megabanks, and exercises stronger regulatory oversight is less likely to generate speculative excesses and more likely to deliver a healthier investment climate.

5. *Minimizing wages is bad for business.* The idea, grounded in microeconomic logic, that

wages are no more than a cost of production has underpinned the drive to make labour markets as flexible as possible. But not only are wages a critical source of demand, their growth can stimulate productivity. Moreover, decent wages are a key component of a strong social contract. Consequently, healthy labour markets require that wages are embedded in robust arrangements of voice and representation and supported through minimum wage and related labour legislation that provides appropriate protection against abusive practices. In the case of developing countries, where underemployment remains an abiding feature of the labour market, targeting measures to tackle informality is of particular importance.

6. *Diversification matters.* No country has made the difficult journey from rural underdevelopment to post-industrial prosperity without employing targeted and selective government policies that seek to shift the production structure towards new sources of growth. The stalled industrial transition in much of the developing world, or worse still "premature deindustrialization", has reinforced their peripheral position in the international division of labour, left them more vulnerable to external shocks and perpetuated high levels of informality. Industrial policies are even more urgent where meeting the climate and digital challenges imply structural and technological leaps and a just transition requires the effective management of stranded activities that ensures new jobs are created in the right locations.

7. *A caring society is a more stable society.* The question of care work is becoming an integral part of any policy agenda for recovering better including transforming paid care work into decent work with the wage levels, benefits and security typically associated with industrial jobs in the core sector of the labour market. But more generally, the design of proactive transformational social policy must go beyond offering simply a residual category of safety nets or floors designed to stop those left behind from falling further. Effectively designed social policies can also be used to accelerate and manage structural transformation, helping to foster technological upgrading and productivity gains underscoring the importance of an integrated approach to policy making for recovering better.

It is clear, as argued more forcefully in previous *Reports*, that policy programmes that build on these broad precepts will need a supportive multilateral system if they are to succeed, with a set of guiding principles aimed at ensuring "prosperity for all" by providing the space for necessary actions at the national level and galvanising global support for collective actions that rest on cooperation across all countries.

The call for reform of the multilateral system, made four decades ago in the first *Trade and Development*

*Report*, to avert an impending development crisis, went unheeded. The imbalances, inequities and insecurities that were beginning to emerge in 1981 have since, with the unleashing of the furies of hyperglobalization, spread further and deeper so that today's crises are now truly global in their reach and impact. With debt levels having risen exponentially over the last four decades, and again during the pandemic, and the climate edging ever closer to a catastrophic tipping point, the urgency of reforming the system has become fiercer than ever.

# Notes

1   It was, of course, also the message of the international New Dealers at Bretton Woods, typified by Morgenthau's recognition that "the Bretton Woods approach is based on the realization that it is to the economic and political advantage of countries such as India and China, and alos of countries such as England and the United States, that the industrialization and betterment of living conditions in the former be achieved with the aid and encouragement of the latter", Morgenthau, 1945.

2   On the intellectual, bureaucratic and political origins of neo-liberalism and its evolution, see Mudge, 2008.

3   While the term was coined by the World Bank in 1981, its more widespread use stems from the establishment of an Emerging Markets Index by the investment bank Morgan Stanley in the late 1980s.

4   The rapid rise of the private capital industry with assets under management of over $7 trillion in 2020, a more than three-fold increase in the decade after the GFC, was indicative of this trend, see Wigglesworth, 2021.

5   The UN Global Policy Model (GPM) is an empirical modelling framework for the analysis of domestic and global interactions between economic variables and policy stances, based on econometric casual-effect relations and a tight stock/flow world accounting framework (https://unctad.org/debt-and-finance/gpm).

6   By design, an economic or financial crisis was not modelled, even though financial fragilities and economic vulnerabilities are clearly emerging that can resemble conditions that triggered crises in the past.

7   This will not mean that government debt ratios will necessarily fall by these means.

8   As with fiscal policy, the scenario has given due consideration to calls to wage protection, job promotion and income support made in some of the

same countries where also a softer approach to fiscal austerity seems to emerge. But as before, the analysis of what is actually in the recipes is, at best, consistent with the view that at some point wage shares may stop from falling but will not significantly rise to catch up with the declining trend.

9   Like with fiscal tightening to reduce debt burdens, the prescription tends to fail, especially on a global scale (Capaldo and Izurieta, 2013).

10   To generate the figure for total external assets, the accounts of financial derivatives were included in net terms. Not doing so would have increased the levels significantly but not changed the trend in a meaningful way.

11   See also Akyüz, 2021.

12   Current account surplus, finance-unconstrained economies include the European Union and other economies of Western Europe, Israel, Japan and the Republic of Korea. Current account deficit, finance-unconstrained economies include Australia, Canada, New Zealand, United Kingdom, and the United States of America. Current account surplus, finance-constrained economies include major developing economies of East Asia (excluding China), of Western Asia (excluding Israel) and the Russian Federation. Current account deficit, finance-constrained economies include all other developing economies.

13   See Chapter I, Box 1.1.

14   This observation resonates with the accounts of the period of buildup of 'petrodollars' during the 1970s and early 1980s, overborrowing and capital flights, especially in commodity and oil exporters (Vos, 1989).

15   As explained in the previous section.

16   It was less visible in earlier episodes where such set of policies were implemented.

17   This includes an agreed bipartisan plan of $1 trillion on physical infrastructure and an additional

$3.5 trillion budget proposal on limited physical infrastructure, childcare, paid leave, health services, and climate-related investments. At the time of writing, the fate of the budget proposal is not yet clear.

18  Since then, most of the leading countries save the United States have abandoned the system of passive taxation (Matheson et al., 2013). Among the major OECD countries only the United States and the Netherlands hold on to the principle of resident taxation – although even that is in some doubt (Avi-Yonah, 2019).

19  Recent studies include IEA (2021), IRENA (2021), Pollin (2020) and, specifically for the U.S., Williams et al., 2020.

20  https://www.whitehouse.gov/briefing-room/statements-releases/2021/04/22/executive-summary-u-s-international-climate-finance-plan/.

21  The energy efficiency estimate is from: https://energyefficiencyimpact.org/. The renewable energy figure is at https://www.bloomberg.com/graphics/climate-change-data-green/investment.html

22  https://www.c2es.org/document/us-state-carbon-pricing-policies/.

23  https://ec.europa.eu/info/strategy/priorities-2019-2024/european-green-deal_en.

24  https://ec.europa.eu/info/publications/delivering-european-green-deal_en.

25  It is still notable that the most current public spending proposal is significantly higher than what had been budgeted previously. Thus, in 2020, the EC projected a total budget of €1 trillion over 2021–2030 for everything, including clean energy investments as well as just transition programs. This included funding from all public and private sources, with about half of the money coming from the EU budget, and the other half provided by a combination of national governments and private investments (https://ec.europa.eu/commission/presscorner/detail/en/qanda_20_24).

26  https://reader.elsevier.com/reader/sd/pii/S0306261921003962?token=898AD8E008D-08C848C1C66228819C4FDE743799A3B9A66 947B82EAB740587B680DE3E2DB11EE3DF96 AE99ACA78C1BB5C&originRegion=us-east-1 &originCreation=20210715214704.

27  https://www.ft.com/content/5e1e5ba5-5b95-445d-9de6-034ad3568d2f

28  In 2018, China and the United Kingdom jointly launched the Green Investment Principles (GIP) for the Belt and Road Initiative.

29  https://www.carbonbrief.org/daily-brief/g7-reaffirmed-goals-but-failed-to-provide-funds-needed-to-reach-them-experts-say.

30  http://www.xinhuanet.com/fortune/caiyan/ksh/137.htm

31  Pollin (2020); see also *TDR 2019*.

# References

Adrian T and Gopinath G (2020). Toward an Integrated Policy Framework for open economies. 13 July. Available at https://blogs.imf.org/2020/07/13/toward-an-integrated-policy-framework-for-open-economies.

Akyüz Y (2021). External balance sheets of emerging economies: Low-yielding assets, high-yielding liabilities. *Review of Keynesian Economics*. 9(2): 232–252.

Avi-Yonah RS (2019). Globalization, tax competition and the fiscal crisis of the welfare state: A Twentieth Anniversary retrospective. Presented at the Taxation and Globalization: A Research Workshop. IDC. Herzliya.

Barbosa-Filho NH and Izurieta A (2020). The risk of a second wave of post-crisis frailty in the world economy. *International Journal of Political Economy*. 49(4): 278–303.

Bernanke B (2004). Remarks by Governor Ben S. Bernanke at the meetings of the Eastern Economic Association. Washington, D.C. 20 February. Available at https://www.federalreserve.gov/boarddocs/speeches/2004/20040220/.

Bhaduri A, Raghavendra S and Guttal V (2015). On the systemic fragility of finance-led growth. *Metroeconomica*. 66(1): 158–186.

BIS (Bank of International Settlements) (2021). *Annual Economic Report*. Basel.

Blair T (2005). Conference speech, Labour Party Conference. 27 September.

Blanchard O, Cerutti E and Summers L (2015). Inflation and activity: Two explorations and their monetary implications. Working Paper No. 21726. National Bureau of Economic Research.

Camdessus M (1997). "Global capital flows: Raising the returns and reducing the risks", speech at World Affairs Council of Los Angeles. 17 June. Available at https://www.imf.org/en/News/Articles/2015/09/28/04/53/spmds9709.

Capaldo J (2015). The Trans-Atlantic Trade and Investment Partnership: European disintegration, unemployment and instability. *Economia e Lavoro*. 49(2): 35–56.

Capaldo J and Izurieta A (2013). The imprudence of labour market flexibilization in a fiscally austere world. *International Labour Review.* 152(1): 1–26.

Capaldo J and Ömer Ö (2021). Trading away industrialization: Context and prospects of the EU-MERCOSUR Agreement. Working Paper No. 52. Global Economic Governance Initiative.

Cobham A (2021). G20 could improve on "one-sided" global tax reform. *Financial Times.* 11 June.

Cobham A, Faccio T, Garcia-Bernardo J, Janský P, Kadet J and Picciotto S (2021). A practical proposal to end corporate tax abuse: METR, a minimum effective tax rate for multinationals. Working Papers No. 8. Institute of Economic Studies (IES).

Costantini O (2015). The cyclically adjusted budget: History and exegesis of a fateful estimate. Working Paper No. 24. Institute for New Economic Thinking.

Costantini O and Seccareccia M (2020). Income distribution, household debt and growth in modern financialized economies. *Journal of Economic Issues.* 54(2): 444–453.

Council of Economic Advisors (2021). Building Back Better: The American Jobs Plan and the American Families Plan. *Issues Brief.* May.

Damgaard J, Elkjaer T and Johannesen N (2019). The rise of phantom investments: Empty corporate shells in tax havens undermine tax collection in advanced, emerging market, and developing economies. *Finance & Development.* 56(3):11–13.

Davies R, Banga R, Kozul-Wright R, Gallogly-Swan K, and Capaldo J (2021). Reforming the International Trading System for recovery, resilience, and inclusive. Research Paper No. 65. UNCTAD.

de Wilde M (2021). Is there a leak in the OECD's Global Minimum Tax Proposals (GLOBE, Pillar Two)? Kluwer International Tax Blog. 1 March. Available at http://kluwertaxblog.com/2021/03/01/is-there-a-leak-in-the-oecds-global-minimum-tax-proposals-globe-pillar-two/.

Delatte AL, Guillin A and Vicard V (2020). Grey zones in global finance: The distorted geography of cross-border investments. Working Paper No. 2020–07. Centre d'Etudes Prospectives et d'Informations Internationales.

Devereux M and Simmler M (2021). Who will pay Amount A? EconPol Policy Brief No. 36. Available at https://www.econpol.eu/publications/policy_brief_36.

Dow S (2017). Central banking in the twenty-first century. *Cambridge Journal of Economics.* 41(6): 1539–1557.

Elliot L (2021). During the pandemic, a new variant of capitalism has emerged. *The Guardian.* 30 July.

Epstein G (2019). *The Political Economy of Central Banking: Contested Control and the Power of Finance, Selected Essays of Gerald Epstein.* Edward Elgar Publishing. Chelthenham.

Fair Tax Mark (2019). The Silicon Six and their $100 billion global tax gap. Available at https://fairtaxmark.net/wp-content/uploads/2019/12/Silicon-Six-Report-5-12-19.pdf.

Ferreira FHG (2021). Inequality in the time of Covid-19. *Finance and Development.* 58(2): 20–23.

Finamore B (2018). *Will China Save the Planet?* John Wiley and Sons. New York.

*Financial Times* (2021). Washington vs Big Tech: Lina Kahn's battle to transform US antitrust. 10 August.

Fukuyama F (1992). *The End of History and the Last Man.* Free Press. New York.

G7 (1981). Declaration of the Ottawa Summit. 21 July. Available at http://www.g7.utoronto.ca/summit/1981ottawa/communique/index.html

G20 (2009). London Summit – Leaders' Statement. 2 April. Available at https://www.imf.org/external/np/sec/pr/2009/pdf/g20_040209.pdf.

G20 (2021). Third Finance Ministers and Central Bank Governors meeting, 9-10 July – Communiqué. Available at: https://www.g20.org/wp-content/uploads/2021/07/Communique-Third-G20-FMC-BG-meeting-9-10-July-2021.pdf.

Gabor D (2021). The Wall Street Consensus. *Development and Change.* 52(3): 429–459.

Galbraith JK (2021). The death of neoliberalism is greatly exaggerated. *Foreign Policy.* 6 April.

Galbraith JK (2008). *The Predator State: How Conservatives Abandoned the Free Market and Why Liberals Should Too.* Free Press. New York.

Georgieva K, Díez FJ, Duval R and Schwarz D (2021). Rising market power—A threat to the recovery? 15 March. Available at https://blogs.imf.org/2019/04/03/how-to-keep-corporate-power-in-check.

Giles C (2021). OECD warns governments to rethink constraints on public spending. *Financial Times.* 4 January.

Godley W and Lavoie M (2007). *Monetary Economics: An Integrated Approach to Credit, Money, Income, Production, and Wealth.* Palgrave Macmillan. Basingstoke.

Gould E and Kandra J (2021). Wages grew in 2020 because the bottom fell out of the low-wage labor market: The State of Working America 2020 wages report. Economic Policy Institute. Washington D.C.

Greenspan A (2005). Risk Transfer and Financial Stability Remarks to the Federal Reserve Bank of Chicago's Forty-first Annual Conference on Bank Structure, Chicago, Illinois. 5 May.

IEA (2021). *Net Zero by 2050.* Available at https://www.iea.org/reports/net-zero-by-2050.

IMF (2020). World Economic Outlook 2020: A Long and Difficult Ascent. October. Washington D.C. International Monetary Fund.

IPCC (2021). AR6 climate change 2021: The physical science basis. Sixth Assessment Report. Available at https://www.ipcc.ch/report/ar6/wg1/.

IRENA (2021). *World Energy Transitions Outlook.* Available at https://irena.org/publications/2021/March/World-Energy-Transitions-Outlook.

Izurieta A, Kohler P and Pizarro J (2018). Financialization, trade, and investment agreements: Through the looking glass or through the realities of income distribution and government policy. Working Paper No. 18-02. UNCTAD and Global Development and Environment Institute.

Jayadev A and Konczal M (2010). When is austerity right?: In boom, not bust. *Challenge.* 53(6): 37–53.

Kohler P and Cripps F (2018). Do trade and investment (agreements) foster development or inequality? Working Paper No. 18-03. Global Development and Environment Institute.

Krogstrup S and Oman W (2019). Macroeconomic and financial policies for climate change mitigation: A review of the literature. Working Paper No. WP/19/185. International Monetary Fund.

Lavoie M and Seccareccia M (2017). Editorial to the special issue: The political economy of the New Fiscalism. *European Journal of Economics and Economic Policies: Intervention.* 14(3): 291–295.

Lucas RE Jr (2003). Macroeconomic priorities. *The American Economic Review.* 93(1):1–14.

Matheson T, Perry VJ and Veung C (2013). Territorial vs. worldwide corporate taxation: Implications for developing countries. Working Paper No. WP/13/205. International Monetary Fund.

Matthews D (2021). The big drop in American poverty during the pandemic, explained. *Vox.* 11 August.

McCombie JSL and Thirlwall AP (1994). *Economic Growth and the Balance-of-Payments Constraint.* Palgrave Macmillan. Basingstoke.

Minsky H (1982). *Can "It" Happen Again? Essays on Instability and Finance.* Routledge. New York.

Morgenthau H (1945). Bretton Woods and international cooperation. *Foreign Affairs.* 23(2): 182–194.

Mudge SL (2008). What is neo-liberalism? *Socio-Economic Review.* 6(4): 703–731.

Nesvetailova A (2007). *Fragile Finance: Debt, Speculation and Crisis in the Age of Global Credit.* Palgrave Macmillan. Basingstoke.

Nye JS (1992). What new world order? *Foreign Affairs.* 71(2): 83–96.

OECD (2021a). *OECD Secretary-General Tax Report to G20 Finance Ministers and Central Bank Governors.* OECD Publishing. Paris. Available at https://oecd.org/tax/oecd-secretary-general-tax-report-g20-finance-ministers-july-2021.pdf.

OECD (2021b). *Perspectives on Global Development 2021: From Protest to Progress?* Organisation for Economic Co-operation and Development. Paris.

Ortiz I and Cummings M (2021). Global austerity alert: Looming budget cuts in 2021–2025 and alternative pathways. Working Paper. Initiative for Policy Dialogue.

Parolin Z, Collyer S, Curran MA, and Wimer C (2021). The potential poverty reduction effect of the American Rescue Plan. Poverty and Social Policy Fact Sheet. 11 March. Center on Poverty and Social Policy.

Phillips R, Pyle J and Palan R (2021). The Amazon method: How to take advantage of the international state system to avoid paying tax. Available at https://left.eu/amazon-method-of-tax-dodging-exposed-in-new-research/.

Picciotto S, Kadet JM, Cobham A, Faccio T, Garcia-Bernardo J and Janský P (2021). For a Better GLOBE: A minimum effective tax rate for multinationals. *Tax Notes International.* 101: 863–868.

Pollin R (2020). An Industrial Policy Framework to Advance a Global Green New Deal. Available at https://www.oxfordhandbooks.com/view/10.1093/oxfordhb/9780198862420.001.0001/oxfordhb-9780198862420-e-16.

Sandbu M (2021). A new Washington Consensus. *Financial Times.* 11 April.

Shaxson N (2019). Tackling tax havens. *Finance and Development.* 56(3): 6–10.

Slobodian Q (2021). Is neoliberalism really dead? *New Statesman.* 27 October.

Storm S and Naastepad CWM (2012). *Macroeconomics Beyond the NAIRU.* Harvard University Press. Cambridge, MA.

Taylor L (2020). *Macroeconomic Inequality from Reagan to Trump: Market Power, Wage Repression, Asset Price Inflation, and Industrial Decline.* Cambridge University Press. Cambridge.

Tooze A (2021). Biden's stimulus is the dawn of a new economic era. *Foreign Policy.* 5 March.

Tooze A (2020). Did Xi just save the world. *Foreign Policy.* 25 September.

UNCTAD (*TDR 1981*). *Trade and Development Report 1981.* (United Nations publication. Sales No. E.81.II.D.9. New York).

UNCTAD (*TDR 1982*). *Trade and Development Report 1982.* (United Nations publication. Sales No. E.82.II.D.12. New York).

UNCTAD (*TDR 1984*). *Trade and Development Report 1984*. (United Nations publication. Sales No. E.84.II.D.23. New York).

UNCTAD (*TDR 1986*). *Trade and Development Report 1986*. (United Nations publication. Sales No. E.86.II.D.5. New York).

UNCTAD (*TDR 1989*). *Trade and Development Report 1989*. (United Nations publication. Sales No. E.89.II.D.14. New York).

UNCTAD (*TDR 1993*). *Trade and Development Report 1993*. (United Nations publication. Sales No. E.93.II.D.10. New York and Geneva).

UNCTAD (*TDR 1994*). *Trade and Development Report 1994*. (United Nations publication. Sales No. E.94.II.D.26. New York and Geneva).

UNCTAD (*TDR 1995*). *Trade and Development Report 1995*. (United Nations publication. Sales No. E.95.II.D.16. New York and Geneva).

UNCTAD (*TDR 1996*). *Trade and Development Report 1996*. (United Nations publication. Sales No. E.96.II.D.6. New York and Geneva).

UNCTAD (*TDR 1997*). *Trade and Development Report 1997: Globalization, Distribution and Growth.* (United Nations publication. Sales No. E.97.II.D.8. New York and Geneva).

UNCTAD (*TDR 1999*). *Trade and Development Report 1999: Fragile Recovery and Risks; Trade, Finance and Growth.* (United Nations publication. Sales No. E.99.II.D.1. New York and Geneva).

UNCTAD (*TDR 2000*). *Trade and Development Report 2000: Global Economic Growth and Imbalances.* (United Nations publication. Sales No. E.00.II.D.19. New York and Geneva).

UNCTAD (*TDR 2002*). *Trade and Development Report 2002: Developing Countries in World Trade.* (United Nations publication. Sales No. E.02.II.D.2. New York and Geneva).

UNCTAD (*TDR 2003*). *Trade and Development Report 2003: Capital Accumulation, Growth and Structural Change.* (United Nations publication. Sales No. E.03.II.D.7. New York and Geneva).

UNCTAD (*TDR 2007*). *Trade and Development Report 2007: Regional Cooperation for Development.* (United Nations publication. Sales No. E.07.II.D.11. New York and Geneva).

UNCTAD (*TDR 2011*). *Trade and Development Report 2011: Post-crisis Policy Challenges in the World Economy* (United Nations publication. Sales No. E.11.II.D.3. New York and Geneva).

UNCTAD (*TDR 2012*). *Trade and Development Report 2012: Policies for Inclusive and Balanced Growth.* (United Nations publication. Sales No. E.12.II.D.6. New York and Geneva).

UNCTAD (*TDR 2013*). *Trade and Development Report 2013: Adjusting to the Changing Dynamics of the World Economy.* (United Nations publication. Sales No. E.13.II.D.3. New York and Geneva).

UNCTAD (*TDR 2014*). *Trade and Development Report 2014: Global Governance and Policy Space for Development.* (United Nations publication. Sales No. E.14.II.D.4. New York and Geneva).

UNCTAD (*TDR 2015*). *Trade and Development Report,2015: Making the International Financial Architecture Work for Development.* (United Nations publication. Sales No. E.15.II.D.4. New York and Geneva).

UNCTAD (*TDR 2016*). *Trade and Development Report 2016: Structural Transformation for Inclusive and Sustained Growth.* (United Nations publication. Sales No. E.16.II.D.5. New York and Geneva).

UNCTAD (*TDR 2017*). *Trade and Development Report, 2017: Beyond Austerity – Towards a Global New Deal.* (United Nations publication. Sales No. E.17.II.D.5. New York and Geneva).

UNCTAD (*TDR 2018*). *Trade and Development Report, 2018: Power, Platforms and the Free Trade Delusion.* (United Nations publication. Sales No. E.18.II.D.7. New York and Geneva).

UNCTAD (*TDR 2019*). *Trade and Development Report, 2019: Financing a Global Green New Deal.* (United Nations publication. Sales No. E.19.II.D.15. Geneva).

UNCTAD (*TDR 2020*). *Trade and Development Report 2020: From global pandemic to prosperity for all: avoiding another lost decade. (*United Nations publication. Sales No. E.20.II.D.30. Geneva).

UNDP (1990). *Human Development Report.* United Nations Development Programme. New York.

UNEP (2021). *Are We Building Back Better? Evidence from 2020 and Pathways to Inclusive Green Recovery Spending.* United Nations Environment Programme. Nairobi.

Volker PA (1978). The Political Economy of the Dollar. The Fred Hirsch lecture sponsored by the Fred Hirsch Memorial Committee at Warwick University. Coventry. 9 November.

Vos R (1989). Ecuador: Windfall gains, unbalanced growth and stabilization.. In: FitzGerald EVK & Vos R eds. *Financing Economic Development: A Structural Approach to Monetary Policy.* Gower. Aldershot:187-232.

Wigglesworth R (2021). Private capital industry soars beyond $7tn. *Financial Times.* 11 June.

Williams J, Jones R and Farbes J (2020). Technology Pathways to net-zero. Available at https://irp-cdn.multiscreensite.com/6f2c9f57/files/uploaded/zero-carbon-action-plan-ch-02.pdf.

Williamson J (1990). What Washington means by policy reform. In: Williamson J ed. *Latin American Adjustment: How Much Has Happened?* Institute for International Economics. Washington, D.C.:7–20.

Williamson J (1993). Democracy and the "Washington Consensus". *World Development.* 21(8): 1329–1336.

Williamson J (2004). The Washington Consensus as policy prescription for development. A lecture in the series Practitioners of Development delivered at the World Bank. 13 January. Available at https://www.piie.com/publications/papers/williamson0204.pdf.

# Annex

**FIGURE 2.A.1** **Stock and housing appreciations in selected countries, first quarter 2000 to first quarter 2021**
*(Real price index, 2010q1 =100)*

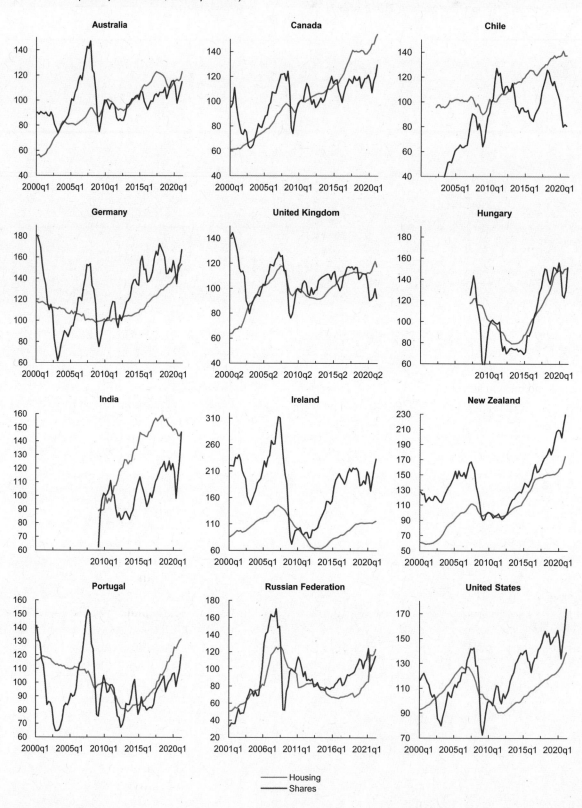

**Source:** OECD data.

# IT'S THE END OF THE WORLD AS WE KNOW IT: SURVEYING THE ADAPTATION LANDSCAPE

## A. Introduction

July 2021 was the hottest month ever recorded on the planet, following on from the hottest year in 2020 which, itself, came after the hottest decade on record. Intense heatwaves, increasingly powerful tropical cyclones, prolonged droughts, rising sea levels, spreading diseases are just some of the threats accompanying the unrelenting rise in global temperatures, bringing with them ever greater economic damage and human suffering. And worse is to come. Even if we get our mitigation efforts together within this decade and manage to keep the global average temperature rise to 1.5°C above pre-industrial levels by the year 2100, the extreme climate events in 2021 serve as a foretaste of what an additional 0.4°C to the average global temperature has in store for communities and countries across the planet.

On current trends, global heating will trigger tipping points in the Earth's natural systems, leading to irreversible changes that will reshape life in this century (IPCC, 2021). Even assuming economic collapse can be avoided, the loss of output over coming decades will be significant everywhere, but particularly in the developing world (SwissRe, 2021); hundreds of millions of people will be forced to move within and across borders (Rigaud et al., 2018) with large parts of the tropical world outside the limits of human adaptation (Zhang et al., 2021); food production will change dramatically (Kumar et al., 2021); access to ever scarcer sources of fresh water will trigger increasing geo-political tensions (WEF, 2019). In short, barring intense action to curb greenhouse gas (GHG) emissions, parts of the planet will simply become uninhabitable for future generations (Wallace-Wells, 2018).

To date, the global policy response to the climate crisis has been divided between mitigation and adaptation measures. *Climate mitigation* focuses on slowing down and reducing emissions of greenhouse gases (GHG), through a mixture of more efficient energy use and the replacement of fossil fuels with renewable sources of energy. *Climate adaptation* centers on harnessing resilience and protection mechanisms to minimize the negative impact of climate change on lives and livelihoods (Ge et al., 2009). While, in practice, the two sets of measures are often difficult to separate, in much of the agenda-setting discussion on climate, adaption has remained a poor cousin of mitigation efforts. This is proving short-sighted and increasingly costly, particularly for developing countries.

The consequences of continued neglect have become more apparent in the aftermath of the health pandemic as talk has turned to building resilience in the face of a global shock. Up until now, climate adaptation policies have been driven by a mixture of the procedural politics surrounding climate conferences, a technocratic approach to policy design and an undue faith in the efficiency of markets to price the way to a sustainable future. The aim has been to meet internationally agreed targets through a better assessment of climate-related risks and their improved management using insurance and other market-based mechanisms. While this approach has yielded some positive results, it has offered too little, too late and no longer stands up to the scale of environmental shocks and the economic damage they are causing.

The chapter is structured as follows. Section B takes account of the measure of the challenge, focusing on the damage to regions and countries around the world and the scale of investment required to meet it. Section C discusses some of the limits of the existing institutional architecture to manage the adaptation challenge. Section D considers how framing the adaptation challenge as one of risk management distracts from the need to position adaptation measures in the context of economic transformation.

# B. Measuring up to the adaptation challenge[1]

The economic impact of climate change comes both through a steady deterioration in the environmental conditions required for everyday life, such as access to water, air quality, and tolerable working temperatures, as well as through shocks that are more temporary in nature, such as wildfires, storms and floods, albeit often with more immediate and devastating consequences. The latter are, arguably, easier to gauge and have certainly garnered more attention. According to the United Nations Office for Disaster Risk Reduction Human Costs of Disaster Report, between 2000 and 2019, 7,348 major recorded disaster events claimed 1.23 million lives, affected 4.2 billion people (many on more than one occasion) with global economic losses totaling $2.97 trillion (CRED and UNDRR, 2020). The numbers are clearly on a rising trend (Figure 3.1).

These disasters cannot be solely attributed to a changing climate. Still, there is no doubting a strong

**FIGURE 3.1** **Disaster impacts 2000–2019 relative to 1980–1999**

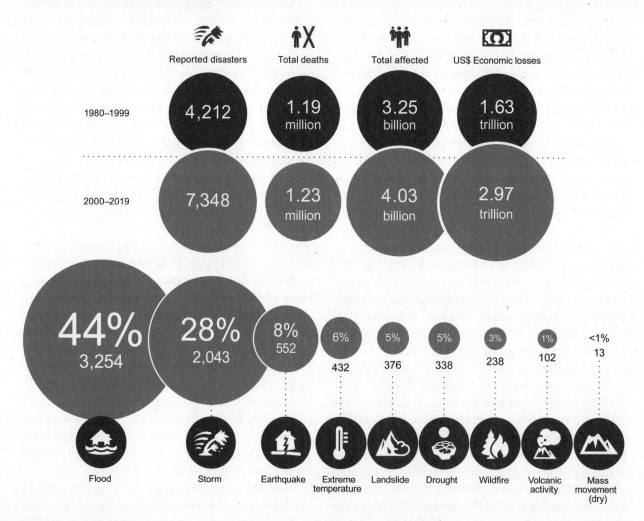

*Source:* CRED and UNDRR 2020.

connection to their increasingly devastating impact (IPCC, 2021).

Emergency Events Database (EM-DAT) data show that storms cost more than any other disaster type in terms of recorded economic damage ($1.39 trillion), followed by floods ($651 billion). In 2020 alone, more than 50 million people were impacted by flooding, droughts and storms (UNEP, 2020). About three-quarter of climate-induced disasters were attributable to floods and storms while heatwaves are becoming more intense and widespread, inducing costs to large swathes of populations in developed and developing countries. Major monsoon floods and tropical cyclones affected more than 2.2 million people in China and 9.6 million in South Asia, including Nepal, India and Bangladesh that cost more than $20 billion in damage across these areas. At the regional level, economic losses in the Americas accounted for 45 per cent of the total losses, followed by Asia (43 per cent) between 2000 and 2019. In the Americas, the U.S. accounts for 78 per cent of total losses with $1.03 trillion in economic losses over the same period, reflecting higher income and replacement costs than in other countries. In Asia, China and Japan account for 38 per cent and 35 per cent of the region's total losses respectively in this timeframe (CRED and UNDRR, 2020).

The damage also follows a clear economic divide. High-income countries tend to have lower numbers of people adversely affected and killed by disaster events, but incur much larger financial losses in absolute terms. Low-income countries report low, but increasing, financial losses per capita and relatively high death tolls per disaster event. Lower-middle and upper-middle income countries make up most disaster events, deaths, and total numbers of people affected; however, they also account for most of the world's population, with Asia standing out as having incurred the largest number of disasters. However, despite making up most of the world's financial losses, high-income countries have the smallest losses as a percentage of GDP. In comparison, least developed countries and Small Island Developing States (SIDS) had the highest losses compared to GDP; the proportion of economic losses is three times higher in low-income compared to high-income countries (CRED and UNDRR, 2020).

Estimates by economists of the rolling damage from climate change have been made with the addition of damage functions to standard growth models. These have produced surprisingly benign results in terms of the loss to global output, even with significant temperature rises, albeit with a steadily worsening assessment as these models have become more complex, integrated and refined (Nordhaus, 2018). Indeed, in his Nobel lecture, William Nordhaus, who has done much to advance "integrated assessment models", concludes, that "economic growth is producing unintended but dangerous changes in the climate and earth systems... (with) unforeseeable consequences".

While using such models to estimate the potential damage is, consequently, a difficult business, their aura of quantitative rigour, precision and reliance on a variety of strong assumptions to allow the modeling to proceed, raises questions about their relevance to the climate challenge (Ackerman, 2018). Even in their more sophisticated versions, these models have been criticized for ignoring tipping points (Keen et al., 2021) and feedback loops (Kikstra, et al., 2021) which leads them to underestimate the scale and persistence of the potential damage from climate change. Moreover, they have little to say about structural inequality or historical patterns of development, particularly the evolving asymmetries in the global economy that shape growth prospects in many developing countries.

There is a further tendency to underestimate the potential threat by distinguishing between manageable and unmanageable system responses and focusing almost exclusively on low-income countries, particularly in tropical regions and coastal states, because of the greater dependence of economic activities on natural ecosystems, which are seen as more difficult to manage than activities and sectors in higher income countries. This dichotomy runs the danger of downplaying, or ignoring altogether, how policy decisions, at all levels of development, can have a profound effect in exacerbating climate threats, including in rural economies with a heavier reliance on the natural ecosystem. As discussed in the previous chapter, the widespread adoption of structural adjustment programmes has resulted in the erosion of public services and investment and tied many developing economies to an even greater dependence on commodity exports, making them even more vulnerable to external shocks. Moreover, this dichotomy, while recognizing the climate-related stresses that some developing countries are already facing, runs the further danger of underestimating the wider damage facing many middle and higher-income developing countries, and indeed, advanced economies, as temperatures rise towards (and above) 1.5°C.

A full picture of the costs and damages of climate change is further complicated by significant under-reporting of data about the economic losses in many developing countries. For instance, one source of discrepancy in the available data concerns heatwaves. According to the Emergency Events Database (EM-DAT), only two heatwaves were recorded in Sub-Saharan Africa between 1900 and 2019 that lead to 71 fatalities (Harrington and Otto, 2020). By contrast, the same database has registered 83 heatwaves in Europe between 1980 and 2019 that resulted in over 140 000 deaths and in more than $12 billion in economic damages. This shows major gaps in data collection, appropriate infrastructure and resources available to national agencies and an overreliance on external parties to collect data in developing regions. What is not in doubt, however, is that the greater the temperature increase the greater the threat of catastrophic events (Figure 3.2).

## 1. Slowing growth, widening gaps

The consequences of rising global temperatures reflect existing structural inequalities within and across countries. The historical responsibility for global greenhouse gas emissions (the principal cause of global warming) lies squarely with the developed nations, which account for around two-thirds of the cumulative total of emissions in the atmosphere compared with just 3 per cent for Africa.[2] And while some developing economies like China, India, Brazil and South Africa have rapidly rising emissions, on a per capita basis they are still behind advanced countries and even the consumption-related emissions of their richest citizens are below their counterparts in advanced economies (Oxfam, 2015).

For many developing countries, rising global temperatures are already compounding a vicious development cycle that has been constraining resource mobilization, weakening adaptive capacities and widening income gaps for decades. Developing countries with underfunded health care systems, underdeveloped infrastructure, undiversified economies and missing state institutions are more exposed not only to potentially large-scale environmental shocks but also a more permanent state of economic stress as a result of climate impacts.

On one estimate, warming temperatures have already, over the period 1961 to 2010, slowed economic growth of (relatively poorer) countries in the middle and lower latitudes, with median losses exceeding 25 per cent over large swaths of the tropics and subtropics where most countries exhibit very high likelihood of negative impacts (Diffenbaugh and Burke, 2019). As Figure 3.3. clearly shows, this situation will only get worse, with rising temperatures hitting growth prospects in developing regions the hardest; and all the more, the higher the increase above the 1.5°C target.

---

**FIGURE 3.2  The Risk of Catastrophic Events Increases with Temperature**

| | Food | Natural Environment | Water | Cities | Infrastructure | Disaster Risk Management |
|---|---|---|---|---|---|---|
| +3.5 °C | Global food supply disruptions | | | More than a **meter of sea level rise** for coastal cities by 2080 | | % of population exposed more than 20 days a year of **deadly heat** by 2100: |
| +3.0 °C | Over **400m people exposed and vulnerable** to crop yield losses | **Permafrost collapse** / **Rain forest dieback** | **10 months average lenght of drought** (up from 2 months at 1.5 °C) | | Significant stress to **global transportation, energy, housing, and other essential infrastructure** that would lead to progressively worse damage with each degree of warming | **74%** |
| +2.5 °C | | Decline due to reduction of geographic range by more than half: | | Annual flood damage losses from sea level rise: | | |
| +2.0 °C | **7–10% loss** of rangeland livestock globally | **18%: insects** **16%: plants** **8%: vertebrates** | **36% increase** in frequency of rainfall extremes over land | **$11.7tn** | | **54%** |
| +1.5 °C | **6% decline** in global average maize crop yield | Extensive coral reef **decline by 70–90%** | **271 million people exposed** to water scarcity | **$10.2tn** | | **48%** |
| +1.0 °C | | | | | | |

*Source:* World Resources Institute, adapted from the IPCC and others.

---

**FIGURE 3.3 Mid-century GDP losses by region generated by global warming**
*(per cent)*

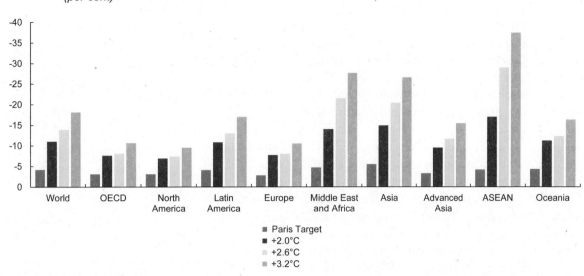

■ Paris Target
■ +2.0°C
□ +2.6°C
■ +3.2°C

*Source:* SwissRe, 2021.

On some accounts, poverty is a better gauge of the impact of climate change, given the compounded vulnerabilities of the poorest sections of society to shocks, their lack of assets to fall back on when they are hit and the constraints they face in building up adaptive capacity (Hallegatte, 2018). While levels of extreme poverty have been declining since the start of the new millennium, climate change is projected to aggravate poverty, notably in the particularly vulnerable developing countries, and create further islands of deprivation in countries with rising inequality, at all levels of development (IPCC, 2018). The World Bank estimates that between 68 million and 132 million people will become impoverished by 2030 due to the accelerating impacts of the climate crisis, and that 143 million people could be forced to internally migrate by 2050 (World Bank, 2020; Rigaud et al., 2018).

Because the vulnerability of the poorest sections of society is multidimensional, so are the channels through which climate change will impact them. Climate change is expected to induce shortages in food supplies and increase agricultural prices exposing millions more people to hunger and water deprivation by 2050 (Global Commission on Adaptation, 2019). The onset of the pandemic which is estimated to have increased the number of people facing hunger and malnutrition by 129 million is a foretaste of what is to come (WFP, 2021). Sub-Saharan Africa will suffer the most, with lower agricultural yields, driving up food insecurity. Likewise in South Asia, especially areas like

Bangladesh and India which are among the most vulnerable countries to natural hazards, as many as 30.6 million will suffer increased poverty levels, compared to East Asia and Pacific (11.8 million people on average), and Latin America and Caribbean (1.9 million people on average) (World Bank, 2020).

The rural poor are particularly sensitive to sea level rises and other extreme weather patterns, especially since the incidence of rural poverty is higher across the board. However, the growing numbers of urban poor in the developing world are also vulnerable given precarious housing conditions and limited access to public services (World Bank, Chapter 1, 2012).

## 2. *Sectoral and regional impacts*

The impact of climate change, and the nature of the adaptation challenge, will vary across regions and sectors of the economy, making a one-size-fits-all response inappropriate. Extremely hot days are expected to primarily increase in the tropics, where temperature variability across years is lowest. Dangerous heatwaves are thus forecast to occur earliest in these regions, and they are expected to become widespread at 1.5°C global warming rise (IPCC, 2018). As the most food insecure region, Sub-Saharan Africa is likely to face deepening challenges. In South Asia, more intense and frequent tropical cyclones, accelerated heatwaves and a rising sea level will continue to generate adverse impacts on the region. Climate-induced disasters in Latin America and the Caribbean will reduce developmental progress. Middle East and North African countries face acute water shortages, where as many as 60 per cent of the region's inhabitants already experience a serious lack of water. East Asia and the Pacific, which have a quarter of the world's population, already suffers from the most severe storms, cyclones and inundation globally, and will likely face the highest levels of climate-induced displacements.

Large portions of populations in low-lying coastal zones – 84 per cent in Africa, 80 per cent in Asia, 71 per cent in Latin America and the Caribbean and 93 per cent in the least developed countries (Neuman et al., 2015) can be especially affected. Critical infrastructure assets and networks like ports, airports, railways and coastal roads will also face devastation by rising sea levels which will cause permanent or even repeated damage and will impede access to food, materials, and other income-generating supplies to people and businesses.

SIDS are being particularly affected (see Table 3.1). For instance, in 2016 Category 4 hurricane Matthew in the Caribbean caused over $1.1 billion in infrastructure damage in Haiti (ECLAC, 2018, p. 27). Similarly, in 2017, almost 90 per cent of building structures on Barbuda were damaged or destroyed by Category 5 Hurricane Irma, which led to a complete evacuation of the island (UNDP, 2018). In the Fiji islands, as many as 30 369 houses, 495 schools, and 88 health clinics and medical facilities were damaged or destroyed and approximately 540 400 people, or approximately 62 per cent of the population, were significantly impacted by the cyclone (Government of Fiji, 2016). Heavy precipitation and consistent rainfall can cause considerable damage to the structural integrity and affect operations of coastal transport infrastructure such as roads, energy, communications, water and sanitation.

For SIDS especially, their middle-income status does not take into account the high risk and economic damage from extreme weather episodes. Caribbean SIDS are among the most indebted in the world, and the level of public debt to GDP is particularly severe in Antigua and Barbuda, Barbados, Grenada, Jamaica and Saint Kitts and Nevis (ECLAC, 2020). This acute level of debt means that they increasingly rely on external financing to meet domestic adaptation needs. SIDS are marginalised through their lop-sided incorporation in

**TABLE 3.1  Top ten countries and territories by economic losses as % of GDP (2000–2019)**

| Countries and territories | Economic losses |
|---|---|
| Dominica | 15.0 |
| Cayman Islands | 9.1 |
| Haiti | 8.0 |
| Grenada | 7.8 |
| Turks and Caicos | 5.8 |
| Bahamas | 4.3 |
| Guyana | 3.6 |
| Puerto Rico | 3.5 |
| Belize | 3.4 |
| Samoa | 2.1 |

*Source:* (CRED and UNDRR, 2020).

the international economic system, failed structural adjustment programs and intensifying financialization. They are, on average, considered 35 per cent more susceptible to economic and financial shocks (UNCTAD, 2021).[3] There has been little movement in this respect from donor countries, lending agencies and the private finance sectors to address the peculiar climate risks that SIDS face, and illustrated, once again, by their lack of coordination on specific debt relief measures in response to Covid-19 shock.

The International Labour Organisation (ILO) estimates that thermal stress will result in an economic loss of $2.4 trillion and 80 million jobs worldwide by 2030 (Kjellstrom and Maître, 2019). There will, however, be uneven distribution of these adverse outcomes, with South Asia and Africa particularly hard hit (Kjellstrom and Maître, 2019). By 2050, costs of climate change impact to urban areas will have risen to more than $ 1 trillion. Therefore, the need to increase adaptation actions in cities and to invest in solutions that have benefits is higher than ever before.

There is a further risk of severe ill-health and disrupted livelihoods for large urban populations due to inland flooding in some regions (IPCC, 2014). The IPCC notes that increases in mortality and morbidity are very likely during periods of extreme heat, particularly for marginalised urban populations and those working outdoors in urban or rural areas. Food insecurity and the collapse of food supply chains are linked to warming, drought, flooding, and precipitation variability, particularly for lower-income and impoverished populations in urban and rural environments. Threats increase for those without adequate essential infrastructure and services or who live in shoddy housing and exposed areas. In urban and rural regions, wage-labor-dependent poor households that are net consumers of food are expected to be particularly affected due to increases in food prices, including in areas with relatively food insecure populations such as Sub-Saharan Africa.

## 3. The Economic Costs of Adaptation

Adaptation costs are typically higher for high-income countries in absolute dollar value terms, but costs are higher relative to gross domestic product for low-income countries. Traditionally, adaptation needs have been measured by the gap between what might happen as the climate changes and the desirable response to meet related shocks (IPCC, 2014). In their initial NDCs, 46 countries included assessments of their adaptation costs totaling $783 billion by 2030 (Bhattacharya et al., 2020). These costs include project financing, income support, technological support, and capacity-building but despite the formal global goal on adaptation enshrined in the Paris Agreement and elaboration in the Cancun Declaration, no single, straightforward metric (or even set of metrics) exists that could be employed to translate the global goal on adaptation into a measurable target (and baseline) at the global level (UNEP, 2020). This is usually because adaptation actions are often defined at the local level and with relevant stakeholders within a country.

Despite these uncertainties surrounding detailed accounting of the adaptation challenge, there is no doubting the consequences of its neglect. In the run up to the Copenhagen COP in 2009, the UNFCCC estimated that annual worldwide costs of adapting to 2 degrees of warming would be between $49 to $171 billion by 2030, with developing countries facing a $34 to $57 billion bill. A decade later, the delay in responding has been costly. Annual adaptation costs in developing countries are now estimated at $70 billion, reaching $140–$300 billion in 2030 and $280–$500 billion in 2050 (UNEP, 2020). Current funding reaches less than a half of current needs and will not reach the 2030 target without a fundamental change of track. Admittedly, adaptation finance and adaptation costs are difficult to compare and estimate for a number of reasons (Pauw et al.,

2020; UNEP, 2020 figure 4.1). Most developing countries make their mitigation and adaptation contributions conditional upon receiving international support finance, technology transfer and/or capacity building.[4]

In general, Pauw et al. (2020) point out that cost estimates for adaptation among the 60 countries they survey varied in terms of quality, sources, estimation techniques with only some fully provided and several others with partial sector-based costs in their NDCs. However, given the available estimates, the adaptation finance gap is widening in relation to costs. As extreme events become more frequent, the gap will be considerable and overall costs will likely increase if we consider the possibility of indirect and unpredictable costs. The major quantitative shortfalls, along with gaps in technical know-how and human resources, remains a binding constraint on implementation of climate action plans (UNEP, 2020), particularly for the least developed countries (see Box 3.1), where the ongoing impacts of climate change and poorly devised responses impede longer-term efforts that address key sectoral goals (see table 3.2).

The Global Commission on Adaptation has noted that even countries which have made use of multilateral and domestic public finance in response to Covid-19 pandemic – amounting to upwards of $10 trillion – have not sufficiently incorporated climate resilience in their recovery programs (Saghir et al., 2020; UNEP, 2020). A recent analysis by the World Resources Institute demonstrated that only 18 of the 66 countries surveyed had explicitly incorporated physical climate risk, adaptation and resilience in their stimulus packages, whether selectively, in specific interventions, or holistically, as a central aspect to their strategy.[5] The 12 countries that specifically cited climate risk management interventions as a primary objective of stimulus spending were Bangladesh, Barbados, Colombia, Fiji, Kenya, Kiribati, Nepal, Niger, the Philippines, Republic of Korea, St. Lucia, and Vanuatu. It is notable that apart from the Republic of Korea, all of these belong to the V20 and all face binding financial constraints on mobilizing resources.[6] The benefits of investing in adaptation are clearly advantageous to both developed and developing economies, but definitely more urgent for developing countries whose climate risks are rising and becoming more complex over time.

**Box 3.1**     National Adaptation Programmes of Action (NAPAs)

Least Developed Countries (LDCs) face disproportionate exposure to climate change and environmental degradation, while these nations also have the least resources and institutional apparatus to recover from climate change impacts. Multiple stressors, such as unequal socioeconomic conditions, high vulnerability, and precarious institutional systems combine to produce low adaptive capacity to impacts of climate change.

Acknowledging this situation, National Adaptation Plans (NAPAs) were launched at the COP7 held in Marakesh in 2001, to address the immediate and urgent adaptation needs of LDCs regarding climate change and sustainable development. Each country's NAPA provides a special funding window and adaptation planning guidance to support LDCs to jumpstart their adaptation plans, tailored to the unique contexts of these nations. Through the NAPA process, LDCs identify priority activities with regard to adaptation to climate change, and propose adaptation projects based on greatest areas of need and urgency, especially those needs for which further delay could increase vulnerability or lead to increased costs at a later stage (Least Developed Countries Expert Group, 2002).

One key objective of NAPAs is to better understand climate variability at a local and regional level and to identify urgent action needed to build adaptive capacity. Strategies do exist at the community level for dealing with climate variability and extreme events. NAPAs therefore involve both expanding current coping range and enhancing resilience to current climate variability and extremes. National Adaptation Plans are then established to develop and implement strategies and programmes to address medium- and long-term adaptation aligned with broader sustainable development objectives. The associated Least Developed Countries Fund (LDCF) operated by the Global Environmental Facility (GEF) supports NAPA implementation, in correspondence with and guidance from the Conference of the Parties (COP). However, the LDC Fund was under-resourced, preventing timely development and implementation of NAPAs. As a consequence, many countries were unable to translate the NAPA plans into clearly defined implementation programmes.

The synthesis of adaptation objectives into national development planning means aligning poverty reduction strategies and overall sustainable development objectives with an understanding of geographical, social and physical criteria of climate change impacts. Eight focus areas were found to be important: 1) conducting a participatory needs assessment; 2) having a clear mandate; 3) having a clear road map for the NAPA process; 4) identifying how adaptation can be integrated into development strategies; 5) establishing effective institutional supports and arrangements; 6) ensuring open, ongoing dialogue with relevant stakeholders, especially marginalised communities; 7) continued assessments for climate risk and vulnerability; and 8) assessing capacity needs for all aspects of the NAPA process, including comprehensive monitoring and evaluation (M&E).

By December 2017, all LDCs had submitted NAPAs and began undertaking their implementation. A review of these programmes suggests their key strengths and successes as well as some challenges, when considering the overall impact of NAPA on building more inclusive, resilient communities, and contributing to sustainable development.

Against this backdrop, there are three key aspects to successful adaptation highlighted by these programmes.

*1.   Integrating adaptive capacities*

Developing the capacity for working at a level of complexity that is commensurate with climate change, and then integrating this with sustainable development processes—itself another complex undertaking—is a very difficult task; yet it appears to be a key factor in successes. Bearing these layers of complexity in mind, LDCs have focused on the challenge of integrating climate change adaptation into national poverty reduction policies and programmes and sustainable development programming. This challenge has been met in various ways, such as, via setting up a climate change adaptation focal point or designing multidisciplinary teams which house the quality and degree of capacity needed for working in an integrative manner, and also promoting and enabling regional synergies for adaptation. For example, in Zambia, a climate change facilitation unit was created to be responsible for harmonizing climate change action within the country, as a way to operationalize the degree of integration needed for effective adaptation. NAPAs that are well-integrated with sustainable development processes at a national level seem to do so by building on the existence of government endorsement and commitment to implementation of these sustainability outcomes. Likewise, Samoa used an integrated approach to combine its priorities identified under the NAPA and strategically plan the implementation of these priorities in line with its national development strategy and policies, in an integrated project with adaptation activities across "four sectors identified in the NAPA, namely: (i) climate health; (ii) agriculture and food security; (iii) ecosystem conservation; and (iv) early warning systems" (Least Developed Countries Expert Group, 2012, p. 55). Developing such integrative adaptive capacity to bring responses to climate change into national and subnational planning processes, engaging with a complexity that is more commensurate with the climate change issue itself, appears as a key factor for success amongst NAPAs to date.

2. *Scaling adaptation*

Urgency and expediency lie at the core of the NAPA concept, and as such, scaling the impact of these programmes is important for their success. The Least Developed Countries Expert Group (2009, p. 30) points out that "Scaling up adaptation is an emerging concept, and can only be fully realized if properly planned… Scaling up also recognizes the linkages between systems both in space and over time, and if implemented properly, would lead to lasting impacts and sustainable benefits." Current research agrees that this cannot just include *scaling out* into greater numbers of initiatives or in replicating projects in greater quantity. Additionally, *scaling up* adaptation efforts into changed institutions and structures is important (Moore et al., 2015), particularly relevant in instilling adaptation objectives in all aspects of development planning. For example, during the implementation of the first NAPA project in Benin, this translated into mainstreaming adaptation practices across sectors, strong national and local coordination, and active involvement of local authorities at the very beginning, which in turn facilitated the mobilization of co-financing and cross-sectoral management (Least Developed Countries Expert Group, 2012, p. 26). 'Scaling up' inserts adaptive thinking and design into the very institutional structures that guide and shape development for the country and in particular specific focus areas with a clear mandate. In addition to scaling out and up, *scaling deep*—into changed values and worldviews—also matters (Moore et al., 2015); such as in fostering ownership and uptake of adaptive practices by local communities and actors. Cambodia for example, undertook a year-long awareness raising campaign with farmers and authorities in target districts in the largely agrarian economy of the country (Least Developed Countries Expert Group, 2012, p. 30). This focus on 'scaling deep' to promote greater awareness and attention to values was carried out alongside other projects for strengthening policy and science in vulnerable regions and building the adaptive capacity with various climate resilient agricultural practices. Such a three-pronged approach to scaling out, scaling up, and scaling deep may be a key component for NAPA success.

3. *Adaptation towards Transformation*

An important link has been made between climate change adaptation and transformation in the fifth assessment report of the Intergovernmental Panel on Climate Change (IPCC, 2014). This stemmed from the acknowledgement that there is a range of adaptive responses, including those that are more reactive and incremental through to actions that are more deliberate and transformative. Some researchers argue that adaptation approaches which merely make adjustments to current development practices risk extending and even reproducing unsustainability and maladaptation. Researchers also note that the vast majority of proposed adaptation strategies aim to inform the short-term tactical decisions for incremental change (Eriksen et al., 2021) but may not account for how climate impacts interconnect with wider processes of change (Ensor et al., 2019). IPCC 2018 underlined this saying "Limiting warming to 1.5 C would require transformative systemic change, integrated with sustainable development [and] would need to be linked to complementary adaptation actions, including transformational adaptation" (Masson-Delmotte et al., 2018, p. 16). The NAPAs that work across this range of adaptive responses, extending into that of transformational adaptation, are therefore better set up for success (IPCC, 2014; O'Brien, 2018). These are inherently long-term processes of change and have multiplier effects in building adaptive capacities and involve new sectoral alignments to meet adaptation goals.

The effective design and implementation of NAPAs depends on their integration into existing national development planning so that climate adaptation can be integrated as a coherent aspect of overall sustainable, equitable development, across regions. Yet often development institutions are not necessarily well set up for such *cross-thematic, cross-programmatic integration*; this constitutes a second major challenge that NAPAs face. The work by the Least Developed Country Expert Group (LEG) to support regional synergies assists in this regard, as well as the UNFCCC's Adaptation Committee which aims to strengthen synergistic engagement with national, regional and international organizations, centres and networks (Least Developed Countries Expert Group, 2015, pp. 16–17).

## C. The disarticulated architecture of climate governance

Developing economies have borne the brunt of the adverse effects of rising global temperatures, with worse to come. However, given their marginalized position in the current architecture of global environmental governance, or more accurately, the unwillingness of negotiating partners to address their concerns, they have not received the required multilateral support to face the adaptation challenge (including for loss and damage). The lack of bold and generous leadership has given rise to a lack of trust which further weakens the international cooperation needed to address the climate challenge in all its dimensions.

Moreover, and unlike the mitigation challenge where the big investment push to transform energy systems is common to all countries, the wide-ranging measures across activities and sectors in response to the adaptation challenge (Table 3.2), vary from country to country depending on local circumstances, ruling out a one size fits all policy approach and underscoring the importance of allowing governments the space to tailor policies to those circumstances.[7]

The ongoing health pandemic, which has focused attention on strengthening resilience to shocks, may yet catalyse a transformation in the climate adaptation challenge, while a series of extreme weather events in 2021, which hit communities in advanced as well as

developing countries with unprecedented losses, has made news headlines. The latest IPCC Report leaves no doubt that more threats to lives, livelihoods and (social and physical) infrastructure will materialize in the near future. Consequently, it has become apparent that properly financed adaptation strategies are vital not only for survival of island nations, but for the protection of human habitats across the planet and at all levels of development.

The Paris Agreement, adopted in 2015 and entered into force in 2016, is intended to enhance the implementation of the UN Framework Convention on Climate Change (UNFCCC) and included, inter alia, an objective "of enhancing adaptive capacity, strengthening resilience and reducing vulnerability to climate change, with a view to contributing to sustainable development and ensuring an adequate adaptation response in the context of the temperature goal",[8] where adaptive capacity refers to the stock of assets which can be drawn upon to support adaptation at a future point (IPCC, 2014). The goal will be achieved by all Parties committing to periodically communicate their nationally-determined contributions (NDCs), including their mitigation

TABLE 3.2    **Potential areas of intervention for climate adaptation**

| Sector | Adaptation measures |
|---|---|
| Urban areas | Creating flood-adapted and resilient infrastructural networks and built environments where people live closer to work or work in safe environments to eliminate excessive transport costs and time, and ensure equitable patterns of work, and to provide emergency safe havens or evacuation sites in the event of floods or extreme weather events. |
| Water | Using and improving rainwater harvesting techniques<br>Improving water storage and distribution facilities and arrangements<br>Investing in irrigation amenities, adjusting drainage management systems, altering tillage practices to preserve water<br>Desalinization<br>Enhanced irrigation plotting, links to farmlands, and efficiency |
| Agriculture | Adjusting planting/ harvesting periods and increasing crop varieties<br>Crop redeployment, forage, and tree species<br>Improved land management systems and techniques, for example, erosion management and soil protection through tree planting<br>Improving land tenure arrangements for small farmers and rural indigenous communities |
| Infrastructure | Improved levees and change in building patterns<br>Creation of wetlands as a buffer against sea-level rise and flooding<br>Climate-proofing of essential public physical infrastructure<br>Creation of accessible and resilient public emergency shelters and evacuation sites |
| Health | Improved capacity to surveil and manage disease outbreaks<br>Improved water and sanitation amenities and management<br>Climate-proofing frontline community public health infrastructure<br>Ensure accessible public health services in times of climate-induced emergencies |
| Transport | Development and relocation of transportation networks and systems<br>Improved coding and planning methods for transport infrastructure to cope with warming and damage |
| Energy systems | Reinforcing generating facilities and grids against flooding, windstorms and heavy rainfall cycles<br>Developing and deploying decentralized, off-grid, micro- or community-based renewable energy power generation facilities |

*Source:* Adapted from UNDESA, 2008.

and adaptation actions, consistent with equity and common but differentiated responsibility and respective capabilities in light of different national circumstances. Parties also committed to reporting on the progress of implementing their NDCs through the Paris Agreement's enhanced transparency framework. Parties' subsequent NDCs under the Paris Agreement would be informed by regular global stocktaking of the state of progress.

In 2010, the 16th Conference of the Parties (COP 16) established the Adaptation Committee as the principal body under the UNFCCC – and the United Nations system more broadly – to provide comprehensive expert advice on adaptation action and support for targeted measures.

It is the sole body under the Convention whose work regularly addresses all facets of the adaptation challenge in a comprehensive manner (United Nations, 2019). The Intergovernmental Panel on Climate Change (IPCC) has subsequently distinguished between incremental and transformational adaptation; the former "maintains the essence and integrity of a system or process at a given scale," whereas the latter "changes the fundamental attributes of a socio-ecological system in anticipation of climate change and its impacts."

The foundational principle of climate negotiations regarding equity under the UNFCCC remains "common but differentiated responsibility", which recognises different levels of responsibility for the climate crisis and for solving it, including transfers of finance and technology from developed to developing countries. Still, tensions in climate negotiations continue around the appropriate scale of transfers among states, as well as the possible adverse impact of policy decisions in advanced countries, with respect to trade measures, intellectual property rights, etc., on the climate response in developing countries (see further Chapter V). Moreover, in the multi-layered framework of decision-making and management around the climate challenge, other actors, at different levels of government, from the private sector, civil society and the scientific community, are involved in advancing a common agenda.

The political forces that have delayed action on mitigation have been extensively discussed, whether framed as an incentive problem linked to the pressure of bridging short-term and long-term decisions (Carney, 2015), a public good problem subject to free riding (Stern, 2007) or a "global commons" problem subject to the undue influence of vested interests, particularly the "winners" from the carbon-based economy (Standing, 2019). Arguably, disagreements around climate mitigation are the main reason why the nexus between national and global decision making has been the focus of attention in climate discussions. Disagreements over the extent to which all Parties should take on mitigation commitments were among the causes of the delays in negotiating a successor to the Kyoto Protocol. The Copenhagen Climate Conference broke down on the failure to deliver such commitments and a further six years were required before the Paris Agreement was signed, on the basis of Nationally Determined Contributions (NDCs) reflecting a just and fair way of operationalising "common but differentiated responsibility and capacities."

The issues of power, conflicting policy preferences, resource allocation, and administrative tensions are no less involved in the adaptation challenge, albeit played out more visibly along the national and sub-national decision-making nexus than is the case with the mitigation challenge (Dolsak and Prakash, 2018). Global monitoring and analysis can certainly help identify those marginalized regions and communities with particularly high levels of vulnerability, including in developed countries. In Nepal, for example, framing of the Himalayan region as particularly vulnerable has prompted external support for its National Adaptation Programme of Action (NAPA).[9] But the national level is still the focal point for mobilizing resources for adaptation action, including for the international community, and remains key for translating global ambition on adaptation to effective action. In this context, the climate challenge is difficult to disentangle from the longstanding development constraints on resource mobilization and which must now include an understanding of the way climate variables constrain development policy at the national level. However, policymakers can still draw some important lessons for the adaptation challenge from the experiences of developing countries over the last four decades of adjusting to exogenous economic shocks:

- If left to make the adjustment themselves, countries will likely be forced to squeeze down incomes, which would result in a prolonged and destabilizing adjustment process, increasing poverty levels, damaging long-term growth prospects and adding to further vulnerabilities.

- Economies that are more diversified (both sector-wise and geographically) tend to show greater resilience with respect to external shocks and recover more quickly, as do economies that are more strategically integrated in the global economy.

•  Societies with greater equality are better able to manage shocks by distributing the burden of adjustment and avoiding the possibly dangerous conflicts that adjustment can trigger.

In this context, the challenge for states is, in part, recognizing adaptation as a cross-cutting issue which needs to be mainstreamed across a variety of line ministries, for example, finance, environment and agriculture. For example, in Malawi, Tanzania and Zambia, institutional structures and availability of resources influence the levels of staff motivation and capacity to design and implement adaptation policies and programmes (Pardoe et al., 2018). The effects of neoliberal policies, burdensome debt instruments and in many cases costly institutional realignments reduce the availability of domestic resources to implement appropriate adaptation policies that further give rise to a reliance on donors for operational budgets (Ciplet and Roberts, 2017; UNCTAD, 2017, 2019). This overreliance limits the capacity of the state to take determined adaptation actions and points to the need for local specification of decisions, increased resource mobilization, and mobilization to change structures over time. In such circumstances, the capacity to act is constrained and leads to selective implementation of adaptation policies (Pardoe et al., 2018).

Global and national level adaptation agendas are likely to require implementation at sub-national levels where local public institutions and civil servants link the state with citizens and thus must negotiate the different interests and trade-offs involved (Funder and Mweemba, 2019). In the context of irregular availability of resources, and particularly where the central state has a weak record of delivering on policy promises, these "interface bureaucrats" have to navigate the different interests involved and be willing to accommodate local priorities in implementation. Representatives of responsible ministries may also have to negotiate space to act within the context of local governments and to engage traditional governance relations through local political leaders (Funder et al., 2018).

A more technocratic framing of adaptation has often tried to sidestep the need for politics of representation that uncovers differential local vulnerability. In this case, many developing countries have raised concern that the top down-mandated participatory processes involved in national climate adaptation policy development contribute to reinforcing existing levels of vulnerability (Nagoda and Nightingale, 2017) and led to calls for greater commitment to locally-led adaptation (Soanes et al., 2021; Mikulewicz, 2018).

Community-based adaptation has a long history as a way of enabling local collective action to address climate risk (Forsyth, 2013). However, community-based adaptation, while potentially offering an alternative option to technocratic fixes, is also inherently political. It can therefore drive or delay changes that take into account systemic risk of climate change. Community spaces are subject to local level power structures and uneven power dynamics among different actors that need to be considered when delivering public and other sources of finance to projects. This has generated particular effects on participatory development approaches adopted by the donor community (Dodman and Mitlin, 2013). These outcomes are part and parcel of a broader approach to economic governance embedded in much climate policy thinking that has fragmented the state and created asymmetries of power and resources and limited the necessary structural changes and equity to communities most in need (Ciplet and Roberts, 2017; Perry, 2020).

The importance of recognising local political economy dynamics in interpreting and fine-tuning an adaptation agenda to suit those circumstances also highlights the diversity of the interested parties involved. At the sub-national level, it is not only local governments, communities and grassroots leaders, but also non-state actors that play a role in implementing adaptation measures. Given resource constraints in many developing countries, the role of multilateral and bilateral donors working in partnership with international NGOs and local civil society organisations often play a key role. Although it tends to receive less attention, in some cases the private sector is also included within coalitions for adaptation. In Kenya, for example, the Climate Change Act encourages collaborations to support climate response, and there are some examples of multistakeholder partnerships involving SMEs (Gannon et al., 2021). However, regardless of the composition, the establishment of partnerships and coalitions is itself a way of (re)producing uneven power relationships at local level that may lead to maladaptation (Naess et al., 2015).

Donors can also play a crucial role in adaptation policy development, especially the financing of projects and disbursements of funds and have to be engaged more than in an arms-length manner. Donor support drives the implementation of global agendas and plays a key role in shaping the emergence and evolution of the national adaptation agendas in several SIDS in the Caribbean and Pacific regions (Perry, 2020; Robinson and Dornan, 2017). Still, as discussed further in subsequent chapters, the use of ODA for climate adaptation carries its own specific challenges linked to policy conditionalities attached to accessing such support, all the more so in the absence of effective multilateral monitoring and assessment of that support, especially including local communities and grassroots organizations.

The recent Leaders' Summit on Climate change hosted by US President Joe Biden held in April 2021, placed a particular emphasis on climate resilience and environmental justice as a major pillar of international support. The US Government has committed to make investments "in underserved and marginalised communities, including indigenous communities, in Canada, Mexico, and the United States to prepare them for climate-related impacts". The plan would focus on small island communities and locally-informed adaptation strategies that draw on culturally-sensitive knowledge and data. In addition, the President proposed providing funding for community-based organizations in the US and abroad to drive local solutions to climate impacts.[10]

Three specific initiatives have been proposed or enhanced, including: (1) the Local2030 Island Network, which connects U.S. island territories with others around the world; (2) the Energy Transitions Initiative – Global, which will seek to support the transformation and resilience of island communities in the Caribbean and Asia-Pacific regions; and (3) the Pacific Climate Ready project and Caribbean Energy and Resilience programs to support SIDS to promote climate-resilient development. At the recent Climate Adaptation Summit, the United Kingdom launched the Adaptation Action Coalition, a group of leading nations that will collaborate with the Race to Resilience initiative and the UN Climate Action team at the COP26 in 2021. Comprising Egypt, Bangladesh, Malawi, the Netherlands, St. Lucia and the UNDP, the Coalition will aim to accelerate efforts to turn political commitment to action on the ground that support the most marginalised and impacted countries.[11]

To what extent these initiatives will prove effective, and how quickly, is a question not only of political will at all levels of decision-making, but of material resources. The challenge of mobilizing resources is discussed in the next chapters. But decision-making, itself, rests on the kind of conceptual framework used to design climate adaptation strategies. The next section addresses this issue in more depth.

## D. Climate adaptation: Risky business?

Adapting to the vagaries of the natural world has been part of the human condition for millennia. As early hunter and gatherer societies transitioned to more sedentary patterns of life, rural societies learnt how to deal with unanticipated environmental events through crop diversification, water storage systems, etc. Equally, the benefits of living in low lying coastal regions have forced human settlements to adapt to the threats that those local climatic conditions can bring, through the development of storm warning systems, flood response mechanisms, etc. Not all attempts at adaptation have succeeded. However, most of those failures have been confined to specific geographical locations and to singular climatic events. By contrast, the contemporary adaptation challenge is both widespread and connected to a wider set of deep-seated social and economic vulnerabilities that have emerged in recent decades (*TDR 2017*; Gallagher and Kozul-Wright, 2019).

The increasing damage from economic shocks, both before and after the GFC, from more frequent extreme climate events, and now from a health pandemic have highlighted the lack of preparedness of policy makers to the inherent fragilities and crises of the contemporary global economy. In response, governments, at all levels of development, have been told to strengthen their resilience to shocks by improving their data gathering and risk assessment techniques to better protect existing assets and by providing temporary financial support when shocks materialise. This approach is appealing because no new methodologies and frameworks appear to be needed. Rather, adopting and adapting already operational approaches is seen as providing a rapid response to the threat to lives and livelihoods.[12]

One review (Sherman et al., 2016) of the different approaches to the adaptation challenge has distinguished between: (1) technocratic risk management (TRM), (2) pro-poor vulnerability reduction (PPVR), and (3) sustainable adaptation (SA). The first two tend to be closely aligned as they tend not to question the underlying development model and the resulting structure of the economy, and instead aim at conserving and protecting the existing assets and the current structure of the economy.[13] That can be termed a conventional, incremental, or a technocratic approach to climate adaptation.

In the technocratic approach, adaptation is seen as the result of mostly technical interventions which are implemented without properly regarding power relations, conflict dynamics or political contexts. Consequently, adaptation measures mostly comprise disaster risk reduction, ecosystem management, agricultural practices, water management, meteorological and early warning system improvements, social safety nets, insurance, and microfinance. That way, adaptation is retrofitted into development assistance. These may provide partial resilience now but by using scarce resources for adaptation to current climate hazards, these interventions preclude other future-oriented interventions and lock in path-dependent dynamics which reproduces current vulnerabilities. Dilling at al. (2015) show that there is no guarantee that adapting to current climate variability would automatically reduce the vulnerability to future climate change.

The use of risk assessment is a well-established tool of economic policymaking where different choices carry different outcomes in terms of benefits and costs. Assuming the alternative outcomes can be calculated with some degree of precision, then policy makers can prepare in advance for the costs of the chosen path through the adoption of various hedging and coping strategies. In measuring the potential costs, economists have distinguished between idiosyncratic risks that are one-off or local in nature, and tend to carry smaller potential costs, and covariant risks, which are more widespread or systemic, tend to be less predictable and carry larger costs. As noted earlier, drawing on conventional economic models tends to focus attention on idiosyncratic risk and ignore systemic risk, paying little attention to longer-term structural trends and tending to underestimate the scale and complexity of the climate challenge, particularly in developing countries.

The extension of this approach to the adaptation challenge can be more explicitly traced to the Sendai Framework for Disaster Risk Reduction that the United Nations General Assembly adopted in 2015 as a blueprint for disaster-related resilience and reacting to human-made hazards (UNGA, 2015). The 2015 adoption of the Paris Agreement also emphasized this approach with its focus on the reduction of risks related to climate change (Opitz-Stapleton et al., 2019).

The weakness of extending a risk-based approach to the adaptation challenge is its reliance on pricing and other market-assessment techniques which bias the approach towards what is predictable and incremental in nature rather than what is uncertain and systemic and that tend to bend the discussion of the appropriate response to coping rather than transforming (UNDESA, 2008; Global Comission on Adaptation, 2019). The IPCC, 2014 Synthesis Report (p.107) is an example: "Existing and emerging economic instruments can foster adaptation by providing incentives for anticipating and reducing impacts (medium confidence). Instruments include public-private finance partnerships, loans, payments for environmental services, improved resource pricing, charges and subsidies, norms and regulations, and risk sharing and transfer mechanisms. This weakness becomes particularly apparent when the understanding of the nature of shocks, and the appropriate response to them, is derived from financial market analysts, where episodic crises are seen as an idiosyncratic threat to existing asset positions, best dealt with by the more effective pricing of risk by adding another layer of market-based instruments (derivatives) which purport to reduce investor uncertainty. Such an approach, under the umbrella term of "de-risking" (*TDR* 2019) calls for the establishment of a 'low-risk' national investment climate through the deepening of capital markets, the creation of large-scale asset classes that can be securitized into safer financial products and the pursuit of transparent economic governance. Policy institutions and think tanks pushing a de-risking agenda have argued that it gives international financial institutions greater scope to attract private investment into otherwise unattractive investment opportunities, including in the area of climate adaptation.

Despite the differences in the nature of climatic and financial shocks, several common assumptions inform the risk-based approach to the adaptation challenges. First, in finance, risk is generally understood as involving a quantifiable divergence of actual from expected outcomes which, given sufficient information, can be effectively measured and properly priced. How much is spent on insuring against risk is then very much a matter of choice reflecting individuals' or communities' attitudes to spending money today in order to insure against damage materialising sometime in the future. Second, while risk drivers may be endogenous (i.e., driven by the behaviour and policies of stakeholders), climate risk tends to be understood as exogenous (i.e. whose origin is outside of the system and therefore beyond the control of a national government or organisation), but predictable.

In the context of the global climate challenge, these core premises carry several critical limitations. The assumption of divisibility of risk overlooks the problem of systemic risk.[14] Despite revisions to financial regulation in the wake of the GFC, post-crisis reforms have underplayed the notion of systemic risk, while epistemic approaches to systemic risk are often contradictory and under-developed. For example, while it is often seen as an external threat caused by improbable and unpredictable exogenous events, systemic risk also arises from endogenous structural weaknesses in complex and highly interconnected systems (Goldin and Vogel, 2010), as well as political decisions. Climate change and accelerating extreme events present a range of complex, systemic risks which cannot be diversified and priced using traditional risk-management tools as they concern social, geo-ecological and political dimensions.

Reflecting this, a revised, "risk and resilience" approach has offered a more comprehensive framework around the complex, interconnected and systemic nature of risk (e.g., Opitz-Stapleton et al., 2019). In this way, based on recent events that are more severe than scientists' modelling predictions, climate risk is even more uncertain and less amenable to quantification and consequent management through traditional risk management instruments. Instead, to cope with complex risk that extreme weather events pose, we may need to shift our understanding from risk events to the *resilience of an impacted system*.

The resulting policy agenda proceeds in five steps: (i) understanding risks, especially complex systemic risks, by identifying the risk drivers and their potential impact; (ii) preventing and mitigating risk, i.e. by addressing the risk drivers by reducing the probability of shocks and avoiding the creation of new risk, especially through ensuring good governance and creating an enabling environment; (iii) reducing the impact of risk by enhancing resilience and lessening vulnerabilities; (iv) managing residual risk through risk sharing, including through insurance and safety nets; and (v) recovering and building back better by adapting to new realities and transiting towards more resilient and sustainable growth and development paths (United Nations, 2021).

The step towards a more integrated approach and systems-based view of policymaking marks an advance from narrow agendas focusing on single risk drivers and narrowly defined vulnerability indicators. Policy implications of this approach most prominently concern "buffering capacity" (Hallegatte, 2014; Caldera-Sanchez et al., 2016), "risk-informed development" (Opitz-Stapleton et al., 2019), or a "risk and resilience framework" (United Nations, 2021). The first two of these approaches are relatively limited and technocratic. "Risk-informed-development" actions emphasize increased understanding of complex risk and acting upon that knowledge. It also recognizes that all decisions involve trade-offs across different development objectives and stakeholders. Building "buffering capacity" emphasizes increased understanding and knowledge creation. But it targets *anticipatory* actions: those aimed at harnessing the ability to anticipate risk and evaluate potential impacts, and at stemming the build-up of vulnerabilities, especially in the domestic economy, to avoid adverse shocks from turning into crises.

Yet even this revised, evolutionary approach to managing climate risk suffers from limitations. If risk results from the *interaction* between threats and underlying conditions, building resilience means creating buffers, rather than changing the wider ecology of risks.

From an economic development perspective, the application of risk-resilience approaches suffers from at least three shortcomings. First, given its roots in financial risk management, the approach privileges a return to (pre-crisis) normality and stability over a dynamic vision of change and new trajectories. In the case of many communities, this 'normality' means a return to persistent inequality. Preservation, in other words, still takes priority over transformation which in the case of climate crisis, is not simply insufficient, but also counterproductive and leads to maladaptation. It occludes the role of a collective set of mobilising actors and policies that may pursue a different set of defined objectives and actions.

Risk-resilience approaches are especially problematic in the current political context, where new social contracts are needed to regain citizens' trust in public policies and multilateral efforts. Tackling current global challenges like climate adaptation requires a new vision of common goals rather than emphasizing the avoidance of risks and worst-case scenarios that emerge from current circumstances. This is, for example, recognised in discussions around a green new deal.

Second, the sequence of crises and the sharpening of inequality and exclusion around the planet suggest that it is not simply a matter of omissions (insufficient information and instruments), but of commission. In the context of climate change, the rules and policies that make contemporary economic globalization and the associated vulnerabilities exclusionary and unstable have been institutionalised over a long period of time. Calculative private financial mechanisms of risk management are unable to address the spectrum of climate dangers, most of which include extreme events, indivisible in their impact and associated uncertainties. Instead, a strategic policy response needs to be built on "active precautionary measures to minimise worst-case risks," which is far beyond milder regulatory measures stemming from conventional probability approaches to risk management and institutional architecture (Ackerman 2018: 163).

Third and relatedly, risk-resilience approaches view the state mainly as a facilitator that sets the incentives and frameworks for self-regulating markets and private-sector initiatives. Within this framework, governments may play three key roles regarding risk (United Nations, 2021): (i) as a risk-bearer of last resort, such as by bailing out insolvent banks and corporates to limit contagion; (ii) as shaping the risk landscape for private investors and other stakeholders, such as by aligning incentives with SDG-relevant risks; and (iii) as seeking risks associated with long-term transformative investments, with a view to de-risking private-sector engagement in such highly uncertain ventures. Governments may also undertake risk-reducing investment to improve coping capacity by creating buffers in terms of increased human capital, social protection, digital infrastructure that improves connectivity and helps to bridge digital divides and, especially, by expanding fiscal space.

These three shortcomings are reflected in the current balance of power (and issues) that frame international efforts to address climate adaptation. Despite our growing knowledge about the threats from rising global temperatures and the resulting adaptation needs, technocratic fixes have so far failed to produce successful adaptation strategies in vulnerable countries (Boyd, 2017). This is, in part, because even if the requisite data is collected and the appropriate technology available, this never just comes "off the shelf" but is (re)produced through social rules (Jasanoff, 2013), including those constructed around intellectual property, which can make accessing and adapting the required technologies a difficult and expensive process for many developing countries. Coping with climate shocks is, moreover, strongly positively correlated with income levels and reflects changes in economic and social structures as countries diversify into more sophisticated and higher productivity activities. The establishment of institutional networks can also build synergies across those activities, and popular deliberation mechanisms can push for increasing the capacity and reach of developmental states to embrace the climate challenge (see next chapter and Gabor, 2020).

A more transformative approach to adaptation, however, will, as discussed in Chapter V, only be possible if the funding required to implement the institutional and structural measures is made available through appropriate mechanisms at both the national and multilateral levels.

## E. Conclusion

This chapter has surveyed the scale and scope of the adaptation challenge and the institutional and policy environment that frames the responses to that challenge. It has set down some broad markers for policy action and reform, suggesting that not only should the political, epistemic and financing components of the climate challenge be addressed through a more integrated framework, but that a more developmental approach to climate is needed, given the persistent underestimation of the adaptation challenge in conventional climate action programmes.

Investing in adaptation will improve the resilience of both advanced and developing economies against rising global temperatures. But while responsibility for the threat resides principally with the former, the damage is felt disproportionately in the latter. Moreover, in many cases, their vulnerability to external shocks has been heightened by the imposition of market-friendly adjustment programmes that have reduced the capacity of the state to respond in a timely and effective manner. Improved knowledge, measurement and monitoring of the adaptation gap is certainly needed, as well as a better understanding of local political and power structures that can obstruct adaptation. The chapter has also shown why current risk-resilience measures drawn from financial markets are inappropriate for framing a transformative adaptation agenda. Rather, retrofitting the developmental state and providing it with greener industrial policies will, as discussed in the next chapter, be critical to advancing such an agenda.

## Notes

1 Adaptation is used here in a broad sense to refer both to managing the adverse effects of climate change, and the related issue of "loss and damage" incurred beyond what adaptation measures can address.

2 See https://ourworldindata.org/co2-emissions

3 See https://dgff2021.unctad.org/foreword/.

4 UNEP notes that estimating adaptation costs is a complex challenge; the stage and process of development changes adaptation costs which can be increased or decreased accordingly; incomplete knowledge about costs of adaptation for some sectors, notably for biodiversity and ecosystem services; indirect and unpredictable climate change impacts can change dynamics and increase certain costs; estimates based on autonomous actions, for instance, if farmers take certain measures that result in improved adaptation, can be severely underestimated, among other reasons. See list in Annex 1 in the Adaptation Gap Report (2020) at https://www.unep.org/resources/adaptation-gap-report-2020.

5 A draft copy of the report is available here: https://www.dropbox.com/s/ayqrjt2xphc7st2/WRI-Are%20COVID%20packages%20building%20resilience%20-%20Jan%2020%202021-%20DRAFT%20FOR%20COMMENT.pdf?dl=0 and cited in (Richmond et al., 2021).

6 The Vulnerable Twenty (V20) Group of Ministers of Finance of the Climate Vulnerable Forum is a dedicated cooperation initiative of economies systemically vulnerable to climate change. The V20 works through dialogue and action to tackle global climate change. Full membership available here: https://www.v-20.org/members.

7 The IPCC has considered adaptation transformation along three axes: (1) transformation inducing fundamental change through the scaling up of adaptation, conceived as a limited, technical intervention with transformative potential; (2) transformation as actions or interventions opened when the limits of incremental adaptation have been reached; (3) transformation seeking to address underlying failures of development, including increasing greenhouse gas emissions by linking adaptation, mitigation, and sustainable development (IPCC, 2014).

8 See: https://unfccc.int/topics/adaptation-and-resilience/the-big-picture/new-elements-and-dimensions-of-adaptation-under-the-paris-agreement-article-7.

9 Support was provided by the Green Climate Fund (GCF), as well as a number of private and foreign government agencies. See here: https://napglobalnetwork.org/wp-content/uploads/2018/07/napgn-en-2018-nepal-nap-process.pdf.

10 See: https://www.whitehouse.gov/briefing-room/statements-releases/2021/04/23/fact-sheet-president-bidens-leaders-summit-on-climate/.

11 See: https://adaptationexchange.org/adaptationActionAgenda.

12 For discussion of risk-resilience approaches in different scientific fields see, for example, Bhamra, Dani and Burnard 2011; Briguglio et al. 2011; Brinkmann et al., 2017; Renn et al., 2020.

13 The two approaches differ in how they conceptualize adaptation and development. The TRM approach sees them as separate (adaptation plus development), while the PPVR sees them jointly (adaptation as development).

14 The latter can be understood as a breakdown of the entire system as opposed to breakdown of its individual components, or a risk that cannot be diversified away (def).

## References

Ackerman F (2017). Worst-Case Economics: Extreme Events in Climate and Finance. Anthem Press. London.

Bhamra R, Dani S and Burnard K (2011). Resilience: The concept, a literature review and future directions. *International Journal of Production Research.* 49(18): 5375–5393.

Bhattacharya A, Calland R, Averchenkova A, Gonzalez L, Martinez-Diaz L and Roolj JV (2020). *Delivering on the $100 billion Climate Finance Commitment and Transforming Climate Finance.* United Nations.

Available at https://www.un.org/sites/un2.un.org/files/100_billion_climate_finance_report.pdf.

Boyd E (2017). Climate adaptation: Holistic thinking beyond technology. *Nature Climate Change* 7(2): 97–98.

Briguglio L, Cordina G, Farrugia N and Vella S (2009). Economic vulnerability and resilience: Concepts and measurements. *Oxford Development Studies*. 7(3): 229–247.

Brinkmann H, Harendt C, Heinemann F and Nover J (2017). Economic resilience: A new concept for policy making? Bertelsmann Stiftung. Available at https://www.bertelsmann-stiftung.de/de/publikationen/publikation/did/inclusive-growth-for-germany-12-economic-resilience-a-new-concept-for-policy-making.

Caldera-Sanchez A, de Serres A, Gori F, Hermansen M and Röhn O (2016). Strengthening economic resilience: insights from the post-1970 record of severe recessions and financial crises. Economic Policy Paper No. 20. Organisation for Economic Co-operation and Development.

Carney M (2015). Breaking the tragedy of the horizon – climate change and financial stability. Speech by Mr Mark Carney, Governor of the Bank of England and Chairman of the Financial Stability Board, at Lloyd's of London. London, 29 September.

Ciplet D and Roberts JT (2017). Climate change and the transition to neoliberal environmental governance. *Global Environmental Change*. 46: 148–156.

CRED and UNDRR (2020). *Human Cost of Disasters: An Overview of the Last 20 years (2000-2019)*. Centre for Research on the Epidemiology of Disaster and United Nations Office for Disaster Risk Reduction (UNDRR). Available at https://www.undrr.org/publication/human-cost-disasters-overview-last-20-years-2000-2019.

Diffenbaugh NS and Burke M (2019). Global warming has increased global economic inequality. *Proceedings of the National Academy of Sciences*. 116(20): 9808–9813. Available at https://www.pnas.org/content/pnas/116/20/9808.full.pdf.

Dilling L, Daly M, Travis WR and Wilhelmi OV (2015). The dynamics of vulnerability: Why adapting to climate variability will not always prepare us for climate change. *WIREs Clim Change*. 6(4): 413–425.

Dodman D and Mitlin D (2013). Challenges for community-based adaptation: Discovering the potential for transformation. *Journal of International Development*. 25(5): 640–659.

Dolsak N and Prakash A (2018). The Politics of Climate Change Adaptation. *Annual Review of Environment and Resources*. 43: 317–341.

ECLAC (2018). *The Caribbean Outlook 2018*. LC/SES.37/14. Economic Commission for Latin America and the Caribbean. Available at https://repositorio.cepal.org/bitstream/handle/11362/43581/4/S1800607_en.pdf.

ECLAC (2020). *The Climate Emergency in Latin America and the Caribbean: The Path Ahead – Resignation or Action?* Economic Commission for Latin America and the Caribbean. Available at https://www.cepal.org/es/publicaciones/45677-la-emergencia-cambio-climatico-america-latina-caribe-seguimos-esperando-la.

Ensor JE, Wennström P, Bhatterai A, Nightingale AJ, Eriksen S and Sillmann J (2019). Asking the right questions in adaptation research and practice: Seeing beyond climate impacts in rural Nepal. *Environmental Science & Policy*. 94: 227–236.

Eriksen S, Schipper ELF, Scoville-Simonds M, Vincent K, Adam HN, Brooks N, Harding B, Khatri D, Lenaerts L, Liverman D, Mills-Novoa M, Mosberg M, Movik S, Muok B, Nightingale A, Ojha H, Sygna L, Taylor M, Vogel C and West JJ (2021). Adaptation interventions and their effect on vulnerability in developing countries: Help, hindrance or irrelevance? *World Development*. 141: 105383. Available at https://doi.org/10.1016/j.worlddev.2020.105383.

Forsyth T (2013). Community-based adaptation: A review of past and future challenges. *WIREs Climate Change*. 4(5): 439–446.

Funder M, Mweemba C and Nyambe I. (2018). The politics of climate change adaptation in development: Authority, resource control and state intervention in rural Zambia. *The Journal of Development Studies*. 54(1): 30-46.

Funder M and Mweemba C E (2019). Interface bureaucrats and the everyday remaking of climate interventions: Evidence from climate change adaptation in Zambia. *Global Environmental Change*. 55: 130–138.

Gabor D (2021). The Wall Street Consensus. *Development and Change*. 52 (3): 429–459.

Gallagher K and Kozul-Wright R (2019). *A New Multilateralism for Shared Prosperity: Geneva Principles for a Global Green New Deal*. UNCTAD. Geneva.

Gannon K, Crick F, Atela J and Conway D (2021). What role for multi-stakeholder partnerships in adaptation to climate change? Experiences from private sector adaptation in Kenya. *Climate Risk Management*. 32:100319.

Ge Q, Qu J, Zeng J and Fang X (2009). Review on international strategies and trends for adaptation to climate change. *Advancement Climate Change Research*. 5: 369–375.

Global Comission on Adaptation (2019). Global Adaptation Report. Adapt now: A global call for leadership on climate resilience. Global Commission on Adaptation. Available at https://gca.org/about-us/the-global-commission-on-adaptation.

Goldin I and T Vogel (2010). Global governance and systemic risk in the 21st century: Lessons from the financial crisis. *Global Policy*. 1 (1): 4–15.

Government of Fiji (2016). *Fiji—Post-Disaster Needs Assessment: Tropical Cyclone Winston*. 20 February. Government of Fiji. Available at https://www.gfdrr.org/sites/default/files/publication/Post%20Disaster%20Needs%20Assessments%20CYCLONE%20WINSTON%20Fiji%202016%20(Online%20Version).pdf.

Hallegatte S (2018). Poverty and climate change: An introduction. *Environment and Development Economics*. 23(3): 217–233.

Harrington LJ and Otto FEL (2020). Reconciling theory with the reality of African heatwaves. *Nature Climate Change*. 10(9): 796–798.

IPCC (2014). *AR5 Climate Change 2014: Impacts, Adaptation, and Vulnerability*. Intergovernmental Panel on Climate Change. Intergovernmental Panel on Climate Change. Available at https://www.ipcc.ch/report/ar5/wg2/.

IPCC (2018). Global Warming of 1.5°C: An IPCC Special Report on the Impacts of Global Warming of 1.5°C Above Pre-industrial Levels and Related Global Greenhouse Gas Emission Pathways, in the Context of Strengthening the Global Response to the Threat of Climate Change, Sustainable Development, and Efforts to Eradicate Poverty. Intergovernmental Panel on Climate Change.

IPCC (2021). AR6 Climate Change 2021: The Physical Science Basis. Intergovernmental Panel on Climate Change.

Jasanoff S (2013). *Science and Public Reason*. Routledge-Earthscan.Abingdon, Oxon.

Keen S (2021). The appallingly bad neoclassical economics of climate change. *Globalizations*. 18(7): 1149–1177.

Kikstra J, Waidelich P, Rising J, Yumashev D, Hope C and Brierley CM (2021). The social cost of carbon dioxide under climate-economy feedbacks and temperature variability. Environmental Research Letters. 16(9):4037 .

Kjellstrom T and Maître N (2019). *Working on a Warmer Planet: The Effect of Heat Stress on Productivity and Decent Work* [Report]. International Labour Organisation. Geneva. Available at http://www.ilo.org/global/publications/books/WCMS_711919/lang--en/index.htm.

Kumar SN, Aggarwal P K, Saxena R, Rani S, Jain S and Chauhan N (2013). An assessment of regional vulnerability of rice to climate change in India. *Climatic Change*. 118(3-4): 683–699.

Least Developed Countries Expert Group (2002). *Annotated guidelines for the preparation of national adaptation programmes of action*. United Nations Framework Convention on Climate Change (UNFCCC). Available at https://unfccc.int/resource/docs/publications/annguid_e.pdf.

Least Developed Countries Expert Group (2009). *Step-By-Step Guide for Implementing National Adaptation Programmes of Action*. FCCC/GEN/250E. United Nations Framework Convention on Climate Change (UNFCCC). Available at http://unfccc.int/resource/docs/publications/ldc_napa2009.pdf.

Least Developed Countries Expert Group (2012). *Best Practices and Lessons Learned in Addressing Adaptation in the Least Developed Countries* [Vol. 2]. FCCC/GEN/278 E. United Nations Framework Convention on Climate Change (UNFCCC). Available at http://unfccc.int/resource/docs/publications/ldc_publication_bbll_2012.pdf.

Least Developed Countries Expert Group (2015). *Regional synergy in addressing adaptation through the national adaptation programmes of action and the national adaptation plan process in least developed countries*. United Nations Framework Convention on Climate Change (UNFCCC). Available at http://unfccc.int/6110.

Masson-Delmotte V., Zhai P, Pörtner H.-O, Roberts D, Skea J, Shukla PR, Pirani A and Moufouma-Okia W (2018). *Global Warming of 1.5C. An IPCC Special Report on the impacts of globa warming of 1.5C above pre-industrtial levels and related greenhouse gas emission pathways, in the context of strengthening the global response to the threat of cliamte change, sustainable development, and efforts to eradicate poverty*. Intergovernmental Panel on Climate Change (IPCC). Available at https://www.ipcc.ch/site/assets/uploads/sites/2/2019/06/SR15_Full_Report_High_Res.pdf.

Mikulewicz M (2018) Politicizing vulnerability and adaptation: On the need to democratize local responses to climate impacts in developing countries. *Climate and Development*. 10(1):18–34.

Moore M-L, Riddell Dand Vocisano D (2015). Scaling out, scaling up, scaling deep: Strategies of non-profits in advancing systemic social innovation. *Journal of Corporate Citizenship*. 58: 67–84.

Næss LO, Newell P, Newsham A, Phillips J and Quan J (2015). Climate policy meets national development: Insights from Kenya and Mozambique. *Global Environmental Change*. 35: 534–544.

Nagoda A and Nightingale J (2017). Participation and power in climate change adaptation policies:

Vulnerability in food security programs in Nepal. *World development.* 100: 85–93.

Neuman B, Vafeidis AT, Zimmermann J and Nicholls RJ (2015). Future coastal population growth and exposure to sea-level rise and coastal flooding - A global assessment. *PLoS One.* 10(6): e0131375.

Nordhaus W (2018). Climate change: The ultimate challenge for economics. The Sveriges Riksbank Prize in Economic Sciences in Memory of Alfred Nobel. Stockholm University.

O'Brien K (2018). Is the 1.5°C target possible? Exploring the three spheres of transformation. *Current Opinion in Environmental Sustainability.* 31: 153–160. Available at https://doi.org/10.1016/j.cosust.2018.04.010.

Opitz-Stapleton S, Nadin R, Kellett J, Calderone M, Quevedo A, Peters K and Mayhew L (2019). *Risk-informed Development: From Crisis to Resilience.* United Nations Development Programme. New York.

Oxfam (2015). Carbon emissions and income inequality. Technical Briefing. Oxfam. Available at https://oxfamilibrary.openrepository.com/bitstream/handle/10546/582545/tb-carbon-emissions-inequality-methodology-021215-en.pdf?sequence=2.

Pardoe J, Vincent K, Conway D, Archer E, Dougill AJ, Mkwambisi D and Tembo-Nhlema D (2018). Evolution of national climate adaptation agendas in Malawi, Tanzania and Zambia: The role of national leadership and international donors. *Regional Environmental Change.* 20:118.

Pauw WP, Castro P, Pickering Jand Bhasin S (2020). Conditional nationally determined contributions in the Paris Agreement: Foothold for equity or Achilles heel? *Climate Policy.* 20(4): 468–484. Available at https://doi.org/10.1080/14693062.2019.1635874.

Perry KK (2020). For politics, people, or the planet? The political economy of fossil fuel reform, energy dependence and climate policy in Haiti. *Energy Research & Social Science.* 63: 101397. Available at https://doi.org/10.1016/j.erss.2019.101397.

Renn O, Laubichler M, Lucas K, Kröger W, Schanze J, Scholz RW and Schweizer PJ (2020). Systemic risks from different perspectives. *Risk Analysis.* Available at https://onlinelibrary.wiley.com/doi/10.1111/risa.13657.

Richmond M, Choi J, Rosane P, Solomon M., Tonkonogy B, Molloy D, Larrain F and Rae JJ (2021). *Adaptation Finance in the Context of Covid-19: The Role of Development Finance in Promoting a Resilient Recovery.* Global Center on Adaptation. Available at https://gca.org/wp-content/uploads/2021/01/GCA-Adaption-in-Finance-Report.pdf.

Rigaud KK, de Sherbinin A, Jones B, Bergmann J, McCusker B, Schewe J, Ober, Heuser S, Adamo S, Clement V and Midgley A (2018). *Groundswell: Preparing for Internal Climate Migration.* World Bank Group. Washington, D.C.

Robinson Sand Dornan M (2017). International financing for climate change adaptation in small island developing states. *Regional Environmental Change.* 17(4): 1103–1115.

Saghir J, Schaeffer M, Chen A, Ijjasz-Vasquez EJ, So Jand Mena Carrasco M (2020). *State and Trends in Adaptation Report 2020: Building Forward Better from Covid-19: Accelerating Action on Climate Adaptation.* Global Center on Adaptation. Available at https://gca.org/wp-content/uploads/2021/03/GCA-State-and-Trends-Report-2020-Online-3.pdf.

Sherman M, Berrang-Ford L, Lwasa SFord J, Namanya DB, Llanos-Cuentas A, Maillet M and Harper S (2016). Drawing the line between adaptation and development: A systematic literature review of planned adaptation in developing countries. *WIREs Climate Change.* 7(5):707–726. https://wires.onlinelibrary.wiley.com/doi/abs/10.1002/wcc.416.

Soanes M, Bahadur A, Shakya C, Rumbaitis del Rio C, Dinshaw A, Coger T, Smith B, Patel S, Huq S, Patel S, Musa M, Rahman F, Gupta S, Dolcemascolo G and Mann T (2021). Principles for locally led adaptation. Issue Paper. International Institute for Environment and Development (IIED). January.

Standing G (2019). *Plunder of the Commons: A Manifesto for Sharing Public Wealth.* Pelican Books. London

Stern N (2007). *The Economics of Climate Change: The Stern Review.* Cambridge University Press. Cambridge.

SwissRe (2021). The economics of climate change: No action not an option. SwissRe Institute. April.

UNCTAD (*TDR 2017*). *Trade and Development Report 2017: Beyond Austerity – Towards a Global New Deal.* (United Nations publication. Sales No. E.17. II.D.5. New York and Geneva).

UNCTAD (*TDR 2018*). *Trade and Development Report 2018: Power, Platforms and the Free Trade Illusion.* (United Nations publication. Sales No. E.18.II.D.7. New York and Geneva).

UNCTAD (*TDR 2019*). *Trade and Development Report 2019: Financing a Green New Deal.* (United Nations publication. Sales No. E.19.II.D.15. Geneva).

UNCTAD (2021). *Development and Globalization: Facts and Figures 2021.* UNCTAD Geneva.

UNDP (2018). From early recovery to long-term resilience in the Caribbean Hurricanes Irma and Maria: One year on. Summary Report. United Nations Development Programme. Available at https://www.latinamerica.undp.org/content/dam/rblac/

UNDP-Recovery-Programme%202%20oct%20 WEB.pdf.

UNDESA (2008). *World Economic and Social Survey 2008: Overcoming Economic Security.* United Nations, Department of Economic and Social Affairs. New York.

UNEP (2020). *Adaptation Gap Report 2020.* United Nations Environment Programme. Available at https://unepdtu.org/wp-content/uploads/2021/01/adaptation-gap-report-2020.pdf.

United Nations (2019). *25 Years of Adaptation under the UNFCCC Report by the Adaptation Committee.* United Nations Climate Change Secretariat. Available at https://unfccc.int/sites/default/files/resource/AC_25%20Years%20of%20Adaptation%20Under%20the%20UNFCCC_2019.pdf.

United Nations (2021). Financing for Sustainable Development Report 2021. Inter-Agency Task Force on Financing for Development. (Sales No. E.21.I.6. New York). Available at https://developmentfinance.un.org/fsdr2021.

Wallace-Wells, D. (2019). "The Uninhabitable Earth: a Story of the Future", Penguin Books, UK.

United Nations General Assembly (2015). Resolution adopted by the General Assembly on 3 June 2015. Document A/RES/69/283.

WEF (2019). Water is a growing source of global conflict. Here's what we need to do. World Economic Forum. Available at https://www.weforum.org/agenda/2019/03/water-is-a-growing-source-of-global-conflict-heres-what-we-need-to-do/.

WFP (2021). *The State of Food Security and Nutrition in the World. 2021: Transforming Food System for Food Security, Improved Nutrition and Affordable Healthy Diets for All.* World Food Programme. Rome.

World Bank (2012). *Climate Change, Disaster Risk, and the Urban Poor: Cities Building Resilience for a Changing World.* World Bank. Washington D.C.

World Bank (2020). *Poverty and Shared Prosperity 2020: Reversals of Fortune.* World Bank Group. Washington, D.C.

Zhang Y, Held I and Fueglistaler S (2021). Projections of tropical heat stress constrained by atmospheric dynamics. Nature Geoscience. 14: 133–137.

# FROM DE-RISKING TO DIVERSIFICATION: MAKING STRUCTURAL CHANGE WORK FOR CLIMATE ADAPTATION

# IV

## A. Introduction

As discussed in the previous chapter, growth prospects in many developing countries are already under threat from climate shocks, with worse to come. Adapting to these shocks is a major policy challenge. The favoured approach has so far emphasized "de-risking" development through a variety of market-based coping measures and relying on the public sector as a benevolent insurer of existing assets. While these may help address some of the immediate consequences of climate shocks, in particular for vulnerable populations, the only lasting solution is to reduce the dependence of developing countries on a small number of climate sensitive activities through a process of structural transformation that can establish more resilient economies.

The success of today's advanced economies, as well as in the catch-up economies of East Asia, rests on sustained economic growth closely tied to structural transformation. At its core, this involves two sets of combined and cumulative processes: a vertical shift in the production structure from the primary sector to manufacturing (and on to high-end services) on the one hand, and a more horizontal move of resources from lower- to higher-productivity and more capital-intensive activities within and across sectors. Together, these processes have, in almost all successful development experiences, facilitated a more diversified pattern of economic activity, raised productivity and led to an improvement across a broad set of social indicators, including poverty reduction.

More diversified economies are also less vulnerable to external shocks which are likely to disrupt the growth and transformation process (OECD/WTO, 2019). This has, in recent years, been apparent with the heightened vulnerability of primary export dependent economies to economic shocks that originate elsewhere in the global economy but it is also the case with climate shocks. Indeed, in many developing countries, particularly those located in tropical and sub-tropical regions, vulnerability to economic and climate shocks are compounding each other, locking countries into an eco-development trap of permanent disruption, economic precarity and slow productivity growth. Breaking out of that trap implies that the climate adaptation challenge in the developing world needs to be approached from a developmental perspective.

Not all past experiences, no matter how attractive, can be easily adapted to contemporary realities. The main problem with turning to history for successful growth experiences is their reliance on fossil fuel-based development paths. Today, developing countries confront the dilemma of having to pursue economic development while keeping emissions and resource consumption within the ecological limits of the planet.

This challenge, in turn, necessitates new strategies that pursue structural transformation in a climate constrained world. As that world wakes up to rebuilding economies after the Covid-19 shock, an opportunity to formulate, agree and implement a set of new policy choices that combine developmental and ecological concerns should not be missed.

Developing country policymakers face this challenge from a position of disadvantage in terms of their ability to mobilise domestic resources, the structural constraints on expanding those resources and their weak or missing institutional capacities and skills, many of which only emerge along with a successful development process. One possible countervailing advantage of economic latecomers is being able to draw on technologies already developed in more advanced economies to help speed up their transformation. This, however, is easier said than done, and an extensive literature has discussed the obstacles to technology transfer facing developing countries, obstacles that are becoming more pronounced in the face of binding environmental constraints.

At one level, many developing countries are less locked-in to fossil fuel-based technologies and to vested interests in public decision-making that may hamper change. Instead, they can build their urban environments, manufacturing industries, energy and transport systems in less carbon-intensive and more environmentally sustainable ways. At the same time, the fragmentation of production processes through the spread of global value chains along with the tightening of intellectual property rights over recent decades are posing even greater obstacles for developing countries in accessing the technologies needed to make that transition, at the same time as they are becoming more exposed to the adverse consequences of a warming climate and the threat of the eco-development trap.

Policy strategies associated with the East Asian development experience – often summarised as the "developmental state" model (e.g., *TDR 2016*; Wade, 2018) – can provide useful guidance in this regard (Poon and Kozul-Wright, 2019). Those strategies, which yielded rapid industrialisation and productivity growth in East Asia in the 1980s and 1990s (and earlier, but more ephemerally, in Latin America), include elements of economic planning and targeted industrial policies, as well as the space required to establish a well-defined national interest, experiment with different policy options and define and negotiate economic priorities across a variety of stakeholders (*TDR 2003*; Beeson, 2006). At the same time, it is clear that today, not only has that space narrowed under the pressures and constraints of hyperglobalization, but the priorities and related trade-offs introduced by adding the environmental dimension of development further complicate efforts to emulate the developmental state model.

This chapter analyses the challenge of structural transformation in the climate-constrained world. It is organized under two broad headings. The initial sections discuss developmental challenges in a historical and comparative setting, using the dual economy model of Sir Arthur Lewis (1954) as a heuristic device to examine how achieving economic development through structural transformation in a climate-constrained world may work, identifying some of the limitations of the original idea. The second examines in more depth how such limitations may be overcome today. It distils policy experiences from successful industrializations and identifies a set of policies (industrial, food and energy security) that can help guide structural transformation while addressing the climate crisis. Taken together, such policies form part of a green developmental state agenda that can respond to developing country priorities in the climate constrained, post-Covid global economic system.

## B. The Lewis model of development for a climate-constrained world

One of the best-known models of economic development was provided by Arthur Lewis (1954). Lewis argued that the driver of economic development was capital accumulation, conditioned by a movement of labour - the abundant production factor in a typical developing country - from the "traditional" or "non-capitalist," low-productivity sector, to the "modern" or "capitalist" sector, characterized by higher productivity, higher wages, and the use of reproducible capital (essentially machines and equipment).

The key condition for this mechanism to work is the existence of surplus labour in the traditional or non-capitalist sector. This surplus ensures that, during an extended period of labour migration, wages in the capitalist sector remain constant because the inflow of workers exceeds demand at the prevailing wage in this sector, determined by the subsistence wage in the traditional sector plus a fixed margin. The resulting surplus of output over wages in the modern sector is captured by the capitalists as profits. The capitalist sector grows, as with ongoing labour migration and constant wages the share of profits in national income rises and parts of the profits are re-invested in the modern sector. This profit-investment nexus gives rise to a virtuous circle of rapid productivity growth, more and better paid jobs, higher household incomes and expanded markets, leading, in turn, to higher levels of investment and thus helping to further boost productivity (Akyüz and Gore, 1996). Once the labour surplus disappears,[1] i.e., an integrated labour market and an integrated economy emerge, rising wages lead to declining returns to investment, and slower growth. The rise in wages may be contained without lowering workers' living standards, by maintaining the availability of wage goods, especially food, at affordable prices which in most cases presupposes productivity and output growth also in agriculture.

A number of the assumptions underlying the Lewis model generated theoretical controversy.[2] In response, Lewis argued that the main objective of his work was not a refinement of abstract models, but an indication of how development, understood as a multidimensional process of economic, social and institutional change, could be tackled in a problem-solving way through instruments of public policy.[3]

A more serious criticism was the view of agriculture as a backward and inherently stagnant sector which ignited interest in a more positive and active role for agriculture development in structural transformation, including through rural institutions and incentives that would spur productivity growth.[4] Timmer (1988) considers that structural transformation starts with rising productivity in agriculture, leading to declining food prices, in turn enabling productivity growth and the development of internationally competitive activities in manufacturing. In other words, this perspective holds that structural transformation depends on rising productivity in both agricultural and non-agricultural sectors, and that the two are connected through backward and forward linkages.

Notwithstanding these criticisms, the Lewis model "remains relevant as an 'ideal type' or heuristic device for the study of economic development through which contemporary patterns of structural transformation and their implications for inclusive growth, wages, profits, employment and productivity can be examined" (Sumner, 2018: 2).

One such examination relates to the use of the main elements of the Lewis model in the analysis of the successful development experiences in East Asia over the past four decades and their potential lessons for current developmental challenges. Although each country needs to tailor its development strategy to its own specific conditions, including historical, cultural and institutional background, certain key elements in the Lewis model, and reflected in the East Asian experience, remain of wider validity. Two of these - the role of capital investment and the capacities of the state – are particularly relevant for the discussion of development challenges in the climate-constrained world today. A third element, the concept of linkages, which was developed, in part, in response to its absence in the original Lewis model, can further enrich that discussion.[5]

## 1. Capital investment

Perhaps the most important feature of the East Asian development experience is the importance of capital investment as a driver of growth-enhancing structural transformation. An expanding modern sector can gradually absorb the labour surplus, while its higher level of productivity supports economic growth. Mobilizing sufficient capital in the initial stages of industrialization may require foreign finance but will increasingly be replaced by a reinvestment of profits into the expanding modern sector, creating a dynamic profit-investment nexus (Akyüz and Gore, 1996). When agriculture is brought into the analysis, it too can become a source of structural transformation as a potential (and often the only) sector to induce growth. Ranis and Fei (1961), argued that agriculture can serve industrialization by generating much-needed foreign exchange to finance imports of capital and intermediate goods, provide a stable domestic market for manufacturing output, and keep the cost of wage goods low (thereby boosting industrial profits and investment).

Capital investment in the modern sector is closely associated with productivity growth: due to scale economies in the modern sector, labour productivity growth is a positive function of the pace of output growth.[6] The positive relationship between capital investment and productivity growth can be boosted further by exports, an element not considered in the Lewis model. This is because increasing investment in sectors that export to developed countries allows production to shift towards products with high income elasticity, while expanding the modern sector requires a large volume of intermediate and capital goods whose imports must be financed with foreign exchange earned through exports. Otherwise, increased external borrowing would raise debt-service ratios which could, in turn, act as a constraint on the growth process.[7]

Similar to the assumption in Lewis (1954) that developing countries can draw on an ever-increasing stock of technologies for the purpose of catching-up with other countries, these mechanisms also imply that productivity growth through technological upgrading largely relies on the transfer, imitation and adaptation of foreign technology that has been successfully used in more advanced economies and whose effective use in developing countries are facilitated by building up domestic technological capacities, local R&D, and better skilled labour. This leads us to the second key element in the Lewis model: the role of the state.

## 2. State capacity

In addition to market mechanisms, Lewis (1954) emphasizes the role of government policies as instrumental to solving a set of successive coordination problems that arise with a process of structural transformation. Specifically, the crucial question in dualistic economies is how to manage the relation between the traditional and the modern sector of the economy.[8] The ability of a government to conceive of and implement policy is defined as state capacity. In the developmental context, and specifically in the case of East Asia, the notion of state capacity includes "precise circumstances, tools, strategies and relationships that distinguish and effectively constitute different national approaches to successful economic development" (Beeson, 2006: 444–445). Successful development outcomes, in turn, depend on the state's ability to institutionalise channels for continual negotiation of economic policies. These channels need to be, on the one hand, aligned with the national interest, but on the other, designed so that the state is not captured by vested economic interests.

Macroeconomic priorities of a developmental state are based on the proactive, pro-investment set of policies, as well as strategic collaboration and coordination between the private sector and the government. The latter is needed to monitor the interdependence between investment and production decisions. These decisions concern identifying the areas where the most significant constraints to investment are; how effectively to channel public and private investment to the high-productivity activities; and monitor whether these investments are managed in such a way as to sustain a high-wage future for citizens and to increase long-term productivity. Such disciplining of investment is ensured through monitorable performance standards and a withdrawal of governmental support that fails to achieve its objective within a given period

of time, as well as through checks on rent-seeking of government officials and entrepreneurs.

While capital formation and stronger state capacity are key pillars of a development state model, there is not one but many variants, of the model, reflecting specific regional, historical and socio-economic factors (Haggard, 2018). And although the 1997–98 crisis in East Asia tarnished the model in some respects, it remains the case that "government signaled the direction, cleared the way, set up the path and – when needed – provided the means" to help countries in the region successfully transition to a sophisticated industrial economy with the active support of a developmental state (Cohen and de Long, 2016: 2).

Even in the agricultural sector, higher productivity is only achievable through significant state support in the form of agricultural extension programmes, such as R&D, and through providing physical infrastructure for water management and irrigation systems, construction of roads for market access, and stabilizing input and output markets through price support schemes (Ranis and Fei, 1961; Johnston and Mellor, 1961). State intervention also targets small to medium farms because of their higher effective demand for domestic production, as opposed to larger and more mechanized farms. These farms tend to use imported inputs for more capital-intensive production technology, which not only depletes foreign reserves but also breaks the forward-backward linkages that are a necessary feature of a cumulative growth process (Adelman, 1984).

Most importantly, state machinery is needed for reallocating the surplus created in the agricultural sector through taxation and manipulating the domestic terms of trade (i.e., to get the prices wrong) in favour of industry. In the absence of the strategic reallocation of the surplus by the state, there is no guarantee of mobilizing the privately owned agrarian surplus coming from millions of separate small and medium-sized producers to strategic sectors for structural transformation.

Externally too, pressures of global economic integration require enhanced state capacity to manage economic integration and protect vulnerable sectors of the economy (Beeson, 2006). While there are potentially strong synergies between investment, exports and productivity growth, particularly with respect to manufacturing activities, positive outcomes are not predetermined; when there is surplus labour, strong import competition, or the exit of less productive firms, trade liberalization can result in declines in aggregate (economy-wide) productivity even as it raises productivity in the industrial sector or among trading firms (McMillan and Rodrik, 2011). The net impact ultimately depends on wider employment dynamics and on whether the productivity growth in industry is outweighed by a larger shift of labour and resources into low productivity work outside the sector. Evidence of such shifts underlie concerns about weak industrialization (including premature de-industrialization) in the developing world in recent decades (*TDR 2003, 2016*; Tregenna, 2009).

With the structure of the economy continuously changing under technological and external market pressures building a network of robust linkages, both domestically and internationally, becomes an even greater economic development challenge to which active industrial and trade policy must adapt accordingly.

### 3. Linkages

The immense appeal of the manufacturing sector lies in its potential to generate productivity and income growth, and because such gains can spread across the economy through production, investment, knowledge, and income linkages. As noted above, a strong link between profits and investment was assumed by the Lewis model and has certainly been key to the success of East Asian later industrializers. Such a link was, however, as much the outcome of active state policies as automatic market forces (Akyüz and Gore, 1996).

Several other linkages that can play an important role in establishing a virtuous pattern of growth and structural transformation deserve mention here. To begin with, expanding production can help build 'backward' linkages (to source inputs for production), and 'forward' linkages in so far as the produced goods are used in other economic activities (Hirschman, 1958). This relates, for instance, to domestically produced pesticides and simple agricultural equipment, as well as agricultural raw materials as inputs for domestic production. Intersectoral linkages emerge as knowledge and efficiency gains spread beyond manufacturing to other sectors of the economy, including primary and service activities (Tregenna, 2010). There also are additional benefits to be gained from adaptability linkages: in manufacturing, which lends itself more to the division of labour, there is a high degree of adaptability towards the use of inputs beyond the immediate industrial niche.

Investment linkages are created when investments in productive capacity, new entrepreneurial ventures, and the related extensions of manufacturing activities in one enterprise or subsector trigger additional investments in other firms or sectors, which otherwise would not occur because the profitability of a specific investment project in a certain area of manufacturing activity often depends on prior or simultaneous investments in a related activity (Rodrik, 2004). In turn, the coordination problem that may result from these interdependencies can be resolved by strategic collaboration between the government and business organizations or between the government and state-owned enterprises.

Income linkages emerge from rising wage incomes generated from industrial expansion; these add to the virtuous cycle through 'consumption linkages', when higher wages trigger higher food demand which, in turn, causes rising demand for domestic inputs to agriculture. Income linkages also operate through supplementary government revenues (i.e., 'fiscal linkages'), which may therefore expand public expenditure. The creation of such income linkages can strengthen the self-reinforcing aspect of industrialization through increasing domestic demand and therefore GDP growth.

The expansion of manufacturing activities and the diversification process more generally as key to successful transformation can be interpreted as the complex intertwining of these linkages and related feedback loops through a process of "cumulative causation" (Myrdal, 1957; Kaldor, 1957). However, one obvious caveat should be pointed out: historically the expansion of manufacturing has tended to rely on patterns of production that damage the environment through pollution and lead to degradation and overexploitation of natural resources and excessive carbon emissions associated with climate change. Indeed, a shift to services-based growth could be advocated precisely in order to avoid the environmental problems that have emerged in some rapidly industrializing countries. However, there are both strong analytical and empirical grounds to assume that the services sector needs to rely on strong intersectoral linkages and interdependencies with a mature manufacturing sector to itself upgrade (*TDR 2016*; Cherif and Hasanov, 2019). In any case, such problems are not intrinsic to the industrialization process: they depend crucially on the choice of technologies, policies and regulations.

# C. Climate change, development and post-Covid recovery

The need for effective state capacity and active policy to manage structural transformation is amplified further by climate change, and so are the challenges of policymaking. A climate-conscious developmental state today must be able to balance the threat of climate change along with the longstanding goals of achieving economic growth and closing the economic and technological gaps with more advanced economies. At the most basic level, addressing climate change makes structural transformation a global task, in which the advanced economies must take the lead in undertaking profound changes in their patterns of production and consumption but where significant structural and technological changes are also necessary even in the least developed countries. But while climate-related structural transformation is needed to address the degradation of the global commons, targeted national policies (and resources) are needed to address the adaptation challenge countries are facing from the rising temperature already baked into current patterns of growth. Aligning these global and national challenges is neither straightforward nor automatic but requires strategic planning and policy intervention. In line with the discussion in the previous section, the integrated policy framework that is required can build around efforts to achieve more diversified economies.

The divergence between global climate objectives and immediate national interests is most evident for countries with large fossil-fuel sectors, as policies to reduce emissions will inevitably depress fossil fuel demand. Political short-termism in the wake of the pandemic can also lead some countries to attract polluting industries from countries with more stringent environmental standards and regulations, with the resulting proceeds providing income that could be used to reduce pollution later. Such a "grow-now-clean-up-later" suggests an environmental Kuznets curve, along which indicators of environmental degradation first rise, and then fall, with increasing per capita income (Stern, 2004). Such an approach may seem particularly attractive considering high uncertainty and considerable up-front investment related to pioneering green technologies that may be shouldered more easily by more advanced economies, as well as a way to force early industrializers to pay their historic debt for past pollution (UNCTAD, 2020a).

At the same time, the urgency to preclude the risk of catastrophic tipping points, combined with the more proactive policies that have been adopted to combat the Covid-19 pandemic, open up an accommodative terrain for action. As this *Report* argues in preceding chapters, responses to the Covid-19 pandemic offer an ideal opportunity for fresh thinking about the public policy agenda and for using stimulus and recovery measures in order to accelerate structural change towards a low-carbon economy. The big policy challenge lies in ensuring that these measures trigger more virtuous growth circles, initiating cumulative technological changes in low-carbon growth sectors, supporting economic diversification, and creating employment opportunities that will be maintained even as temperatures rise.

To examine how this more accommodative terrain may be used for these purposes, we extend the guiding principles of the Lewis model in relation to the climate adaptation challenges and outline possible policy impacts on structural transformation in three scenarios: (i) continuing with business as usual; (ii) focusing climate-adaptation action on changes in consumer behaviour and other factors affecting trade; and (iii) approaching climate adaptation in a cohesive, integrated manner.

Scenarios 1 and 2 are not mutually exclusive. They each contain a series of risks to development and equitable growth, which we analyse below. Our analysis suggests that only a cohesive, integrated strategy towards climate-oriented structural transformation will deliver the type of development sustainable in a climate-constrained world. Given that climate constraints require structural transformation to include a shift from high- to low-carbon technologies as a further crucial step, structural transformation in a climate-constrained world can only succeed when it is approached in an integrated, cohesive manner, with a universal shift towards low-carbon technology occurring alongside productivity growth, expanding employment opportunities, and rising living standards for all citizens throughout the world.

## (a) Scenario 1. Business as usual as a constraint on structural transformation: the case of agriculture

Many developing countries are already experiencing the constraint of a changing climate on structural transformation and income growth. This is most clearly the case where agricultural activity is still a major source of income, and where the dependence on temperature, precipitation and other climate variables is uniquely significant among economic sectors. These factors combine to undermine resource bases and cause a global loss of agricultural production (FAO, 2021a).

While great uncertainty about the net impact of climate change on global agriculture remains, evidence suggests that the agricultural and forestry sectors in developing countries are particularly vulnerable to climate change. Part of this results from within the agricultural sector. Due to significant emissions from fertilizer application, intensive livestock and manure management, and the burning of agricultural residuals and savanna for land clearing, industrial agriculture has contributed to soil overexploitation and degradation, as well as to desertification, deforestation, and water pollution.

At the same time, the greater importance of agriculture for their economies, and the smaller size of their farms, often occupying marginal land areas, can limit the ability of developing countries to cope with even small changes in temperature and precipitation. As a result, many developing regions will be exposed to significant reductions in agricultural output and in average yields of food items, as well as an erosion of arable land. Model simulations indicate that, depending on crop adaptability, climate change could cause yield losses of 5–25 per cent in food production that could trigger an increase in projected levels of average aggregated world crop commodity prices by 12–18 percent by 2050 (Rosegrant et al., 2021).

Especially in places where these features occur in situations of high or rising population density, climate change will impair economic activities in agriculture and forestry and increase the likelihood of social conflict, with both factors incentivizing large-scale migration from rural to urban areas. Contrary to the Lewis model, where rural-urban migration is voluntary and driven by sectoral differences in labour-market outcomes, this migration is involuntary. It may also be "pre-mature" (Godfrey, 1979) in the sense that labour migration is decoupled from productivity growth and instead results from degrading agricultural areas ocurring before the industrial sector is able to gainfully absorb the migrants, i.e., before migrants can find employment in activities with substantial profit and re-investment opportunities (e.g., Barrett et al., 2021). Such pre-mature migration also can cause rising food prices, with adverse consequences

on the purchasing power of urban workers and the international competitiveness of manufacturing firms. As a result, climate-change related labour migration causes a risk of swelling urban informal sectors with employment and income precarity and little potential for productivity growth.[9]

Some of these developments are already apparent in recent structural transformation experiences in Africa. Regarding agriculture, there is great heterogeneity across developing countries and the absolute climate-related loss of agricultural production over the period 2008–2018 was particularly high in Asia, with China accounting for more than half of the global loss. However, the severity of agricultural production losses is most evident when expressed in terms of the share of potential production: on this measure, African economies have lost up to 8 per cent, considerably higher than losses at the global level (FAO, 2021a). Moreover, agricultural development in Africa was driven not by productivity increases but mainly by area expansion and intensification that have resulted in widespread land degradation and soil nutrient depletion (Badiane, Diao and Jayne, 2021).[10]

Both these developments have contributed to people leaving farming. Yet the resulting decline of labour in agriculture as a share of total employment has not been accompanied by a meaningful growth of well-paying jobs in large-scale manufacturing activity. Rather, it has been accompanied by fast growth in occupations related to construction, food trade and personal care services, often in the form of informal urban activities. This means that premature labour migration from agriculture has been related to the rise of what Lewis (1979) had called an "in-between" urban sector (Diao and McMillan, 2018; Kruse et al., 2021).

In addition to persistent high inflation related to food price increases (Alper et al., 2016) – including from lower-than-expected food production, the non-tradability of major food staples, and generally fragile agricultural sectors – an important reason why a large-scale modern manufacturing sector has not emerged in sub-Saharan Africa may be the nature of technologies available to African firms.[11] Recent evidence for Ethiopia and the United Republic of Tanzania indicates that the few large-scale manufacturing firms that exist in these countries have adopted significantly more capital-intensive technologies than would be expected in terms of these countries' income levels or relative factor endowments (Diao et al., 2021). This bias towards capital-intensive technology may result from the spread of global value chains and the resulting homogenising effect on technology adoption around the world. To compete with production in much richer countries it became indispensable for African firms to adopt the capital-intensive technologies developed in advanced economies that allowed them to boost productivity but not to expand employment opportunities that could have absorbed labour migration from agriculture.

The existence of an "in-between" urban sector raises more general questions regarding the relationship between the informal sector and climate mitigation. Literature suggests that informal sectors facilitate a green economy, for example, in terms of waste management, recycling and processing waste into new products; agri-food markets by encouraging the use of local green technologies in smallholder farming and by providing better affordable food, which in turn may allow consumers to undertake green investments; use of biomass energy; the upgrading of housing and infrastructure where achieving greater energy efficiency often requires labour-intensive works; and in the form of home-based work that compared to formal employment requires less transport, space and utilities, including electricity (e.g., Benson, 2014; Chen and Raveendran, 2014; Özgür, et al., 2021).

At the same time, the diffused and unorganized character of informal sectors make it more onerous for authorities to track and enforce environmental regulations. Given this circumvention of environmental regulation and the finding of an inverse relationship between environmental pollution and the intensity of government regulations, most informal economic activities intensify environmental degradation (Brown et al., 2014). Moreover, informal manufacturing sectors are usually made up of small-scale firms that lack the capital base for investment in clean or energy-efficient technologies (e.g., Timilsana and Malla, 2021). But depending on the linkages between formal and informal enterprises, the circumvention of environmental regulation may sometimes be intentional, perhaps even enabled by the authorities, with formal enterprises outsourcing environmentally burdensome activities to informal enterprises to cut production costs and, in some cases, maintain international competitiveness.[12] Urban informality also tends to encourage informal settlements or slums. These areas suffer from the lack of decent sanitation services and facilities and their locations both create and expose their inhabitants to climate-related hazards, especially flooding and landslides.

Taken together, measures designed to achieve economic development through structural transformation in a climate-constrained world will need to achieve sufficiently productive agriculture to ensure food security at affordable prices. Such measures include, but are not confined to, halting deforestation and land degradation, and, at the same time, improving access to technology in manufacturing and in agriculture that would enable productivity growth and employment generation.

## (b) Scenario 2. Environmental sustainability vs. structural transformation: the case of consumer behaviour and trade

Growing environmental concerns have increasingly been reflected, particularly in advanced economies, in consumer demands that firms prioritize social and environmental sustainability along their supply chains. Recent evidence indicates an increasing scrutiny from consumers and regulators regarding firms' environmental standards but also that most firms have yet to achieve sufficient visibility of their supply chains and put processes in place that would allow them to undertake meaningful action commensurate to their mission or purpose statements (Villena and Gioia, 2020).

A strengthening of environmental sustainability measures could adversely affect structural transformation in developing countries to the extent that, over the next three years, lead firms refocus on the manufacturing links in their supply chains, and, in particular, on improving environmental sustainability by moving some of those links onshore or make more localized as part of their general objective of reducing overall shipping miles (Oxford Economics, 2021). The likely extent of reshoring, in both the short and the long run, is still unclear (Barbieri et al., 2020). However, such measures are likely to hamper structural transformation through export-oriented manufacturing that has played an important role in the successful experiences in East Asia particularly because the supply chains with the highest end-to-end emissions include sectors such as textiles and garments, plastics, electronics, and automobiles (WEF, 2021).

Structural change through export-oriented manufacturing may also be harmed once it is realized that it is erroneous to believe that services is a low-emissions sector and that the increasing shift in consumption patterns of developed countries towards services is a means of decoupling economic growth from environmental damages. Emission accounts which include upstream value-chain emissions in the form of inputs procured by service providers for five developed economies reveal that their services sector accounts for around one fifth of these economies' total emissions. This is because service provision requires inputs from manufacturing – electronics, pharmaceutics, materials and machinery – sectors that produce emissions and that often take the form of imported inputs and intermediates (Roberts et al., 2021).

While such trade-related consumer-based accounts are gaining importance, there is little evidence to suggest that global maritime transport is a main contributor to CO2-emissions. Indeed, other modes of transport, and in particular road transport, are significantly more polluting, with international maritime transport generating less than 10 per cent of the emissions of the transport sector (IEA, 2019).

Climate change can also hamper developing countries' manufactured exports by the damage that natural hazard events (such as sea level change, increased storm intensities and rising temperatures) cause to ports and maritime supply chains, which enable global commerce. Even though prospective damages are sizeable,[13] only a few countries have implemented required adaptation strategies. Uncertainties in climate projections, high upfront costs, and often unquantifiable benefits of adaptation measures imply that such investment can make a port more attractive for some time but eventually will prove to be no more than stop-gap measures because they do not solve the underlying cause of climate change (Becker et al., 2018). Nevertheless, many developing countries may be at a disadvantage as smaller ports are likely to have the least resources for required investments and may lose their local port functions in a process towards consolidation of port infrastructure at the regional level.

Structural transformation through export-oriented manufacturing will also become more challenging if developed countries establish carbon border adjustment mechanisms (CBAMs), i.e., tax imported goods based on domestic carbon prices and the greenhouse gases emitted abroad to make them.[14] By imposing the same price on carbon emissions from domestic and foreign production, such mechanisms would set limits on the carbon content in traded goods. As such, they would be particularly onerous for the many developing countries that rely on coal-based electricity as an energy source for their manufacturing activities.

One major objective of CBAM is to avoid so-called "carbon leakage", i.e., a shift of polluting industries to jurisdictions with less stringent emission regulations that might occur with an increase in domestic carbon prices. Such increases are generally considered to be required to attain recently set tighter climate objectives – such as reducing emissions by 2030 from 40 per cent to 55 per cent, as adopted by the EU (European Commission, 2021a) – while not causing further de-industrialization in developed countries. This objective also indicates that securing manufacturing employment and activity play a central role in the climate measures of developed countries.

But should carbon border adjustment mechanisms be implemented, much of their impact on structural transformation in developing countries will depend on their detailed technical specifications, with one of the major legal challenges being to make these mechanisms compatible with WTO rules. However, independent of these details, the principle of these mechanisms is to impose on developing countries the environmental standards that developed countries are choosing. This goes against the principle of common but differentiated responsibility enshrined in the Paris Agreement. Moreover, should the revenues from these mechanisms be used in developed countries, rather than be invested in climate adaption in developing countries, they would turn basic principles of climate finance on their head.[15]

## (c) Scenario 3. Low-carbon technology and structural change: the need for a cohesive approach

It has traditionally been considered that latecomers to structural transformation have an advantage over early industrializers because they can quickly and less riskily adopt technologies, methods of production, and management techniques that have been developed in advanced countries. The hypothesis of an "advantage of backwardness" postulates that the more distant a country is from the world's technology frontiers, the greater the potential benefits it can reap from this advantage (Gerschenkron, 1962). This is because adopting existing technology is easier and faster than relying on innovation, which is costlier, more uncertain and highly-knowledge intensive.[16]

However, a strategy of relying on the adoption of technology from advanced economies has become much less attractive because many of these technologies are related to burning fossil fuels. Developing countries that rely on importing carbon-rich technologies risk getting locked into unsustainable production patterns and may have to face very high costs of switching to low-carbon technologies in the future, as the urgency of climate adaptation only increases.

Engaging in low-carbon technologies early in the process of structural transformation avoids the building of high-emission production structures and associated high switching costs in the future. Policy frameworks that mutually reinforce structural change and the adoption of low-carbon technologies reduce the risk of a technological lock-in, especially where low-carbon solutions allow for easy retrofit options and ensure interoperability with existing structures. Moreover, early engagement in low-carbon solutions provides opportunities for augmenting fixed assets in economic activities that can provide and rapidly scale up advantages in international production directed towards new and expanding markets, which either require compliance with high environmental standards or where consumers are willing to pay higher prices for products that emanate from environmentally sustainable production (UNCTAD, 2020a).

This means that, in a climate-constrained world, latecomers to structural transformation might enjoy an "advantage of backwardness" not because they can access proven technologies from advanced countries but because they face less switching costs from their lower level of stranded assets and locked-in carbon-intensive technologies. As a result, their technological challenge is less the gainful appropriation of technologies from advanced economies and retracing the steps taken by already-industrialized countries, than to raise the pace of capital formation by leapfrogging into new low-carbon technologies that are appropriate for their specific economic and ecological conditions.

One way to accelerate capital formation and leapfrog to carbon-low technologies relates to international technology transfer. However, literature suggests that the transfer of low-carbon technology on commercial terms works well among developed countries, while developing countries continue to be exposed to a range of economic, financial, and technical barriers – such as subsidies to fossil-fuel technologies, lacking access to appropriate finance, and an absence of energy efficiency regulations or other incentives for the adoption of low-carbon technology – that prevent private commercial transactions to take place between developed and developing countries (Trærup et al., 2018). These findings are supported by

evidence from trade data. While trade in low-carbon technologies (LCTs) has increased more than global trade over the past three decades, developed countries continue to account for most of both exports and imports of LCTs, even though China has become the world's largest importer and exporter of LCTs. China has also become the leader in foreign direct investment in renewable energy technology, i.e., the only category for which comprehensive FDI-data are available (Pigato et al., 2020).

An analysis of recent patent data (e.g., Corrocher et al., 2021) indicates a remarkable process of growth in green patenting in successful latecomer countries – especially China, but also the Republic of Korea, and Taiwan Province of China. Perhaps most importantly, the recent literature suggests that intellectual property rights (IPRs) do not have a positive impact on technology transfer to developing countries in recent years (e.g., Kirchherr and Urban, 2018). Indeed, a report on LCT transfer concludes that the "analysis presented in this report finds that strong IPR protections have no significant effect on LCT transfer from either high-income or developing countries" (Pigato et al., 2020: xxiii). This finding undermines the traditional case for strong patent protection, based on the argument that strong protection of IPRs promotes the transfer and dissemination of technology. Combined with the general need of a global sharing of the intellectual property that underpins LCT to achieve climate objectives, this finding supports calls for a general waiver of IPRs on LCT like that for Covid-19 vaccines, as further discussed below.

Leapfrogging to low-carbon technologies based on domestic efforts has the potential to yield important benefits in the long run. This is partly because improved environmental performance enhances the attractiveness of suppliers in supply chains, and because it provides opportunities to exploit early mover advantages, at least relative to other latecomers, as markets are not yet taken by incumbents and market entry barriers are lower because technologies are not yet protected by patents.

Many low-carbon technologies are intrinsically local because the nature of their energy source depends on an economy's specific ecological conditions. This implies that new low-carbon technologies have less of a need for retrofitting than new versions of fossil fuel-based technologies would have. Building structural change on fossil fuel-technologies now would be particularly exposed to the risk of asset stranding.

Technological leapfrogging as part of an integrated strategy that combines structural transformation and climate adaptation may rely on what has been called "green windows of opportunity" with features that markedly differ from traditional windows of opportunity for rapid structural change (e.g., Lee and Malherba, 2017). Considering that windows of opportunity for rapid structural transformation may result from "changes to the prevailing techno-economic paradigm, changes in market demand or major modifications to government regulations or policy interventions" (Lema et al., 2020: 1195), case-study evidence indicates that, compared to traditional windows of opportunity, green windows of opportunities stand out due to a relatively more important role of government policies, strong knock-on effects on new market demand (e.g., through government procurement) and technological change (e.g., by inducing mission-guided public R&D programmes), and a relatively greater importance of local conditions and domestic markets (e.g., because of the intrinsically local character of related energy sources, mentioned above) even when the external environment and external market opportunities play an important role.

The greater role of government policies has been reflected in the well-known Porter hypothesis, which states that "properly designed environmental standards can trigger innovation that may partially or more than fully offset the costs of complying with them" (Porter and van der Linde, 1995: 98). Some studies have found only mixed support for this hypothesis in that environmental regulations induce innovation activity in cleaner technologies but that the direct benefits from these innovations do not appear to be large enough to outweigh the costs of regulations. It is important to note that this finding comes from analyses that study the impact of environmental regulations on firm competitiveness in isolation (Dechezleprêtre and Sato, 2018).

By contrast, a recent review of the literature on the impact of investment in clean technologies on sectoral production costs and productivity growth concludes that "most studies examining the relationships between green/clean technologies and productivity show a positive relation", that this is true especially for the manufacturing sector, that large firms have a greater capacity to make such investments, and that the "primary factors behind the growth of green/clean investment are policies and measures introduced by the government in response to environmental concerns, particularly global climate change" (Timilsina and Malla, 2021: 3, 39).

Leapfrogging towards low-carbon technologies also faces important challenges. Apart from building the required technological capabilities, an important challenge for public policies is to ensure that public investment crowds-in private investment in a way that capital accumulation supports structural transformation and employment generation. In other words, policy coherence – combining clear climate commitments with policy measures that demonstrate decisive following through on those commitments – is probably the most important single factor that supports an integrated approach to structural transformation and climate adaptation.

This poses questions as to what a pandemic-related greater permissiveness of proactive policies and the important role that government policy plays in the promotion of green paths to structural transformation imply for concrete policy measures and how these measures can be financed. This is the focus of the second part of this Chapter.

## D. Policies to combine structural transformation and climate adaptation strategies

Neither climate mitigation, nor climate adaptation, are necessarily a drag on economic development. Instead, they can become cylinders in a new engine of growth, which emphasizes the simultaneous achievement of structural transformation (productivity growth, technological upgrading, more and better paid jobs) and the benefits of environmental preservation (avoiding the negative effects of global warming).

The preceding discussion has also shown that, much like industrialization, addressing climate constraints requires far-reaching structural transformation of productive activities, where a climate-conscious structural transformation must include a shift from high- to low-carbon intensive activities. As such, diversification, not de-risking, needs to be put at the centre of the climate adaptation agenda.

This part of the chapter first discusses the impact of climate constraints on industrial policies. It then looks at complementary national policies, with an emphasis on fiscal policy and the role of central banks, and ends on discussing the role of the State in moving towards a low-carbon economy. International policy issues related to trade and finance are the subject of the next chapter.

## 1. Industrial policy revisited

The debate on industrial policy has a long history both in terms of theoretical background and forms of application.[17] Its recent return to prominence in policy discussions is less the result of new analytical insights, and more related to a reassessment of policies that were guided by the Washington Consensus. The lop-sided emphasis on government failures that allegedly cause proactive policies to harm rather than support development, has produced outcomes that have not only fallen short of their own promises but also of successful development experiences that relied on more interventionist policies, leading to a more generalized reappreciation of the role of the state and a related inspection of how industrial policy can be used best. Another reason is the growing recognition that the urgent large-scale transformations related to climate change adaptation cannot be achieved without active government support (e.g., Gallagher and Kozul-Wright, 2019; European Commission, 2021b). Given that moving towards a low-carbon economy implies a reshaping of economic structures, applying key principles of successful industrial policymaking can provide valuable insights for climate change adaptation policies.

Industrial policy may be defined in numerous ways, but most definitions refer to "targeted and selective government policies to shift the production structure towards activities and sectors with higher productivity, better paid jobs and greater technological potential" (*TDR 2016*: 176). Green industrial policy has a wider scope. It aims not only at shifting the economic structure towards higher-productivity activities, but at aligning productivity-enhancing structural transformation with shifts from high carbon-intensive to low carbon-intensive resource-efficient activities, and particularly at exploiting the synergies between these two processes of structural transformation.[18]

The greening of industrial policies comes with additional challenges. Of greatest importance among these additional challenges are that green industrial policy (i) provides a clear normative direction towards "good" technologies that can guide a conscious steering of investment and technological change towards low-carbon activities; and (ii) has significantly greater ambition. This greater ambition is reflected not only in aiming at transforming the entire economy and doing so with considerable urgency in a short period of time to avoid environmental tipping points, but also in its need for broader economic and societal support in the face of higher global temperatures and a more disruptive climate, as further discussed below.

The traditional challenges related to structural transformation combined with these two additional challenges call for a results-driven framework and an approach to industrial policy where policymakers aim at shaping markets and "have the opportunity to determine the *direction* of growth by making strategic investments, coordinating actions across many different sectors, and nurturing new industrial landscapes that the private sector can develop further" (Mazzucato and Kattel, 2020: 312; emphasis in original). In this approach, transformations that unlock the synergies of industrialization and shifts towards low-carbon activities may be considered a global public good, which is generated collectively by a range of actors and in whose generation both the state and the private sector, as well as ordinary citizens, have active roles to play.

The remainder of this section discusses the implications of this perspective of green industrial policy for the objectives of policymakers and for basic principles of effective policymaking aimed at these objectives.

### (a) Selected objectives of green industrial policies

#### i. Energy security

Avoiding the worst effects of climate change makes it imperative to succeed in a large-scale transition to clean and renewable energy. It has been estimated that reaching net-zero carbon emissions by 2050 will involve a reduction of fossil fuel-based energy from almost four-fifths of total energy supply today to around one-fifth. In its stead, wind, solar, geothermal, hydro and bioenergy would have to provide two-thirds of the total (IEA, 2021). The clean-energy transition will arguably have the biggest impact on structural transformation because fossil fuel-based energy has been the backbone of industrial activities.

Most technologies needed to achieve the transition to clean energy and the resulting deep cuts in global emissions by 2030 are today commercially available (Pollin, 2020) and their adoption has already contributed to a large reduction in the cost of energy production over the last decade. According to IRENA (2021), costs of electricity from utility-scale solar photovoltaics (PV) fell 85 per cent between 2010 and 2020, and most of new wind and solar projects produced cheaper energy than coal plants in 2020. Lazard (2020) estimates that onshore wind and utility-scale solar energy became cost-competitive with conventional generation of energy several years ago on a new-built basis, and that the cost of storage of renewable energy has also diminished rapidly. Based on recent trends, further reductions of costs can be expected regarding renewable energy production and storage. In the same vein, Mathews (2020) argues that the costs of solar PV have been falling by 28.5 percent for every doubling of production.

Obstacles to achieving further transformation have been mainly social and political (Pollin, 2020). Especially in developed countries, these obstacles include the high cost in the form of stranded assets that would be implied by disrupting environmentally unsustainable technological pathways. One result of attempts to avoid such costs may be the continued large subsidies for fossil fuels. Recent estimates indicate that, over the period 2017–2019, G20 governments provided an annual average support of $584 billion to the production and consumption of fossil fuels at home and abroad, in the form of direct budgetary transfers and tax expenditure, price support, public finance, and SOE investment (IISD, 2020), with coal and petroleum together account for 85 percent of global fossil-fuel subsidies (Coady et al., 2019).

Removing these obstacles in developing countries will not only foster structural transformation towards a low-carbon economy but also support industrial development. The equipment to generate renewable energy (wind turbines, solar photovoltaic cells, batteries) are products of manufacturing and, just as traditional manufactures, are likely to enjoy increasing returns to scale from learning by doing and, especially as the turn towards renewable energy accelerates, expanding markets (Mathews, 2020). As such, the switch to renewable energy can help foster industrialization, while advancing the energy transition (initially through the diversification of energy sources), reducing the vulnerability of energy security to changes in global fuel prices, and

freeing scarce foreign exchange for imports of capital goods and technologies that will further support industrialization.

Morocco is one example of a developing country that has adopted a comprehensive strategy aimed at industrialization based on low-carbon, resource efficient technologies.[19] Starting from the desire to diversify the energy mix and reduce the share of imported fossil fuels in energy supply, Morocco adopted ambitious renewable energy targets in 2008 and created a favourable legal framework, training and research programmes, a project development and implementation agency, and dedicated public funds to finance required investment. While initially targeting use of renewable energy in housing and agriculture, the government also began providing tax reductions and other investment incentives for manufacturers to adopt domestic renewable energy sources and to manufacture parts and components for renewable energy and energy-efficiency technologies, with a view to creating a market for renewables and foster the development of a local industry. While the strategy has supported employment creation and domestic manufacturing, insufficient coordination of individual policy measures has hampered a scaling-up of the initiatives and their outcomes (Auktor, 2017).

China's engagement in renewable energy production has also initially aimed at building energy security. But the judicious coordination of a wide range of industrial policy measures (such as tax incentives, domestic capability formation and standard setting, and the provision by development banks of finance at discounted rates in priority activities) has propelled China to a globally leading provider of manufactured low-carbon energy devices (Mathews, 2020). This has been the case particularly for solar photovoltaic products, which can be mass manufactured and provide an easier entry point for developing countries into emerging low-carbon technologies than, for example, wind power equipment where the high transport cost of some components, or the requirement for local maintenance and servicing of specific turbine models, require rapidly growing domestic demand to support the development of manufacturing activities (Binz et al., 2020).

China's rapid development of low-carbon energy sources has also supported the country's technological shift from internal combustion engines to electric automobile technology, with an emphasis on cars and two-wheelers. Proactively engaging in this shift has been considered an opportunity for catching-up in global automotive technology and production, in addition to addressing urban air pollution. The government has supported this shift on the demand side through generous purchase subsidies, tax exemptions, public procurement and the creation of a public electric grid company tasked to build an infrastructure of charging stations for electric vehicles, as well as on the supply side through dedicated research programme on lithium-ion batteries, electric vehicle quotas for carmakers, stricter fuel economy requirements, new technological and environmental regulations, etc. These measures have made China a leading global market for electric vehicles. While Chinese manufacturers have so far mainly covered the low-end product range, the government's stronger emphasis on research, stricter technology standards, and consolidation of the fragmented auto and battery industries are set to result in rapid upgrading (Altenburg et al., 2017). Particularly the recycling and reuse of batteries will provide further manufacturing opportunities, as discussed in the following section.

## ii.   Resource security

Achieving resource security relates to the concept of a "circular economy", which relies on the insight that resource use must be decoupled from output growth to ensure that the global economy can grow, and the growing global population be fed without an ever-increasing demand on Earth's finite resources. This decoupling can be achieved by replacing the traditional linear path of resource use with a circular economy that can be characterized by 3Rs – reduce, reuse, recycle.

The linear path of resource use relies on extracting resources from nature at one end of the process and dumping the residues back into the natural world at the other end. Doing so creates the threat of unmanageable waste and shortages of key resources, including water and rare minerals and metals.[20] A circular economy aims to slow the depletion of non-renewable natural resources, reduce environmental damage from their extraction and processing, and reduce pollution from their use and disposal. It seeks to do this by increasing the efficiency and productivity of resource use and by reducing the share of material that is not reused. It also aims to change product design to foster reuse, refurbishing and repair, rather than their disposal.

Moving to a circular economy may be defined as representing "a change of paradigm in the way that human society is interrelated with nature and aims to prevent the depletion of resources, close energy and material loops, and facilitate sustainable development" (Prieto-Sandoval, Jaca and Ormazabal, 2017: 610). In this definition, geographic proximity is a key component of the circular economy. As such, it provides a new entry point for industrialization as the circular use of resources is based on disassembling and re-manufacturing resources which, like more traditional manufacturing processes, may be subject to increasing economies of scale and result in a decline of the costs of recirculated materials to below the cost of newly extracted materials (Mathews, 2020).

The reuse of resource waste from domestic manufacturing processes can be enhanced by the promotion of a global circular economy that provides opportunities for developing countries to export re-manufactured products. However, such support can materialize only if an emerging global circular economy is not one where developed economies reduce their carbon footprints by dumping their waste and scrap on developing countries or by outsourcing carbon-intensive recycling and re-manufacturing stages of the circular economy to developing countries and tax resulting re-imports through carbon border adjustment mechanisms, or where they themselves undertake recycling and re-manufacturing activities and export to developing countries production inputs or final consumer goods at prices that make developing country producers of new goods and materials uncompetitive. Avoiding such outcomes requires appropriate trade policy measures to provide a developmental frame for a global circular economy, as addressed in chapter 5 of this *Report*.

## iii.   Low-carbon agriculture and food security

Current modes of food production, which are based on intensive industrial agriculture that rely on high inputs of fertilizers and pesticides and dominated by large-scale specialized farms – cause substantial environmental burden, in addition to being characterized by a lack of secured access to food and the widespread occurrence of forms of malnutrition (FAO et al., 2021). Agri-food systems (including crops, livestock, fisheries, aquaculture, agroforestry and forestry) account for about one-third of total anthropogenic greenhouse gas emissions (Crippa et al., 2021). Moreover, industrial agriculture, fish farming and forestry is often related to export-oriented global value chains, with product demands imperfectly suited to local soil conditions, resulting in soil degradation, overfishing and the replacement of natural wildlife systems with food crops or animal feed.

One approach to adapting agriculture to climate constraints is through climate-smart agriculture. This approach builds on sustainable agriculture approaches, using principles of ecosystem and sustainable land and water management and landscape analysis, and assessments of the use of resources and energy in agricultural production systems and food systems. It does not rely on a set of practices that can be universally applied, but rather involves different elements that are embedded in specific contexts and tailored to meet local needs.[21]

This comprehensive approach will bring benefits in terms of adapting agriculture to climate change but may not be sufficient. In an analysis of different scenarios for reducing emissions from agriculture by 2030 to limit warming in 2100 to 2 degrees Celsius above pre-industrial levels, Wollenberg et al. (2016) find that plausible development pathways fall far short of that goal, and that more transformative technical and policy options would be needed.

More radical approaches include the production of food from microbes. The resulting microbial biomass is rich in proteins and other nutrients. One huge benefit of this method, which is still in its infancy, is that brewing microbes through precision fermentation can move production of food from fields to factories and thus reduce the need for farmland and intensive agriculture, reducing the environmental impact of food production and allowing land use for other purposes in the process. Another is higher efficiency than in traditional agriculture. In terms of caloric and protein yields per land area, microbial production can reach an over 10-fold higher protein yield and at least twice the caloric yield compared to any staple crop (Leger et al., 2021). Moreover, as with other manufacturing activities, the costs decline as producers move along the learning curve and productivity increases.

It remains uncertain which, if any, of these innovations will eventually make strides into global agricultural production in the decades to come. But if they do, the environmental sustainability of food production is very likely to increase drastically at the global scale. However, it is concerning that these innovations will further detract from the universal availability of affordable nutritious food in developing countries. These innovations tend to be owned and applied in developed countries, with likely adverse impacts on developing countries' net food import balances. And

if these shifts to less carbon-intensive modes of food production cause food price increase in developing countries, they will also have an adverse impact on their low-carbon industrialization pathways.

Most importantly, these changes would largely eliminate farmers and hand food production and food security over to large digital and agro-industrial corporations that mostly reside in developed countries. This further expansion of corporate power would be made worse by using the land that has been freed-up by moving food production to labs as carbon sinks in which global financial capital can invest to reduce their net carbon footprint by offsetting their own emissions without actually reducing them (e.g., Oxfam, 2021). What is needed instead are agroecological approaches that can tackle climate change and ensure food security while at the same time ensure decent income of local farming communities.

## (b) Lessons for effective industrial policymaking

Critics of industrial policy query the practical implementation of industrial policy, typically pointing to information asymmetries between government officials and entrepreneurs, as well as rent seeking by government officials and industry lobbyists (Oqubay et al., 2020). Here, the lessons of successful structural transformation in developed countries and in the East Asian developing economies provide useful insights (see also *TDR 2006, 2016, 2018*).

A first such lesson is the need for *strong administrative and institutional capacities* for the government to formulate industrial policy and lead structural transformation. Experience with the Covid-19 pandemic and the uncertainties associated with climate adaptation suggest that governments should also possess dynamic capabilities to be able to anticipate and learn from events. One recent suggestion (Mazzucato and Kattel, 2020) applies such dynamic capabilities to five areas: foresight and anticipatory governance; handling partial and at times contradictory evidence; mechanisms for "mesh governance" (governance which includes multiple tiers); quickly repurpose existing infrastructure; and learning from other governments.

A second lesson is about *mechanisms of accountability* of policymakers and implementation agencies, such as through reporting requirements and other obligations to disclose information, combined with more general checks through auditing, independent courts and the press. As noted by Altenburg and Rodrik (2017: 10), "[a]ccountability serves not only to prevent corruption, favouritism and other forms of collusive behaviour but also helps to legitimize appropriate industrial policies." Combined, the second and third lessons constitute reciprocal control mechanisms.

A third lesson involves embeddedness – the *close relationships between entrepreneurs and government officials* that can ensure a mutual exchange of information and common understandings. Embeddedness will be particularly important for green industrial policies because climate adaptation involves a grand societal transition to new economic pathways. This societal transition involves a broader set of stakeholders and tends to create a larger number of disadvantaged parts of the population, especially those affected by disruptive energy policies in sectors, such as the scrapping of fossil-fuel subsidies. Given the already large income and wealth inequalities across and within many developed and developing countries, targeting, designing and phasing-in of green industrial policies must avoid further increases of inequality and, instead, reflect broad societal consensus.

A final, and related, lesson concerns disciplining devices that the State uses to *sanction abuse* of its support and to *discontinue* failing projects and activities. Disciplining abuse requires clearly defined objectives, measurable performance indicators, appropriate monitoring and evaluation routines, and government autonomy in deciding where and when to apply disciplining devices, as well as where and what experimental approaches to apply, and where and when to change course if something goes wrong.

## 2. Fiscal policy

The accelerated investment in green infrastructure and low-carbon technologies that climate adaptation requires will not be possible without fiscal expansion and a rebalancing of the structure of public expenditure towards an emphasis on low-carbon activities. In this context public procurement, which has always been a major part of public policy, is a powerful policy tool governments can use strategically as a major purchaser (*TDR 2016*, Chapter VI).

Expanded and restructured public spending will need to aim both at an increase in public investment, such as to foster the transition to renewable energy sources, and an increase in government transfers, required to address the adverse effects of the shift away from fossil fuel-based production modes and ensure that a low-carbon economy is more inclusive than the fossil fuel-based economy of the past few decades. One important distinctive factor of transitions to low-carbon paths of structural transformations is that expansionary fiscal policies that include green stimulus measures tend to have higher fiscal multipliers (*TDR 2019*). This is the case particularly in developing countries where the stock of public capital as a share of GDP is generally low, so that the higher direct output effect of increased public investment combines with a larger crowding-in effect on private investment to result in larger fiscal multipliers (Izquieredo et al., 2019).

Fiscal multipliers will also be higher where fiscal expansion is accompanied by an increasing role of public banking. The mandates of development and other public banks that value long-term development outcomes and sustainable economic transformations facilitate crowding-in of private investment (*TDR 2019*). This is the case, for example, because the broad range of activities that require investment for climate adaptation requires strategic collaboration between the government and private investors that aims at coordinating investment activities, where the interdependence of individual investment decisions makes the investments and profits of one entrepreneur partly dependent on the investment decisions of others.

Another distinctive benefit of green fiscal expansion is higher employment benefits. This is because expanding low-carbon sectors tend to be more labour-intensive than shrinking high-carbon sectors. A recent study estimated that renewable energy, energy efficiency and grid enhancement will create around 19 million new jobs worldwide by 2050. As the job losses in the fossil fuel sector will be around 7.4 million, the net addition will be 11.6 million jobs (Gielen et al., 2019; see also IMF, 2020). The greater job-generation capacity of a green path towards structural transformation may be of particular importance for economies where labour migration resulted in an expanding urban informal sector, including because existing technologies were too capital intensive for these economies' structural conditions, as for instance, in parts of Africa.

## 3. The role of central banks

Central banks around the world have been gradually adapting their operations, and in some cases, their mandates, to better reflect the financial risks related to climate change and reduce the threat of a "Minsky climate moment" (e.g., *TDR 2019*). A global Network for Greening the Financial System has brought together more than 80 central banks and financial institutions to explore various means by which central banks can play their role as both leaders of the financial system and also investors. These include integrating climate risks into prudential and monetary frameworks and insisting on regular climate stress tests and disclosure across the financial system.

However, as UNCTAD and others have noted before, this is encouraging but not sufficient. Helping to mitigate risk is the minimum that is needed to encourage positive investment in transformative activities and processes that will assist countries adapt to climate change and reduce emissions overall. Others have also argued that central banks need to align their current Covid-19 responses to avoid locking-in to high carbon recovery as they attempt to maintain financial stability (Dikau, Robins, and Volz, 2020; McDonald et al., 2020). Liquidity enhancing stimulus measures that are not aligned with the ambitions of the Paris Agreement can exacerbate already existing climate-related risks in the portfolios of financial institutions and across the financial system as a whole. Moreover, as governments around the world think about easing off the stimulus put in place since Covid-19, care will be needed to ensure this does not further increase climate related risks, nor the costs of capital for already struggling developing countries.

Some central banks have gone further, by putting in place macro prudential policies and positively guiding capital in a more carbon-sensitive way. A number of developing countries have been very active in this new direction for several years already (Campiglio et. al., 2017; Dikau et al., 2020; *TDR 2019*; Volz 2017). The People's Bank of China, in particular, has long used financial policies and directed credit to support green industrial policies, but banks in much smaller economies have also been experimental and innovative in terms of capital creation and direction. These are, however, more related to providing finance for climate mitigation than adaptation, reflecting the fact that even when interest rates are low the funds are still given as a loan not a grant. Banks are in the business of banking; even when offering loans at concessional terms, they are not normally seen as grant giving bodies nor philanthropists. This is not to say that they cannot be the engine of finance for other institutions that are

grant giving bodies and philanthropists, especially in advanced economies.

Given the scale of adaptation needs and the fact that those who suffer the most are the least able to pay for them, it is clear that advanced and more resilient economies will be the main source of finance. As central banks around the world were able to help support governments directly during the Covid pandemic, post-Covid recovery period presents an opportunity to consider to what extent central banks could also follow this path to supporting government development ministries, aid agencies and development banks.

At the very least, central banks could do more to ensure they do not continue to support carbon-intensive and maladaptive activities – which means a change in the current programme. While governments around the world have reduced sharply their financing flows to the fossil fuel and petrochemical industries since the Copenhagen COP, central banks remain the primary conduit for that finance – accounting for some $26 billion out of a total $38 billion of public funding that began since 2009 and remains active today, in the sense that transactions and bonds have yet to mature (Barrowclough and Finkill, 2021). This sends the wrong signal to the markets and to society.

This has continued during the recent Covid-19 period when central banks purchased corporate bonds on an unprecedented scale as part of their emergency operations to increase liquidity and avoid economic paralysis. Surveys of central bank Covid-19 recovery packages find that many are biased towards fossil fuel finance and did not attempt to tilt away from the sector (Oil Change International, 2021), even though several have active research and policy interests raising awareness of the contradiction.

UNCTAD and Lund University research similarly finds that Covid-19 recovery purchases by major central banks are often at odds with their governments' green ambition.[22] In extending the supportive public function of the central banks to climate needs, BoE (2021) notes that incentives could be used to influence companies to achieve net zero, and these could be ratcheted up over time. At the same time, the Bank also notes that disinvesting out of high-carbon companies means it would lose an opportunity to influence its policy; and recent Covid-19 recovery support schemes suggest that this needs to be an explicit goal or it might not happen. Support to the fossil fuel industry was typically given without any conditions but the opposite occurred when funds were given to firms in the renewables sector (Tearfund, 2021). The growing awareness of these issues is encouraging, but going the further step - to consider how central banks in advanced economies could help finance adaptation in less developed ones - has not been high on the radar screen.

In addition to properly regulating the financial sector, central banks should use a fuller range of tools to create and guide finance to green activities. More specifically, they should stop implicitly supporting high carbon emitters and penalising low-carbon activities. Collateral policy is one of the main tools towards greener central banking: central banks should also adjust their collateral regulations and accept financial institutions' green bonds as collateral.

## 4. Towards a green developmental state

While there is broad agreement on the need to widen economic policy objectives to include environmental adaptation, disagreements continue as to the role and scope of the State in attaining these objectives. Taking its cue from framing the adaptation challenge as one of risk management, one school of thought argues that most of the heavy lifting should be done by the private sector, with the role of the State focussed on distilling environmental objectives into bankable projects and de-risking these projects such that global private financial capital invests in them. In addition to long-standing beliefs that State involvement creates, rather than resolves, economic problems, this approach assumes that efficient resource allocation and maximizing economic welfare is supported best by the creative forces of markets. In this view, pro-active State action comes in as a last resort, when de-risking fails to produce investable projects (see also Chapter III of this *Report*).

An alternative view of the role of the State starts from the recognition that climate adaptation requires *transformation,* rather than the preservation of existing assets, i.e., the core of the risk-management approach. This is akin to the notion discussed earlier of a "developmental State" in East Asia's rapid industrialization and economic catch-up. To be applicable to the challenges of climate adaptation, policymakers need to recognize changes in the development agenda. This especially concerns the ways structural transformation and rapid economic growth connect with the global challenge of climate change to ensure sustainable low-carbon development. While this agenda continues to see technological and industrial upgrading and raising levels of material prosperity as

key development objectives, these objectives need to be reconciled with environmental sustainability goals.

As a result, the traditional concept of the East Asian developmental State has evolved and been adapted for several reasons. In East Asia itself, the successful industrialization strategy and the economies' moving up to middle- or even high-income status reduced the importance of capital accumulation and increased the role of innovation and technological advance for economic growth. At the same time, rising household incomes made constraints on consumption more difficult to maintain, while strengthening the desire of citizens for greater participation in society not least because of the environmental degradation associated with rapid industrial growth.[23] Internationally, the reorganisation of global production around global value chains made domestic firms increasingly beholden to the guidance of MNCs, in the process becoming detached from agreements with the state. The tightening of rules and regulations in international trade and investment agreements reduced the policy space for some of the industrial policy measures East Asian economies had applied, while the increased financialization of the global economy made achieving macroeconomic and financial stability more complex (*TDR 2006, 2014*).

Domestically and internationally, beginning in the 1990s, these changes prompted traditional East Asian developmental States into a set of liberalization measures and regulatory changes which helped to usher in the 1997-98 financial crisis in the region (*TDR 1998*). Despite the origins of the crisis, the response in international policy circles, including the international financial institutions, was to further demonise the developmental State and promote the idea of "doing business" properly. This perspective is not only premised on questionable assumptions about market dynamics but also equates the developmental State with specific policy measures and freezes the concept in space and time. It fails to recognize that at its core "is not the existence of intervention per se but rather the *developmental ambition and elite consensus that* frames that intervention and the existence of institutional capacities that help translate ambition into more or less effective policy outcomes", and while, with regard to the Republic of Korea, "the type of conditions placed by the government on industry support has evolved in tandem with changing objectives, there is little evidence to suggest that the Korean state has abandoned such practices in science-based industries" (Thurbon, 2014: XI, XIV; emphasis in original).[24]

Indeed, the Green Growth Strategy that the Republic of Korea adopted in 2008 may be characterized as "an eco-oriented development strategy with an activist industrial policy dimension" (Dent, 2018: 1200). It has allowed, *inter alia*, for the development of world-class smart-grid systems based on local technologies and the assumption by the Republic of Korea of global leadership in key energy storage technologies, including lithium-ion batteries and hydrogen fuel cells (e.g., Dent, 2018; Kim, 2021). This means that, rather than dismissing the role of the developmental State, these changes have made the concept evolve to what may be called an "East Asian eco-development state" (Harrell and Haddad, 2021) or, more generally, a "green developmental state".

This re-orientation towards a green developmental State maintains the core elements of the traditional developmental state model (see *TDR 1996*; Wade, 2018), such as: (i) the developmental mindset of the political leadership centred on structural differences between economic sectors and targeted at long-term economic catch-up as a powerful shaper of the state's development strategy; (ii) a policy approach that emphasizes an active and coordinating role of the State in structural transformation applied through regulation and an incentive structure where state support is conditioned on performance requirements and an industrial policy aimed at technological upgrading and the creation of well-paying jobs – i.e., where the quality and modalities of interventions matter, not their quantity; and (iii) an institutional architecture that relies on a competent and mission-oriented bureaucracy that is independent from special-interest pressures while being in close contact with the private sector.

There are also important departures from the traditional model of state dirigisme. Perhaps the most important distinction is that policymakers must succeed in the *creation* of green industrial activities while simultaneously achieving the *destruction* of incumbent fossil fuel-intensive activities. Navigating these distinct but interrelated objectives will require a broader range of policy measures, based on the recognition that the industrial structure of developing countries in today's technology-induced global economy cannot flourish without a knowledge- and innovation-based development strategy.

Policymakers will also require societal support that goes far beyond the industrial elite. The combination of the constructive and the destructive elements of structural transformation towards a low-carbon economy requires an alliance between the state and society that extends to workers, who the traditional developmental State co-opted by creating high-wage jobs, and that pays greater attention to the spatial dimension of development and consequently a larger focus on rural areas and the role of agricultural development. Only such more balanced socio-economic alliances can defeat the influence of certain elite and interest groups that are heavily linked to carbon-intensive growth whose perpetuation would make it impossible for governments to apply a long-term green development-oriented approach (Oatley and Blyth, 2021).

Better balanced socio-economic alliances are also necessary because civil society has become a more proactive and empowered form of agency in the development process. As noted by Dent (2014: 1204), "[l]ow-carbon development is as much a societal process as an economic one, encompassing individual lifestyle and choice issues at the micro level as well as macro-level industrial and infrastructural strategies." This means that a green developmental State must explicitly aim to build state-society networks that are based on social participation, deliberation, and consensus and at the same time cover wide parts of the society. Building this new and broader legitimacy base complicates the move towards a green developmental State, even though these wider groups may share the common interests more than the corporate elite where vested interests and financial losses related to stranded assets may prevail.

Another important difference between the traditional and green developmental State lies in its international dimension. The developmental State has been a strategic political choice of countries aiming to compete in the global economy, but this has mainly been in the form of export targets and attracting FDI. By contrast, given today's hyper-globalization, policymakers also need to put in place capital-account management measures to insulate the domestic financial system from global financial instability. Moreover, the goals of today's developmentalism derive ultimately from the global agenda of decarbonising economic activity and international efforts to tackle climate change. Therefore, linking nationally devised and implemented strategies is part of a much larger international climate action project, and national strategies will need to reference their contribution to wider international endeavours on low-carbon development, such as the Paris Agreement (*TDR 2019*).

It is also important to note that a State focusing on de-risking will narrow the policy space of a green developmental State, as de-risking often implies a constraint on the very policy instruments that a green developmental State would apply. For example, regulatory de-risking would make it more difficult to maintain vertically integrated, state-owned energy utilities, to redirect subsidies from fossil-fuel to renewable energy providers, such as via feed-in tariffs, or to ensure guaranteed grid access for renewable energy sources. Moreover, financial de-risking would target green-oriented grants, tax relief, or debt-based instruments, while it would promote financial globalization with an emphasis on portfolio flows (rather than FDI as in traditional developmental States), which will tend to hamper macroeconomic

and financial stability. It would also divert scarce fiscal resources from public investment towards backstopping public-private partnerships, such as to compensate a private operator for demand shortfalls in the payable use of infrastructure, or if a government introduces regulations, such as higher minimum wages, that might reduce private sector profitability.[25]

These international aspects of climate adaptation policies call for a new multilateralism that is enabled to provide the global public good needed to deliver shared prosperity and a healthy planet and to ensure that no nation's pursuit of its economic and environmental goals infringes on the ability of other nations to pursue them. This is discussed further in the following chapter.

# E. Conclusion

Structural transformation, characterized by a shift in the production structure from the primary sector to manufacturing, has traditionally been the most successful way of achieving rapid economic growth. This avenue was followed by the now advanced economies, as well as a few successful late industrializers in East Asia. This traditional fossil fuel-intensive model, however, cannot satisfy the aspirations of the many other developing countries that are trying to upgrade their national incomes through industrialization because it would take emissions and resource consumption beyond the limits of the planet's ecological capacity.

The answer to this problem is not to forsake manufacturing development, and diversification strategies more generally, in developing countries. Rather, it is to build a low-carbon industrial system, powered by renewable energy sources and green technologies, and where economic activities within and across sectors are interconnected through resource-efficient linkages. Such a solution maintains manufacturing as a central objective because important elements of structural transformation towards a low-carbon economy are closely inter-related with industrialization. The energy transition and an emergent circular economy provide opportunities for a reduction of the carbon footprint of traditional manufacturing, as well as for the manufacturing of devices for a low-carbon economy themselves.

The transition to renewable energy and engagement with the circular economy can increase the scope

for industrialization for a broad range of developing economies because they decouple economic activities from natural resource use. Sources of renewable energy – such as sunshine, wind and water – are more equally distributed than economically exploitable deposits of fossil fuels, and the circular economy allows extracting resources from used products and waste, thereby reducing the required quantity of new resources. Many activities related to renewable energy production and the circular economy can economically operate at low scale, opening business opportunities for small firms and rural areas. This will not only help to diversify economic production structures and reduce many countries' dependence on the production of a narrow range of primary commodities, but it can enlarge developing countries' tax bases and foster domestic resource mobilization as a source of development finance. These activities can also help to relax countries' balance-of-payments constraints. Relying on domestic production of energy and food requirements, thereby reducing the import of virgin raw materials, may allow for a sizable reduction of imports, which will liberate scarce foreign exchange for imports of capital goods for industrialization and economic catch-up.

None of these transformations are likely to occur without a developmental State. Successful structural transformations have generally relied on proactive government policies. Climate change adaptation implies system-wide changes that cannot occur without an integrated policy approach that addresses the multiple challenges of industrialization in a climate-constrained world, synchronously and cohesively. In addition to undertaking large-scale public investment and financing the investment push required for green structural transformation through green financial instruments, it will involve green industrial policy and state-society relations that not only break existing fossil-fuel interests but also establish clear rules, the enforcement of which can govern the new green investment trajectories and ensure a legitimacy base that can rely on a wide range of societal groups.

# Notes

1   Or, in other words, the economy attains the so-called "Lewis turning point".

2   Much of the criticism relates to Lewis' questioning of the neoclassical approach to labour and its focus on homogeneous one-sector economies, and his explicit reference to classical economics and historical experience (Sumner, 2018).

3   Lewis (1979) extended his original approach by adding an "in-between" sector to the dual economy model. This sector includes a heterogenous range of small-scale enterprises in urban areas that operate in manufacturing, transportation, construction, and a wide range of services. They often are unregistered and constitute part of the informal sector. While these enterprises provide valuable employment, their capital base and levels of technology and productivity are generally lower than in the modern sector.

4   Lewis (1954) had, in fact, stressed that the traditional, non-capitalist sector should not only be identified with agriculture or rural areas, but includes all those economic activities that do not use reproducible capital. This criticism also gave rise to the so-called "urban bias" hypothesis (Lipton, 1977; Bates, 1988) that sees poverty in developing countries as concentrated in rural areas and as a direct result of how government policy manages the relationship between traditional and modern sectors, further discussed below.

5   The concept is closely associated with the contribution to development economics of Albert Hirschman.

6   This relationship is known as the "Verdoorn law" which is based on the observation that a key characteristic of manufacturing is its greater potential for the division of labour, which gives rise to scale economies.

7   Primary exports can also be an initial source of foreign-exchange earnings. However, in addition to issues related to the availability of affordable food, mentioned above, this mechanism may be constrained by the non-tradability of major food staples.

8   The failure of African economies to achieve structural transformation to a similar extent as East Asian economies has often been related to differences in managing the relation between the two sectors. Post-independence African governments were said to have an "urban bias" by concentrating infrastructure in urban areas, over-taxing rural areas, and tilting relative prices in favour of urban pursuits (Lipton, 1977; Bates, 1988). But see Karshenas (2001) who concludes that the major policy failure in Africa during the 1970s and 1980s was not the rate of agricultural taxation per se, but rather the failure to put money back into agriculture to increase productivity and thus nurture an increase in the net agricultural surplus.

9   In poor economies where the process of industrialization is in its infancy or where the income incentives for migration are low for other reasons, climate change may tighten the liquidity constraints of rural dwellers to the extent that they cannot afford migration (e.g., Selod and Shilpi, 2021). Where this is the case, climate change is likely to abort structural transformation and cause large swaths of rural populations to be trapped in poverty.

10   Land degradation and soil nutrient depletion have also resulted from so-called "land grabbing", where land, with its available water potential, is acquired by private and public actors, including sovereign governments, often with a view to securing their own national food security and biofuel needs. These acquisitions often occur in areas with weak land tenure regulations and with local governments in need of fiscal revenues, accompanied by little compensation for dispossessed local communities and little consideration for sustainable land use (e.g., Batterbury and Ndi, 2018).

11   The continued divergence of structural transformation in Africa from experiences in East Asia is clearly related to a broad set of reasons that also include macroeconomic and institutional factors. The account here is limited to main elements of the Lewis model.

12   In a sense, this is the other side of the same coin regarding attempts to transit to low-carbon value chains from end to end, discussed below. See Rani (2020) for a general discussion of informal

employment for cost-cutting reasons, motivated by labour regulations or costly environmental or social protection policies.

13 For recent evidence on the cost of climate-related port disruptions, see, e.g., Verschuur et al., 2020. See also UNCTAD, 2020b.

14 For the mechanism envisaged by the United States, see the President's 2021 Trade Policy Agenda and 2020 Annual Report of the President of the United States on the Trade Agreements Program, March 2021, https://ustr.gov/sites/default/files/files/reports/2021/2021%20Trade%20Agenda/Online%20PDF%202021%20Trade%20Policy%20Agenda%20and%202020%20Annual%20Report.pdf; for the European Union, see the proposal for a new Carbon Border Adjustment Mechanism, adopted by the Commission on 14 July 2021, https://ec.europa.eu/taxation_customs/green-taxation-0/carbon-border-adjustment-mechanism_en; for further discussion of this proposal, see UNCTAD, 2021.

15 According to media reports, the European Union plans to use the expected annual revenue of Euro 10bn from its planned carbon border tax mechanisms to repay debt incurred for its recovery measures; see Mehreen Khan "EU carbon border tax will raise nearly Euro10bn annually", *Financial Times*, 6 July 2021, https://www.ft.com/content/7a812f4d-a093-4f1a-9a2f-877c41811486.

16 The more recent literature argues that the advantage of backwardness can benefit only those countries that are not too far behind because many poorer countries require a level of domestic technological capabilities that is sufficiently high to gainfully use advanced technologies (e.g., Oqubay and Ohno, 2019). This helps to understand why many least developed countries have not benefitted from their "advantage of backwardness".

17 For a review of this debate see *TDR 2006, 2016*; Cherif and Hasanov, 2019; Oqubay et al., 2020.

18 For detailed discussion of definitions and concepts related to green industrial policy, see Altenburg and Rodrik, 2017; Harrison et al., 2017; and Tagliapietra and Veugelers, 2019.

19 For a more general assessment of the potential to link renewable energy and manufacturing in Egypt, Morocco, and Tunisia, see EIB, 2015.

20 See OECD, 2019, for a recent account of the use of material resources since 1970 and projections until 2060.

21 See FAO, 2017, with country-specific examples in FAO, 2021b.

22 'Pathways to Breaking the Fossil Fuel Lock-In'. Sources: Bank of England (2020). Asset Purchase Facility (APF): Additional Corporate Bond Purchases – Market Notice 2 April. Available at https://www.bankofengland.co.uk/markets/market-notices/2020/asset-purchase-facility-additional-corporate-bond-purchases [Accessed 19 July 2021]; European Central Bank (2021). Pandemic Emergency Purchase Programme. Available at https://www.ecb.europa.eu/mopo/implement/pepp/html/index.en.html [Accessed 15 August 2021]; US FED (2021). Board of Governors of the Federal Reserve System. The Fed - Secondary Market Corporate Credit Facility. Available at https://www.federalreserve.gov/monetarypolicy/smccf.htm [Accessed 23 June 2021].

23 This environmental degradation has a domestic component in the form of polluted cities, soils and rivers, as well as high greenhouse gas emissions, but also an international component in the form of deforestation in those countries that provide wood for the construction and furniture industries, or soybeans for animal feed.

24 For detailed discussion of the alleged death of the developmental State see, for example, Thurbon 2014; Wade 2018.

25 For more detailed discussion of these issues, see Gabor, 2021.

# References

Adelman I (1984). Beyond export-led growth. *World Development*. 12(9): 937–949.

Akyüz Y and Gore C (1996). The investment-profits nexus in East Asian industrialization. *World Development*. 24(3): 461–470.

Alper E, Hobdari NA and Uppal A (2016). Food inflation in sub-Saharan Africa: Causes and policy implications. Working Paper No. 16/247. International Monetary Fund. Available at https://www.imf.org/en/Publications/WP/Issues/2016/12/31/Food-Inflation-in-Sub-Saharan-Africa-Causes-and-Policy-Implications-44492.

Altenburg T, Feng K and Shen Q (2017). Electric mobility and the quest for automobile industry upgrading in China. In: Altenburg T and Assmann C, eds. *Green Industrial Policy: Concept, Policies, Country Experiences*. UN Environment; German Development Institute / Deutsches Institut für Entwicklungspolitk (DIE). Geneva. Bonn: 186–198.

Altenburg T and Rodrik D (2017). Green industrial policy: Accelerating structural change towards wealthy green economies. In: Altenburg T and Assmann C, eds. *Green Industrial Policy: Concept, Policies, Country Experiences.* UN Environment; German Development Institute / Deutsches Institut für Entwicklungspolitk (DIE). Geneva. Bonn: 1–20.

Auktor GV (2017). Renewable energy as a trigger for industrial development in Morocco. In: Altenburg T and Assmann C, eds. *Green Industrial Policy: Concept, Policies, Country Experiences.* UN Environment; German Development Institute / Deutsches Institut für Entwicklungspolitk (DIE). Geneva. Bonn: 154–165.

Badiane O, Diao X and Jayne T (2021). Africa's unfolding agricultural transformation. In: Otsuka K and Fan S, eds. *Agricultural Development: New Perspectives in a Changing World.* International Food Policy Research Institute (IFPRI). Washington, D.C.: 153–192.

Barbieri P, Boffelli A, Elia S, Fratocchi L, Kalchschmidt M and Samson, (2020). What can we learn about reshoring after Covid-19? *Operations Management Research.* 13: 131–136.

Barrett CB, Ortiz-Bobea A and Pham T (2021). Structural transformation, agriculture, climate, and the environment. Structural Transformation and Economic Growth Pathfinding Paper. Available at https://steg.cepr.org/publications/structural-transformation-agriculture-climate-and-environment.

Barrowclough D and Finkill G (2021, forthcoming). Banks, bonds and the petrochemicals/plastics industry – Greening the path from Copenhagen Agreement, Covid-19 and beyond. Research Paper No. 69. UNCTAD.

Bates RH (1988). Governments and agricultural markets in Africa. In: Bates RH, ed. *Towards a Political Economy of Development: A Rational Choice Perspective.* University of California Press. Berkeley: 331–358.

Batterbury SPJ and Ndi F (2018). Land grabbing in Africa. In: Binns T, Lynch K and Nel E, eds. *The Routledge Handbook of African Development.* Routledge. London: 573–582.

Becker A, Ng AKY, McEvoy D and Mullett J (2018). Implications of climate change for shipping: Ports and supply chains. *WIREs Climate Change.* 9(2): e508.

Beeson M (2006). Politics and markets in East Asia: Is the developmental state compatible with globalization. In: Stubbs R and Underhill GRH, eds. *Political Economy and the Changing Global Order.* Oxford University Press. Oxford: 443–453.

Benson E (2014). Informal and green? The forgotten voice in the transition to a green economy. Discussion Paper. International Institute for Environment and Development. Available at https://pubs.iied.org/16566iied.

Binz C, Gosens J, Yap XS and Yu Z (2020). Catch-up dynamics in early industry lifecycle stages - a typology and comparative case studies in four clean-tech industries. *Industrial and Corporate Change.* 29(5): 1257–1275.

Brown D, McGranahan G and Dodman D (2014). Urban informality and building a more inclusive, resilient and green economy. Working Paper., International Institute for Environment and Development. Available at https://pubs.iied.org/10722iied.

Campiglio E, Godwin A, Kemp-Benedict E and Matikainen S (2017). The tightening links between financial systems and the low-carbon transition. In: Arestis P and Swayer M, eds. *Economic Policies Since the Global Financial Crisis.* Palgrave Macmillan. Basingstoke: 313–356.

Chen M and Raveendran G (2014). Urban employment trends in India: Recent trends and patterns. Working Paper No 7. Women in Informal Employment: Globalizing and Organizing (WIEGO). Available at https://www.wiego.org/publications/urban-employment-india-recent-trends-and-patterns.

Cherif R and Hasanov F (2019). The return of the policy that shall not be named: Principles of true industrial policy. Working Paper No. 19/74. International Monetary Fund.

Coady D, Parry I, Le NP and Shang B (2019). Global fossil fuel subsidies remain large: an update based on country-level estimates. Working Paper No. 19/89. International Monetary Fund. Available at https://www.imf.org/en/Publications/WP/Issues/2019/05/02/Global-Fossil-Fuel-Subsidies-Remain-Large-An-Update-Based-on-Country-Level-Estimates-46509.

Cohen S and de Long BJ (2016). *Concrete Economics: The Hamilton Approach to Economic Growth and Policy.* Harvard Business Review Press. Cambridge.

Corrocher N, Malerba F and Morrison A (2021). Technological regimes, patent growth, and catching-up in green technologies. *Industrial and Corporate Change.* Forthcoming. Available at https://doi.org/10.1093/icc/dtab025.

Crippa M, Solazzo E, Guizzardi D, Monforti-Ferrario F, Tubiello FN and Leip A (2021). Food systems are responsible for a third of global anthropogenic GHG emissions. *Nature Food.* 2(3): 198–209.

Dechezleprêtre A and Sato M (2018). Green policies and firms' competitiveness. Issue Paper. OECD Green Growth and Sustainable Development Forum. Available at https://www.oecd.org/greengrowth/GGSD_2018_Competitiveness%20Issue%20Paper_WEB.pdf.

Dent CM (2018). East Asia's new developmentalism: State capacity, climate change and low-carbon development. *Third World Quarterly*. 39(6): 1191–1210.

Diao X, Ellis M, McMillan M and Rodrik D (2021). Africa's Manufacturing Puzzle: Evidence from Tanzanian and Ethiopian Firms. Working Paper No. 28344. National Bureau of Economic Research.

Diao X and McMillan M (2018). Toward an understanding of economic growth in Africa: A reinterpretation of the Lewis model. *World Development*. 109: 511–522.

Dikau S, Robins N and Volz U (2020). A toolbox for sustainable crisis response measures for central banks and supervisors: Lessons for practice. INSPIRE Briefing Paper. Grantham Research Institute on Climate Change and the Environment, London School of Economics and Political Science and SOAS Centre for Sustainable Finance, SOAS University of London.

European Commission (2021a). Legislative Train Schedule: A European Green Deal. Carbon Border Adjustment Mechanism as part of the European Green Deal / Before 2021-07. Accessed 18 August 2021. Available at https://www.europarl.europa.eu/legislative-train/theme-a-european-green-deal/file-carbon-border-adjustment-mechanism.

European Commission (2021b). Updating the 2020 New Industrial Strategy: Building a stronger Single Market for Europe's recovery. Document COM(2021) 350 final. 5 May. Available at https://ec.europa.eu/info/sites/default/files/communication-industrial-strategy-update-2020_en.pdf.

EIB (2015). Evaluating Renewable Energy Manufacturing Potential in the Mediterranean Partner Countries. European Investment Bank. Available at https://www.eib.org/attachments/femip_study_evaluating_renewable_energy_manufacturing_potential_en.pdf.

FAO (2017). Climate-Smart Agriculture Sourcebook Summary Second edition. Food and Agriculture Organization. Rome. Available at http://www.fao.org/3/i7994e/i7994e.pdf.

FAO (2021a). *The Impact of Disasters and Crises on Agriculture and Food Security: 2021*. Food and Agriculture Organiaztion. Rome. Available at https://doi.org/10.4060/cb3673en.

FAO (2021b). *Climate-smart Agriculture Case Studies 2021: Projects from around the World*. Food and Agriculture Organization. Rome. Available at https://doi.org/10.4060/cb5359en.

FAO, IFAD, UNICEF, WFP and WHO (2021). *The State of Food Security and Nutrition in the World 2021: Transforming Food Systems for Food Security, improved Nutrition and Affordable Healthy Diets for all*. Food and Agriculture Organization. Rome. Available at https://doi.org/10.4060/cb4474en.

Gabor D (2021). The Wall Street consensus. *Development and Change*. 52(3): 429–459.

Gallagher KP and Kozul-Wright R (2019). *A New Multilateralism: Geneva Principles for a Global Green New Deal*. Boston University and UNCTAD. Boston and Geneva. Available at https://unctad.org/webflyer/new-multilateralism-shared-prosperity-geneva-principles-global-green-new-deal.

Gerschenkron A (1962). *Economic Backwardness in Historical Perspective*. Harvard University Press. Cambridge.

Gielen D, Boshell F, Saygin D, Bazilian MD, Wagner N and Gorini R (2019). The role of renewable energy in the global energy transformation. *Energy Strategy Reviews*. 24: 38–50.

Godfrey M (1979). Rural-urban migration in a "Lewis-model" context. *The Manchester School*. 47(3): 230–247.

Harrell S and Haddad MA (2021). The evolution of the East Asian eco-developmental state. *The Asia-Pacific Journal*. 19(6): article 5557.

Harrison A, Martin LA and Nataraj S (2017). Green industrial policy in emerging markets. *Annual Review of Resource Economics*. 9: 253–274.

Hirschman AO (1958). *The Strategy of Economic Development*. Yale University Press. New Haven, CT.

IEA (2019). *CO2 emissions from fuel combustion. Highlights*. International Energy Agency. Paris. Available at https://iea.blob.core.windows.net/assets/eb3b2e8d-28e0-47fd-a8ba-160f7ed42bc3/CO2_Emissions_from_Fuel_Combustion_2019_Highlights.pdf.

IEA (2021). *Net Zero by 2050: A Roadmap for the Global Energy Sector*. International Energy Agency. Paris. Available at https://www.iea.org/reports/net-zero-by-2050.

IISD (2020). Doubling Back and Doubling Down: G20 scorecard on fossil fuel funding. International Institute for Sustainable Development. Winnipeg. Available at https://www.iisd.org/system/files/2020-11/g20-scorecard-report.pdf.

IMF (2020). *World Economic Outlook – October, Chapter 3: Mitigating Climate Change*. International Monetary Fund. Washington D.C.

IRENA (2021). *Renewable Power Generation Costs in 2020*. International Renewable Energy Agency. Abu Dhabi. Available at https://www.irena.org/publications/2021/Jun/Renewable-Power-Costs-in-2020.

Izquieredo A, Lama R, Medina JP, Puig J, Riera-Crichton D, Vegh C and Vuletin G (2019). Is the public investment multiplier higher in developing countries? An empirical investigation. Working Paper No. 26478. National Bureau of Economic Research

Johnston BF and Mellor JW (1961). The role of agriculture in economic development. *The American Economic Review. 51*(4): 566–593. Available at http://www.jstor.org/stable/1812786.

Kaldor N (1957). A model of economic growth. *The Economic Journal. 67*(268): 591–624.

Karshenas M (2001). Agriculture and economic development in sub-Sharan Africa and Asia. *Cambridge Journal of Economics*. 25(3): 315–342.

Kim SY (2021). National competitive advantage and energy transitions in Korea and Taiwan. *New Political Economy*. 26(3): 359–375.

Kirchherr J and Urban F (2018). Technology transfer and cooperation for low carbon energy technology: Analysing 30 years of scholarship and proposing a research agenda. *Energy Policy*. 119: 600–609.

Kruse H, Mensah E, Sen K and de Vries G (2021). A manufacturing renaissance? Industrialization trends in the developing world. Working Paper No. 2021/28 United Nations University / World Institute for Development Economies Research. Available at https://www.wider.unu.edu/sites/default/files/Publications/Working-paper/PDF/wp2021-28-manufacturing-renaissance-industrialization-trends-developing-world.pdf.

Lazard (2020). Levelized Cost of Energy and Levelized Cost of Storage – 2020. Available at https://www.lazard.com/perspective/levelized-cost-of-energy-and-levelized-cost-of-storage-2020/.

Lee K and Malerba F (2017). Catch-up cycles and changes in industrial leadership: windows of opportunity and responses of firms and countries in the evolution of sectoral systems. *Research Policy*. 46(2): 338–351.

Leger D, Matassa S, Noor E, Shepon A, Milo R and Bar-Even A (2021). Photovoltaic-driven microbial protein production can use land and sunlight more efficiently than conventional crops. *Proceedings of the National Academy of Sciences*. 118 (26): e2015025118. Available at https://www.pnas.org/content/118/26/e2015025118

Lema R, Fu X and Rabellotti R (2020). Green windows of opportunity: latecomer development in the age of transformation toward sustainability. *Industrial and Corporate Change*. 29(5): 1193–1209.

Lewis WA (1954). Economic development with unlimited supplies of labour. *The Manchester School*. 22(2): 139–191.

Lewis WA (1979). The dual economy revisited. *The Manchester School*. 47(3): 211–229.

Lipton M (1977). *Why Poor People Stay Poor: A Study of Urban Bias in World Development*. Temple Smith. London.

Oxford Economics (2021). *The Sustainable Supply Chain Paradox: Balancing the Bottom Line with the Green Line*, Oxford Economics Research. Oxford.

Mathews JA (2020). Greening industrial policy. In: Oqubay A, Cramer C, Chang HJ and Kozul-Wright R, eds. *The Oxford Handbook of Industrial Policy*. Oxford University Press. Oxford: 266–283.

Mazzucato M and Kattel R (2020). Grand challenges, industrial policy, and public value. In: Oqubay A, Cramer C, Chang HJ and Kozul-Wright R, eds. *The Oxford Handbook of Industrial Policy*. Oxford University Press. Oxford: 311–336.

McDonald D, Marois T and Barrowclough D (2020). *Public Banks and Covid-19: Combatting the Pandemic with Public Finance*. Municipal Services programme, Eurodad and UNCTAD. Kingston, Geneva and Brussels.

McMillan M and Rodrik D (2011). Globalization, structural change and productivity growth. In: Bacchetta M and Jansen M, eds, *Making Globalization Socially Sustainable*. International Labour Organization and World Trade Organization. Geneva: 49–84.

Myrdal G (1957). *Economic Theory and Underdeveloped Regions*. University Paperbacks. Methuen. London.

OECD (2019). *Global Material Resources Outlook to 2060: Economic Drivers and Environmental Consequences*. OECD Publishing. Paris.

OECD/WTO (2019). *Aid for Trade at a Glance 2019: Economic Diversification and Empowerment*. OECD Publishing. Paris.

Özgür G, Elgin C and Elveren AY (2021). Is informality a barrier to sustainable development? *Sustainable Development*. 29(1): 45–65.

Oatley T and Blyth M (2021). The death of the carbon coalition. *Foreign Policy*. 12 February.

Oqubay A, Cramer C, Chang HJ and Kozul-Wright R, eds. (2020). *The Oxford Handbook of Industrial Policy*. Oxford University Press. Oxford.

Oqubay A and Ohno K, eds. (2019). *How Nations Learn; Technological Learning, Industrial Policy, and Catch-up*. Oxford University Press. Oxford.

Oxfam (2021). Tightening the net: Net zero climate targets – implications for land and food equity. Briefing Paper. Oxfam International.

Pigato MA, Black SJ, Dussaux D, Mao Z, McKenna M, Rafaty R and Touboul S (2020). *Technology Transfer and Innovation for Low-carbon Development*. International Development in Focus. World Bank. Washington, D.C.

Pollin R (2020). An industrial policy framework to advance a global green new deal. In: Oqubay A, Cramer C, Chang HJ and Kozul-Wright R, eds. *The Oxford Handbook of Industrial Policy*. Oxford University Press. Oxford: 394–428.

Poon D and Kozul-Wright R (2019). Learning from East Asia: Catch-up and the making of China's developmental state. In: Oqubay A and Ohno K, eds. *How Nations Learn. Technological Learning, Industrial Policy, and Catch-up.* Oxford University Press. Oxford: 38–62.

Porter ME and van der Linde C (1995). Toward a new conception of the environment competitiveness relationship. *Journal of Economic Perspectives.* 9(4): 97–118.

Prieto-Sandoval V, Jaca C and Ormazabal M (2018). Towards a consensus on the circular economy *Journal of Cleaner Production.* 179: 605–615.

Rani U (2020). Old and new forms of informal employment. In: Chen M and Carré F, eds. *The Informal Economy Revisited. Examining the Past, Envisioning the Future.* Routledge. London and New York: 88–91.

Ranis G and Fei JCH (1961). A theory of economic development. *The American Economic Review.* 51(4): 533–565.

Roberts SH, Foran BD, Axon CJ and Stamp AV (2021). Is the service industry really low-carbon? Energy, jobs and realistic country GHG emissions reductions. *Applied Energy.*, 292: 116878.

Rodrik D (2004). Industrial policies for the twenty-first century. Research Working Paper No. 04-047. John F. Kennedy School of Government.

Rosegrant MW, Wiebe KD, Sulser TB, Mason-D'Croz D and Willenbockel D (2021). Climate change and agricultural development. In: Otsuka K and Fan S, eds *Agricultural Development: New Perspectives in a Changing World.* International Food Policy Research Institute (IFPRI). Washington, D.C.: 629–660. Available at https://doi.org/10.2499/9780896293830_19.

Selod H and Shilpi F (2021). Rural-urban migration in developing countries: Lessons from the Literature. Policy Research Working Paper No. 9662. World Bank. Available at https://openknowledge.worldbank.org/handle/10986/35610.

Stern DI (2004). The rise and fall of the environmental Kuznets curve. *World Development.* 32(8): 1419–1439.

Sumner A (2018). Is the Lewis model of economic development still relevant to developing countries? *Global Policy Journal.* Opinion. 20 April. Available at https://www.globalpolicyjournal.com/blog/20/04/2018/lewis-model-economic-development-still-relevant-developing-countries.

Tagliapietra S and Veugelers R (2019). *A Green Industrial Policy for Europe.* Blueprint Series 31. Bruegel. Brussels. Available at https://www.bruegel.org/wp-content/uploads/2020/12/Bruegel_Blueprint_31_Complete_151220.pdf

Tearfund (2021). Cleaning up their act? G7 fossil fuel investments in a time of green recovery. Report. Tearfund.. Available at https://learn.tearfund.org/en/resources/policy-reports/cleaning-up-their-act.

Thurbon E (2014). The resurgence of the developmental state: A conceptual defence. *Critique Internationale.* 63(2): 59–75.

Timilsana G and Malla S (2021). Do investments in clean technology reduce production costs? Insights from the literature. Policy Research Working Paper No. 9714. World Bank. Available at https://openknowledge.worldbank.org/handle/10986/35885.

Timmer CP (1988). The agricultural transformation. In: Chenery H and Srinivasan TN, eds. *Handbook of Development Economics*, Volume 1. Elsevier. Amsterdam: 275–331.

Tregenna F (2009). Characterising deindustrialisation: An analysis of changes in manufacturing employment and GDP internationally. *Cambridge Journal of Economics.* 33 (3): 433–466.

Tregenna F (2010). How significant is intersectoral outsourcing of employment in South Africa? *Industrial and Corporate Change.* 19 (5): 1427–1457.

Trærup SLM, Greersen SL and Knudsen C (2018). Mapping barriers and enabling environments in technology needs assessments, nationally determined contributions, and technical assistance of the Climate Technology Centre and Network. Document TEC/2018/17/4. Available at https://unepdtu.org/publications/mapping-barriers-and-enabling-environments-in-technology-needs-assessments-nationally-determined-contributions-and-technical-assistance-of-the-climate-technology-centre-and-network/.

UNCTAD (*TDR 1996*). *Trade and Development Report 1996 – Part II: Rethinking Development Strategies: Some Lessons from the East Asian Experience.* (United Nations publication. Sales No. E.96.II.D.6. New York and Geneva).

UNCTAD (*TDR 1998*). *Trade and Development Report 1998: Financial Instability, Grow in Africa.* (United Nations publication. Sales No. E.98.II.D.6. New York and Geneva).

UNCTAD (*TDR 2003*). *Trade and Development Report 2003: Capital Accumulation, Growth and Structural Change.* (United Nations publication. Sales No. E.03.II.D.7. New York and Geneva).

UNCTAD (*TDR 2006*). Trade and Development Report 2006: Global Partnership and National Policies for Development. (United Nations publication. Sales No. E.06.II.D.6. New York and Geneva).

UNCTAD (*TDR 2014*). *Trade and Development Report 2014: Global Governance and Policy Space for*

*Development*. (United Nations publication. Sales No. E.14.II.D.4. New York and Geneva).

UNCTAD (*TDR 2016*). *Trade and Development Report 2016: Structural Transformation for Inclusive and Sustainable Growth*. (United Nations publication. Sales No. E.16.II.D.5. New York and Geneva).

UNCTAD (*TDR 2019*). *Trade and Development Report 2019 : Financing a Green New Deal*. (United Nations publication. Sales No. E.19.II.D.15. New York and Geneva).

UNCTAD (2018). *World Investment Report 2018:Investment and New Industrial Policies*. (United Nations publication. E.18.II.D.4. New York and Geneva).

UNCTAD (2020a). *Transforming Trade and Development in a Fractured, Post-Pandemic World: Report of the Secretary General of UNCTAD to the Fifteenth Session of the Conference*. (United Nations publication. Sales No.E.20.II.D. Geneva).

UNCTAD (2020b). *Climate Change Impacts and Adaptation for Coastal Transport Infrastructure: A Compilation of Policies and Practices*. Transport and Trade Facilitation Series No 12. UNCTAD/DTL/TLB/2019/1. (United Nations publication. Sales No. E.20.II.D.10. Geneva).

UNCTAD (2021). A European Union Carbon Border Adjustment Mechanism: Implications for developing countries. Geneva. Available at https://unctad.org/system/files/official-document/osginf2021d2_en.pdf.

Verschuur J, Koks EE and Hall JW (2020). Port disruptions due to natural disasters: Insights into port and logistics resilience. *Transportation Research Part D: Transport and Environment*. 85: 102393.

Villena VH and Gioia DA (2020). A more sustainable supply chain. *Harvard Business Review*. March-April: 1–11.

Volz U (2017). On the role of central banks in enhancing green finance. Inquiry Working Paper No. 17/01. UN Environment Inquiry:.Design of a Sustainable Financial System Available at https://eprints.soas.ac.uk/23817/1/On_the_Role_of_Central_Banks_in_Enhancing_Green_Finance%281%29.pdf.

Wade RH (2018). The developmental state: dead or alive? *Development and Change*. 49(2): 518–546.

Wollenberg E, Richards M; Smith P, Havl P, Obersteiner M; Tubiello FN, Herold M, Gerber P, Carter S, Reisinger A, Van Vuuren DP, Dickie A, Neufeldt H, Sander BO, Wassmann R, Sommer R, Amonette JE, Falcucci A, Herrero M, Opio C, Roman-Cuesta RM, Stehfest E, Westhoek H, Ortiz-Monasterio I, Sapkota T, Rufino MA, Thornton P, Verchot L, West PC, Soussana JF, Baedeker T, Sadler M, Vermeulen S and Campbell BM (2016). Reducing emissions from agriculture to meet the 2°C target. *Global Change Biology*. 22(12): 3859–3864. Available at https://doi.org/10.1111/gcb.13340.

WEF (2021). *Net-Zero Challenge: The Supply Chain Opportunity*. World Economic Forum in collaboration with Boston Consulting Group. Geneva, Available at https://www.weforum.org/reports/net-zero-challenge-the-supply-chain-opportunity.

# ADAPTATION GOVERNANCE: CHALLENGES IN INTERNATIONAL TRADE AND FINANCE

# V

## A. Introduction

In recent *Trade and Development Reports*, UNCTAD has outlined the case for a Global Green New Deal to tackle the multiple challenges facing the international community. At its heart is the call for a massive and coordinated investment and jobs push for a cleaner and more efficient global energy system. But as with its erstwhile namesake, this recovery strategy for the planet is linked to regulatory and redistributional measures which should also assume a global dimension. These include measures (and related institutional reforms) aimed at curbing the undue power and predatory practices of large financial and non-financial corporations, reducing the wealth and income inequalities that have created fragmented societies and distorted economies, and ensuring that resilience to unforeseen shocks is guaranteed for the many, not just the privileged few.

The previous chapters of this *Report* explained that at the national level, pursuing a Green New Deal requires recovering policy options (and the space to implement them) lost to the undue reliance on market forces. During the last forty years, two key assumptions have guided economic policy in many countries: first, that the private sector is uniquely placed, and should be left alone, to boost national incomes through its focus on cost competitiveness, guided by market efficiency, and second, that fiscal austerity is the best tool available to policymakers to correct macroeconomic imbalances that might alter market outcomes.

As a result, the global economy has been fundamentally transformed, shrinking the public space while unleashing the forces of financialization and rentierism. It has not, however, delivered the promise of a more vibrant, inclusive and stable economic system. This failure has been particularly evident with respect to investment, both public and private, where the trend, in many countries, has been stagnation or decline over this period, while a prolonged disconnect between wage and productivity growth in most countries, along with the degradation of public services, has produced widening socio-economic gaps (*TDR 2017, 2020*).

The unprecedented government response to the pandemic is an implicit recognition that both the need and the room for a policy shift is greater than previously acknowledged. Chapter II offered a series of lessons that should guide policy forces, beyond the context of the current crisis and recovery. Among these, the recognition that "no one is safe until everyone is safe" speaks directly to the extension of the resilience challenge to climate adaptation.

But there are significant differences across countries in their capacity to respond to that challenge. In particular, the pandemic has exposed the gulf between developed and developing countries when it comes to the space they have to mobilize the resources needed to respond to unforeseen shocks. This has unavoidable implications not only for a big investment push into new sources of energy, but also for their capacity to respond to the growing threat from rising global temperatures.

The intensification of climate threats facing developing countries is not of their own making. Given this history, as well as the tight external constraints on their efforts to mobilize resources, they cannot be expected to put their own house in order without significant financial and technological support from the international community. As noted in Chapter III, the principle of common but differentiated responsibilities is intended to ensure that advanced countries provide that support, commensurate with the economic benefits they have reaped from pumping two centuries' worth of greenhouse gases into the atmosphere. The best vehicle for mobilizing and coordinating that support remains the multilateral system.

Previous *Reports* have stressed that the current multilateral architecture will need to undergo reforms to be able to address the multiple crises facing developing countries, in the time frame, and with the ambition, that has been set by the international community. In part, this means getting the institutions established in the years between 1944 and 1947 back to what their original designers intended (Gallagher and Kozul-Wright, 2021). Yet even assuming we are in "a Bretton Woods moment" (Georgieva, 2020), this cannot be an exercise in simply winding the clock back, given the weaknesses and asymmetries in the original design (particularly on matters of economic development). In 2021-22, creating a new multilateralism for shared prosperity is just as, and arguably even more, demanding a task than it was at the end of the Second World War. The global economy is now larger, more complex and fragile; the competing demands for resources are greater; and the voices that have to be listened to, in particular from the developing world, are more diverse.

Building back better will require a rethinking of public policy at the national level, along with a renewal of public institutions and a revitalization of the social contract, combined with new principles of cooperation and leadership at the global level. Strengthening the ambition and capacities of the developmental state is, as discussed in the preceding chapter, a necessary condition for developing economies when undertaking the structural changes needed to build resilience, without exacerbating the climate crisis and causing further environmental damage. But developing countries need collective support at the international level to complement and bolster their domestic efforts at resource mobilization. Progress on both fronts, can, if effectively coordinated, advance an agenda that works for all people and the planet.

This chapter analyses two major multilateral areas of the climate adaptation challenge: international trade rules and the financial system. As explained earlier in this *Report*, climate adaptation has been overshadowed by commitments to climate mitigation and reduction targets for greenhouse gas emissions. This asymmetry has been replicated in the wider trade and financial architecture, which have not delivered the opportunities and funding needed for a resilient, and climate conscious growth in developing economies. Existing rules and principles do not accommodate the technological, economic and financing needs of developing economies facing the adaptation challenge. Below we review these challenges and mechanisms in detail, and outline proposals for policy changes.

## B. Climate adaptation and the international trading system

With a shrinking timeline to stabilize the climate and advance the SDGs, all countries should find ways to both promote and discipline trade and investment in line with their Paris Agreement commitments and with the principle of common but differentiated responsibilities. But many of the initiatives that are gaining momentum in the reform of the international trading system continue to adhere to a lopsided liberalization agenda. This agenda has thus far neither delivered on the promise of development nor been associated with reduced emissions. Pursuing it further is likely to undermine any notion of a just transition by disadvantaging developing countries that have least responsibility for climate-related damages.

### 1. Trade and environment in the WTO and other trade agreements

Issues around trade and environment have again gained momentum in the World Trade Organization (WTO) since November 2020, when a group of 23 members (EU as one of them) initiated 'trade and environmental sustainability structured discussions' (TESSD) with an intention to report concrete deliverables, initiatives and next steps to the ministers at the 12th Ministerial Conference.[1] Since then, in various meetings, proposals have been tabled on liberalizing trade in environmental goods and services; reforming environmentally harmful subsidies; carbon border adjustment mechanism and climate actions; and circular economy and biodiversity.[2]

The Preamble to the Marrakesh Agreement emphasizes the need for "…expanding the production of and trade in goods and services, while allowing for the optimal use of the world's resources in accordance with the objective of sustainable development, seeking both to protect and preserve the environment and to enhance the means for doing so in a manner consistent with their respective needs and concerns at different levels of economic development."[3]

In line with this objective, paragraph 31 (iii) of the Doha Ministerial Declaration called for negotiations on "the reduction or, as appropriate, elimination of tariffs and non-tariff barriers to environmental goods and services"[4] and paragraph 32 called for particular attention to be given to the effect of environmental measures on market access of developing and least-developed countries, aiming at a triple win situation beneficial to trade, environment, and development.

Formal negotiations on a plurilateral Environmental Goods Agreement were launched at WTO in July 2014 but only two developing countries joined these negotiations, which stalled in 2016. Some of the reasons for developing countries not joining the negotiations included a missing development dimension, the inclusion in the lists of goods with multiple non-environmental uses that primarily supported the export interests of developed countries, and the fear that trade liberalization discriminates against their products based on non-environmental and social concerns (Khor et al., 2017; de Melo and Solleder, 2020).

Outside of the WTO, climate concerns have been reflected in the trading system primarily as non-binding sustainability chapters in bilateral or plurilateral trade agreements. These chapters have arguably had limited impact on encouraging climate action (Lowe, 2019) but mainly helped to secure the regulatory advantage of wealthy regions as global standard-setters (Goldberg 2019). The 2021 G7 Trade Ministers' communiqué also included the commitment to "make trade part of the solution" to climate change, in particular highlighting environmentally destructive agricultural practices and the issue of carbon leakage whereby high-emitting industries move operations from regions with stricter regulation to those with lower standards,

undermining the goal of reducing global greenhouse gas emissions (G7 Trade Ministers' Communiqué, 2021). Preventing carbon leakage has been high on the agenda of advanced economies, due to concerns that their higher environmental standards provide an unfair trade advantage for countries with less strict environmental regulation, and they have been demanding to 'level-the-playing-field' (United States Congress, 1992). One such measure is the proposed carbon tariff or Carbon Border Adjustment Mechanism (CBAM), which has been under consideration in the United Kingdom, the United States, and Canada, and is already part of the European Union's flagship policy in aligning trade and climate, i.e., the Green Deal (European Commission, 2021).

The G7-communiqué also highlighted the trade ministers' united position against 'unfair trade' and 'non-market policies and practices' including industrial subsidies and forced technology transfer, even though these same countries have used these policies in their own successful development process. The G7 has also called for an overhaul of the principle of special and differential treatment (SDT), essentially calling for a contraction in privileges with more targeted and specific measures. SDT was adopted to allow developing countries to benefit from non-reciprocal tariff reductions and granted some special rights and privileges to them to mitigate the disadvantages they face in the international trading system and to help them with implementing multilateral trade agreements (Kozul-Wright et al., 2019). With developing countries standing on the edge of another lost decade in the aftermath of the pandemic, it is a clear contradiction for the world's most advanced economies to restrict what policy space is available to them through SDT or industrial policy tools while expecting them to meet increasingly demanding climate goals.

These more recent unilateral proposals were preceded by the beginning of negotiations of a plurilateral Agreement on Climate Change, Trade and Sustainability (ACCTS) which has brought together six 'first-mover' countries (Costa Rica, Fiji, Iceland, New Zealand, Norway, and Switzerland) to build momentum around aligning trade and climate issues. While these negotiations are ongoing and have not yet resulted in a formal trade agreement with enforceable rules and regulations, they signal the approach that these countries plan to take on trade and climate, namely reducing tariffs on environmental goods and services, eliminating fossil fuel subsidies, and developing guidelines on voluntary eco-labelling schemes.[5]

## 2. Carbon border adjustment mechanism in the era of global value chains

The interconnectedness of the global economy and the fragmentation of production process make it difficult to gauge any specific country's carbon footprint accurately because a sizable share of $CO_2$ emissions in developing countries are generated in the production of consumer goods for developed countries. The organization of global production through global value chains (GVCs) has led to many carbon emitting production activities to be shifted to developing countries, while associated low-carbon pre-production and post-production activities have been retained in developed countries (*TDR 2018*). The comparative energy efficiency in the North is therefore closely linked to the energy inefficiency in the South.

According to data on the amount of carbon emissions embodied in final demand and international gross trade published in Yamano and Guilhoto (2020) for 65 countries and the period 2005–2015, of the total global $CO_2$ emitted in 2015, around 27 per cent is linked to international trade and concentrated in seven industries (mining and extraction of energy producing products; textiles, wearing apparel, leather and related products; chemicals and non-metallic mineral products; basic metals and fabricated metal products; computers, electronic and electrical equipment; machinery and equipment; and motor vehicles, trailers and semi-trailers). These are also the industries with a higher proportion of trade through GVCs. An analysis of these data reveals three additional features.

First, the share of non-OECD countries in global $CO_2$ emissions embodied in global domestic final demand and in global gross exports is 57 per cent and 69 per cent, respectively. However, removing China's share (25 per cent) from non-OECD aggregates makes the share of non-OECD decline to 32 per cent in $CO_2$ emissions embodied in global final demand, i.e., below that in the OECD countries (43 per cent). Similarly, the share of non-OECD countries less China in $CO_2$ emissions embodied in global gross exports is almost half of that in the OECD countries, i.e., only 16 per cent as compared to 31 per cent (Figure 5.1).

Second, average per capita $CO_2$ emissions based on production declined over the period 2005–2015 in OECD countries, but remained much higher than those in the non-OECD countries in 2015. Most of the developed economies like Australia, Canada, European Union, Germany, Japan, and the United States, have higher $CO_2$ emissions per capita

---

**FIGURE 5.1** **$CO_2$ emissions in domestic final demand and gross exports, OECD and non-OECD countries, 2015**

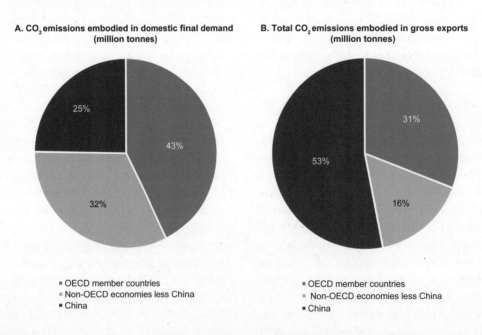

A. $CO_2$ emissions embodied in domestic final demand (million tonnes)

B. Total $CO_2$ emissions embodied in gross exports (million tonnes)

- OECD member countries
- Non-OECD economies less China
- China

*Source:* UNCTAD secretariat calculations, based on OECD, https://www.oecd.org/sti/ind/carbondioxideemissionsembodiedininternationaltrade.htm.

compared to developing countries like China, India, Indonesia, and Malaysia.

Third, $CO_2$ emissions in gross exports of OECD countries to non-OECD countries have grown much faster than the $CO_2$ emissions in their imports from non-OECD countries in the period 2005–2015. This trend is consistent across almost all industries and

services (Figure 5.2). The fact that despite their lower emission levels, $CO_2$ emissions in the gross exports of OECD countries have grown faster than $CO_2$ emissions in their gross imports, is indicative of the growing inter-connectedness in the global economy which makes it impossible to disentangle high-carbon and low-carbon emitters in global value chains.

**FIGURE 5.2** **Growth in $CO_2$ emissions in gross exports and gross imports of OECD-countries from non-OECD countries, 2005–2015**
*(tonnes, millions)*

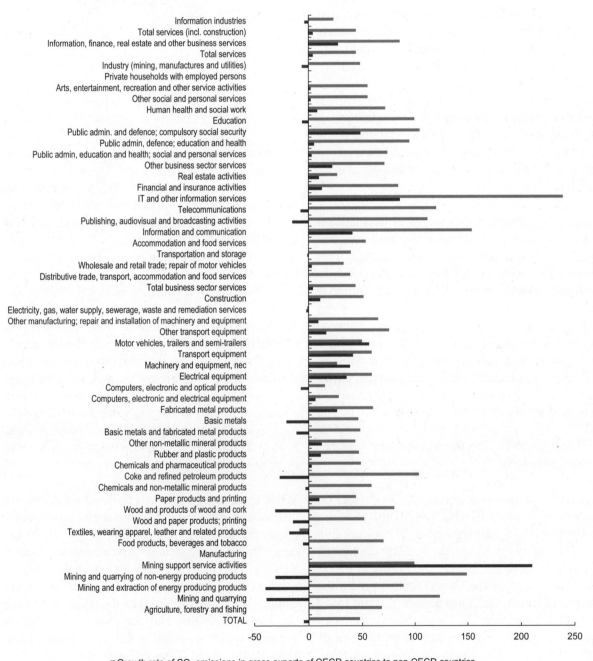

■ Growth rate of $CO_2$ emissions in gross exports of OECD countries to non-OECD countries
■ Growth rate of $CO_2$ emissions in gross exports of non-OECD countries to OECD countries

*Source:* See Figure 5.1.

At the same time, should carbon border adjustment mechanisms actually be implemented, much of their impact on structural transformation in developing countries will depend on their detailed technical specifications, with one of the major legal challenges being to make these mechanisms compatible with WTO rules. Yet, independent of these details, the principle on which these mechanisms are based is to impose on developing countries the environmental standards that developed countries are choosing. This goes against the principle of common but differentiated responsibility enshrined in the Paris Agreement. Moreover, should the revenues from these mechanisms be used in developed countries, rather than invested in climate adaption in developing countries, they would turn basic principles of climate finance on their head.[6]

In this context, it is notable that "[s]ince 1995, carbon emissions embodied in trade have been increasing both in absolute value and as a share of global emissions. However, the volume of global trade has grown more rapidly than carbon emissions embodied in it" (OECDb, 2019: 10).

In 2015, $CO_2$ emissions embodied in international trade (8.8 Gt) as a share of total global emissions was only 27.2 per cent (Yamano and Guilhoto 2020). This indicates that carbon emissions generated to produce goods and services consumed domestically comprise a much higher share in global carbon emissions than those that are internationally traded. National policies for climate adaptation can therefore play a much greater role than international trade policies. Nevertheless, proposals have been advanced by some of the developed countries to liberalize trade in environmental goods and services (e.g. WTO, 2021).

### 3. Push to liberalize environmental goods and services

The Combined List of Environmental Goods (CLEG) that was elaborated by OECD (2019b) provides the Harmonized System 6-digit level codes of 248 environmentally related goods. In 2019, the top ten exporters of these goods were the European Union followed by China, the United States, Japan, the Republic of Korea, the United Kingdom, China Hong Kong SAR, Singapore, Canada and Switzerland with a combined share of 88 per cent of global exports (Table 5.1), most developing countries were net importers of these products.

Tariffs on these environmentally related goods are on average 5 to 6 per cent in developing countries with

**TABLE 5.1  Top exporters of environmentally related goods**

|  | Exports (mn $) | Share in total exports (percentage) |
|---|---|---|
| European Union (EU27) | 510 210 | 38.8 |
| China | 279 877 | 21.3 |
| United States | 106 252 | 8.1 |
| Japan | 85 738 | 6.5 |
| Republic of Korea | 46 524 | 3.5 |
| United Kingdom | 36 760 | 2.8 |
| China Hong Kong SAR | 27 282 | 2.1 |
| Singapore | 26 360 | 2.0 |
| Canada | 20 440 | 1.6 |
| Switzerland | 17 847 | 1.4 |
| **Memo item:** Total of the above | 1 157 290 | 87.9 |

*Source:* UNCTAD secretariat calculations, based on World Bank *World Integrated Trade Solution (WITS)* database, and United Nations *Comtrade* database.

maximum tariffs exceeding 100 per cent on some products, while they are below 1 per cent in most developed countries (OECD, 2019). For example, passenger motor vehicles (HS code 8703.90) are also listed in CLEG as an environmental good, which is levied a tariff of 125 per cent in India, 100 per cent in Pakistan, 80 per cent in Nepal and 51 per cent in Egypt.

In 2019, tariff revenue collected on these goods by developing countries amounted to $15 billion (using applied duties). Trade liberalization in these products will therefore entail a substantial loss of tariff revenue for developing countries. This may have substantial adverse effects especially now when domestic sources of finance are urgently needed both to fight the Covid-19 pandemic and address climate change. Table 5.2 presents estimated annual tariff revenues in these products for 99 developing countries.

While there is no consensus on what goods should be included in the list of environmental goods, environmental services were already classified for the negotiations on the General Agreement on Trade in Services (GATS). Negotiations on environmental services have traditionally taken place under the Council for Trade in Services focusing on sewage services, refuse disposal services and sanitation services, which are listed in the environmental services sector of the Services Sectoral Classification List (GATT, 1991). However, there are attempts to widen the scope of environmental services to include services like engineering, architecture, design, general management, construction (OECD, 2017). Any

TABLE 5.2    Tariff revenue from environmental goods, developing economies, 2019

| | Weighted average tariff rate | Maximum tariff rate | Imports of environmental goods ('000 $) | Tariff revenue ('000 $) | | Weighted average tariff rate | Maximum tariff rate | Imports of environmental goods ('000 $) | Tariff revenue ('000 $) |
|---|---|---|---|---|---|---|---|---|---|
| Algeria | 10.2 | 60 | 5 936 180 | 606 678 | Lao PDR | 0.3 | 20 | 651 445 | 2 150 |
| Angola | 3.3 | 50 | 1 680 473 | 55 120 | Lebanon | 3.4 | 20 | 693 714 | 23 517 |
| Anguila | 14.7 | 20 | 8 979 | 1 323 | Lesotho | 0.2 | 30 | 283 544 | 482 |
| Antigua and Barbuda | 10.9 | 35 | 55 488 | 6 065 | Macao | 0.0 | 0 | 187 547 | 0 |
| Argentina | 9.8 | 35 | 6 292 625 | 619 194 | Madagascar | 5.7 | 20 | 191 376 | 10 889 |
| Armenia | 2.9 | 15 | 301 507 | 8 804 | Malawi | 4.6 | 25 | 82 154 | 3 763 |
| Aruba | 11.6 | 50 | 70 954 | 8 195 | Maldives | 20.9 | 400 | 312 341 | 65 217 |
| Azerbaijan | 5.3 | 15 | 1 569 400 | 83 649 | Mali | 8.2 | 20 | 168 101 | 13 734 |
| Bahrain | 3.2 | 5 | 1 407 649 | 44 341 | Mauritania | 8.8 | 20 | 184 151 | 16 224 |
| Bangladesh | 8.0 | 25 | 2 349 383 | 187 246 | Mauritius | 0.5 | 30 | 348 394 | 1 881 |
| Belize | 7.3 | 45 | 59 056 | 4 287 | Mongolia | 5.0 | 20 | 493 144 | 24 559 |
| Benin | 7.6 | 20 | 100 845 | 7 614 | Montserrat | 10.5 | 35 | 3 859 | 403 |
| Bhutan | 1.1 | 100 | 63 192 | 695 | Morocco | 2.1 | 25 | 3 199 868 | 68 157 |
| Bolivia | 2.9 | 20 | 1 624 712 | 46 629 | Myanmar | 1.3 | 30 | 995 940 | 12 648 |
| Botswana | 1.4 | 30 | 266 854 | 3 816 | Namibia | 0.7 | 30 | 373 416 | 2 689 |
| Brazil | 10.5 | 35 | 15 557 060 | 1 630 380 | Nauru | 10.5 | 30 | 5 024 | 529 |
| Brunei | 0.0 | 5 | 900 181 | 270 | Nepal | 9.6 | 80 | 465 351 | 44 813 |
| Burkina Faso | 8.1 | 20 | 179 222 | 14 535 | Nicaragua | 1.5 | 15 | 311 005 | 4 789 |
| Burundi | 8.9 | 35 | 16 597 | 1 472 | Niger | 9.2 | 20 | 86 909 | 7 987 |
| Cameroon | 13.9 | 30 | 316 419 | 44 014 | Oman | 2.1 | 5 | 3 522 949 | 73 982 |
| Cape Verde | 6.1 | 40 | 58 834 | 3 589 | Pakistan | 11.5 | 100 | 4 220 456 | 483 664 |
| Chile | 0.4 | 6 | 4 604 802 | 20 261 | Palau | 3.0 | 3 | 10 470 | 314 |
| China | 3.7 | 15 | 151 613 712 | 5 655 191 | Papua New Guinea | 1.9 | 25 | 409 901 | 7 870 |
| Colombia | 1.6 | 35 | 3 404 373 | 55 491 | Paraguay | 4.2 | 20 | 541 667 | 22 642 |
| Comoros | 12.2 | 20 | 2 706 | 329 | Peru | 0.1 | 11 | 3 055 895 | 2 139 |
| Congo, Dem. Rep. | 9.3 | 20 | 393 356 | 36 543 | Philippines | 1.2 | 30 | 8 667 970 | 104 016 |
| Cook Islands | 0.0 | 0 | 8 580 | 0 | Qatar | 3.4 | 5 | 3 184 188 | 107 307 |
| Costa Rica | 0.8 | 14 | 993 988 | 8 151 | Rwanda | 6.4 | 35 | 306 986 | 19 524 |
| Cote d'Ivoire | 8.6 | 20 | 787 451 | 67 721 | Sao Tome and Principe | 8.8 | 20 | 4 248 | 372 |
| Cuba | 10.0 | 30 | 475 653 | 47 660 | Senegal | 8.5 | 20 | 680 144 | 57 948 |
| Ecuador | 6.8 | 35 | 1 419 910 | 96 128 | Seychelles | 0.0 | 25 | 105 682 | 0 |
| Egypt, Arab Rep. | 2.4 | 135 | 3 659 071 | 88 915 | Singapore | 0.0 | 0 | 25 144 184 | 0 |
| El Salvador | 1.4 | 30 | 509 218 | 7 180 | Solomon Islands | 8.1 | 15 | 26 787 | 2 156 |
| Eswatini | 0.4 | 30 | 9 9071 | 406 | South Africa | 2.1 | 30 | 5 633 598 | 118 869 |
| Fiji | 7.9 | 32 | 149 789 | 11 848 | Sri Lanka | 5.7 | 30 | 1 072 420 | 60 806 |
| French Polynesia | 5.0 | 13 | 99 797 | 4 990 | St. Kitts and Nevis | 11.9 | 45 | 19 830 | 2 354 |
| Gabon | 12.5 | 30 | 249 306 | 31 039 | St. Lucia | 5.5 | 50 | 50 521 | 2 784 |
| Ghana | 8.3 | 20 | 938 607 | 78 280 | St. Vincent & Grenadines | 8.7 | 35 | 21 893 | 1 900 |
| Grenada | 7.1 | 35 | 16 788 | 1 195 | Suriname | 6.3 | 30 | 155 882 | 9 852 |
| Guinea | 8.1 | 20 | 216 794 | 17 539 | Taiwan, Prov. of China | 2.0 | 18 | 17 070 441 | 334 581 |
| Guinea-Bissau | 8.8 | 20 | 12 872 | 1 134 | United Republic of Tanzania | 6.2 | 35 | 724 055 | 44 819 |
| Guyana | 6.1 | 45 | 220 345 | 13 529 | Togo | 12.6 | 20 | 136 060 | 17 184 |
| Hong Kong, China SAR | 0.0 | 0 | 30 341 851 | 0 | Turkey | 0.6 | 16 | 13 607 372 | 84 366 |
| India | 6.4 | 125 | 25 710 053 | 1 645 443 | Uganda | 6.1 | 35 | 426 025 | 26 158 |
| Indonesia | 1.6 | 50 | 15 567 797 | 244 414 | United Arab Emirates | 4.0 | 5 | 15 153 056 | 612 183 |
| Iran, Islamic Rep. | 12.4 | 55 | 5 207 631 | 643 142 | Uruguay | 6.3 | 23 | 496 472 | 31 178 |
| Kazakhstan | 1.4 | 15 | 7 748 942 | 106 935 | Venezuela | 11.4 | 26 | 282 817 | 32 241 |
| Kenya | 8.0 | 35 | 539 190 | 42 973 | Vietnam | 1.0 | 70 | 21 151 174 | 217 857 |
| Kuwait | 3.9 | 5 | 4 971 529 | 191 901 | Wallis and Futura Isl. | 0.4 | 10 | 2355 | 10 |
| Kyrgyz Republic | 2.6 | 20 | 237 716 | 6 157 | | | | | |

*Source:* UNCTAD secretariat calculations, based on World Bank World Integrated Trade Solution (WITS) database, and UN-TRAINS. Tariff revenue calculated on basis of applied duties.

resulting commitments in these services will take away the flexibility that the positive list approach in the GATS offered to the developing countries in terms of liberalizing their services trade. Furthermore, there is a risk that forcing liberalization of vital public utilities and bringing it under private sector can lead to negative development outcomes, because this creates an environment of conflicted interests, because public goods are delivered for profit. This will further restrict developing countries' ability to use public procurement as a policy tool to achieve social objectives.

## 4. Can international trading rules promote the circular economy?

Recently in the WTO, developed countries have been pursuing the narrative on 'circular economy' to gain market access into the developing countries. It has sometimes been argued that trade liberalization is indispensable to move towards a circular economy, particularly because trade restrictions in the form of export bans may hinder circular economy activities related to reuse, repair, refurbishment, remanufacturing and recycling (OECD, 2018).

Calls for the liberalization of trade in remanufactured or recycled goods and waste date back to 2004 when the issues of non-tariff barriers affecting trade in remanufactured goods such as medical and heavy equipment and motor vehicles and parts were first raised (WTO, 2004). Some of the non-tariff barriers identified at the time with respect to remanufactured goods were: requirements to provide a "refurbished certificate" signed by the consulate in the country of origin guaranteeing that the imported product is "like new"; prohibitions on imports of remanufactured goods if the equivalent goods are manufactured domestically or if they can be substituted for goods manufactured domestically; requirements that imported remanufactured goods meet a "special needs" test; and certification requirements from a chartered engineer that spare parts have at least 80 per cent of their original life remaining. To remove these restrictions and liberalize trade in remanufactured goods, some WTO Members proposed a Ministerial Decision on Trade in Remanufactured Goods in 2010 (WTO, 2010).

The proposed Ministerial Decision was rejected mainly because some developing countries raised concern about the possible adverse impacts of these imports on producers of new goods in their countries and on the transfer of new technologies. The danger

was that second-hand, refurbished, or remanufactured goods may lock developing economies into outdated and less efficient technological solutions and therefore would delay the achievement of environmental goals (Steinfatt, 2020). Concerns were also raised on liberalizing trade in waste and scrap as that would put additional pressure on the waste management systems of developing countries, especially those which lack a sound regulatory framework for waste management and the associated infrastructure capacities. Developing countries argued that restrictions like export bans on metal waste and scrap were used to promote domestic processing and value added. Furthermore, imports of second-hand clothes and footwear were found to have significant negative impacts on the revamping of the textiles and leather industries, especially in Africa. They were also found to have adverse impacts on consumer health, human dignity, and culture (Wetengere, 2018).

While moving towards a circular economy is, therefore, vital to contain resource use and environmental degradation, there is little reason to combine the moves required to do this with trade liberalization. Instead, a circular economy may be best achieved through appropriate domestic regulatory policies, as discussed in the previous chapter.

## 5. The way forward on the trade and environment agenda

While climate adaptation remains a priority for developing countries, greenhouse emissions in traded goods and services account for only 27 per cent of global carbon emissions. This points to a rather limited scope for trade policy to contribute to a global green growth agenda, with trade policy only serving as a complementary tool for attaining environmentally sustainable growth. Rather than building a trade and environment agenda on trade liberalization, making the most of the coherence between special different treatment (SDT) and the UNFCCC principle of 'common but differentiated responsibilities' (CBDR) may offer a better point of departure for a development-oriented approach to the trade-climate nexus.

While SDT is designed to expand policy space for developing countries to tackle the specific challenges they face in integrating into the global trading system, CBDR recognizes that advanced economies bear most of the responsibility for historic emissions that have caused climate change, and therefore should shoulder most of the burden to respond to the impacts of climate change and tackle its root causes. The convergence of SDT and CBDR, both of which acknowledge systemic asymmetries, leads to a vastly different agenda for aligning trade and climate. Such an agenda emphasizes the expansion of policy space for green industrial policy; the enhancement of flexibilities regarding the protection of intellectual property rights and of incentives fostering technology transfer for climate and environment-related goods; a strengthening of transition support for developing countries to accelerate the adoption of renewable energy sources; and an expansion of financial support that exceeds the $100 billion climate finance target agreed in the UNFCCC process for developing countries to meet climate goals.

### (a) Expanding policy space for climate and development

A first step in aligning SDT and CBDR would be to widen non-reciprocal SDT measures to expand policy space for climate and development initiatives. A limited climate waiver of WTO trade and environment rules combined with a 'peace clause' for disputes on trade-related environmental measures of developing countries could be one route forward. A narrowly defined waiver and peace clause would give countries the assurance that they will not face disputes for climate and development-friendly initiatives such as prioritizing a transition to renewable energy, green procurement, and green jobs programmes – all initiatives that advanced economies are also prioritizing but that could be challenged under the WTO-dispute mechanism.[7]

While legal tools such as waivers and peace clauses will help diminishing the number of restrictive rules and the extent of regulatory chill, as well as expanding the policy space for developing countries, unilateral action in advanced economies can provide further room for maneuver. Incentive-based approaches, such as optional preference schemes that provide ringfenced climate financing additional to ODA or preferential market access in exchange for progress towards nationally determined contributions (NDCs), could accelerate climate action without recurring to punitive measures with anti-developmental effects.

### (b) Climate and intellectual property rights

Recent evidence suggests that intellectual property rights protection does not promote the transfer of low-carbon technology (Pigato et. al. 2020), suggesting that an alleviation of intellectual property

rights protection may be the best way to ensure global dissemination of low-carbon technologies. This calls for a multilateral arrangement that reflects the commitment to "shared responsibility" and makes low-carbon technologies widely accessible.

As a step towards such an arrangement, the international community could support initiatives to transform rules governing intellectual property rights, such as through a WTO Ministerial Declaration on TRIPS and Climate Change, with a view to expanding TRIPS flexibilities for developing countries in relation to climate-related goods and services. The Doha Declaration on the TRIPS Agreement and Public Health adopted by the WTO Ministerial Conference of 2001 reaffirmed flexibility of TRIPS member states in circumventing patent rights for better access to essential medicines. This could provide a basis for innovative mechanisms for promoting access to patent-protected critical green technologies. Other initiatives that could support this agenda include the open-sourcing of key green technologies as global public goods, South-South cooperation on low-emission research and design, and green investment strategies that include technology transfer.

### (c) Climate finance and trade

Concerning the relationship between climate finance and trade, existing proposals for Carbon Border Adjustment Mechanisms (CBAMs) and tariff eliminations on environmental goods and services are likely to disproportionately impact resource mobilization in developing countries whose total economic output is currently more carbon-intensive than that in developed countries and for whom tariffs make up a greater proportion of government revenue. New financing support could be provided through a Trade and Environment Fund, as proposed by some WTO members (WTO, 2011). Such a Fund could finance the incremental costs of sourcing critical technologies, provide grants for specific green technologies, finance joint research, development and demonstrations, as well as the establishment of technology transfer centres, exchanges and mechanisms.

Should negotiations on carbon tariffs proceed at the WTO, it will be important to ensure that this issue remains in the multilateral rules-based system. No decision should be taken between smaller groups of developed economies, as this would risk further undermining the trust of other WTO members, particularly those impacted most, in the ability of the multilateral trading system and global climate initiatives to support the achievement of developmental objectives.

While it is not clear whether currently considered forms of a CBAM would be compliant with WTO rules, any such mechanism will best serve the interests of global climate commitments and development goals if it includes a redistributive mechanism that redirects new tariff revenue to dedicated financing for green transitions in developing countries. Moreover, any imposition of tax or elimination of tariffs should be commensurate with the level of economic development, national objectives and needs of developing countries, and adequate transition periods should be built in that to allow for phased implementation of obligations for developing and least-developed countries. But most importantly, any requirement for governments in the Global South should be contingent on the more effective policies outlined above regarding expanded policy space, enhanced intellectual property rights flexibilities and new sources of climate finance to avoid a catastrophic impact on development initiatives.

## C. Financing climate adaptation: issues, instruments, institutions

Facing up to the climate challenge, both mitigation and adaptation, requires an unprecedented degree of investment, on a global scale.[8] As noted in Chapter III of this *Report*, estimates converge around a global clean energy investment push in the range of 2–3 per cent of world output per year, and lasting well into the next decade, if the increase in global temperatures is to be kept to between 1.5 and 2 degrees. Assuming the transition will be a just one, which would include sufficient financing for adaptation purposes, then the higher end of that range would seem the appropriate target. This amounts to something in the order of $2.5 trillion per year. To put that into perspective, the OECD countries issued $18 trillion in debt in 2020 in response to the Covid-19 crisis.[9]

A study commissioned by the UN Environmental Programme (UNEP, 2020) estimates that the annual requirement for climate adaptation and resilience investments could vary between $140 and $300 billion by 2030 and $280–$500 billion in 2050. According to the World Bank, building climate-resilient infrastructure in the power, water and sanitation, and transport sectors in low- and middle-income countries will require between $11 to $65 billion a year by 2030 (Timisel, 2021: 3). At present, scaling up development finance is seen as a largely static reallocation exercise to direct existing financial resources (or savings) to meet the SDGs including for climate mitigation and adaptation. At the heart of this agenda is the idea that available public finance should be used to "leverage" international private finance, through blended financing instruments that allow investors to hedge against risk and, more generally, by "embarking on system-wide insurance and diversification of risk to create a large-scale asset class and mobilize significantly greater private sector participation" (EPG-GFG, 2018: 30).

Rather than encouraging developing countries to build domestic banking and financial systems that can manage domestic credit creation for development, and advocating measures to reduce their exposure to volatile international financial markets, this agenda focuses on how best to increase developing countries' attractiveness for global private wealth holders and to safeguard international investor (and creditor) risk through "financial innovation" to diversify and insure such risk "throughout the system". As recent research shows, this effectively means shifting most of this risk onto the public realm (Attridge and Engen, 2019).

The political economy of climate financing entails two specific consequences for developing countries' financing needs. First, where financing for climate investments is aid dependent, they have had to compete with other donor priorities, particularly those more closely linked to poverty reduction, as well as being subject to the variable constraints on donor budgets. As a result, actual funds committed for climate-related finance have not been close to what is required to address the scale of the climate challenge.

Second, as climate investments have come to rely on market-based financial instruments for raising capital, the dominant paradigm of risk management, as laid out in Chapter III of this *Report*, has prioritized profit-making activities in climate mitigation, leaving climate adaptation needs largely overlooked and under-funded. Even with respect to mitigation efforts, existing climate governance system assumes investor rationality as a given; prioritizes "market discipline" and understand climate change as financial stability risk which demands risk disclosure (Christophers , 2017: 1108). In this type of governance, financialization has shifted power away from the public sector to the market – that is, to funds and fund managers managing public, private and blended finance, with a consequent reduction in the quality of accountability and transparency (Bracking and Leffel, 2021; Christophers, 2019).

Previous *Reports* have highlighted a number of concerns stemming from this climate governance and specifically from letting the financial markets determine climate-oriented investment priorities.[10] The pandemic has only confirmed that the management of public goods (and bads) requires the lead be taken by governments through dedicated public policy, investments and services.

As detailed further below, the experience of many developing countries shows that public, multilateral development initiatives have yielded greater success in building resilience at national and local levels. However, such funding often suffers from insufficient and unreliable source of capital and a lack of coordination across multiple actors. As a result, finance for adaptation purposes is caught between under-financed public mechanisms on the one side, and hyper-charged but unreliable private mechanisms, on the other.

It is clear that a more structural solution is needed to address the challenge of climate governance broadly, and climate adaptation needs in particular. Such a change needs to be guided strategically at national levels, by developmental states, in line with local needs, but there is a necessary, and larger role than is currently the case for international financial institutions in mobilizing and coordinating resources in support of that change.

This section analyses the landscape and record of green finance initiatives to date, before developing specific policy recommendations. Our analysis shows that financing the climate adaptation gap in developing countries requires both a massive scaling up of grant-based and concessional finance, as well as increased certainty that the funds raised will benefit the intended users and purposes. The concluding section outlines some steps in the direction of necessary policy reform.

## 1. The role of ODA and climate funds

Providing ample – and ideally grant-based or highly concessional – international climate finance is

### TABLE 5.3 Stock and flows of climate finance (by donor reports)

| *Annual flows of climate finance* | |
| --- | --- |
| Pledged at Cancun (2009) and Copenhagen (2010) | $100 billion |
| Paid flows of funds reported to UNFCCC and OECD (2017) | $56 billion |
| Paid flows of funds reported to UNFCCC and OECD (2018) | $63 billion |
| OXFAM estimate of effective climate-specific net assistance | $19-22 billion |
| *Estimated Stock of finance from Climate Funds under the UNFCCC* | |
| Green Climate Fund (since 2009)* | $5.6 billion |
| LDC Fund (since 2001) | $1.6 billion |
| Adaptation Fund (since 2001) | $0.8 billion |
| Special Climate Change Fund (since 2001) | $0.3 billion |

**Source:** Oxfam (2020), Vincent (2021).
**Note:** *The phrase "since 2009" refers to the year of this fund's inception; same with the other dates. The figures above these come from the Oxfam report.

the cornerstone of global cooperation on climate change (Oxfam, 2020; UNCTAD, 2019, 2020). It is important not only because of the urgency and costs of the problem, and not only because its nature as a "public bad" demands collective action, but because many of the countries worst hit by changing climatic conditions, and most in need of adaptation investment, are the least responsible for causing those changes.

The key dilemma facing these countries is that financing climate adaptation is not as likely to generate income-earning opportunities as compared to mitigation. Moreover, even if funds were divided equally between the two broad categories, the total size of the envelope from ODA and contributions to dedicated global climate funds is too small for what is needed (Table 5.3).

Donor reports of public climate finance to the UNFCCC and OECD show that even though sums are rising, they still fall well short of the $100 billion per year by 2020 pledged in Copenhagen in 2009 and Cancun 2010. Of the $79.6 bn assistance provided by developed countries in 2019, one quarter was for adaptation purposes (OECD, 2021). Moreover, on some measures the effective funds are even less than half the amount reported (Oxfam, 2020). Counting only the grant equivalent and not loans, guarantees or non-grant instruments that bring with them future debt service payments, interest and administrative costs, the net financial value to recipient countries in 2017-18 fell to $19–$22.5 billion from the reported figure of $60bn (ibid). Some individual donor countries gave 100 per cent of aid in the form of grants;[11] yet grants from other donors ranged from less than one third and up to only one half of their total package – meaning that the net contribution to poor countries' ability to finance climate change adaptation is much less than it appears. Of the total funding received, only around 20 per cent came as grants (ibid); the rest came in loans and other non-grant instruments that could significantly increase the debt burden of recipient countries – many of whom are LDCs and SIDS.

The need for global public funds to scale up adaptation finance is reinforced by a survey carried out by the Climate Policy Initiative in 2019 (Buchner et al., 2019, updated 2020). The survey found that in 2017–2018, total grants came to only $29 billion, all of which was provided by public sources; the small amount of low-cost loans came to 93 per cent from public sources (in particular, DFIs), and a very large amount of market-rate loans reached as much as $316 billion.[12] The vast majority of loan finance raised was directed to mitigation (93 per cent) and only 5 per cent to adaptation. More positively, the absolute value of adaptation funds was rising as was the value of joint adaptation-mitigation funds (2 per cent of the total) reflecting, perhaps, a better understanding of the integrated nature of the problem. Nonetheless, CPI concludes that a "tectonic plate shift" is still needed in both public and private financing, especially of adaptation (ibid:26). Figure 5.3. illustrates this; the CPI survey includes only certified bonds which is a small proportion of the total bonds described by their issuers as "green".

The United States has recently pledged to double by 2024 its annual public climate finance to developing countries (relative to the average commitment made during 2013–2016), including increasing three-fold its annual adaptation financing.[13] This would take the US pledge to where it was almost seven years ago when it made a similar commitment. At the recent 2021 Climate Adaptation Summit,[14] France reaffirmed that €2 billion, or one-third of France's climate contributions, will be directed at climate adaptation. Germany also committed €270 million extra for climate-vulnerable countries.

Notwithstanding these pledges, the persistent failure of advanced countries to meet the 0.7 per cent ODA target is a major obstacle to achieving climate-related goals. The lack of dependable, core financial support particularly affects countries that lack the domestic

**FIGURE 5.3  Adaptation vs mitigation finance estimates**

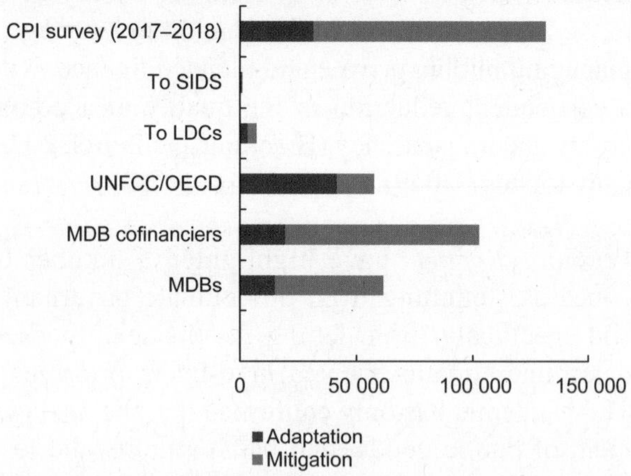

**Source:** Derived from Buchner et al. (2019), Oxfam (2020), AfDB (2019).
**Note:** CPI survey includes only certified bonds.

resources for even the most fundamental activities, such as waste disposal and water treatment services, which are unlikely to be attractive as private investments. Even before the Covid era, lack of investment in these activities had a climate change urgency, e.g., the lack of publicly provided fresh water provokes demand for water sold in bottles – usually single-use plastic – which ends up polluting the oceans. The recent G7 communiqué committed to "strengthening adaptation and resilience to protect people from the impacts of climate change," but provided little indication of how that might happen beyond encouraging "further development of disaster risk finance markets... in line with the InsuResilience Global Partnership and Risk-Informed Early Action Partnership (REAP)." Instead, a commitment by just these seven countries to meet the 0.7 per cent ODA target would generate an additional $150bn annually, albeit still at the bottom of the range needed.

## 2. Debt relief for adaptive development

Previous *Reports* have shown that the Agenda 2030 is undeliverable in many developing countries under their existing burden of debt (*TDR 2015, 2019*). Moreover, warming global temperatures will only worsen their prospects, fueling an even more vicious circle in developing countries, as the adverse impact on growth prospects heightens their perceived credit risks, leading to a downgrade in their credit ratings and higher borrowing costs, adding hundreds of billions of dollars in debt servicing over the coming years (Klusak et al., 2021). For many vulnerable developing countries this will add insult to the injuries already caused by unfair credit conditions.

When financial and debt distress reaches levels that require intervention, effective and fair sovereign debt restructuring mechanisms are essential to preserving a constructive role for developmental credit creation and debt in the future. The current *ad hoc* frameworks for sovereign debt restructurings are costly, fragmented and fraught with inefficiencies and perverse incentives, largely tilting the balance of power in favour of creditors (*TDR 2015*: chap. VI; Guzman et al., 2016).

As UNCTAD has long argued, many poorer developing countries and SIDSs, now regularly exposed to natural disasters related to climate change, need temporary debt moratoriums and automatic mechanisms to extend such moratoriums on debt servicing to safeguard government expenditure on essential social spending, such as health, education and sanitation, when such events occur. The pandemic has seen moves in this direction, through the DSSI, albeit on far too small a scale.

An obvious place to begin linking debt relief to climate adaptation would be with economies that are already experiencing serious damage from rising global temperatures (see Box 5.1). Prime Minister Sheik Hasina of Bangladesh has called for a reassessment of the debt burdens of climate vulnerable countries in response to the imminent climate collapse predicted in the report.[15] As a founding member of the Group of Twenty Finance Ministers of Vulnerable Countries (the V20), Bangladesh and the group of 48 countries who self-identify as climate vulnerable, have much to be concerned about.[16] Left unchecked, rising global temperatures will lead to two-thirds of Bangladesh's land mass being inundated with sea water within 30 years. Viet Nam, another V20 country, faces a prospect that within the same time span, 80–90 per cent of the country will be covered by sea water each year; only once will be enough to dislodge Viet Nam as the producer of a third of the world's rice. Sea level rises of this sort will displace more than 100 million people in South Asia alone.[17]

The external debt of V20 countries stands at under $1 trillion, and forgiveness or relief of a substantial part of this would provide the fiscal space to begin to address adaptation investment and the climate related SDGs. The London Agreement of 1953 which relieved post-war Germany of half its outstanding debt and limited its debt servicing requirement to 3 per cent of the value of annual exports could provide the blueprint for a negotiated settlement between these vulnerable countries and their creditors (*TDR 2015*: 134).

---

**Box 5.1**    Shades of vulnerability – Climate, finance and SDG dimensions facing the V20 countries

While their classification as low- and middle-income developing countries already suggests vulnerability,[18] a closer examination suggests that the V20 countries are relatively more vulnerable than their reference groups in three fundamental ways: financial, climatic, and developmental vulnerabilities self-reinforce to undermine the prospects of V20 countries to emerge from climate collapse with their economies and populations intact. In each of these aspects, the V20 have little self-determination – they are not responsible for the climate degradation, or the high interest rates they face in international capital markets, and they are unlikely to be able to mobilize sufficient domestic resources to meet the developmental needs encapsulated in the SDGs.

Around 70 per cent (33 countries) of the V20 countries are considered Poverty Reduction and Growth Trust (PRGT)-eligible countries, which can access concessional finance due to tier low-income status. Of these, 32 are eligible for the G20 Debt Servicing Suspension Initiative (DSSI) – set in place in the wake of the Covid-19 pandemic.[19] While this has provided some small measure of relief, it was clearly not enough, with 25 of the 33 V20 DSSI countries in debt distress, or in high-risk of debt distress by June 2021.[20] Figure 5.B1.1 (left panel) shows that V20 countries have higher levels of external debt to GDP (40 per cent) than other LICs and MICs (26 per cent) on average, and similar levels of external debt servicing (as a share of export earnings – at 16 per cent). However, the right panel of Figure 5.B1.1 shows that the non-DSSI V20 countries – excluded like many other MICs from concessional finance – have the highest levels of indebtedness (as measured by the external debt to GDP ratio), at almost 45 per cent. In the case of public debt, it appears that V20 countries pay a premium to access capital markets, with a recent paper from Buhr et al. (2021) suggesting that V20 countries pay an additional 117 basis points or nearly 10 per cent more on overall interest costs, as a consequence of climate change effects being transmitted to sovereigns' credit profiles through weaker economic activity, damage to infrastructure, rising social costs associated with climate shocks (access to health and food) and population displacement.

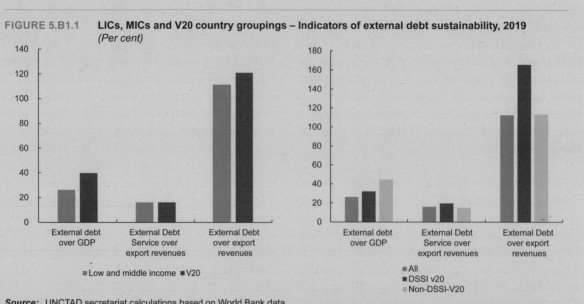

**FIGURE 5.B1.1  LICs, MICs and V20 country groupings – Indicators of external debt sustainability, 2019**
*(Per cent)*

*Source:* UNCTAD secretariat calculations based on World Bank data.
  *Note:*  No debt data for Barbados, Kiribati, Marshall Islands, Palau, South Sudan, and Tuvalu. WB do not carry data for Palestine.

While the much-anticipated 2021 SDR allocation to all developing countries – including the V20 countries – offers some potential relief, for the non-DSSI V20 countries, the new SDR allocation will not make a big dent in indebtedness, making up just over 2 percent of their 2019 external debt, compared to 2.4 per cent for all MICs (see Table 5.B1.1).

**TABLE 5.B1.1 Projected SDR allocations – all LICs and MICs and the V20**

| All LICS and MICS | | | | | V20 | | | |
|---|---|---|---|---|---|---|---|---|
| SDR allocation as a share of 2019 external debt | Number of countries | 2021 Allocation (billion USD) | 2019 total external debt (billion USD) | SDR over total debt (per cent) | Number of countries | 2021 Allocation (billion USD) | 2019 total external debt (billion USD) | SDR over total debt (per cent) |
| LICs | 26 | 8 | 151 | 5.40 | 12 | 5 | 86 | 5.46 |
| MICs | 105 | 198 | 8.220 | 2.41 | 33 | 19 | 899 | 2.07 |

*Source:* Oxfam (2020), Vincent (2021).

The Notre Dame Global Adaptation Index and Climate vulnerability Index[21] is gaining prominence in terms of measuring climate vulnerability (eg. Tiedemann et. al., 2021) and includes an assessment of the propensity or predisposition of human societies to be negatively impacted by climate hazards in one index, and climate change readiness, defined as the ability to make effective use of investments for adaptation actions, in another. According to these measures, the vulnerability of 74 per cent of V20 countries falls below that of the global average, as compared to 53 per cent of MICs. Moreover, MICs that are neither DSSI nor V20 countries perform best on the Readiness index (more of them exceed the global average value of readiness) and only 31 per cent are relatively vulnerable (see Figure 5.B3.2)  LICs are more vulnerable and have least readiness (Zero per cent are more ready than the global average). The adaptation readiness of V20 countries matches that of all MICS at 28 per cent, and slightly more DSSI V20 countries (27 per cent) exceed the global average than for DSSI eligible countries (17 per cent). It is possible the identification of V20 countries as climate vulnerable has already directed their investments to adapt.

Archimedes famously indicated that in order to change the world, one needs a lever and a place to stand.[22] The V20 – by virtue of their identification as the climate vulnerable South – have a place to stand. One potential way to extend their lever would be to redress exclusion of vulnerable countries from concessional finance – on the grounds that they have exceeded some national income threshold. By adding climate vulnerability as a criterion to the PRGT selection, for example, could potentially mean access to concessional finance, and a lower cost of credit. Another would be to enact a regular (possibly annual) SDR allocation to climate vulnerable countries as suggested in Chapter I, Box 1.3 and a third would be to begin a process of debt relief, targeting countries whose climate vulnerability undermines their capacity to adapt.

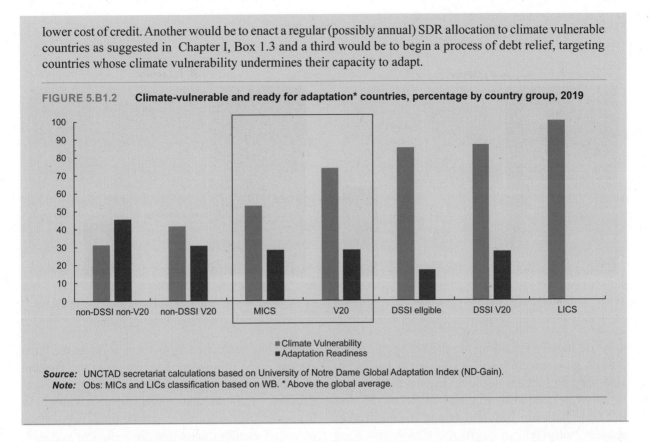

**FIGURE 5.B1.2    Climate-vulnerable and ready for adaptation\* countries, percentage by country group, 2019**

■ Climate Vulnerability
■ Adaptation Readiness

***Source:*** UNCTAD secretariat calculations based on University of Notre Dame Global Adaptation Index (ND-Gain).
***Note:*** Obs: MICs and LICs classification based on WB. \* Above the global average.

## 3. The topography of green finance: instruments and institutions

Notwithstanding the political prioritization of market-based mechanisms in global climate governance, private capital has neither been sufficient nor willing to address the climate challenge. Existing research lists a long series of obstacles that prevent private actors from engaging with climate projects at a fuller scale. These include the lack of quantifiable incentives, low returns to corporate social responsivity practices, perceived high risks of low-carbon technologies by private financial institutions, a mismatch between long-term payback period and the short-term horizons of most private investors, inability to evaluate projects and their climate-related consequences, as well as a shortage of 'bankable' low carbon, adaptation, and resilience projects (see Bhandary et al., 2021). Political, institutional and legal barriers to private investments also play a major role, especially when coordination is lacking at the international level (ibid: 530). This section reviews key instruments used by the private sector and evaluates their role in funding climate adaptation needs.

### (a) Green bonds

Of all the activities in the fast-growing green finance space, the so-called green bonds have attracted the highest profile, in financial quarters at least. This is unsurprising, given that since 2007 – when the first green bond was launched by the European Investment Bank (EIB) – estimates for the sector now range from $754 billion to $1.1 trillion in loosely defined climate or climate-aligned bonds (CBI, 2021). While much of this may be window-dressing or worse (Guardian, 2021), the considerably smaller $100 billion category of "Certified Climate Bonds (CBI, 2021) is still large compared to the other sources of finance discussed above.[23] In 2020 alone, the total issuance reached a record level of $300 billion (in comparison to less than $50 billion in 2014 and 2015, an increase of almost 700 per cent) a value already achieved in the first-half of 2021. Green bonds also dominate the certified green finance market.[24] Yet even with this rapid growth, the green bond market represents only 5 per cent of the total issuance and 4.3 per cent of the amount outstanding in the international capital market. In other words, although the world is awash with capital, the challenge is how to direct it to productive purposes – in this particular case, towards adaptation that meets the additionality criteria.

Green bonds are, by their nature, often considered to be more suitable for green investments with higher short-term profitability. This may be in part because

**FIGURE 5.4  Green bonds: accumulated issuances, 2014–2020**
*(Billions of US dollars)*

**A. By Issuer**

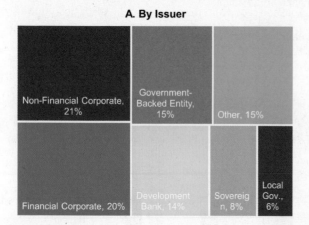

**B. By sector**

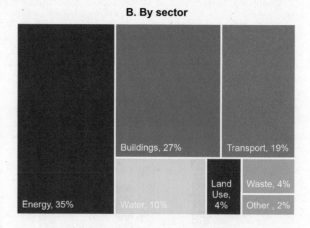

*Source:* UNCTAD secretariat calculations, based on OECD, https://www.oecd.org/sti/ind/carbondioxideemissionsembodiedininternationaltrade.htm.

they are mostly issued by the private sector, even though governments and development banks are still very significant sources (Figure 5.4). More research is needed to examine in detail the distinctions between different bonds from different issuers, but given that green bonds do not need to be asset-backed (asset defined *a priori*) and can also be asset-linked (asset defined after the fact), there is a lingering concern about the possibility of "greenwashing", that is, the practice of channelling proceeds from green bonds towards projects or activities having negligible or even negative environmental benefits that can be maladaptive. While some bond label certificates do help to ensure that financed activities are green, existing frameworks are non-binding and lack enforcement mechanisms (Deschryver and Mariz, 2020; Noor, 2019). Moreover, even if bonds have the benefit of a significant 'greenium' – a question on which there is still no consensus[25] – as long as adaptation-oriented activities do not generate profit, especially in the short-term, such sources of finance are unlikely to be a solution for developing countries. Although the distinction between adaptation and mitigation has not been formally made in these kinds of instruments, looking at the categories of activities and issuers shown in Figure 5.4, it is evident that adaptation account for a tiny proportion of the whole.

*(b) Nature-based swaps and funds*

Can developing countries use their natural resources as a way to get the finance needed for climate adaptation? Keeping the majority of fossil fuels in the ground has been cited as one way to meet the Paris Agreement – prompting a revisiting of the concept of debt-for-nature swaps that were used in previous decades. This could be something of a win-win in the sense that the countries get the funds needed and emission-creating activities are halted or reduced; recipient countries could even be protected from the volatile swings in commodity prices that will happen anyway as investors pull their funds out of "sunk assets". However, once again these proposals need to deal with the fact that adaptation is not likely to be a revenue-earning activity, as compared to mitigation.

The current call for a renewal of debt for nature deals rests in part on the historical experience of their use by at least 30 countries across the globe, mostly in the 1980s and 1990s. Compared to other sources of finance the amounts cited are small – in the order of $2.6 billion to $6 billion over the three decades since their inception in 1987, according to some estimates, Recent examples include the Seychelles Sovereign Debt swap of $21.6 million in 2016, which was innovative as it included philanthropic donors and impact investors, and contained a government policy commitment for marine conservation (World Ocean Initiative, 2020). Other recent examples include debt-for nature swaps between the United States and Indonesia (in 2011 and 2014) under a Tropical Forests Conservation Act programme, one of which was included under the REDD+ (See Box 5.2). However, while actual activity has declined since the earlier decades, some country proposals have been more ambitious, including Commonwealth Secretarian proposals for debt swaps to finance climate change adaptation and mitigation for small states. Other recent examples have been used in countries ranging from Bhutan to Fiji and South Korea.

Compared to previous decades, however, debt-for-nature swaps seemed loosing favour during the 2000s – a trend attributed by some to the stronger world economy and to the impacts of debt restructuring and debt forgiveness programmes of the 1980s and 1990s, and by others to the concerns of creditor countries that suffered from the global financial crisis including the United States, European Union and Japan (Ito et al., 2018; Sheikh, 2018).

---

**Box 5.2    What makes a bank green?**

To be effective, a "green" bank should stand out clearly compared to other banks in terms of its mandate, its loan portfolio, and the terms and conditions of its lending. The *mandate* in particular should be dedicated to green developmental outcomes and in line with international commitments including the SDGs and Paris Agreement, even if this is somewhat flexibly defined and can evolve over time as banks develop capacity and country needs change. Some banks highlight the goal of investing in the most promising new technologies. Some are rather supposed to focus on the needs of poor households in this area (e.g., Hawaii GEMS). This is important because the mandate and role drive public banks' activities and focus their investment decisions, including the types of clients and sectors to target. They also allow stakeholders to hold banks and management to account for the impact of their investments and commitment to community.

The *operational strategy* or business model must be consistent with its mandate. This refers to how the bank raises its finance, including the mix between public and private funding, which, in turn, will affect the extent to which it offers concessional loans and can deliver environmental and development outcomes. Surveys suggest that the vast majority of green banks offer loans, most of which are priced lower than the market rate. But even when rates are favourable compared to the market, this obligation may be a challenge for developing countries to meet. A smaller proportion offer finance in other ways such as equity or guarantees, and an even smaller number offer grant finance.[26] It appears that all green banks offer technical assistance. This contribution is important as expert banks can help governments design the framework of climate change adaptation, including strategies relating to regulation and pricing policies etc. (Griffiths-Jones, 2021). *Financial sustainability* is also important for all banks. This does not mean maximizing profitability and requires a different lexicon for performance measurement. The long-term financial sustainability of a green bank should not undermine its ability to invest in higher risk areas or projects where development returns are high but profitability is low – as is likely to be the norm when it comes to adaptation.

Most green banks are stand-alone entities set up by government legislation and capitalized by government appropriations. Some (e.g. the United States) are funded through a transfer, for example the transfer of electricity bills (Connecticut Green Bank and New York Green Bank). Striking a balance between the appropriate level of returns for a bank to remain viable, and the broader social and environmental demands of non-profit adaptation remains a challenge however.[27]

Some hints as to how green banks could create this path are evident from the recent experience of Covid-19. Public banks around the world responded immediately and often dramatically to support their governments' efforts to secure economic relief and resilience during the stand-still caused by lockdown. A rapid review carried out by UNCTAD during the early months of lockdown found that local, national and regional public banks around the world stretched out to produce a fast and strong counter-cyclical effect.[28] Some changed their mandates and procedures to meet the urgent needs; many scaled up their lending capacities by issuing bonds or accessing international markets, sometimes for the first time; virtually all offered finance on concessional or favourable conditions as well as technical advice. Those with a long institutional history, mandates that were supported by adequate finance and appropriate performance metrics were in the best position to respond effectively. Financing the adaptation to climate change has many parallels with this experience.

---

Schemes of the size of the Polish EcoFund have not been seen again yet – perhaps reflecting the charged timing of this debt-for-environment initiative, which came just as Poland was in transition away from central planning (Caliari, 2020). The debt-for-environment initiative was carefully prepared in parallel to negotiations on the shape of the wider economy and institutions (OECD, 2007: 23). Paris Club creditors agreed to additional bilateral debt swaps that were arranged not as a one-off swap of the entire debt stock. Rather, the Polish government transferred every year a percentage of the debt repayment due to a local financing facility the EcoFund, which then managed the spending to be given as grant support for projects in Poland, addressing transboundary air pollution of sulphur and nitrogen oxides; pollution and eutrophication of the Baltic Sea; global climate change gases; biological diversity; and waste management and the reclamation of contaminated soil. Over the years additional swaps were arranged with other creditors, each on different terms, and altogether the scheme generated an unprecedented amount of over half a billion dollars – an amount that dwarfs all other debt-for-environment or nature swaps in the world (OECD, 1998).

Debt swaps represented an alternative to deeper sovereign debt restructurings in countries with high but sustainable debt burdens (i.e. those that do not face a solvency problem). Debt swap programs can be effective in addressing different debt compositions in developing economies and, in particular, exposure to large commercial debts and large public debt stocks. A disadvantage of debt swaps can be high transaction and monitoring costs for project-based swap programmes. They are complex to implement, and swaps in the past have taken from 2 to 4 years to negotiate between all parties – many of which involve a recipient government, a donor government, and local and donor country conservation groups. However, these can potentially be mitigated under coordinating regional initiatives, such as ECLAC's Debt for Climate Adaptation Initiative for the Caribbean and ESCAP's Debt Swap Mechanism for the Western Asia region, both recently launched.

Nature Performance Bonds (F4BI 2020) are another nature-based way being used to recapitalize sovereign debt. Any new debt would receive Brady type credit enhancement in exchange for commitments to spend the money on SDG-type investments – secured by bond issues by MFIs or SDRs from the IMF. The original Brady Plan was organized extremely quickly, yet this partly is because the debtor countries essentially refused to pay and their bargaining power was high. It is not clear if this proposal could work when it is not banks that are owed money but rather institutional investors who offer it. Supporters of this approach insist that such a policy should be linked with country programmes that are designed by the recipient countries, and with conditionalities that are designed by them as well (see Caliari, 2020; Griffiths-Jones, 1992; OECD, 2007, among others). Once again however, it is not clear how to translate these into adaptation, which does not provide recipient countries with an income stream. In addition, one needs to be careful given the nature of the arrangements being proposed that limit the policy space of developing countries. They may place even greater power in the hands of bondholders and international financiers, and the latter may apply conditionalities and constrict democratic decision-making on the part of the debtor country.

# D. Banks and climate finance

## 1. Dedicated green banks

Nearly all the public banks established since 2010 have "green" in the title or high up in their mandate (see Box 5.3). By some estimates they have lent about $24.5 billion since their inception (Whitney et al., 2020). The figure does not include established banks with a green desk or with green lending within their normal activities – such as the new public banks that emerged after the 2007-2008 crisis, including the Asian Infrastructure Investment Bank. Many governments have expressed an interest in establishing a green bank, as in the case of current discussions in the United States for a new national development bank with a green mandate. Others are looking to establish a green facility within an existing bank. Survey evidence suggests that typically it is the Ministry of Finance, or a country's central bank, that champions the idea, as opposed to the Ministry of Environment or the private sector. The main motive of investing in climate related activities is the second, not the first,

priority. It is therefore not clear whether this will be a significant source of finance for adaptation activities, as compared to mitigation. In the State of Green Banks report, adaptation activities appear in a minority of related investments (Exhibit 9, Whitney et al., 2020: 30). Other long-standing public and development banks have boosted their green credentials; for example, the EIB recent declaration that 50 per cent of all new lending from 2025 must be low-carbon and no investments will be allowed that are not consistent with the Paris Agreement.

The Banco Popular in Costa Rica, established in 1969 by the Costa Rican government to promote economic development, for example, has been involved as a "finance catalyzer" in a project designed to help marginalized people and communities adapt to the frequent droughts that are attributed to changing climate. Based on grant financing, watershed protection and better management of water use are among the adaptation strategies that it supports. Banco Popular, working with the Government of Costa Rica and agro-processing companies, came up with a $9.8 million grant as co-financing alongside the $8.8 million grant provided by the Green Climate Fund (GFC).

The German public development bank KFW has long argued it was not enough to address the causes of climate change by reducing emissions, because the impacts of climate change are already being felt in many countries. In the years 2013–2018 it invested 23.6 billion euro in climate related projects in developing countries, of which around 25 per cent was devoted to adaptation and resilience building projects. Among these projects included monitoring of glaciers in Pakistan, flood protection in Mozambique and hydrological monitoring in Jordan. As with the Costa Rican example above, these national banks operate in cooperation with other institutions: a recent project for flood protection in Bangladesh saw the KFW deliver $15 million (from the German Federal Ministry of Economic Cooperation and Development), alongside $40 million from the GCF with the Government of Bangladesh contributed $25 million.

## 2. Multilateral development banks with a climate change agenda

Development banks are well positioned to respond to the adaptation challenge compared to other sources of finance, as their remit usually specifically authorizes them to provide finance for the long-term, at lower rates and on more advantageous terms. When it comes to these investments the private sector will hardly support as necessary, illustrating the systemic problem related to adaptation and non-profit-centred ambitions. To date, development banks have provided most of the concessional loans and grant-based finance. Not all MDBs and RDBs have been consistent in this regard, but their role is critical given current predictions and worsening scenario in light of the IPCC 2021 report.

This type of public financing needs to increase in areas that so far have been under-resourced, especially in regional projects where many climate projects are considered less feasible for private or revenue-seeking purposes. Partly compensating for the limitations of under-capitalized national banks, MDBs have been steadily increasing their climate finance activities in the years since the Paris Agreement. Many pledged to re-direct their financing decisions and investment portfolios to be consistent with climate change adaptation and mitigation goals. The 12 largest MDBs committed to five Voluntary

Principles for Mainstreaming Climate Change and by October 2020 as many as 48 institutions had followed suit.

The key principle of providing financing for MDBs in vision, if not yet in practice, has moved beyond the issue of simply increasing lending for climate-oriented or green projects. Now, MDBs and other members of the International Development Finance Club (IDFC) vow to "shift from financing climate activities in incremental ways to making climate change – both in terms of opportunities and risk – a core consideration and a "lens" through which institutions deploy capital" (Climate Action in Financial Institutions, 2018; Murphy and Parry, 2020). This is a major change in focus that aims to mainstream climate considerations and align banks' entire financing and investment portfolios with the Paris Agreement. These intended changes constitute a bigger and more complex ambition than mobilizing and tracking climate finance contributions to the $100 billion pledge made in 2009.

But the goal of scaling up is yet to be achieved. In 2019, nine MDBs announced their target to increase collective global climate investment to at least $65 billion per year by 2025, and within this timeframe to double the portion designated for adaptation purposes to $18 billion per year (ADB et al., 2019: 1). They plan also to increase co-financing to $110 billion, of which less than half is anticipated being mobilized by private direct sources. By 2020, the total committed was $66 billion (ADB et al., 2020: 3), however, at the same time, even as all banks announced ambitious plans for increased spending over the coming years, some 6 out of 8 lent less in 2020 than the year before. Only the World Bank and the European Investment Bank increased total climate finance spending in the last year. This is a particular concern for low-income countries, which received just $38 billion total finance in 2020, which is a fall from the year beforehand ($41.5 billion) (ibid: 7). This could potentially reflect the unanticipated spending due to the economic impact of Covid-19, although this rationale was mentioned specifically in only one or two bank cases. So, while there has been a sizeable increase since 2015, there is still a long way to go.[29] Securing adequate finance is not just about the *amount* of money lent, but also its *purpose* within the broad spectrum of climate related activities. MDBs themselves note the need to scale up the share going to adaptation, which currently counts for just 26 per cent of total lending. This proportion is up 2 percentage points from 2019 and while the absolute values show a marginal increase in 2020 from $15 billion to $16 billion, they are still below the stated target (Table 5.4). This is especially important for least developed countries and lower middle-income countries that are already struggling to cope with some effects of climate change, which find it more difficult to attract finances from other sources, and which are more in need to make the transformative leap into industrialization (ideally, green) and to fund activities that can earn sustainable revenues in the future.

Preliminary evidence suggests that banks whose beneficiary members include more low-income countries such as the African Development Bank and the Islamic Development Banks, devoted the highest proportion of finances to adaptation at 56 per cent and 47 per cent respectively, in 2019 and 63 per cent and 65 per cent by 2020 (AfDB ibid). In contrast, the European Investment Bank, with a more North Atlantic focus, spent only 4 per cent on adaptation in 2019 rising to 10 per cent in 2020, and the rest on potentially game-changing mitigation. Similarly, the European Bank of Reconstruction and Development directed most of its finance to mitigation. Until low-income countries will also benefit from getting into the new technologies and new markets that mitigation entails, long-standing inequalities will be further cemented.

It is also evident that co-financing remains more prevalent in mitigation activities than for adaptation ones in 2020 compared to 2019, reflecting the fact that the former are revenue-earning in nature; although at the same time, perhaps unsurprisingly, this year both co-financing and private borrowings have fallen significantly while public borrowing rose – reflecting concerns that the short-term needs of this year's health and economic crisis should not derail longer term development financing needs (see Chapters I and II of this *Report*). It is also notable that, when it comes to co-financing, alongside the public MDBs, it is other public sources of finance that provide the lion's share – especially with regards to low-income countries (Table 5.5).

Assuming the private sector remains reluctant to make the investments needed, even alongside significant public sector co-finance from MDBs, donors, domestic public sources and others – where is this necessary acceleration in capital availability to come from? A greater pool of available climate adaptation financing (with more grants and highly

### TABLE 5.4 MDBs climate finance components, 2020

|  | MDB climate finance ($ million) | Per cent of total | Climate co-finance ($ million) | Per cent of total |
|---|---|---|---|---|
| Adaptation | 16 100 | 26 | 19 954 | 23 |
| Mitigation | 49 945 | 81 | 65 130 | 77 |
| Public borrower | 46 687 | 71 | 53 413 | 63 |
| Private borrower | 19 358 | 31 | 31 672 | 37 |
| **Total** | **66 045** | **100** | **85 084** | **100** |

*Source:* Derived from AfDB et al. (2019, 2020).

### TABLE 5.5 Climate co-financing partners to MDBs, 2020
*($ million)*

| Finance mobilization | Low- and middle-income countries | High-income countries | Total |
|---|---|---|---|
| Private direct | 3 556 | 2 354 | 5 910 |
| Private indirect | 6 345 | 19 417 | 25 762 |
| Total private co-finance | 9 901 | 21 771 | 31 672 |
| Public direct | 8 366 | 1 658 | 10 024 |
| *Public co-finance* | | | |
| Other MDBs | 8 150 | 813 | 8 962 |
| IDFC members | 1 774 | 251 | 2 026 |
| Other international public | 1 946 | 4 477 | 6 423 |
| Other domestic public | 6 182 | 19 796 | 25 978 |
| Total public direct and co-finance | 26 418 | 26 995 | 53 413 |

*Source:* Derived from AfDB et al. (2020, 2019).

concessional loans) requires that MDBs scale up their total lending capacities considerably. One way of financing this could be through the revenues earned from their mitigation loans, but this will take too long to be of use to countries in urgent need of adaptation investments today. Also, some under-capitalized MDBs are already struggling to maintain viability as it is.

Other routes for scaling up have been suggested in the past, including by previous *Reports*. One is for the owner members to increase their paid-in capitalization – this route perhaps has the greatest potential if political will is there. Another is to take on new members, especially members from higher income countries that can make a larger capital contribution; or to revise MDB mandates and operational rules to allow banks to increase the leverage of the funds they already have. UNCTAD has long argued for this (*TDR 2019*) and the precedent has been made

**TABLE 5.6    Summary of the financing landscape**

| Mechanisms/Institutions | Examples | Issues |
|---|---|---|
| ODA $19-$63 billion depending on source. | OECD DAC, payments to UNFCCC | ODA is still way below the sums pledged. Much is given not as grants, and is more directed to mitigation than adaptation. |
| Global funds $8.3bn | Green Climate Fund, Adaptation Fund, LDCs and others | Insufficient funds for the needs. |
| MDBs $46 billion | | Mostly for mitigation, not all banks are as reliable or effective as others. Banks especially undercapitalized and weak in areas where the needs are greatest. |
| Grants or debt for nature - $2.6 bn since inception | Most in LAC since 1980s; Indonesia, Seychelles; REDD+ schemes. | Complex to implement, high transactions costs – takes 2-4 years to negotiate between all the parties. Need long-term financial commitment, vulnerable to currency devaluation.  Role of local and international conservation groups. |
| Sovereign and corporate green bonds $100 billion certified out of loosely defined green market $754 bn. | Developing country green bond issuances are increasing (Bhutan, Fiji, China); Liberty Bond issuances in advanced economies. | ESG highly debatable; Asset linked not asset backed; even if domestic bonds still raise currency vulnerability; Many are not concessional; Countries say they lack capacity to manage them; all the other problems with other bonds and currency risks etc |
| Green banks $24.5 bn since inception; more if include green lending (AIIB, NDB MDBs etc) World Bank). | Discussion for a new United States green bank just one of many. | Risk of privatization if make too much or too little returns.... Are these actually the best bet? |
| Central banks | Many examples from developing countries. NGFS. | COVID programmes are not pro-climate, may instead bring about maladaptation. |
| Conservation trust funds | More than 80 in place globally, e.g. Caribbean Biodiversity Fund est. 2018 with endowment of $43 million and now managing $70 million (endowment fund and sinking fund). | |
| Other market – auctioning of allowances | Payment for entry to marine EEZs, payment for fishing licenses (Indonesia $31 million in 2018, Kiribati $117m in access fees).  Cruise ship levies – Antigua and Barbados $1.2 m in 2018 by a $1.50 per person tax. | These are nature-related fund raising activities but may be needed to pay for other fiscal uses not adaptation. |

already during the Covid period. When southern-led MDBs scaled up lending during the early phases of the Covid-19 pandemic, they did it by reallocating existing portfolios and borrowing from members' sovereign wealth funds, adapting mandates, redefining key priorities and changing functions (MacDonald et al., 2020: 361-375). One South-South institution increased its lending capacity by as much as 60 per cent to meet the urgent needs (Ibid).

Another possible source of multilateral funding would be to repurpose SDRs for long-term environmental and country-specific adjustment plans, including preservation targets and emission reductions, as well as the required investments and budgets to meet these targets. This could provide a flexible and, in principle, unlimited financing mechanism for long-standing calls, by UNCTAD and others, for a global environmental protection fund that can provide predictable and stable emergency funding without strict policy conditionalities or limiting eligibility criteria.

International capital markets can still be used to scale up quickly, and most MDBs do rely on them.[30] Since 2008, when the World Bank issued the first green bond following demand from a group of Swedish pension funds for high quality (AAA) liquid products that could also have a positive impact (World Bank, 2008).[31] The Bank has issued 185 green bonds in 23 currencies worth an equivalent of $15 billion, and many other MDBs have followed suit, including Southern-led ones.[32] A high profile and similar boom in demand for green bonds is taking place in the national and corporate space, although there are many reasons to think it is as much more about the search for yields in a low return environment than a concern to have concrete impact. MDBs could rather utilize at least some of these funds in a better way given that they are actively engaged in green-backed projects. It is quite likely that many investors with a genuine interest in supporting climate-related finance would prefer to buy issuances from the World Bank and other MDBs. However, it is notable that these arrangements are usually beyond the realm of individuals or smaller funds.

# E. Policy recommendations

The triple imperative of scaling up climate finance, directing it to where it is needed, and ensuring favorable conditions for developing countries in both trade (delinking international trade rules from climate adaptation policies) and funding (long maturities, grants or concessional terms) needs to be approached through a number of specific policy reforms, some of which are listed below.

At present, assistance from the international community for climate adaptation continues to rely on a combination of short-term aid, longer-term conditionalities of fiscal consolidation and preventative self-insurance schemes against catastrophic risk. This, however, is woefully insufficient to address the systemic impact of recurrent and increasingly frequent climate change-related shocks.

By its nature, the challenge of climate adaptation puts the onus on grant-based finance or highly concessional lending mechanisms as key to meeting the adaptation challenge. At the same time, any finance provided will work best if integrated under an overarching financial and industrial policy designed and implemented by a climate conscious developmental state (see Chapter IV).

This is, therefore, the *first priority* of a strategic approach to climate adaptation. A climate conscious developmental State should be catalyzing and not just addressing "market failures", nor relegating itself to "de-risking" the opportunity for others to make profit and take more than their share of the benefit. The systemic risk involved here requires a regulator and coordinator of private green finance, as with the financial sector generally. These must be seen as a means to avoid the destructive tendencies of today's ultra-liquid financial sector, where the embedded search for yield is inconsistent with the needs of climate mitigation, let alone the more challenging needs of adaptation.

Most adaptation efforts are also required at the local level (DCF Alliance, 2019). The vast majority of adaptation finance appear to be channeled to large financial institutions geared towards large-scale projects that do not necessarily support local efforts or meet local-level adaptation priorities. Locally-led climate finance efforts need to be driven by principles that ensure the most effective way of responding to governance and climate challenges and risks, including: i) community-led planning that is anchored within and supportive of existing devolved institutions, and that promotes ii) social inclusion of climate-marginalized people; iii) a process that is flexible and adaptive management towards the creation of resilience investments, with iv) an emphasis on public goods provisioning (DCF Alliance, 2019: 4).

Until the right balance is found, all the best intentions will be high-jacked or side-tracked. As shown above, to date, the emergence of green bonds, a carbon trading market or even the uses of Covid-19 recovery funds, has not done enough to help developing countries adapt to climate change (Gallagher and Carlin, 2020). Two levels of reforms for financing the adaption challenge can be identified: first, steps in support of a climate conscious developmental state to mobilise financial resources for mitigation and adaptation investments, and second, reforming the approach to climate governance internationally.

The first set of reforms should focus on the following:

- **Assistance**. ODA commitments and pledges need to be met and go further, to increase the proportion of additive finance designated for climate change adaptation and resilience building. *Grants and extremely concessional* *loans* are essential for adaptation. These could be financed by a green bond and a tax *à la Tobin*, or through the repurposing of fossil fuel subsidies. This must take account of specific country requirements in least developed countries and lower-middle income countries and fossil-fuel exporting economies that need a gradual restructuring of these carbon-intensive industries and an appropriate safety net system to meet climate debt.

- **Debt relief and debt cancellation** for developing countries should be put on the climate agenda. The delivery of the Agenda 2030 was already in doubt before the Covid-19 crisis given the burden of debt being carried by many developing countries but in the post-Covid era these countries face even greater challenges in addressing their climate resilience needs. An obvious starting point would be the debt of the V20 countries, but linking the climate and debt crises highlights the need for systemic reforms to the international debt architecture.

- **Banking.** Well-financed *green public and development banks*, staffed by experts in climate change issues, at municipal, national and regional levels, are needed. Mandates and performance indicators should be aligned with that purpose. The multilateral development banks need additional capital to support more green investments and less fossil fuel or polluting activities and their activities aligned with the Paris Agreement and their "build forward better" commitments, withdrawing from oil, coal and gas and building in transition processes that support people and those industries to make the leap. Policy conditionalities will need to be pruned back and their AAA straitjacket should be relaxed to support experimental or new green technologies and enterprises. G7 countries should use their shareholder power to guide MDB in this direction. *Regional Development banks* and multilateral development banks could also buy developing countries' green bonds, guaranteeing a more stable demand for such bonds and easier access to long-term capital for developing countries. This could also have a favourable impact on their yields and, consequently, help to mitigate the external service burden, to an extent.

- **Bond markets.** Affordable access to long-term funding is essential for developing countries in meeting developmental and climate needs, and green bond market is a key ways to help raise such long-term financing. Yet regulatory standards lag behind the growth of the green bond market: many disclosure commitments are voluntary, mechanisms to protect issuer and bondholder rights are under-developed; mechanisms to avoid greenwashing should be in place. These deficiencies need to be addressed by the private sector, as well as national and international regulators. *Appropriate standards* and enforcement of rules need to be agreed upon and introduced to make sure that green bonds stay green; that green savings bonds issued by national governments *respond to the needs* of local population; that the use of green bonds is properly *monitored and enforced* by the issuing governments; that both *investors and bond issuers are protected* over the lifetime of the bond; that *greenwashing is identified and penalised*; certification standards need to be transparent, harmonised and properly implemented. Given the scale of the challenge, the regulatory framework for the green bond market needs to be supported by *correspondent levels of financing and staffing*, at national and international levels.

The *second* priority would be declaring climate change adaptation a public good (cf. Timisel, 2021), at the international level, and establishing appropriate mechanisms to govern it. Such a recognition would reflect the reality already experienced by the developing economies struggling to green their exports and fund climate adaptation needs, and enable them to access and adapt green technologies to their national growth trajectories. Internationally, a Climate Adaptation Fund, as proposed by some countries in the WTO,[33] can help countries in greening their exports. A Trade and Environment Fund could fund the incremental costs of sourcing critical technologies, provide grants for specific green technologies, finance joint research, development and demonstrations and fund establishment of technology transfer centers, exchanges and mechanisms. This measure would also deliver the necessary institutional coordination at the international level, for the much needed financial, technological and economic needs of climate conscious development.

# F. Conclusion

With the growing intensity of major extreme events, adaptation must be prioritized. Institutional reforms that are required must build towards a move away from the principles of a regulatory, market-enabling state, and towards a developmental green state which would be in control of its own long-term priorities in climate adaptation and economic trajectories.

Trade has an important role to play in shaping sustainable development paths. However, attempts to liberalize trade in areas of export interests of the developed world, and relying on actions like CBAM can only undermine the ability of developing countries to use trade as a mean of development.

Facilitating climate adaptation in developing countries through trade agreements will require green technology transfers without restrictive patents, appropriate SDT in environmental goods and services so that providers of these goods and services in developing world can have level playing field and preserving policy space to encourage export diversification.

Since $CO_2$ emissions embodied in international trade as a share of total emissions is not more than 27 per cent, trade rules need to be de-linked from climate adaptation objectives, especially in the WTO, and countries should be provided with sufficient policy space to implement their national policies for climate adaptation. There is a need to pursue incentive-based approaches like declaring green technology transfers and limiting patents on these technologies.

The year of the pandemic may yet prove to be transformative on the way to formulating a more ambitious approach to financing the adaptation challenges, but hurdles are high and time has run out. It is encouraging to see the United States announcing its commitment of $5.7 billion in annual climate finance for developing countries by 2024. Yet, "in the context of both the need and the money being spent at home, this is an error term...the lack of a truly global response to the pandemic augurs badly for common action of climate" (Wolf, 2021).

A much more visible and leading hand for public financial institutions at all levels is essential. Some seventy-five years ago, the Marshall Plan helped deliver shared prosperity among the war-torn economies. Today, climate change is a challenge to humanity that requires a similar integrated, anticipatory and strategic approach. A menu options has been discussed in this chapter. However, a global, green-oriented structural fund would support realignment of developing countries and deliver funding for both adaptation and mitigation initiatives as an urgent priority. This would generate dividends not only for the developing countries, but for advanced economies too. It will help building counter-cyclical buffers, enhance resilience and inclusion in communities at local and national levels, and enable growth towards a pattern that can keep global temperature rises below the critical 1.5°C.

# Notes

1. WT/CTE/W/249.
2. https://sdg.iisd.org/commentary/policy-briefs/wto-members-assess-mc12-options-for-trade-environmental-sustainability-work/.
3. See https://www.wto.org/english/docs_e/legal_e/04-wto_e.htm.
4. See https://www.wto.org/english/thewto_e/minist_e/min01_e/mindecl_e.htm.
5. https://www.mfat.govt.nz/en/media-and-resources/climate-change-ministers-express-support-for-the-agreement-on-climate-change-trade-and-sustainability-at-cop25/.
6. According to media reports, the European Union plans to use the expected annual revenue of €10bn from its planned carbon border tax mechanisms to repay debt incurred for its recovery measures; *Financial Times* (2021). EU carbon border tax will raise nearly €10bn annually. 6 July.
7. Depending on its design, such a climate waiver and/or peace clause could also help to tackle the regulatory chill resulting from legal mechanisms such as Investor-State Dispute Settlement (ISDS) which disproportionately expand the purview of investors over the public policy-making process, often at the expense of climate

and development-friendly initiatives (Tienhara, 2017).

8   *Mitigation* finance is directed to general activities that reduce greenhouse emissions and are compatible with low emission development, such as renewable electricity generation or energy-efficient construction. *Adaptation* finance is, rather, linked to particular projects and location specific loans that directly impact vulnerability to climate change, such as improving the resilience of small island states to natural disasters.

9   As noted in Chapter III, with respect to investing in mitigation there are multiple potential sources of financing to ensure that countries can meet the required investment target. See further *TDR 2019*.

10  Further on the limits and dangers of relying on private finance to take the lead on sustainable investment, see Fancy, 2021.

11  This includes Australia, some European Union institutions and the Netherlands. Denmark, Sweden and Switzerland gave over 95 per cent of their contribution in the form of grants. At the same time, for countries that gave significantly much larger sums in total, such as Germany and Japan, their smaller relative proportion in grant form did yield a significant amount in absolute terms (Oxfam, 2020:10). The main point is that grant provision from all sources needs to increase.

12  https://www.climatepolicyinitiative.org/publication/global-landscape-of-climate-finance-2019/.

13  In 2015, the United States pledged to double its adaptation funding through multilateral and bilateral channels to $800 million per year to developing countries by 2020. See: https://2009-2017.state.gov/r/pa/prs/ps/2015/12/250495.htm. From 2010 to 2015, total adaptation financing was US$2.57 billion, averaging US$428 million (US State Department, n.d.). See President Biden's latest announcement here: https://www.whitehouse.gov/briefing-room/statements-releases/2021/04/23/fact-sheet-president-bidens-leaders-summit-on-climate/.

14  See: https://adaptationexchange.org/adaptationActionAgenda.

15  Statement in Response to the Sixth Assessment Report of the IPCC, 2021. 10 August 2021.

16  Started in 2009, but formally established in Lima, Peru in 2015, the 48 countries represent 1.3 billion people and include Afghanistan, Bangladesh, Barbados, Bhutan, Burkina Faso, Cambodia, Comoros, Colombia, Costa Rica, Democratic Republic of the Congo, Dominican Republic, Ethiopia, Fiji, Gambia, Ghana, Grenada, Guatemala, Haiti, Honduras, Kenya, Kiribati, Lebanon, Madagascar, Malawi, Maldives, Marshall Islands, Mongolia, Morocco,

Nepal, Niger, Papua New Guinea, Palau, Palestine, Philippines, Rwanda, Saint Lucia, Samoa, Senegal, Sri Lanka, South Sudan, Sudan, United Republic of Tanzania, Timor-Leste, Tuvalu, Vanuatu, Vietnam, Yemen. See https://www.v-20.org/members.

17  Sir David King, Head of the Centre for Climate Repair, Oxford, recorded in FT podcast "Can Climate damage be repaired?" 12 August 2021. Available at https://www.ft.com/content/5804b93f-8b80-40c4-9b30-3d8b9bf8da3d.

18  We employ the World bank categorization of countries in this discussion.

19  Sudan being the exception.

20  See: https://www.imf.org/external/Pubs/ft/dsa/DSAlist.pdf.

21  Methodology can be found here: https://gain.nd.edu/assets/254377/nd_gain_technical_document_2015.pdf.

22  "Give me a place to stand, and a lever long enough, and I will move the world".

23  According to the Climate Bond Initiative (CBI), "rigorous scientific criteria ensure that bonds and loans with certification, are consistent with the 2 degrees Celsius warming limit in the Paris Agreement".

24  There are also ESG debt instruments that are not certified and labelled as green, social and sustainability bonds. The uncertified green debt instruments are called climate or climate-aligned bonds.

25  See, for example: Ehlers and Packer, 2017; Zerbib, 2016; Larcker and Watts, 2019; Hachenberg and Schiereck, 2018; Kapraun et al., 2019.

26  Based on a sample of 27 green banks by Whitney et al., (2020).

27  One part of the path may be to target committed, small scale investors, not just the big institutional. The Connecticut Green Bank CGB, established in 2011 and with a focus on renewable energy, recently launched an innovative bond programme purchasable in $1 000 tranches on 15-year terms to households and 'ordinary citizens' with the assurance the funds would be used to finance rooftop solar systems. The bond issuance was sold out within two weeks, with demand exceeding the bank's supply.

28  Carried out by UNCTAD in mid-2020 in collaboration with Eurodad, the Municipal Services Project and a team of 24 researchers and four regional public bank and finance associations, this was the first review of public banks and their response to Covid-19. It can be found at https://unctad.org/webflyer/public-banks-and-covid-19-combatting-pandemic-public-finance.

29  The pledged $65 billion for 2019 appears like a big increase over previous years but this is in part because it includes EIB lending to European

countries, not previously included. When only emerging and developing countries are included, the 2019 lending commitment shows a smaller increase, from $43.1 billion to $46.5 billion.

30    The ISDB issued a special Covid Sukuk and borrowed from other MDBs; the NDB also issued a special Coronavirus bond.

31    https://www.worldbank.org/en/events/2018/11/16/from-evolution-to-revolution-10-years-of-green-bonds.

32    Demand remains high and new bonds are typically heavily over-subscribed even when very large, as seen with a recent offer in May 2021 of a $2.5 billion five-year AAA rated Sustainable Development Bond. Paying an annual yield of 0.963 per cent, it had one of the lowest spreads in the sector and was taken up mostly by central banks and official institutions (buying 63 per cent of the issue). Pension funds and asset managers also took a portion (18 per cent). https://www.worldbank.org/en/news/press-release/2021/05/18/world-bank-usd-2_5-billion-5-year-bond-mobilizes-finance-for-sustainable-development.

33    The trade and environment Fund was proposed by China and India in 2011. For details see: https://docs.wto.org/dol2fe/Pages/FE_Search/FE_S_S009-DP.aspx?language=E&CatalogueIdList=104702,98548,101134,90606,71962,99113,92836,94001,92436,58038&CurrentCatalogueIdIndex=0&FullTextHash=&HasEnglishRecord=True&HasFrenchRecord=True&HasSpanishRecord=True.

# References

AfDB, ADB, AIIB, EBRD, EIB, IDBG, IsDB and WBG (2019). Joint Report on Multilateral Development Banks' Climate Finance 2019. African Development Bank (AfDB), the Asian Development Bank (ADB), the Asian Infrastructure Investment Bank (AIIB), the European Bank for Reconstruction and Development (EBRD), the European Investment Bank (EIB), the Inter-American Development Bank Group (IDBG), the Islamic Development Bank (IsDB) and the World Bank Group (WBG). Available at https://publications.iadb.org/publications/english/document/2019-Joint-Report-on-Multilateral-Development-Banks-Climate-Finance.pdf.

AfDB, ADB, AIIB, EBRD, EIB, IDBG, IsDB and WBG (2020). Joint Report on Multilateral Development Banks' Climate Finance 2020. African Development Bank (AfDB), the Asian Development Bank (ADB), the Asian Infrastructure Investment Bank (AIIB), the European Bank for Reconstruction and Development (EBRD), the European Investment Bank (EIB), the Inter-American Development Bank Group (IDBG), the Islamic Development Bank (IsDB) and the World Bank Group (WBG). Available at https://www.afdb.org/en/documents/2020-joint-report-multilateral-development-banks-climate-finance.

Attridge S and Engen L (2019). Blended finance in the poorest economies: The need for a better approach. Overseas Development Institute Report. London. April. Available at https://www.odi.org/publications/11303-blended-finance-poorest-countries-need-better-approach (accessed 19 October 2021).

Barrowclough D (2020). South-South public finance: A rapid review of cooperation and resilience to face Covid-19. In: McDonald DA, Marois T and Barrowclough D, eds. *Public Banks And Covid-19: Combatting The Pandemic With Public Finance.* Municipal Services Project, UNCTAD and Eurodad. Kingston, Geneva, Brussels.

Bhandary R , Gallagher KS and Zhang F (2021). Climate finance policy in practice: A review of the evidence. *Climate Policy.* 21(4): 529–545.

Bracking S and Leffel B (2021). Climate finance governance: Fit for purpose? *Climate Change.* 12(4):e709. Available at doi: https://doi.org/10.1002/wcc.709

Buchner B, Clark A, Falconer A, Macquarie R, Meattle C, Tolentino R and Wetherbee C. (2019). Global Landscape of Climate Finance 2019. Climate Policy Initiative.Available at https://www.climatepolicyinitiative.org/wp-content/uploads/2019/11/2019-Global-Landscape-of-Climate-Finance.pdf.

Buhr B, Volz U, Donovan C, Kling D , Lo Y, Mirinde V and N Pullin N (2021). *Climate Change and the Cost of Capital in Developing Countries: Assessing the Impact of Climate Risks on Sovereign Borrowing Costs.* Available at https://www.v-20.org/category/resources/publications/cost-of-capital.

Caliari A (2020). Linking debt relief and sustainable development: Lessons from experience. Background Paper No. 2. Debt Relief for Green and Inclusive Recovery Project. Available at https://drgr.org/files/2020/11/BackgroungPaper2-Lessons-from-Experience.pdf.

Christophers B (2017). Climate change and financial instability: Risk disclosure and problems of neoliberal governance. *Annals of the American Association of Geographers.* 107(5): 1108-1127.

Christophers B (2019). Environmental beta or how institutional investors think about climate change and fossil fuel risk. *Annals of the America Association of Geographers.* 109(3): 754–774.

Climate Action in Financial Institutions (2018). Principles for mainstreaming climate action. Available at https://www.mainstreamingclimate.org.

DCF Alliance (2019). The devolved climate finance mechanisms: Principles, implementation and lessons from four semi-arid countries. Available at https://pubs.iied.org/g04424.

De Melo J and Solleder JM (2020). The EGA negotiations: Why they are important, why they are stalled, and challenges ahead. *Journal of World Trade.* 54(3): 333–347.

Deschryver P and de Mariz F (2020). What future for the green bond market? How can policymakers, companies, and investors unlock the potential of the green bond market? *Journal of Risk and Financial Management.* 13(3):1–26. Available at https://ideas.repec.org/a/gam/jjrfmx/v13y2020i3p61-d336328.html.

Ehlers T and Packer F (2017). Green bond finance and certification. Quarterly Review. Bank for International Settlements.

EPG-GFG (2018). Report of the G20 Eminent Persons Group on Global Financial Governance. Global Finance Governance. Available at https://www.globalfinancialgovernance.org/report-of-the-g20-epg-on-gfg/.

European Commission (2021). Legislative Train Schedule: A European Green Deal. Carbon border adjustment mechanism as part of the European Green Deal, before 2021-07. Accessed 18 August 2021. Available at https://www.europarl.europa.eu/legislative-train/theme-a-european-green-deal/file-carbon-border-adjustment-mechanism

GATT (1991). Services Sectoral Classification List. Document MTN.GNG/W/120. 10 July.

Gallagher KP and Carlin FM (2020). *The Role of the IMF in the Fight Against COVID: The IMF COVID Response Index.* Global Development Policy Center. Available at https://www.bu.edu/gdp/2020/09/15/the-role-of-imf-in-the-fight-against-covid-19-the-imf-covid-19-response-index/.

Gallagher K and Kozul-Wright R (2021). *The Case for a New Bretton Woods.* Polity Press. Cambridge.

Georgieva K (2020). A new Bretton Woods moment. Speech. 15 October. Available at https://www.imf.org/en/News/Articles/2020/10/15/sp101520-a-new-bretton-woods-moment.

Goldberg E (2019). Regulatory cooperation – a reality check. Associate Working Paper No. 115. Mossavar-Rahmani Center for Business and Government.

.Available at https://www.hks.harvard.edu/centers/mrcbg/publications/awp/awp115.

G7 Trade Ministers' Communiqué (2021). The Joint Communiqué issued by the G7 countries at the G7 Trade Track on 28 May 2021. United Kingdom Department for International Trade. Available at https://www.gov.uk/government/news/g7-trade-ministers-communique.

Griffiths-Jones S (1992). Conversion of official bilateral debt: the Opportunities and issues. In: *Proceedings of the World Bank Annual Conference on Development Economics 1992.* World Bank. Washington, D.C. Available at http://www.stephanygj.net/papers/ConversionOfOfficialBilateralDebt1993.pdf.

*Guardian* (2021). Green investing 'is definitely not going to work', says ex-BlackRock executive. 3 March. Available at https://www.theguardian.com/business/2021/mar/30/tariq-fancy-environmentally-friendly-green-investing.

Guzman M and Stiglitz JE (2016). Creating a framework for sovereign debt restructuring that works. In: Guzman M, Ocampo JA and Stiglitz JE, eds. *Too Little, Too Late: The Quest to Resolve Sovereign Debt Crisis.* Columbia University Press. New York: 3–32.

Hachenberg B and Schiereck D (2018). Are green bonds priced differently from conventional bonds? *Journal of Asset Management* 19(6): 371–383.

Ito H, Sekiguchi R and Yamawake T (2018). Debt swaps for financing education: Exploration of new funding resources. *Cogent Economics & Finance.* 6(1):1563025.

Kapraun J, Latino C, Scheins C and Schlag C (2019). (In)-Credibly green: Which bonds trade at a green bond remium? (April 29, 21). Proceedings of Paris December 2019 Finance Meeting EUROFIDAI - ESSEC.

Khor M, Montes MF, Williams M and Yu VPB (2017). Promoting sustainable development by addressing the impacts of Climate Change response measures on developing countries. Research Paper No. 81. South Centre.Available at https://martinkhor.org/wp-content/uploads/2019/10/RP81_Promoting-Sustainable-Development-by-Addressing-the-Impacts-of-Climate-Change-Response-Measures-on-Developing-Countries_EN-1.pdf.

Klusak P, Agarwala M, Burke M, Kraemer M and Mohaddes K (2021). Rising temperatures, falling ratings: The effect of climate change on sovereign creditworthiness. Working Papers in Economics No. 2127. University of Cambridge.

Kozul-Wright R, Banga R, Fortunato P, Maystre N, Poon D and Wang D (2019). From development to differentiation: Just how much has the world changed. Research Paper No. 33. UNCTAD, Available at https://unctad.org/system/files/official-document/ser-rp-2019d5_en.pdf.

Larcker DF and Watts E (2019). Where's the Greenium? Working Paper No. 239. Stanford University Graduate School of Business.

Lowe S (2019). The EU should reconsider its approach to trade and sustainable development. Centre for European Reform. 31 October. Available at https://www.cer.eu/insights/eu-should-reconsider-its-approach-trade-and-sustainable-development.

Murphy D and Parry J (2020). *Filling the Gap: A review of Multilateral Development Banks' efforts to scale up financing for climate adaptation*. International Institute for Sustainable Development (IISD). Manitoba.

Noor R (2019). Global Overview and Market Analysis of Green Bond. MIT Climate. Available at https://climate.mit.edu/posts/global-overview-and-market-analysis-green-bond (accessed on 18 February 2021).

OECD (1998). Swapping debt for the environment: The Polish Ecofund. Organisation for Economic Co-operation and Development.

OECD (2007). *Lessons Learnt from Experience with Debt-for-Evironment Swaps in Economies in Transition*. Organisation for Economic Co-operation and Development. Paris.

OECD (2017). Trade in services related to the environment. Document COM/TAD/ENV/JWPTE(2015)61/FINAL COM/TAD/ENV/JWPTE(2015)61/FINAL. 27 March.

OECD (2018). International trade and the transition to a more resource efficient and circular economy – concept paper. Document COM/TAD/ENV/JWPTE(2017)3/FINAL.

OECD (2019). Report on a set of policy indicators on trade and environment. Document COM/TAD/ENV/JWPTE(2018)2/FINAL.

OECD (2021). *Climate Finance Provided and Mobilised by Developed Countries: Aggregate Trends Updated with 2019 Data*. Available at https://www.oecd.org/env/climate-finance-provided-and-mobilised-by-developed-countries-aggregate-trends-updated-with-2019-data-03590fb7-en.htm.

Oxfam (2020). Climate Finance Shadow Report 2020: Assessing Progress Towards the $100 billion commitment. Oxford: Oxfam International.

Pigato M, Black S, Dussaux D, Mao Z, McKenna M, Rafaty R and Touboul S (2020). *Technology Transfer and Innovation for Low-Carbon Development*. World Bank Group. Washington, D.C.

Sheikh PA (2018). Debt-for-Nature initiatives and the Tropical Forest Conservation Act (TFCA): Status and implementation. Report. Congressional Research Service. Government of the United States.

Steinfatt K (2020). Trade policies for a circular economy: What can we learn from WTO experience? Staff Working Paper ERSD-2020-10. World Trade Organization Available at https://www.wto.org/english/res_e/reser_e/ersd202010_e.htm.

Tiedemann J, Piatkov V, Prihardini D, Benitez JC and Zdzienick A. (2021). Meeting the Sustainable Development Goals in small developing states with climate vulnerabilities: Cost and financing. Working Paper No. 21/62. International Monetary Fund.

Tienhara K (2017). Regulatory chill in a warming world: The threat to climate policy posed by investor-state dispute settlement. *Transnational Environmental Law*. 7(2): 229–250. Available at https://doi.org/10.1017/S2047102517000309.

Timisel C (2021). Financing climate change adaptation: International initiatives. *Sustainability*. 13(12). 6515.

UNCTAD (*TDR 2015*). *Trade and Development Report 2015: Structural Transformation for Inclusive and Sustained Growth*. (United Nations publication. Sales No. E.16.II.D.5. New York and Geneva).

UNCTAD (*TDR 2017*). *Trade and Development Report 2017: Beyond Austerity – Towards a Global New Deal*. (United Nations publication. Sales No. E.17.II.D.5. New York and Geneva).

UNCTAD (*TDR 2018*). *Trade and Development Report 2018: Power, Platforms and the Free Trade Delusion*. (United Nations publication. Sales No. E.18.II.D.7. New York and Geneva).

UNCTAD (*TDR 2019*). *Trade and Development Report 2019: Financing a Green New Deal*. (United Nations publication. Sales No. E.19.II.D.15. Geneva).

UNCTAD (*TDR 2020*). *Trade and Development Report, 2020: From Global Pandemic to Prosperity for All: Avoiding another Lost Decade*. (United Nations publication. Sales No. E.20.II.D.30. New York and Geneva).

UNEP (2020). *AdaptationGap Report 2020*. United Nations Environment Programme. Available at https://unepdtu.org/wp-content/uploads/2021/01/adaptation-gap-report-2020.pdf.

United States Congress,(1992). . *Trade and Environment: Conflicts and Opportunities*. Office of Technology Assessment. OTA-BP-ITE-94. U.S. Government Printing Office. Washington, D.C.

US State Department (2015). *Overview of the Global Climate Change Initiative U.S. Climate Finance 2010–2015*. United States Department of State. Available at https://2009-2017.state.gov/documents/organization/250737.pdf.

Vincent K (2021). Political Economy of Adaptation. Unpublished background paper prepared for Trade and Development Report 2021.

Wetengere KK (2018). Is the banning of importation of second-hand clothes and shoes a panacea to industrialization in East Africa? *African Journal of Economic Review.* 6(1): 119–141.

Whitney A, Grbusic T, Meisel J, Cid AB, Sims Dand Bodnar P (2020). *State of Green Banks 2020.* Rocky Mountain Institute. Available at https://rmi.org/insight/state-of-green-banks-2020/

Wolf M (2021). The G20 has failed to meet its challenges. *Financial Times.* 13 July.

World Bank (2020). *Poverty and Shared Prosperity 2020: Reversals of Fortune.* World Bank Group. Washington, D.C.

World Ocean Initiative (2020). "Seychelles swaps debt for nature". Blue Finance blog. 8 April 2020. Available at https://ocean.economist.com/blue-finance/articles/seychelles-swaps-debt-for-nature.

WTO (2004). Non-tariff barrier notifications. Negotiating Group on Market Access. TN/MA/W/46/Add.8/Rev.1. 18 November. World Trade Organization.

WTO (2010). Market access for non-agricultural products. Negotiating Text on Liberalizing Trade in Remanufactured Goods. Communication from Japan, Switzerland, and the United States. Document TN/MA/W/18/Add.16/Rev.4. 9 July. World Trade Organization.

WTO (2011). WTO negotiations on environmental goods and services: Addressing the development dimension for a "triple-win" outcome. TN/TE/W/79. World Trade Organization.

WTO (2021). Trade and environmental sustainability structured discussions – Communication by the European Union. Document INF/TE/SSD/W/7. World Trade Organization.

Yamano N and Guilhoto J (2020). $CO_2$ emissions embodied in international trade and domestic final demand: Methodology and results using the OECD Inter-Country Input-Output Database. Science, Technology and Industry Working Papers No. 2020/11. Organisation for Economic Co-operation and Development OECD. Available at https://doi.org/10.1787/8f2963b8-en.

Zerbib OD (2016). Is there a green bond premium? The yield differential between green and conventional bonds. *The Journal of Banking and Finance.* 98(2019): 39-60. As The effect of pro-environmental preferences on bond prices: Evidence from green bonds.

# TRADE AND DEVELOPMENT REPORT
## Past issues